Planks of Reason

Essays on the Horror Film

Revised Edition

Edited by
Barry Keith Grant
and Christopher Sharrett

The Scarecrow Press, Inc.
Lanham, Maryland • Toronto • Oxford
2004

SCARECROW PRESS, INC.

Published in the United States of America
by Scarecrow Press, Inc.
A wholly owned subsidary of
The Rowman & Littlefield Publishing Group, Inc.
4501 Forbes Boulevard, Suite 200, Lanham, Maryland 20706
www.scarecrowpress.com

PO Box 317
Oxford
OX2 9RU, UK

British Library Cataloguing in Publication Information Available

Library of Congress Cataloging-in-Publication Data

Planks of reason : essays on the horror film / edited by Barry Keith Grant
and Christopher Sharrett.—Rev. ed.
    p.   cm.
  Includes bibliographical references.
  ISBN 0-8108-5013-3 (alk. paper)
  1. Horror films—History and criticism.   I. Grant, Barry Keith, 1947–   .
II. Sharrett, Christopher.
PN1995.9.H6P56   2004
791.43′6164—dc22   2004006623

∞ ™ The paper used in this publication meets the minimum requirements of
American National Standard for Information Sciences—Permanence of Paper
for Printed Library Materials, ANSI/NISO Z39.48-1992. Manufactured in
the United States of America.

For our parents,
Sumner and Helen Grant
and
Victor and Mildred Sharrett

Contents

Acknowledgments

Mikita Brottman's "Ritual, Tension and Relief: The Terror of *The Tingler*" originally appeared in a somewhat different version in *Film Quarterly* 50, no. 4 (Summer 1997): 2–10. Used with permission of the author and *Film Quarterly*.

Morris Dickstein's "The Aesthetics of Fright" originally appeared in *American Film* 5, no. 10 (September 1980): 32–37, 56–59. Copyright 1980 by Morris Dickstein. Reprinted with permission of *American Film*.

Barry Keith Grant's "Rich and Strange: The Yuppie Horror Film" originally appeared in slightly different form in *Journal of Film and Video* 48, nos. 1–2 (Spring/Summer 1996): 4–16. Copyright 1996 by Barry K. Grant.

Bruce Kawin's "The Mummy's Pool" originally appeared in *Dreamworks* 1, no. 4 (Summer 1981): 291–301. Copyright 1981 by *Dreamworks*. Reprinted with permission of *Dreamworks* and the author.

Steve Neale's "*Halloween*: Suspense, Aggression and the Look" originally appeared in *Framework*, no. 14 (1981): 25–29. Copyright 1981 by *Framework*. Reprinted with permission of *Framework*.

Dana Polan's "Eros and Syphilization: The Contemporary Horror Film" originally appeared in a shorter version as "Eros and Syphilization" in *Tabloid: A Review of Mass Culture and Everyday Life*, no. 5 (Winter 1982): 31–34. Copyright 1982 by Dana Polan. Reprinted with permission of *Tabloid* and the author.

Sharon Russell's "The Witch in Film: Myth and Reality" originally appeared in *Film Reader 3* (Evanston, Ill.: Northwestern University,

1978): 80–89. Copyright 1978 by The Silver Screen. Reprinted with permission of *Film Reader* and the author.

Christopher Sharrett's "The Idea of Apocalypse in *The Texas Chainsaw Massacre*" is slightly revised from the first edition. Copyright 1983 and 2003 by Christopher Sharrett. Used with permission of the author.

J. P. Telotte's "Faith and Idolatry in the Horror Film" originally appeared in *Literature/Film Quarterly* 8, no. 3 (1980): 143–55. Reprinted with permission of *Literature/Film Quarterly* and the author.

Robin Wood's "An Introduction to the American Horror Film" appeared originally as the introduction to *The American Nightmare*, ed. Robin Wood and Richard Lippe (Toronto: Festival of Festivals, 1979): 7–28. Copyright 1979 by Robin Wood, Richard Lippe, and Festival of Festivals. Reprinted with permission.

Rick Worland's "AIP's *Pit and the Pendulum*: Poe as Drive-In Gothic" is a slightly different version of chapter 8 in the author's book *Horror Films*, forthcoming from Cambridge University Press. Used with the kind permission of Cambridge University Press.

Bonnie Zimmerman's "Daughters of Darkness: The Lesbian Vampire on Film" originally appeared as "Daughters of Darkness: Lesbian Vampires" in *Jump Cut*, nos. 24/25 (1981): 23–24. Copyright 1981 by *Jump Cut*. Reprinted with permission of *Jump Cut* and the author.

Finally, the editors would like to thank Becky Massa for her initial support of a revised edition of *Planks of Reason*, Stephen Ryan for arranging for and accepting this edition, and Kellie Hagan for seeing the project through to publication. Thanks also to Olga Klimova and Curtis Maloley, graduate student research assistants in the interdisciplinary M.A. program in popular culture at Brock University, for preparing the index.

Introduction

The original edition of *Planks of Reason*, published in 1984, seems in retrospect to be a kind of homage to the "golden age" of the American horror film, as this genre played an increasing role in film culture and American life. This age, generally considered the period from Hitchcock's *Psycho* (1960) until the Reagan era, saw the breakthrough work of Tobe Hooper, Wes Craven, George Romero, David Cronenberg, Larry Cohen, and others whose notion of horror contained a radical challenge to society, a rejection of middle-class notions of normality, and a monstrous sense of otherness. Their important horror films appeared at the height of the Vietnam/Watergate era and its aftermath, almost all containing some form of critique of that time.

Having said this, it must be noted, of course, that the notion of a single "golden age" of horror is problematical. The genre was always a distinguished contribution to film art, its sardonic treatment of bourgeois life at least incipient from *The Cabinet of Dr. Caligari* (1919) through the remarkable Universal Studios renderings of the Frankenstein and Dracula narratives, the works of Val Lewton, the arrival of British horror from Hammer Studios, and the undervalued Edgar Allan Poe adaptations by Roger Corman. At the same time, the genre's major deficit was always its lack of "respectability," its relegation to lowbrow status on the tacit assumption, shared by journalistic reviewers and much of the public, that the genre was rather equivalent to pornography. Its supposedly base impulses were considered counter to those associated with the ambitions of high art, or at least the tastes of a public conditioned by the fare sanctioned by the press and various sectors of official culture.

If this book had a single role in its original edition as the first academic critical anthology on horror, it was in establishing the genre's legitimacy within academic culture as the genre itself proved its significance in films such as *Night of the Living Dead* (1968), *Sisters* (1972), *The Texas Chainsaw Massacre* (1974), *It's Alive* (1974), *The Hills Have Eyes* (1977), *Dawn of the Dead* (1978), *God Told Me To* (aka *Demon*, 1979), and *Videodrome* (1982). Academic writing about horror has, unfortunately, done relatively little to retrieve horror from the lowbrow designation to which it has again been rather deliberately assigned by the film industry. The proliferation of teen-kill pics and the franchising of Freddy, Jason, and other horror film characters through the 1980s and '90s have effectively taken the radical *frisson* from horror. Rarely does a horror film today have the socially allegorical function of Romero's remarkable zombie films; indeed, one would be hard-pressed to find in contemporary horror even marginally interesting characters whose function is something more than target or wielder of ax, knife, or machete. The attempt to return to the spirit of raw, unvarnished independent horror through low-budget films such as *The Blair Witch Project* (1999) most often turn out to be contrived, poorly conceived exercises that thrive primarily through the shenanigans of Internet hype and an accepting, ahistorical audience that has come to expect so little, settling for the good "boo" that hostile critics always claimed the genre was about in its essence.

Horror's situation in the new century reflects merely the increased intellectual impoverishment and neoconservatism of the New Hollywood, the fading of a relatively independent, oppositional cinema (in which horror flourished at the end of the studio system), and the replacement of script and concept with special effects undergirding the "rollercoaster" experience of the new multiplex cinema. The 1999 remake of Robert Wise's extraordinary *The Haunting* (1963) makes the point easily enough. Wise's film was a sophisticated exploration of female repression, a portrait of a woman's psychological unraveling (according to screenwriter Nelson Gidding) caused, as the narrative suggests from its earliest scenes, by the suffocating, patriarchal, nuclear family—an oppression the film cannot quite condemn. *The Haunting* introduces lesbian sex as an alternative to heterosexual, patriarchal family life in a manner not predicated on repulsion (certainly not with the casting of Claire Bloom as Julie Harris's prospective partner), even if the film hasn't the courage to follow through on its assertions. Jan de Bont's remake, on the other hand, avoids all such comment, and all the original's subtlety. Wise's film suggested a "haunted" unconscious by sublimely suggestive moments of terror rather than hit-over-the-head special effects for which the industry currently opts.

Marcus Nispel's remake of *The Texas Chainsaw Massacre* (2003) is an even more egregious case in point. The film contains the contours of the plot from Hooper's pivotal 1974 original, and even aspects of the original's macabre iconography. But Nispel's film has none of the lunatic absurdity of Hooper's film, none of the sense of the close narrative connection between the "normal" family of young travelers, with its deranged and mistreated brother Franklin, and Leatherface's cannibal clan. Nor does the film contain anything like the original's resonance as a cultural reflection of its political-historical moment. The Vietnam/Watergate era seeped into every image of Hooper's desiccated, overlit wasteland through a variety of brilliant touches, none of which is noticed by Nispel's film. And like much postmodern art, the new *Texas Chainsaw Massacre* cares nothing for humanity as a whole, with its monsters merely shallow grotesques and its normal folk simply targets for the killers. Current horror seems to share a particular look that might be identified with the world of rock video, not surprising since numerous filmmakers—David Fincher is representative—began in that form of mass media. This look, which also owes much to *Blade Runner* (1982), is characterized by a world of eternal night, with day photography saturated with a gray-blue gloom over a collapsing urban technoscape. Cronenberg is a central figure in the conception of the overcast, doomed postmodern landscape, the style reaching its most common and identifiable aspect with Jonathan Demme's *The Silence of the Lambs* (1991) and David Fincher's *Se7en* (1995) and *Fight Club* (1999). It offers a sense of fatalist apocalypticism projecting a nihilist vision rebuking radical change. The look has gained strong currency and acceptance within the genre and by audiences, its most regular manifestations being the *Hellraiser* films of Clive Barker and those who assist with the franchise. This territory has been charted, perhaps to a fault, by numerous critics of the fantastic.

With his *Hellraiser* films, art books, comic books, Tortured Souls action figures, and other paraphernalia, Barker is among the more canonized figures of postmodern horror. It has been argued that Barker is an heir to the traditions of 1970s radical horror, his vision transgressive in the iconography of the Cenobites and the world pictured around them. Along with films such as Dee Snider's *Strangeland* (1998), the *Hellraiser* films, so the argument goes, embody the new fringe culture of body piercing, scarification, tattooing—the subcultural semiotics of the "new primitivism," explicitly exploited in John Carpenter's *Ghosts of Mars* (2001). Accepting that this is a reasonable way of reading the films (which demands that we overlook the strong puritannical themes of *Hellraiser* and all its sequels), a question arises as to what constitutes the postmodern counterculture, if the term has any meaning. The new horror of Barker and others, and the "urban primitive" youth culture that seems to embrace his work, suggests little more than the extreme alienation of our society, a notion implicit in horror at its inception. The culture of body piercing (putting aside arcane notions of neoprimitivism, hardly a plausible notion in so atomized a culture) demonstrates an acquiescence in the self-destruction that is part of the logic of the capitalist state. The more important features of self-mutilation—as a cry for help by the young and a need to reawaken an obliterated sense of self—have nothing to do with the new horror, which overwhelmingly sides with acquiescence.

In this collection, with the exception of co-editor Christopher Sharrett's piece on *The Texas Chainsaw Massacre*, the essays are reprinted as they appeared in the first edition. This writing characterized both the history of the genre from its beginnings through the early 1980s and the critical thinking about horror at that time and in our view is a crucial part of the book's value, then and now. Hence, only a few essays have been dropped from the original edition and several new ones added to fill some of the gaps in the collection's overall historical coverage of the genre as well as the periods of the book's focus.

The first four essays—by Bruce Kawin, J. P. Telotte, Dennis Giles, and Morris Dickstein—seek to define from different perspectives the appeal of horror films as well as to map out some of the genre's iconography, conventions, and techniques. Kawin's essay, which begins part 1, also sets it apart from the other genre with which the horror film most frequently overlaps: the science fiction film. Telotte and Giles both focus on the experience of horror in the cinema in terms of seeing, the former taking a phenomenological approach based on film's ability to lure us into its imaginary worlds, and the latter by emphasizing the concept of pleasure as a tension between seeing and the blockage or delay of vision. Dickstein also approaches the genre in terms of its unique spectatorial experience, but argues for horror as a ritualized way of dealing with fear and anxiety.

Sharon Russell, Bonnie Zimmerman, and Lester Friedman examine character types and representations in horror in terms of gender, sexuality and race, respectively. In the 1980s, each of these essays offered new directions for exploring the significance and meaning of the horror film, and in turn expanded our sense of what the genre is about. Robin Wood's influential overview of the genre then puts into an ideological perspective many of the issues concerning horror raised in the preceding essays, as well as in several of the essays in part 2. Dana Polan's examination of sexuality in one historically contemporaneous group of horror films from the 1970s in terms of the opposition between the monstrous and the human is one of those essays clearly indebted to Wood. The essay by Barry Keith Grant that concludes part 1 looks at a historically specific cycle of horror of the 1980s, exploring how its generic conventions have been adapted to a particular cultural moment, the Reagan era.

Part 2 comprises criticism focusing on individual horror films and employing a range of critical approaches. Detailed formal questions concerning the articulation of horror are explored in the essays by Edward Lowry and Richard deCordova on *White Zombie* (1932), D. N. Rodowick on Craven's *The Hills Have Eyes*, and Steve Neale on John Carpenter's *Halloween* (1978). Other essays look at particular horror films within the historical context of their production: Noel Carroll convincingly explicates *King Kong* (1933) within its Depression-era context, Jonathan Lemkin examines *Jaws* (1975) as a contemporary expression of the American sensibility in terms of landscape, and Lane Roth interprets both *Nosferatu* (1922) and *Horror of Dracula* (1958) as indicative of the different times in which these two vampire films were made. Sharrett reads the original *The Texas Chainsaw Massacre* as an expression of a recurrent American apocalypticism during the turbulent Vietnam/Watergate era.

Films by horror auteurs are discussed in the essays by Janice R. Welsch and Syndy M. Conger (James Whale's *Frankenstein* [1931] and *Bride of Frankenstein* [1935]), Mikita Brottman (William Castle's *The Tingler* [1959]), Rick Worland (Roger Corman's *Pit and the Pendulum* [1961]), and Mary B. Campbell (David Cronenberg). Brottman deals with male hysteria and the psycho-sexual elements in Castle's film heretofore seen as mere exploitation. Similarly, Worland examines the Freudian and Gothic elements of Corman's Poe adaptation, as well as the function of Vincent Price's persona within the Poe cycle. Campbell's essay was one of the first scholarly analyses to consider seriously the location of David Cronenberg's films within the tradition of horror, staking out the terrain of body horror subsequently explored by a number of other scholars. Finally, Ruth Goldberg establishes the importance of Nakata Hideo's highly influential film *Ringu* (1998) to the huge wave of postmodern Japanese horror and, in comparing it with *The Exorcist* (1973), raises crucial questions regarding horror within the context of national cinema.

Introductions typically end with the old saw about material not covered. However, no one book could hope to cover the historical range and stylistic diversity of horror, and this one contains, for example, no stylistic analyses of Val Lewton's horror films, or those of Abbott and Costello, or other national horror traditions such as Italian *giallo* or kiwi Gothic. Regrettable as these omissions are, we think that particularly important for future work on horror would be the exploration of ways that horror has penetrated international and art cinema, not so much to investigate the legacy of Hitchcock, Whale, Lewton, Romero et al., but to recognize the pervasiveness of the horrific within contemporary international cinema, a new sense of horror not as something special or supernatural but as part of everyday life, even as some of these best representations remain rather marginal to the dominant North American cineplex culture.

Michael Haneke's *The Piano Teacher/La Pianiste* (2001), for example, can easily be called a work of modern horror, its central themes having much in common with the most radical emblems of the genre (*Psycho,*1960; *Sisters*; *God Told Me To*) in its extraordinary meditation on repression, the fate of the female in an age that has dispensed with feminism, and the whole of the western cultural canon as enforcer of oppression as much as it is a possible (marginal) path toward liberation in the current climate. Haneke's film certainly has a good deal more to say about the politics of self-mutilation than *Hellraiser* or *Strangeland*. Catherine Breillat, particularly in *A ma soeur* (*Fat Girl*, 2001), has developed a comparable approach to horror focusing on the detailed gender politics of seduction and sex. Her mixture of detached long takes and sexual violence, both explicit and subtle, has been taken up in several other films, including *Baise-Moi* (2000) and Bruno Dumont's *29 Palms* (2003). And Gaspar Noe's *Irreversible* (2002) almost universally dismissed as the basest pornography, seems a *cri de coeur* repudiating gender relations with a violence and bitterness that hearkens to Dostoevsky and Genet. The style of the film, a kind of updating of the off-kilter vision of Expressionism, associates the horror genre with the new European cinema.

If *Irreversible* goes no further than the nihilism of certain of the 1970s horror films, it at least avoids the consolations that the modern cinema has readopted, as well as the easy notions of the monstrous also reacquired by commercial genre filmmaking. It is perhaps instructive that the apocalyptic vision of the horror film's stellar period is now accepted as commonplace by many of the most intelligent and interesting international filmmakers, who see horror as the only sensible response to the murderous conditions of patriarchal, late capitalist civilization.

1
DEFINITIONS
AND APPROACHES

1

The Mummy's Pool

Bruce Kawin

> Helen: Have I been asleep? I had—strange dreams. Dreams of
> ancient Egypt, I think. There was someone like you in them.
> Ardeth Bey: My pool is sometimes troubled. One sees strange
> fantasies in the water. But they pass, like dreams.
>
> —*The Mummy*

> Sir John Talbot: All astronomers are amateurs. When it comes to
> the heavens, there's only one professional.
>
> —*The Wolf Man*

Karl Freund's *The Mummy* (1932), George Waggner's *The Wolf Man*
(1941), Reginald LeBorg's *The Mummy's Ghost* (1944), and Peter
Weir's *The Last Wave* (1978) point to some very interesting connections among horror films, nightmares, and prophetic dreams—
connections that might help explain what horror films do and why
they remain interesting to viewers who probably stopped believing in
Dracula along with Santa Claus. To clarify some of these points—such
as the relations between displacement and reflexivity, prophecy and the
attractions of being the "first victim," catharsis and the Land of the
Dead, reincarnation and repression—it is necessary to define the elementary ways in which films are like dreams and the broad characteristics of horror film as a genre.

Watching a film and having a dream are both passive and active

3

events. The dreamer/audience is physically cushioned in a darkened room, most of his movements restricted to slight shifts of position in a bed or chair, and mentally in various degrees of alertness, watching a visual process that often tells a story and often masks/presents some type of thought. In both cases the eyes move and the mind exercises creative attention. The dreamer might be considered more creative since the dream manifests his own thought processes, but the role of the film audience is also an active one since the viewer creates his own experience of the work: we all have different interpretations of *Persona* not because the film is difficult, but because we interact with the signs in the generation of meaning and because our attention is selective. Although the dreamer is completely responsible for the dream, he usually avoids this awareness and casts himself in the role of participant or spectator; although the filmmakers are responsible for the movie, the viewer decides which film to attend and so chooses the general content of his experience. Thus dreamer and filmgoer approach a middle ground of pseudo-responsibility for what is watched. Both dreams and films include verbal and visual information but are effectively dominated by the limits of pictorialization. Film is primarily a visual medium, and the stories and symbols in dreams are subject not only to condensation, displacement, and secondary revision, but also to translation into pictorial and concrete representability, according to Freud.[1] In *Mindscreen*[2] I have attempted to show how the visual fields of film and dream are analogous, particularly in the ways each field indicates the "off-screen" activity of a consciousness. In a film this "narrating" mind may be that of the artist, of a character within the fiction, or of the work's self-awareness: "mindscreen" generally refers to the visual and sometimes aural field of such a consciousness, as opposed, for instance, to "subjective camera," which imitates the visual field of the physical eye of a character. A dream is the mindscreen of its dreamer, as the color section of *The Wizard of Oz* (1939) is the mindscreen of Dorothy and as *Persona* (1966) is the mindscreen of its own systemic self-consciousness. A film like Wise's *The Curse of the Cat People* (1944) plays with the question of whether the ghost is "real" or an aspect of the mindscreen of the child.

One goes to a horror film in order to have a nightmare—not simply a frightening dream, but a dream whose undercurrent of anxiety both presents and masks the desire to fulfill and be punished for certain conventionally unacceptable impulses. This may be a matter of unconscious wish-fulfillment, following Freud: of confronting a hidden evil in the culture, as in *Alien* (1979) or *The Stepford Wives* (1975); or of voyaging through the Land of the Dead and indulging a nostalgia for ritual, as we shall see when we turn to Frazer. Horror films function as nightmares for the individual viewer, as diagnostic eruptions for repressive societies, and as exorcistic or transcendent pagan rituals for supposedly postpagan cultures. They can be analyzed in all these ways because they represent a unique juncture of personal, social, and mythic structure and because each of these structures has a conscious/official and an unconscious/repressed dualism, whose dialectic finds expression in the act of masking.

The clearest way to define the horror film genre is to compare it with that of science fiction, since the two are regularly confused with each other and often draw on the same materials (*Alien*, for instance, is a monster movie set in outer space). In what may seem like an unnecessarily long digression, I would like to show how horror and science fiction tend to present radically opposite interpretations of what may look like comparable situations, because the closed-system worldview of horror may be a key to its personal and societal dreamwork.

Genres are determined not by plot-elements so much as by attitudes toward plot-elements. Horror and science fiction are different because of their attitudes toward curiosity and the openness of systems, and comparable in that both tend to organize themselves around some confrontation between an unknown and a would-be knower. To lay to rest the usual assumption that a film is science fiction if it has scientists in it and horror if it has monsters, let us look quickly at a science fiction film, *The Day the Earth Stood Still*, and a horror film, *The Thing*, both of which are 1951 Cold War American studio films about flying saucers with highly intelligent pilots.

The Day the Earth Stood Still (directed by Robert Wise) is the story of a spaceman, Klaatu (Michael Rennie), who sets down his flying saucer in Washington, D.C., with the intention of putting Earth on notice: anything resembling nuclear violence will be punished by the obliteration of the planet, courtesy of a race of interstellar robot police. The spaceman has three forces to contend with: the army, which wants to destroy him; the scientists, who are willing to listen to him; and a woman (Patricia Neal), who understands and helps him. The central scientist (Sam Jaffe) is a kooky but open-minded and serious figure. Although it is suggested that earthlings understand violence better than most kinds of communication, they do respond to a nonviolent demonstration of Klaatu's power, and he does manage to deliver his message—perhaps at the expense of his life. The film's bias is in favor of open-minded communication, personal integrity, nonviolence, science, and friendship. The major villain (Hugh Marlowe) is a man who values personal fame and power more than integrity and love; he is willing to turn Klaatu over to the army, which shoots first and asks questions later—even if it means losing Neal, his fiancée.

The Thing (from Another World) (directed by Christian Nyby with considerable assistance from the producer, Howard Hawks) is deliberately formulaic, and so it is valuable as a key to the genre. It is the story of a team of military men sent to an Arctic station at the request of its scientists, to investigate what turns out to be the crash of a flying saucer. The saucer's pilot (James Arness) is a bloodsucking vegetable that is described as intelligent but spends most of its time yelling and killing and leaving evidence of plans for conquest. The minor villain is a scientist (Robert Corthwaite) who wants to communicate with the Thing rather than destroy it and who admires the alien race for its lack of sexual emotion. The Thing, however, has no interest in the scientist; and the human community (from which the scientist wishes to exclude himself), led by an efficient, hard-headed, and sexually active captain (Kenneth Tobey), manages to electrocute the "super carrot." The film's bias is in favor of that friendly, witty, sexy, and professionally effective—Hawksian—human community, and opposed to the dark forces that lurk outside (the Thing as *Beowulf*'s Grendel). The film also opposes the lack of a balanced professionalism (the scientist who becomes indifferent to the human community and whose professionalism approaches the fanatical, as opposed to the effective captain and the klutzy but less seriously flawed reporter), and what was meant in that paranoid time by the term *Communism* (we are all one big vegetable or zombie with each cell equally conscious). This is how the oppositions between these two movies stack up:

Army versus Scientists. In both films the army and the scientists are in conflict with each other. The army sees the alien as a threatening invader to be defended against and, if necessary or possible, destroyed. The scientists see the alien as a visitor with superior knowledge, to be learned from and, if possible, joined. In *The Thing*, the army is right and the scientist is an obsessive visionary who gets in the way of what obviously needs to be done. In *The Day*, the scientists are right and the army is an impulsive force that is almost responsible for the end of the world (hardly a far-fetched perspective).

Violence versus Intelligence. The Thing is nonverbal and destructive; Klaatu is articulate and would prefer to be nonviolent. The army, which meets violence with violence, is correct in *The Thing* and wrong in *The Day* because of the nature of the alien; but what I am suggesting here is that the alien has its nature because of each genre's implicit attitude toward the unknown. The curious scientist is a positive force in *The Day* and a negative force in *The Thing*, for the same reasons.

Closing versus Opening. Both horror and science fiction open our sense of the possible (mummies can live, men can turn into wolves, Martians can visit), especially in terms of community (the Creature walks among us). Most horror films are oriented toward the restoration of the status quo rather than toward any permanent opening. *The Day* is about man's opportunity to join an interstellar political system; it opens the community's boundaries and leaves them open. *The Thing* is about the expulsion of an intruder and ends with a warning to "watch the skies" in case more monsters show up; in other words, the community is opened against its will and attempts to reclose. What the horrified community has generally learned from the opening is to be on guard and that chaos can be repressed.

Inhuman versus Human. Science fiction is open to the potential value of the inhuman: one can learn from it, take a trip with it (*Close Encounters of the Third Kind,* 1977), include it in a larger sense of what is. Horror is fascinated by transmutations between human and inhuman (wolfmen, etc.), but the inhuman characteristics decisively mandate destruction. This can be rephrased as Uncivilized versus Civilized or as Id versus Superego, suggesting the way a horror film allows forbidden desire to find masked expression before it is destroyed by more decisive repression. The Id attempts to include itself in the wholeness of the dream-picture but is perceived as a threat and expelled from the community of what is human. It is not too heavy a borrowing from *The Republic* to observe that the Gestalts of an artwork, a person, and a society are comparable. *The Wolf Man* expresses and exorcises the Id-force of uncontrolled aggression in its own system (the werewolf), in Larry Talbot (his werewolf phases), and in the community (the destabilizing forces of rape, murder, gypsy liminality, and aristocratic privilege—Talbot often behaves as if he had *droit du seigneur* when courting the engaged Gwen). In *Invasion of the Body Snatchers* (1956), the egoless, emotionless attitude of the "pods" is as undesirable in Becky as it is in the culture.

Communication versus Silence. This links most of the above. The Thing doesn't talk; Klaatu does. (Or: Romero's Living Dead are completely nonverbal, while the climax *of Close Encounters* is an exchange of languages.) What one can talk with, one can generally deal with. Communication is vital in *The Day*, absurd in *The Thing*. The opened community can be curious about and learn from the outsiders, while the closed community talks only among itself. Horror emphasizes the dread of knowing, the danger of curiosity, while science fiction emphasizes the danger and irresponsibility of the closed mind. Science fiction appeals to consciousness, horror to the unconscious.

In Gestalt terms, any dream (or fantasy or artwork) involves the projection of aspects of the self and the arrangement or interplay of those projections in a structure that corresponds to the whole self; the therapist's task is to help the dreamer re-own the projections. If I dream that I am walking in the desert and see a flower, a therapist might have me speak in the voice of the flower and then in the voice of the desert, to help me realize that they are as much myself as that image of the wandering observer and that the whole scene is a display of my wholeness. In this sense, the science fiction Gestalt features a split-off creative hope that, once re-owned, can lead to an open, growthful, positive system. The horror Gestalt features a split-off destructive element that will be feared until it is re-owned, at which point the system can become stable. In most horror films, however, the negative projection is not re-owned but rejected and repressed: the Blob is frozen but can never be killed; the Mummy is burned but reappears in sequels; and in *Alien* the monster is destroyed but the corporate evil survives. Repression solves nothing, but (coupled with the momentary wish-fulfillment) gives a temporary sense of relief. Henry Frankenstein (leaving the novel out of this) may attempt to reverse the Original Sin and reenter the community by acquiescing to the horror cliche that "there are things we are not meant to know"—except that his initial hubristic motive was not just to figure out eternity but to create life without the help of any Eve (he wants to "be as God" in a double sense), and when in the sequel he manages to get married it is a sure bet that some Dr. Praetorius will "force" him into an all-male effort to create a bride for the monster, Henry's split-off rejected/rejecting child-self.

In the dreamworld of movies, horror films come under two headings: in the Freudian sense, they are anxiety dreams or nightmares; anthropologically they express a nostalgia for contact with the spirit world. In his *Introductory Lectures on Psycho-Analysis*, Freud observed that "the attitude of the dreamer towards his wishes is a peculiar one: he rejects them, censors them, in short, he will have none of them. Their fulfillment, then, can afford him no pleasure, rather the opposite, and here experience shows that this 'opposite,' which has still to be explained, takes the form of *anxiety*."[3]

In *The Wolf Man*, this process is extremely clear. Larry Talbot (Lon Chaney Jr.) is a big, Americanized engineer who is being groomed by his short and controlling father, Sir John (Claude Rains), to take over Talbot castle and the role of village Baron. Larry meets Gwen (Evelyn Ankers) and comes on like a "wolf," despite her being engaged to his father's gamekeeper (a model of controlled animal aggression, who is suited for the civilized institution of marriage). After he is bitten by a gypsy werewolf (Bela Lugosi), Larry splits into a wolf and a man. The man experiences pain and anxiety at the prospect of acting out his unconscious desires; at the climax, the wolf begins to attack Gwen and then abandons her for more pressing game, Sir John. Larry insures he will be punished for this, for although he has given Gwen his own protective medallion, he has given his father the silver-headed wolf cane that can kill him. *The Wolf Man* is a transparently Oedipal nightmare, a full playing out of castration anxiety, and a clear example of how some horror films are analogous to one kind of dream. Although it can be said that *The Wolf Man* is the dream of the screenwriter (Curt Siodmak, who went on to dream the similar *Bride of the Gorilla*, 1951), it could also be analyzed as Larry's dramatized dreamworld—or, taking a cue from *Beauty and the Beast,* as Gwen's projection of the two sides of her sexuality, werewolf and gamekeeper; but it is also obviously the dream of the audience, which has decided to let its own unconscious desires find as-if expression, with the scariness of the film carrying the dream's anxiety quotient and the killing of the beast appearing to vindicate repression.

There is yet another side to all this. Sir John (a prize-winning researcher) believes in God, the universal "professional"; his religious sense is conventionally patriarchal, and Larry's Oedipal rebellion includes his participation in an erupting/repressed religion, gypsy superstition. (Recall the scene where Larry is too upset to join his father in church.) Whereas Sir John believes that all this is in Larry's mind and that werewolfery can be explained as a split between "the good and evil in a man's soul," with the evil finding expression in a fantasy of animality, the film attempts to prove him wrong. Sir John finds that all this is not a dream, that the wolf he has killed is his son. In this sense, the horror film asserts the survival of "paganism" (the gypsies are right) and the inadequacy of science ("all astronomers are amateurs," a theme recognizable in *The Thing*)—a return to magic. Judaeo-Christianity represses, in this sense, the mystical unconscious that the horror-system allows to be expressed. (All this opens the possibility of a Jungian reading as well.) We may recall Van Helsing's pronouncement in *Dracula* (1931), that "the strength of the vampire is that people will not believe in him."

In *The Golden Bough*, Frazer observed that dreams are often considered instances of contact with the spirits of the dead and that such dreams may serve as keys to the future and (through the symbolism of mistletoe, placed under pillows to induce prophetic dreams[4] and, as "the golden bough," an illuminating open-sesame) to the Underworld. Freud, too, mentions the ancient concept of "true and valuable dreams which were sent to the dreamer as warnings, or to foretell future events,"[5] and there is a considerable surviving literature of dreaming as genuine out-of-body travel, usually on the astral plane.[6] A medieval poem like *Pearl* (in which the poet mourns the death of his daughter and then has a dream of her full-grown in heaven) can be Electra-cuted by any number of Freudian readings, but its appeal and point are clearly in the way it presents itself as a genuine visionary experience.

Horror films appeal to this kind of dreaming through the figures of seer and "first victim," and thus to the audience's desire to glimpse the truth, no matter how horrible. (A Freudian might translate this into the desire to learn about sex and be punished for it, which is often a legitimate reading.) In science fiction, the visionary is usually rewarded; in horror, punished. Peter Weir's *The Last Wave* (one of the few great horror films of the decade, perhaps matched only by *Spirit of the Beehive* and *Don't Look Now* [both 1973]) is the story of an Australian lawyer named David (Richard Chamberlain) who defends a group of aborigines involved in a ritual murder, one of whom (Gulpilil) begins to appear in his dreams. These dreams put him in touch with a parallel world ("the other side," in Western terminology) and remind him of his childhood experiences of night travel and prophetic dreaming. Eventually David discovers that he is a member of a race of priests and that the aborigines are expecting a great wave to destroy the intruding white civilization. As soon as he accepts his true vocation, David sees the wave and becomes its first victim. The wish such a horror film fulfills is that of *seeing*, and the worldview it confirms is that "the other side" is real. In other words, David is a surrogate for the audience's desire to have, through watching a horror film, a spiritual vision. The satisfaction of being the "first victim" is that one knows the hidden truth.

In the greatest of all horror films, Dreyer's *Vampyr* (1932), the world and "the other side" continuously overlap, and a dream within this dreamworld reveals to the hero the identity of the vampire. It is within this dream—of nearly being buried in a coffin whose window is clearly a reference to the frame of the movie-screen, so that the audience is cast as the victim/dreamer of the film-as-horror-object—that the hero is most in danger. The survival of Dreyer's dreamer and the death of Weir's visionary show that the crucial issue is not the destruction of the seer, but the threat of victimization. They also show that, although the more common impulse in the horror film is to exorcise the demon and save the community (*Vampyr, Jaws* [1975], *The Thing, Tarantula* [1955], *The Blob* [1958], *Frankenstein* [1931], etc.), there is a parallel track in which the community is rightfully destroyed (*The Last Wave, Dawn of the Dead* [1978], *Dr. Strangelove* [1964]).

"The other side" may be a parallel spirit-world or it may be the Underworld, the Land of the Dead; in horror films these are usually comparable. At the climax of *The Last Wave*, David finds that he is a reincarnated priest, in a sense his own ghost. In *Apocalypse Now* (1979), which advertises its indebtedness to *The Golden Bough*, the possibility of the community's being restored by the exorcism of Kurtz is overwhelmingly ironic, since the truths of the Underworld have more integrity than the lies of the conscious Establishment, and the transfigured seer can never rejoin "their fucking army." So although there are many horror films that play on the dangerous attractions of prophecy and spirit-contact, the cathartic journey into the Land of the Dead presents itself as the larger category and as the key to all the patterns observed so far, especially if one makes the link between death and rigidity of unconscious fixations. Freud's work on the relations between compulsive repetition and the death instinct (*Beyond the Pleasure Principle*) is very useful here, but the more luminous juncture is that between the Mummy films and *The Golden Bough*.

The Mummy opens with the best "first victim" scene I know of. An expedition has discovered a mummy, Imhotep (Boris Karloff), and with him a sealed casket bearing a formidable curse. While two senior Egyptologists (one a straight scientist, one superstitious) discuss whether to open the box, the junior researcher, left alone, opens it and finds the Scroll of Thoth. Mouthing an impromptu translation under his breath, he inadvertently raises the Mummy from the dead. Imhotep takes the scroll and exits, leaving a terminal madman in his wake. Here the desire to discover what is forbidden is related to the thrills of danger and self-destruction that are part of the cathartic masochism of attending horror films and having nightmares, and the mechanism of releasing an unconscious deathless force is tied into the legend of Isis and Osiris.

According to Frazer, the spell of Thoth was first used by Isis to raise her son Horus from the dead. When her brother/husband Osiris was murdered and dismembered, Isis had the aid of several gods and relatives in reassembling the body parts (except for his genitals) and raising him from the dead. Revived, Osiris became the King of the Underworld, Lord of Eternity, and Ruler of the Dead. The rituals Isis practiced were imitated in Egyptian burial ceremonies so that the deceased might be born again in the Underworld (although Osiris, the first mummy, was supposed to have been revived in this world, too).[7]

In Freund's film, this is condensed into Isis' using the Scroll of Thoth to revive Osiris from the dead. The story is that Imhotep had tried to read the scroll over the body of his beloved Anckesenamon, a priestess of Isis and daughter of the Pharaoh; for this attempted sacrilege, Imhotep had been buried alive along with the scroll, which could thus never again be used. Revived and in possession of the scroll, however, Imhotep (now calling himself Ardeth Bey) sets out to find the reincarnation of Anckesenamon, who turns out to be Helen Grosvener (Zita Johann). He nearly convinces her to die and be reborn as a living mummy like himself, but at the last moment Helen decides to live rather than to let her ancient identity dominate her (i.e., she chooses health over neurosis) and appeals to Isis to teach her again the spells she has forgotten over the ages. The statue of Isis responds to the spells and kills the Mummy; this implies that it was not enough for Helen simply to reject Imhotep, that she had to integrate her Helen and her Anckesenamon aspects in order to come into her full power. This is very similar to what Imhotep wanted her to do, except that he would have had her proceed from that integration to a fuller Anckesenamon rather than to a fuller Helen.

What this shows is that there is no safety in ignoring the Id/Underworld/monster (the attitude of the ineffectual patsy in most horror films, e.g., the mayor in *Jaws* and Helen's modern boyfriend [David Manners] in *The Mummy*), but that there is considerable strength in confronting the danger and surviving that deeply acknowledged contact—in other words, re-owning the projection. In this sense, horror films are valuable and cathartic, for they may offer the possibility of participating in the acting out of an unacknowledged wish or fear in a context of resolution rather than of repression. This is of course what happens to Helen and not to the Mummy. He is a walking repetition compulsion, determined to complete his frustrated sacrilege and consummate his romance (the sexist aspects of all this are quite blatant in the film). He would have her "go through moments of horror for an eternity of love," but what he means by love is the insatiability of unconscious drives (which are, to be fair, often involved in fantasies of eternal romance). There is value, then, not in being Imhotep but in, like Helen and like the audience, *almost* being Imhotep.

We are now back to Osiris and Frazer. One of the major points of *The Golden Bough* is that the agricultural year and the sacred year are closely related in a great many cultures, and that the myth of the death and resurrection of Osiris (like that of Jesus, whose death and resurrection occur in the spring) may have served the Egyptians as an explanation or prompter (through ritual reenactment) of the land's return to life in the spring after its death in the winter. The parallel with horror films should be immediately obvious: one enters the Land of the Dead, gives death temporary dominion in order to emerge reborn and refreshed. Horror films are the Land of the Dead, the visionary/ghost-world where shades and demons have power; one goes to the theatre as to the Underworld, becomes Imhotep or Helen on an as-if basis, undergoes a catharsis, and steps back into the light of day (if it happens to be a matinee, which is how most children see horror films and form lasting impressions of the paradigmatic content of the experience). For Osiris, this transit left him in a position of power over the Underworld, and it will be remembered that Jesus, too, harrowed Hell when he died; thus for the community, the benefits include an assured sense of the existence of divinity and a reborn economy, and for the god, the benefits include life and power. But not all dreams, not all winters, and not all horror films have such happy resolutions. The stories of Osiris and Jesus do not depend on repression. A Freudian dream solves little or nothing until it is understood in analysis; simply to allow the unconscious wish to find masked fulfillment does not remodel the psyche. Left to his own devices, the Mummy will simply repeat his compulsive and insatiable project in sequel after sequel, like an incarnation of neurosis itself. So it is valuable to have a character within the film who can, like Helen, acknowledge the unconscious drive and go on from there into an integrated life—or a dreamer who can re-own projections and live a free, healthy, flexible future.

This reduces itself to a question of audience intention, since even a film like *The Thing* or *The Wolf Man*, in which the horror-object is simply repressed/killed and the community reasserts its boundaries, can serve its audience as a visit to the Land of the Dead. The overall structure of such a visit may be cathartic in the same way that to dream may promote psychic health regardless of dream content. One could, in any case, go to *The Wolf Man* because one would enjoy participating in a fantasy of uncontrolled aggression and victimization (which is why most people went to *Jaws* and *Alien* and *The Texas Chainsaw Massacre*, 1974). But once there, one has the option of feeling that one's private beast has been purged and will require no further playground, or of enjoying the punishment and anxiety that attend unconscious wish-fulfillment and planning to attend another horror film the next time one feels in conflict about such desires. The latter is clearly more in line with Freud's reading of dreamwork, and with my outline of closed-system behavior, and it is doubtless the more common experience of horror films. Yet the former response is possible and legitimate, and it strikes me as being encouraged in those films that call the viewer's attention to the fact that he is watching a horror film and pretending to believe it, much as the analyst may attempt to engage the patient's ego while interpreting a dream. This is the method of *Vampyr* and of the bizarre, neglected, wonderful *Mummy's Ghost*.

The intervening sequels—*The Mummy's Hand* (1940) and *The Mummy's Tomb* (1942)—changed many of the terms of the story. The Mummy, Kharis, is now presented as having tried to raise the Princess Ananka by giving her the fluid from nine tana leaves; his tongue is torn out (Kharis is silent, unlike Ardeth Bey), and he is buried with a box of the leaves and charged with guarding her tomb for eternity. The Banning expedition discovers Ananka and ships her mummy back to the Scripps Museum in America, despite considerable interference from Kharis, who has been revived by a cult of priests (led by George Zucco). Kharis' motives are to keep the dead Ananka with him (neurotic possessiveness) and to defend the integrity of the Ancient Gods (against whom he rebelled in the first place). Therefore in these two films he is fulfilling the curse made against himself and has no strategy for reviving Ananka. The climax of these films comes when the priest (George Zucco in *Hand*, Turhan Bey in *Tomb*) decides to administer tana fluid to himself and the nearest heroine (who is never Ananka), but is foiled or killed, after which the Mummy is burned and the community of Americans restored. So if Kharis represents anything here, it is the deathless persistence of compulsive fixation that may have begun in sexual desire but has become only an undead, rigid, destructive, rejecting anger.

The Mummy's Ghost may be a brilliant parody of the series, a self-deconstructing masterpiece, or simply what used to be called a really good bad movie. It exploits every formula it can, turning them against themselves, right up to the climax where the monster, for once, gets the

The Mummy's Tomb, 1942. The Mummy Kharis (Lon Chaney Jr.) as compulsive fixation. From the editors' collection.

girl. It begins in the tombs of Arkham (a reference to Lovecraft?), where Zucco explains his role to the new priest, Yusef Bey (John Carradine). When told of his mission, Yusef Bey says incredulously, "Kharis—still *lives*?" His "you've got to be putting me on" tone puts the film in sync with the audience immediately, as the sequel declares its awareness of being a formulaic sequel or its worldly equivalent. Next we see Professor Norman explaining to his college students the legend of Kharis, who was supposedly destroyed in their own town, Mapleton. A student argues, "Maybe it was a man made up as a mummy, to keep the legend alive." The student is of course right, in a way he could not guess but the audience can. The professor, however, insists that he saw the monster (i.e., this is a horror-filmlike world and these dangers are real). This scientist is, of course, the first victim.

The romantic lead, Tom Harvey (Robert Lowery), has a crush on an Egyptian, Amina Monzouri (Ramsay Ames), who is working on the college staff; he also has a little dog named Peanuts. Whenever Amina thinks of Egypt, she gets a chill, but Tom insists that Egypt is just like any other modern country. Tom is the all-time ineffectual patsy of the formula, blindly confident in the status quo of modern America and uncomplicated marriage, while Amina is in conflict about her destiny, which is called Egypt but means sex and death—"forbidden love." When Kharis is on his way to kill Professor Norman, his shadow crosses her sleeping face and Amina walks in a trance to the site of the murder. When she is found in the morning, her wrist bears the birthmark of Ananka and her hair has a white streak. The next evening, Tom manages to convince Amina to neck with him in his car; while they kiss, Kharis' shadow crosses her face again.

By this time, Yusef Bey has brought Kharis to the museum. Downstairs a guard prepares to relax, hanging his hat on a realistic statue of a woman (i.e., he doesn't believe art is real), opening a crime magazine, and turning on the radio ("This is *The Hour of Death*. The forces of evil stand at the threshold. A man shall die tonight. . . . Did you ever meet a killer, my friend? You will tonight—"). The guard is a surrogate for the horror audience, which enjoys pretending that horrors exist, and a play on and against the suspension of disbelief—because the lies on the radio describe the truth of his situation. The reflexivity of this picture allows it to disarm the audience completely, since it continually calls attention to the fact that it is just a ghost story and just as continually presents its horrors as *real anyway*.

Upstairs, Kharis finally touches the mummy of Ananka; there is a straight cut to Amina in bed, waking and screaming; straight cut back to a collapsed pile of wrappings. Ananka's soul has been reborn in Amina, again to seek its salvation. (This would frustrate the curse—for in this version of the story, Ananka and Kharis are equally culpable for their forbidden love, and the priests' motives include keeping either of them from working out their karma through reincarnation.) The site of Amina's joining her repressed Ananka is, as usual, implicitly sexual. A friend reassures her that she "must have been having a nightmare." Back at the museum, Kharis kills the guard ("gunshots—crash—," the radio had said: the guard shoots Kharis and then is smashed against a glass door before being strangled).

Kharis finds Amina in bed and takes her away, unconscious, to a shack where Yusef Bey waits. Yusef Bey soon tells her that she is Ananka, and points to Kharis as an example of eternal unfulfillment and restlessness; she faints, and in her sleep her hair turns completely white. Then Yusef Bey decides to give her and himself the tana fluid— the most blatant instance of formula (or compulsive role-playing) in the whole film, coming absolutely out of nowhere—and Kharis kills him. Peanuts has led Tom to the scene, and Kharis knocks him out; then he carries Amina into the swamp (in New England?—again, more formula than "reality"). Tom is joined by the sheriff's posse (which has been digging a pit for the Mummy and burning tana leaves—another fakeout, since the Mummy transcends his compulsive desire for the fluid and walks on with his romantic burden, i.e., the fixed pattern of his sexual desire is stronger than the fixed pattern of the movie's formula; this pit business would have served as a typical solution in many films of the period). A formulaic rush to the rescue ensues— reminiscent of the torchlight parades in *Frankenstein* and *The Mummy's Tomb*—with Peanuts and Tom and the posse all chasing the Mummy. Such crosscut chase scenes have signified climax and resolution since Griffith, and aside from the St. Bartholomew's Day Massacre sequence of *Intolerance* (1916), there are very few examples of failed climactic chases in the whole history of film. One of the most troubling closes *The Mummy's Ghost*.

Because the chase does fail, and in a masterful way. As Kharis carries her, Amina becomes entirely Ananka: her flesh dries, her frame contracts, but she is still alive. Imhotep's project has been fulfilled (Kharis, too, has returned to his origins): the two lovers are united as living mummies. This rare moment of absolute fulfillment of forbidden love, which Amina has been shrinking from and growing toward, and which

Kharis has been yearning after for 3,000 years, is immediately succeeded by their deaths—they drown in the swamp. The posse stands
there looking beaten; Tom (who has seen Ananka's face) is a wreck;
Peanuts is alone on the swampbank cocking his puzzled head. There is
a sudden feeling of "what happened!" Suddenly a real horror has
asserted itself—Amina has given herself over to her unconscious drives;
the Mummy has abducted her and gotten away with it; all the formulas
have failed at once. And at this point a George Zucco voice-over
intones the curse: "The fate of those who defy the will of the Ancient
Gods will be a cruel and violent death." (This is what Derrida would
recognize as a good place to begin deconstructing the film, except that
the film has already done it for us.) Although it seems that Ananka
has repeated her sin rather than sought her salvation, and therefore is
properly punished (Freud again), there is no denying the satisfactions
of romantic apotheosis. Except if one views it from a feminist perspective, whereby Amina could be seen as surrendering to the deadly
obsessions of her abductor, utterly identifying with her state of victimization; the horror of her no-win situation is that her only alternative
to Kharis, in this culture, would be to play the role of Tom's wife.
Whether Amina is seen as joining her demon lover or as the victim of
a cosmic rape, it is still clear that the curse, as formulated, is not in
control, and that horror has triumphed.

Behaving according to formula is one aspect of repetition compulsion and of neurosis. In this film, the force of Kharis's and Ananka's
unconscious desires is so strong that they at least balance and perhaps
make irrelevant the repressive curse. (To say that Amina has these
"desires" is to say that she behaves like a Freudian construct of masochistic femininity; if one abandons the feminist reading, one is left
with the less complex observation that she allows the aspects of her
sexuality that frighten her to find complete expression.) Kharis is so
compulsive that he wins, even if briefly, and the formulaic aspects of
the genre are turned against themselves; the community is not restored.
The audience is unable to take comfort from the expected formulaic
resolution and has been made aware of the presence of formula all
along: so the possibility exists that this film educates its audience
(engages the ego in self-consciousness) rather than encouraging it only
to participate in unconscious wish-fulfillment (while, as usual, having
it both ways and fulfilling the wish completely). As it reminds the
audience that it is a formulaic film, *The Mummy's Ghost* is like a
dream, one of whose major strategies has been undermined—since one

of the basic functions of displacement and secondary revision is not just to mask the desire but to keep the dreamer asleep, to keep the dreamer from realizing what these masked desires are and that they are his own. Like the most intense nightmares, *The Mummy's Ghost* awakens the audience in a moment of anxious clarity and fulfillment. It may be, to reverse the phrase, that the sleep of monsters breeds reason.

NOTES

1. Sigmund Freud, "The Dream Work," *The Interpretation of Dreams*, in *The Basic Writings of Sigmund Freud*, ed. and trans. A. A. Brill (New York: Random House/Modern Library, 1938), 319–68.

2. Bruce Kawin, *Mindscreen: Bergman, Godard, and First-Person Film* (Princeton, N.J.: Princeton University Press, 1978).

3. Freud, "The Psychology of the Dream Processes," *The Interpretation of Dreams*, 520n.

4. Sir James George Frazer, *The Golden Bough* (New York: Macmillan, 1963), 818–19.

5. Freud, *The Interpretation of Dreams*, 184.

6. For an interesting and unusual approach to the question of night travel, see John-Roger, *Dreams* (New York: Baraka Press, 1976).

7. Frazer, *The Golden Bough*, 422–26.

2

Faith and Idolatry in the Horror Film

J. P. Telotte

> It is at the same time true that the world is *what we see* and that,
> nonetheless, we must learn to see it—first in the sense that we
> must match this vision with knowledge, take possession of it, *say*
> what *we* and what *seeing* are, act therefore as if we knew nothing
> about it, as if here we still had everything to learn. It is said that
> to cover one's eyes so as to not see a danger is to not believe in the
> things, to believe only in the private world; but this is rather to
> believe that what is for us is absolutely, that a world we have suc-
> ceeded in seeing as without danger is without danger.
>
> —Maurice Merleau-Ponty

As these statements by Merleau-Ponty indicate, perception in great
part determines how we conceive of the world we inhabit and our place
in it. By seeing, we invoke what he terms a "perceptual faith,"[1] or belief
that what we view is not illusion but truth itself, that the world freely
opens itself up, enabling us to understand both it and ourselves. The
visual arts, and especially film, would seem to involve a similar acces-
sion, for film's stock in trade is images which "could be"—surrogates
or extensions of the phenomena we commonly perceive about us. Film
criticism, however, has largely neglected its audience's perceptual
involvement, as V. F. Perkins notes in his study *Film as Film*, where he

suggests that we "redirect attention to the movie as it is seen, by shifting the emphasis back from creation to perception."[2]

Phenomenology and the critical approach it has offered students of literature might well be the key to this shift of emphasis in film criticism. Following Perkins' lead, therefore, I wish to apply such an approach to a common movie experience, specifically our encounter with the horror film, to account for this film/viewer interaction. Two sides of this visual process must be considered: first, the normal audience experience of the genre, and second, the focus on perception within the structure of one film, Hitchcock's *Psycho* (1960). What I intend to demonstrate through this approach is that the most effective horror films operate from a distinctly visual bias emanating from that "perceptual faith" Merleau-Ponty notes, and that this visual participation best explains why we find this particular genre so satisfying—in short, why we enjoy being scared by such films.

As the phenomenologists tell us, nothing valid can be learned about a particular object or event so long as we fail to take into account our consciousness of it, and specifically that act of perception which brought it to our consciousness; as Merleau-Ponty asserted, knowledge cannot admit any "cleavage" between subject and object, but must "make the contact between the observer and the observed enter into the definition of the 'real.'"[3] Hence, a proper phenomenological approach directs our attention to the self as it participates in that world it inhabits and perceives. To this end, the basic methodology of phenomenological analysis calls for examinations in two directions: "on the one hand, they are noematic descriptions that take as a guiding clue the essential difference between species, regions, etc.; on the other hand, they are noetic descriptions of conscious acts that intend a being of this or that type."[4] In layman's terminology, we are asked to examine both the world as it reflects back upon ourselves and our own understandings of that world—including the contributions of our consciousness to its makeup. The result, we hope, is a deeper understanding of our involvement with the phenomena around us, and perhaps even a qualitatively better level of participation in that human environment.

In America at least, this critical model has probably had its most successful application in literary criticism. As Dudley Andrew suggests, its failure to "catch on" in film studies may be due in great part to the extensive hold which structuralism has taken in this field, especially with the prior absence of any equally rigorous alternative approach.[5]

Because of its demonstrated openness to a variety of critical methods, genre study may afford the best opportunity for applying this approach, particularly since the genre movie is so manifestly a phenomenon whose significance derives from its audience's consciousness of and participation in its basic formulas.

In every movie experience, as André Bazin notes, perception becomes the key to "an imaginary space which demands participation and identification" of us.[6] With the horror film, though, composed as it is of what often must seem pointedly unreal images, we might expect some dispensation from these "demands." Since this genre still works its magic so easily upon us, however, we must wonder whether there is something within its substance or structure which, despite any momentary sense of disbelief, can yet engage us in its special realm and circumstances. In the modern realistic mode of this genre, in such films as *Psycho* (1960), *Sisters* (1972), or even *Halloween* (1978), this question may be less bothersome, since such films make every effort to place their terrors within a realistic context, to suggest that their dark and eerie landscapes, the threatening shadows and noises, are essentially coterminous with our own, supposedly well-known and safe world. While that question becomes less troubling with such films, it is still a pertinent one. A film like *Psycho* may face a simpler task than a *Dracula* (1931), for we immediately perceive its world as having much in common with our own; we are therefore more prepared to immerse ourselves in its realistic circumstances and thus obligingly set ourselves up for its shocks. Regardless of the mode, however, this genre seems to work its spell through a specific approach to the phenomena with which it normally concerns itself,[7] our fears of the repressed, the abnormal, threats to the human proposition. Basically, monsters do not a horror film make; rather, the special ingredients are an emphasis on our perceptual participation in the world depicted, often accompanied by a "perception imagery," underscoring the film's concern with the manner in which we see the world and our place in it.[8]

Such a desire for participation in the world we view around us is, as Owen Barfield has pointed out, a natural human impulse, and its satisfaction is a key to living what the existentialists would term an "authentic existence." This participation is normally evoked by our perceptions, since the "everyday world is a system of collective representations" whose reality is "for the most part dependent upon the percipient."[9] In most cases, therefore, we achieve a satisfying sense of placement in and participation with our world through our perceptions, provided, as Barfield cautions, that we view things in the proper perspective. Since we assist in their creation, in the establishing of their essence, those images we see should be considered to be "of the same nature as the perceiving self," and not "objects wholly extrinsic to man with an origin and evolution of their own independent of man's evolution and origin."

The horror film, more than any other genre, I would suggest, depends quite heavily on such an evocation of audience participation, because whatever chills it elicits have their source in the movie's ability to convince us that its threats have some measure of reality about them. They exist within a context of their own making, a world which we, in unspoken agreement, certify as a real, although aberrant, part of our own environment; hence, they represent a threat not just to our existences, but to our very human nature. Properly speaking, they signify a perversion of that participation into what Barfield terms "idolatry"—the worship of appearances or objects which seem little better than appearances since they are "wholly extrinsic to man," almost of another order of existence. Starting from what is conceived to be our normal world, the realistic horror film seeks to evoke a sense of *otherness*, but it is an otherness which, we are told, has its source in ourselves. As its horrors gradually emerge from the very fabric of our society, from our families, even from within our spirits and psyches, we become fascinated with this newly revealed dimension in our lives. The modern horror film thus discloses a sudden radical schism in our "faith," but it does so, like any spiritual trial, to strengthen our resolve; it seeks to foster a longing for some renewal of human participation by revealing the dangers of its opposite, this idolatry. By means of those visual "collective representations" through which it works, then, the horror film seems to invite our participation on the one hand, only to suddenly plunge us into another, alienated world—a world of "idols"—on the other.

I do not mean to suggest that such films encourage a worship of monsters or horrors of any sort, although assuredly some creatures like Dracula, defanged with the passage of years and the advent of a more sophisticated audience, have become almost idolized after the fashion of real-life movie stars, as is evidenced in the spate of vampire films—*Love at First Bite*, *Nosferatu* (both 1978), and *Dracula* (1979)—in which Dracula is less a creature of loathing than a figure evoking fascination, even a measure of sympathy in his "plight." While the horror film does picture a world antipathetic to the normal, it is an antipathy finally to life itself, for it shows life drained of all value and living things reduced to mere objects or superficies—as, for example, the furniture composed of human remains in *The Texas Chainsaw Massacre* (1974)—the victims of some ultimate threat to the vital principle. The idol we are in danger of worshipping, therefore, is the god of objecthood, of oblivion to human concerns. By attending such films to be scared we thus become temporarily involved in an idolatry of sorts, for we celebrate deviation from the human and the destruction of that vital participation, erecting in its place a distorting mirror through which we see ourselves as objects deprived of life and abandoned among a world of similar objects. The end result is fortunately an aversion, yet it seems to be an aversion we clearly relish.

Behind this predilection seems to be the feeling that, if we temporarily succumb to this idolatry, we might eventually recoup our original, participative vision which often seems so precarious, as if by first bathing our eyes in horror, we could cleanse them for a new perspective on life. So the horrific images evoke what we could term a propitious terror, one which helps us cope with the normal tensions and threats implicit in modern life. As Robin Wood notes, these horrors "are not meaningless; they represent attempts to resolve those tensions in more radical ways than our consciousness can countenance."[10] What I would like to isolate at this point is the manner in which we resolve these tensions to once again vitally participate with our world.

Specific modes of perception and perception imagery—essentially the syntagmatic and paradigmatic axes of the film structure—contribute to the creation and the resolution of that horrific tension. For instance, one of the most frequent and compelling images in the horror film repertoire is that of the wide, staring eyes of some victim, expressing stark terror or disbelief and attesting to an ultimate threat to the human proposition. To maximize the effect of this image, though, the movie most often reverses what is a standard film technique and, in fact, the natural sequence of events. Normally an action is presented and then commented upon by reaction shots; the cause is shown and then its effect. The horror film, however, tends to reverse the process, offering the reaction shot first and thus fostering a chilling suspense by holding the terrors in abeyance for a moment; furthermore, such an arrangement upsets our ordinary cause–effect orientation. What is eventually betrayed by those expressive eyes of the reaction shot is the onset of some unbelievable terror, something which stubbornly refuses to be accounted for by our normal perceptual patterns. Simultaneously, then, this sequence distorts our common, orderly approach to events (our rational understanding of them), while its key image suggests a sudden, supreme taxing of our perceptions, as if only by being opened to their fullest could the eyes, somehow, process this sudden, new, and threatening appearance. What should be more apparent, then, is that the horror film often achieves its ends by creating a sense of our own involvement in or contribution to its world of terror. For instance, in a film like *Halloween*, the audience is forced for a time to identify itself with a killer through the subjective opening sequence, shot so as to turn the murderer's perspective into an analogue of the audience's viewpoint. Little Michael, the murderer here, is a viewer himself, cut off from that which he sees, as he stands outside his house, voyeuristically watching his sister "make out" with her boyfriend. Afterwards, he inexplicably—perhaps through possession, madness, or even frustration—carries out his own assault on his sister, attacking her with a long, phallic knife in a horrifying travesty of the sexual encounter he has only partially witnessed and totally misunderstood.

But John Carpenter is hardly content with compelling his audience to engage in this temporary and extremely disconcerting identification. Throughout the rest of the movie he insistently intrudes image correlatives for that mode of seeing with which he introduced us into this world of horror. The opening close-up of a jack-o'-lantern's glaring eye is followed by frequent references to the killer's unnatural eyes—"the devil's eyes," as the doctor describes them—by close-ups of his victims' dead, staring eyes, and by repeated compositions in depth which consistently reveal some threat lurking just behind or beyond a foreground character's perspective. The film thereby calls our attention to the way in which we perceive its horrors and underscores that manner of seeing with specific imagery of a failed or improper vision. By film's end we are afraid *not* to see, to turn our eyes away, for fear that this "thing" which has several times seemed vanquished will rise again, once again to threaten our precariously stable world. In *Halloween*, then, we investigate not only a specific visual field of horrors, but also its consequences for ourselves, viewers potentially every bit as vulnerable as the victims in the film. The end product of this realistic horror genre is a phenomenological analysis of our participation in that mysterious and threatening world which it so matter of factly evokes.

As *Halloween* simply demonstrates, both the imagery and its sequential arrangement work to suggest how easily and fully our normal world of appearances can be shattered by the intrusion of a harsh, new reality. And with this suborning of our commonplace perceptions of reality comes the onset of that idolatry. We are cast into a world of dark, mysterious, and inexplicable phenomena, and it is one to which we pay the ultimate homage of fear. Propitiously, this predicament is something of a "fortunate fall," for by our descent into idolatry we finally can become better participants in our world. With this distortion of our normal perceptual patterns comes an enlarging of our processing capacities; our vision of the world becomes more encompassing, able to account not only for the everyday configurations of life, but also for those often denied patterns of death. This is what R. H. W. Dillard describes as "the bold method of the horror film."[11] It engages us in a "pageantry" of death and horror, confronting us with precisely the perceptions we need to effectively extend our vision of reality and eventually render our world a more accurately human one.

As we witness this pageant, its horrific images eventually urge a new level of participation by encouraging us to see our natural place in a world of normalcy, light, and life. When the horror film does present us with a tantalizing image, one seeming to immediately invite our participation, it is usually a case of deceit, a trick to lull our perceptions into a sense of normalcy and thus make the onset of that terror all the more unsettling. This is frequently the case in *Halloween*, where the mundane activity—washing clothes or watching television, for instance—consistently becomes a springboard into terror. The premier case, though, is easily the famous shower scene in *Psycho*, where the nude figure of Marion Crane invites the eye to indulge itself voyeuristically, only to be violently repelled by the slaughter it soon after witnesses. Of course, the horror film usually depends on images which freely acknowledge their otherness, figures which, as Frank McConnell suggests, project a certain "absurd presence" deriving from their general lack of the "depth" we see in the things of our world.[12] These images emerge from what he terms a "two-dimensional tableau," a realm clearly alien to the one man inhabits; and at least part of that powerful presence derives from their implicit threat to reduce us to equally inhuman forms inhabiting a shadow world. Apparently, the threat in *Psycho* is just such a two-dimensional figure, almost what we might term a caricature, Norman Bates dressed as his mother. Obviously, this fact does not make Marion's death any less real, but it increases the horror by effectively plunging us into an unexpectedly different world, a world of objects or idols. One consequence is that we are momentarily drawn into the action on the side of the threatened, the inhabitant of our human realm, participating with this identifiably human element in its encounter with this *thing*, this threatening otherness.

Since this encounter is implicitly the story behind *Psycho*, let me turn to its basic outline for a more detailed illustration of the perception/participation nexus of the horror film. Perkins has previously noted that *Psycho* is practically a study of perception, and particularly a special form of perception, that of the "prying eye."[13] Since the camera's view is inevitably our own, we immediately become implicated in this prying activity through the boom shots with which the film opens. The camera tracks up to and through a window to introduce us to Marion and Sam, two lovers in a seedy hotel. This voyeuristic perspective is repeated with the subjective shot of Marion undressing in the Bates Motel, as we watch with Norman Bates through his peephole in the wall. And again, from within Marion's shower, we fix our stare first upon her naked body; although as we watch, we are disconcertingly jolted by the shadowy approach of a threatening figure. Even though we are aware of this impending threat long before Marion is, we must maintain our voyeuristic position and helplessly witness her brutal murder. Our very impotence in this situation, however, should then thrust home a truth about the level of perception we have so easily and comfortably slipped into.

Rather than a participative vision and attitude, we have opted unconsciously for a kind of idolatry, and surely one of Hitchcock's points here, as in most of his films, is the hazard posed by such a lack of awareness. The voyeur, as we know, takes his gratification not from his involvement in an action or with people, but from his divorce from the situation or abdication from any demands of involvement. Thus our perceptions of Marion throughout the first half of *Psycho* tend to coincide with Barfield's definition of idolatry as a "tendency to abstract the sense data from the whole representation and seek that for its own sake, transmuting the admired image into a desired object."[14] What we witness through much of *Psycho*, then, is a failure of that vital participation, the transformation of the human into an object—of visual pleasure, sexual desire, and finally homicidal mania. The potential consequences of this human failing are manifest. Once a person is shorn of his humanity and reduced to nothing more than an object, he is hardly still alive. Looks, perhaps, can kill after all.

Hitchcock's particular strategy is to awaken us to this danger by

Psycho, 1960. Marion Crane (Janet Leigh) meets Norman Bates (Anthony Perkins).
Still courtesy of Jerry Ohlinger's Movie Material Store.

manifesting our common alienation from a proper perception of the
world and our place in it. Marion Crane previously estranges herself
from normal society by taking $40,000 from her employer to finance
her future with Sam. Apparently she feels that, given their present economic situation, their only hope for the future lies in attempting to
"steal" happiness. While driving to Fairvale to meet Sam, however,
Marion's eyes become bleary—again shown through a series of subjective shots from her perspective, intercut with close-ups of her face and
blinking eyes—so that she can no longer see the road clearly.[15] The
visual failing precipitates her calamitous stop at the Bates Motel. We
understand this blurring to be a natural consequence of Marion's
fatigue and the stress she is under, but a further conclusion, one in
keeping with the visual interpretation here outlined, might also be
drawn. Up to this point Marion has grievously abused her perceptions,
her view of the world and her own place in it. She has now reached a
situation where, both literally and metaphorically, she can no longer

clearly "see" her way. At this critical point, her senses warn her to stop and reconsider, to re-*view* her actions.

This visual motif receives its fullest development in the shower murder sequence which begins, appropriately, with the extreme close-up of Norman Bates' eye, voyeuristically staring at Marion as she undresses. Circular, eye-like images thereafter accumulate rapidly throughout the sequence, as Hitchcock focuses our attention alternately on the toilet bowl, shower head, bathtub drain, and finally Marion's dead, staring eye—as empty and lifeless as all of the *objects* with which it has been juxtaposed. No longer capable of seeing and responding to that world around her, Marion's blank eyes forcefully emphasize the consequences of abusing one's perception, while at the same time they underscore the logical alternative to a vital participation in the world one inhabits. Confronted with such a horrific experience, Marion's eyes have more than they can handle; forced to process more information than can ordinarily be accounted for, specifically this inexplicable onslaught, her eyes have, so to speak, been burned out, and her active participation in a human world has been rendered impossible.

Before that final juxtaposition of eye and drain—of two equally empty wells—Marion slumps down in the shower, staring into the camera in a "look of outward regard" as she reaches out towards us for aid. Her dying stare, however, never quite engages our eyes, never totally manages to implicate us in her death, and her hand meets with only the flimsiest of support in the shower curtain, which then gives way with her weight. After being almost completely drawn into Marion's situation, and after ourselves being visually assaulted by the quick-cut intensity of her murder, we pull back with the camera, perhaps even a bit pleased to divorce ourselves from this horrific scene and its accusatory images. Yet Hitchcock does not let his viewers get away so easily, for complicity is, after all, the story told by these image patterns and by the recurring voyeuristic perspectives we engage in. He still confronts us with the close-ups of Marion's burned-out eye, with its blank gaze into the camera continuing to reprimand us for distorting something human—just like ourselves—into an object, for so easily abdicating from a human participation.

It is this blank eye which, I believe, carries the thematic weight of *Psycho*. After Marion's murder, similar image patterns ensue; for instance, Norman spies on both the detective Arbogast, who is searching for Marion, and Sam and Lila, but in neither case does Hitchcock use the subjective shot which would identify our perspective with Norman's. Instead, he distances us a bit from the action, which is made all the easier by the loss of our surrogate identity which Marion had formerly provided. In Arbogast's murder he further emphasizes our withdrawal through a series of high, overhead shots which effectively mask the murderer's identity. Only the close-ups of Arbogast's eyes, staring in disbelief as he is stabbed, suddenly call back that earlier sense of our complicity in these actions and the full weight of the threat which they pose. When Lila seems about to fall victim to a similar attack, Hitchcock effectively varies part of his pattern. Just before Norman appears with his knife upraised, Lila discovers the skeleton of his mother; a close-up shot underscores the empty eye sockets of her skull and hints at Lila's eventual fate. Only the interposition of Sam, a caring and willing participant in her plight, saves Lila from the same fatal pattern seen in the case of her sister and Arbogast.

The basic threat which such realistic horror films revolve about, and which *Psycho* so clearly and forcefully demonstrates, then, is a distinctly perceptual one, emphasizing the necessity for our participation in the world we inhabit. We might keep in mind that the normal means of expressing fear, of *enacting* it in the horror film especially, is with the eyes opened wide, stating, far better than any screams could, the stark terror evoked by some revealed threat. And as both Marion and Arbogast so effectively attest, few people die in horror films with their eyes closed. The reason is that, in their failure to respond any longer to the stimulus of light or life, those blankly staring eyes become emblematic of death itself. Having lost his capacity for visually participating with the world he inhabits, for processing the normal patterns of life, man has effectively departed from the living and become little more than an object himself. Furthermore, it is by means of those same staring eyes that the horror film challenges its viewers to respond to this threatening otherness; it dares its audience to smash the idols to reassert a world of life in place of one of dead and objective phenomena.

It may be paramountly for this reason that we find the horror film such a paradoxically pleasurable experience. At one and the same time it asks us to shape a richer human situation and seems to affirm our controlling ability to achieve such a positive result. Movies like *Psycho*, for instance, permit us to bask our eyes in the horrific without danger of suffering that same burned-out effect, that is, with no immediate fear of the ultimate threat—death. We are, in fact, fully in control, as most children implicitly understand. When those depicted or suggested horrors become too realistically threatening, we may simply shut our eyes, cover them with our hands, or avert them from the screen until the danger is past. Our eyes, in short, endow us with a mastery over the situation, freeing us to witness previously unimagined horrors, to create and celebrate the persistence of life, or deny existence to its opposite. We thus pay to view the unseemly, since with our ticket we recapture the power of that childlike perspective; and, too, it brings the comforting knowledge that we can leave that threatening world when the show is over or at any time during the horror's hegemony. It is a temporally and visually limited threat we submit to, and having survived it or reaffirmed our mastery over it, we can exit to a world which, by comparison, seems bright and beautiful, a proper field of vision—a proper arena for life—once more.

What we take with us from these films is a deeper perceptual awareness of life and of our involvement in its complexities. Corresponding to the vital patterns with which we are familiar, there are, as is now thrust home, equivalent patterns of death and dissolution. However, I do not mean to suggest that the genre affords us simply a tragic view, designed to make us more accustomed to the human condition of transience. More precisely, from this initial experience and awareness we are encouraged to renew our participation in the world we inhabit. As we move from a dark environment abounding in psychic horrors, spiritual demons, or monsters created by our society or way of life into a human world of light and normalcy, we cannot help but react accordingly. Rid of such terrors, even if only temporarily, we almost eagerly participate in what must seem now a more vital world and certainly a more humanly hospitable one.

For many horror films, though—especially *Psycho, Halloween,* and most of the Val Lewton productions of the 1940s—this fearsome atmosphere is never totally dispelled. The horror is, for a time, able to be submerged or exorcised, but as *Halloween* demonstrates, although we stab the killer, put out his dehumanizing eye, or pump him full of bullets, he may once again arise to continue his harrowing escapades if we relax our vigilance or dismiss the threat which his very existence represents. That terror clearly promises to rear its head again some day and once more shatter our normal world, so we had best be prepared. Perhaps the relative frequency of sequels and remakes in the horror genre offers a further testimony to this fact. The close of *Psycho* offers a classic example of the persistence of terror which this genre often evokes. As the movie ends, the visual threat seems completely evapo-

rated, for the voice of reason in the person of the psychiatrist Dr. Rich-
man takes over, fully explaining Norman's psychosis and thereby
reestablishing for us a world which seems comfortingly rational. By
bringing the horrifying, the irrational, under the control of words and
theory, by making it easily explicable, the horror itself is not totally
eradicated, but is made to seem like only a momentary aberration
within the normal world, and one which could not possibly extend its
threat any further, for instance, into our own, everyday lives. The final
close-up of Norman, visually metamorphosing into his mother as her
personality takes complete control, however, tends to discompose any
such feelings of security. As the camera once again tracks in on an isolated figure, we alone see the truth of Norman's condition, and his
eyes, staring directly into the camera, challenge us to cope with the
horror he represents. His staring face finally dissolves into a shot of
Marion's car being hauled out of the swamp where Norman had hidden it. In its trunk, we know, Marion's corpse will be found, so we
recognize too that more frightening visions are still in store; only the
arbitrary ending of the film at this point saves us from having to witness these additional horrific images.

By insisting on the incessant nature of these threats, the horror film
in general and *Psycho* in particular caution us to guard our new-found
sense of human participation. There are clearly further threats to be
encountered, the genre suggests, other horrors to be overcome, still
more idols waiting to be smashed. Our task is therefore to remain
equally insistent on the persistence of life. A film like *Psycho* warns
that we face a world in which we must continually affirm our own participation, remain strong in our faith, lest, like the Israelites of old, we
willingly slip back into the path of idolatry. As Norman Bates' transformation attests, the otherness in ourselves lurks just beneath the normal human veneer and threatens to resurface some day with all its
horrors. However, since we individually fashion our world, as well as
the conditions under which we inhabit it, through our perceptions, the
burden can be borne. The realistic horror film affirms that our eyes—
and finally our humanity—can take it, can accept the frail human situation and from this vision create a proper context for life.

Admittedly, no film is simply a visual event, and the horror film
which I have focused on is no exception. What I have tried to suggest,
though, is that the realistic mode of the horror film, in its most effective, chilling moments, apparently works from a distinctly visual bias
which strives to emphasize certain images and image patterns. A

greater orientation toward language, of course, would hardly be appropriate, since it would tend to corroborate the "normal" world in which we dwell, suggesting a triumph of the sane, the rational, the understandable, over those chaotic, irrational forces which from time to time erupt through the calm surface of our human world. Since, however, the most horrific effect is often achieved when that chaotic world is *not* completely dispelled, when we leave the theater still partially in the grip of those dark forces, temporarily unsure whether we can ever fully restore normalcy's reign, a visual primacy is practically demanded for best effect. Hitchcock, perhaps better than any other director, understands this formula, so his forays into the genre effectively terrify, even while they evoke a sense of humanity, a feeling of our collective participation in the world he has visualized for us. As even this tentative phenomenological assessment demonstrates, the horror film, especially in its realistic mode, poses a great challenge to the manner in which we see the world and our place in it. However, this burden is one we can accept willingly, because from this onerous charge we may learn to extend our world, to enrich our human experience, and finally, to engage ourselves properly once more in the complex and persistent patterns of life.

NOTES

1. Maurice Merleau-Ponty, *The Visible and the Invisible*, trans. Alphonso Lingis (Evanston, Ill.: Northwestern University Press, 1968), 28. Merleau-Ponty's extended definition of that *perceptual faith* reads as follows: "It is our experience, prior to every opinion, of inhabiting the world by our body, of inhabiting the truth by our whole selves, without there being need to choose nor even to distinguish between the assurance of seeing and the assurance of seeing the truth, because in principle they are one and the same thing."

2. V. F. Perkins, *Film as Film* (Baltimore, Md.: Penguin, 1972), 27. Several recent essays have sought to provide a structuralist explanation of the relationship between the film and its audience. One example is Robert T. Eberwein's "Spectator-Viewer," *Wide Angle* 2, no. 2 (1978): 4–9, which suggests that "the act of vision itself" often "becomes part of the signifier," a notion in line with my contention that a specific mode which demands a visual bias—such as the horror film—would naturally involve a complementary imagery demonstrating that bias.

3. Merleau-Ponty, 16.

4. Joseph J. Kockelmans, "Husserl's Phenomenological Philosophy in the

Light of Contemporary Criticism," in *Phenomenology*, ed. Kockelmans (Garden City, N.J.: Doubleday, 1967), 225.

5. In his essay, "The Neglected Tradition of Phenomenology in Film Theory," *Wide Angle* 2, no. 2 (1978): 44–49, Andrew describes the failure of American critics to follow an earlier European "tradition" of phenomenological film study and suggests that now the time may be right for a reexamination of its potential, particularly in light of the hermeneutics of Paul Ricoeur.

6. André Bazin, "Marginal Notes on *Eroticism in the Cinema*," in *What Is Cinema?*, vol. 2, ed. and trans. Hugh Gray (Berkeley: University of California Press, 1971), 174.

7. As D. L. White notes in his essay "The Poetics of Horror: More than Meets the Eye," in *Film Genre: Theory and Criticism*, ed. Barry K. Grant (Metuchen, N.J.: Scarecrow, 1977), 131, "the arousing of our fear of death by itself is not enough to produce horror; horror requires a certain manipulation of that fear."

8. Gaston Bachelard has offered perhaps a more poetic explanation for the manner in which such perception imagery is generated, noting that "in the most diverse forms, on the most varied occasions, in the works of authors most alien to each other, we see an endless exchange recurring between vision and the visible. Everything that makes us see, sees," in *On Poetic Imagination and Reverie*, trans. Colette Gaudin (Indianapolis: Bobbs-Merrill, 1971), 78.

9. Owen Barfield, *Saving the Appearances: A Study in Idolatry* (New York: Harcourt, Brace, Jovanovich, 1965), 19, 21, 42, 65.

10. Robin Wood, "Return of the Repressed," *Film Comment* 14, no. 4 (July–August 1978): 26. According to Wood, it is "the shared structures of a common ideology" which enable the "personal dreams of their makers and the collective dreams of their audiences" to come together in the horror film. Just what he means by a "common ideology," however, is left open to question. While it seems to have clear Freudian connotations, it could also suggest certain shared human feelings which might form the basis for our common "participation" in the world.

11. R. H. W. Dillard, "The Pageantry of Death," in *Focus on the Horror Film*, ed. Roy Huss and T. J. Ross (Englewood Cliffs, N.J.: Prentice Hall, 1972), 37. Dillard's metaphor for the effect of the horror film seems particularly fitting for that perception/participation nexus which I am attempting to outline: "The mirror the horror film holds up to death is the distorting mirror of a deserted funhouse which frightens us out of fear and frees our fancy to find the truth more surely."

12. Frank McConnell, "Rough Beasts Slouching," in *Focus on the Horror Film*, 31, 32.

13. Perkins, *Film as Film*, 111.

14. Barfield, *Saving the Appearances*, 110–11. Barfield's description here has a clear analogue in Wood's explanation of the horror film, particularly when

he talks of its tendency toward "possessiveness," often of a sexually perverted form (p. 32).

15. We might note that the private eye sent to find Marion notes a similar failing before he is killed by Norman Bates. His comment that "I've been to so many motels that my eyes are bleary with neon" helps prepare us for the visual parallel which Hitchcock subtly creates between Arbogast and Marion, especially for the similar pattern of their murders.

3

Conditions of Pleasure in Horror Cinema

Dennis Giles

Contemporary film theory has begun a movement away from study of a film *in itself*—as an autonomous text—towards the analysis of its social, economic, and psychological context. Over the past decade, Marxist and psychoanalytic studies have proliferated in the journals precisely because they attempt to consider cinema not as a finished product but as a process of production. Cinema is seen less as an aesthetic object than as a communication with a viewing subject who has adapted *to* the text and who, in part, has been produced *by* the institution of cinema itself. What many of us study is the cooperation between the industry and the viewer in the event of movie-going. This shift of emphasis in film theory toward the role and the "place" of the viewer is paralleled in literary study by the work of the German reception theorists Iser, Jauss, and Stierle, among others. I believe that their approach can be enormously useful in understanding the interaction between the off-screen viewer and the onscreen text. However, the work of these men deals primarily with questions of "meaning." My interrogation of horror cinema is centered, instead, on the question of pleasure.

PART 1

Reception theory proposes that meaning does not lie *in* the film but is the result of a "cooperative enterprise" between the producers/exhibitors of the movie and those who choose to receive it.[1] Viewing is as much an action as a passion. There is no total consumption of a movie, no ideal viewer who completely shares the complex of codes "put in" the film by its artists, the industry and the culture that produced it. But this is not to say that meanings (in which I include emotional responses) are wholly individual or situational. The viewer does not impose *any* meaning whatsoever upon the text. Rather, the film guides the viewer's responses, initiating "performances" of meaning. The text proposes, the viewer disposes. Viewers "realize" the text according to their own interests, but in order to enjoy the movie, they collaborate with the text in such a way that the spectators' interests and those of the industry coincide.[2]

What the film industry sells to the viewer is not a material *thing* but an experience, or a promise, of pleasure. To study the pleasure economy of cinema is, then, to investigate how the industry produces and patterns texts that yield enjoyment to the viewer as well as a return of capital. These are texts that lure the viewer to the movies by offering "dangerous" visions of potentially traumatic material—violent, erotic, or otherwise excessive scenes from which, outside the theatre, we are expected to turn away in shame, guilt, or emotional turmoil. Yet at the same time that it threatens to transgress prohibitions, the industry promises a vision that the viewer knows will be psychologically and ideologically *safe*. By the terms of the viewing contract, desire will be engaged, then domesticated by the textual strategies; fear will be aroused, then controlled. In short, the industry offers the viewer a well-defended fantasy, rather than the lawless vision described by Metz.[3] As the psychoanalyst J. B. Pontalis says, "the dream screen should not only be understood as a surface for projection, it is also a surface for protection—it forms a screen."[4] Cinema is never the raw vision of desire, but a compromised text that defends itself (and the viewer) against its own promise (or threat). In other words, the experience of cinema is simultaneously a screening and a screening-off.[5]

What I call the *good movie experience* is simply a satisfying session at the movies. It is the experience of pleasure felt when everything in the movie seems to work *for* the viewer, while the work the viewer performs seems effortless. It is when the movie moves the viewer where he/she wants to go, when the movie is understood and enjoyed in favorable conditions of reception. The good movie experience is the result of a viewing contract scrupulously observed by the producers, the exhibitors, and the consumers of the show.

I prefer the mundane adjective *good* to describe the experience in place of a more technical construction, because I wish to lean on the sense the terms *good mother* and *good dream* have taken in psychoanalysis, implying a sense of satisfaction for a subject who does not merely spectate but actively participates in the good of the experience.[6] It is an experience in which the subject not only receives the pleasure of the text but also co-produces it. But the primary reason to use this adjective is that when viewers have experienced pleasure at the movies, when they feel the movie has done what it is supposed to do, they exclaim, simply, "That's a good movie," collapsing all the various satisfactions into this single term.

My question here is: how can horror films provide this good movie experience? Outside the theater, fear, fright, and anxiety are not pleasant experiences. We suffer these emotional states, but we take no pleasure in them. Yet in the horror cinema, viewers enjoy being terrorized. The "bad" experience has become a "good" one. My question is not *why*? but *how*? More precisely, how are the sounds and images of this genre developed so that the viewer can gain pleasure in fear? And how do I, the viewer, work *with* the film to gain the pleasure it offers? How do I allow the movie to move me, to play with my emotions; how do I put myself into *its* field of play? Especially in contemporary horror—post-*Psycho* (1960)—how do I gain pleasure from the spectacle of rape, mutilation, enslavement, or death?

Clearly, there are many who find *no* pleasure in the terror film—only disgust. Some are unable to defend themselves against the horror of the images; the emotions aroused become too intense for viewers to accept, even though they know that the experience is fictional, that it is "only a movie." Other viewers displace themselves from the fiction by laughter, intentionally misreading the emotional cues of the text, refusing to play by the rules of its game.

When I was an undergraduate at Northwestern, my lover irritated me by her behavior at horror films. During the most terrifying scenes she would put her hands over her eyes. "I can't watch it," she would say; then, "tell me what's happening!" Apparently, there came a point at which the movie moved her too much—a point at which she was too open, too receptive, to the images. There came a point of stress—of overload—at which she had to defend herself against the speech of the film. But not against all of its discourse. She still *heard* the horror—the groans of the monster, the screams of the victim, the pulse of the music. She chose to block her vision, not her ears. She wanted to see the movie, but she also wanted *not* to see when it began to deliver the vision it promised or threatened.

Metz, Heath, Baudry, and Mulvey have elaborated on the theory of the scopophilic drive as a major source of cinema pleasure—the viewer as voyeur, who watches the supposedly private acts of others from his/her hidden position in darkness.[7] But, to my knowledge, what has *not* been explored is the pleasure in *not seeing*—the delayed, blocked, or partial vision that seems so central to the strategy of horror cinema. In the "good dream," according to Masud Khan, the very structure of the dream enables the dreamer to achieve a "benign distancing" from traumatic images or ideas which, in the bad dream, would wake the dreamer in a panic.[8] Films are less dreams of a private subject than public fantasies appropriated by the viewer. But Laplanche, Pontalis, and Lagache have stressed that, while fantasy is the *mise-en-scène* of desire—of the wish—it is also produced by the subject's defenses *against* desire.[9] It is censored, distorted; the pleasurable fantasy is also the product of fear. As a compromised text, it protects the subject from the full implications of his/her unconscious (and primal) fantasies, while at the same time, it speaks these fantasies in a revised, "civilized" form. Others have spoken of cinema pleasure as the representation of desire, but little has been said about how specific films, genres, or cinema as an institution are the site of defensive operations.

PART 2

The contemporary terror film is often accused of visual excess—of showing too much too often. It is said to place excessive reliance on what Stephen King has called the "gross-out"—scenes engineered as sheer stimulus/response, producing shock and revulsion, as when the creature bursts from the chest of its human host in *Alien* (1979).[10] The full vision of the object of fright may be extended indefinitely in such films as *The Texas Chainsaw Massacre* (1974) or *The Exorcist* (1973), but in other films the image is only a brief payoff that proves that the thing is truly terrifying, that the promise of horror can and will be delivered. Typically, the moment of full vision fades once more into a sequence of imagery that anticipates the return of the terrible object but evades it—refuses to face it openly. The quality of the effect changes as well. Presumably, the viewer's "excess" emotion of fright and disgust yields to a more diffuse anxiety in which dread of the return of full vision is commingled with desire for its return to the screen. It is this anticipatory vision—showing little or nothing of the true object of terror—that interests me here.

These are scenes that promise the monstrous, but no monster is visible. The viewer senses a terrible presence in the articulation of imagery, but the images themselves display only an *absence* of the terrible object, or the possibility that it may become visible. These are scenes invested with potential; scenes that toy with and frustrate the wish to see; veiled scenes of partial, blocked, or inadequate vision; delayed visions, even apparently empty visions in which one sees clearly, but there is nothing *significant* to see, no apparent purpose to the image.

The articulation of imagery from film to film is so flexible, so dependent on context, that I hesitate to speak of set visual codes. Better, perhaps, to call these images *figures*—devices or patterns of *figuration*—leaning on arguments advanced by Lyotard. Rather than being a decorative or ornamental "turn" (trope) of the discourse, as classical rhetoric would have it, the *figure* allows a more primary, preconscious or unconscious fantasy to contaminate and rework the ordered surface of the ostensible text.[11] The figure is a kind of overflow from an invisible scene onto the imagery of the film, so that what Heidegger or the expressionists might call the *stimmung*—the mood or "attunement" of the image—is bent by fear, desire and anticipation so that it "speaks" something more than it shows.[12] The figure of the delayed, partial, or empty vision ambiguates the image; it overlays the explicit significance of the scene with a monstrous presence which belongs to an *other* scene—a scene off-screen, and not fully conscious. The range of the imagery is so broad I can offer only an incomplete catalog of figures organized into loose categories.

In the first group of relatively common, straightforward figures, the viewer knows that the monster is already here, in the scene (in the room), about to attack the victim or actually attacking. However, the look at the monster is denied or frustrated. In the first instance, he (I say "he" because the monster is usually male) is excluded from the shot by framing. In *Alien* and *The Prophecy* (1979), the camera holds the victim in extreme close-up (ECU) "choker" shot just before the attack moves into its opening stages. We see the victim's reaction but the reverse-angle vision of the threat is withheld. If and when the reverse angle is added to the figure, the first shot has become an instance of delayed or suspended vision. *Friday the 13th, Part 2* (1981) teases the viewer by cutting from an attack in progress to peaceful or playful scenes elsewhere in the camp, only to return, after several of these delaying shots, to the attack or its aftermath. The monster himself is visually present in the first part of the film only as a pair of feet in the foreground of the shot.

Another instance of the on-scene threat is the familiar shot, infinitely variable, in which the image of the monster is obscured by mist (*The Fog*, 1979), smoke (*Curse of the Demon*, aka *Night of the Demon*, 1957), or by the shadows of a chiaroscuro lighting pattern. *Poltergeist* (1982) transforms the convention by means of a masking "spectral light" (as one of the characters terms it). Overlit and overexposed shots, the light glaring into the camera, evoke an ambiguous *stimmung* of combined threat and wonder.[13]

In the second figural category, the potential victim approaches a site that the viewer believes to be inhabited by the monster. This figure prolongs the approach, dwells on the simple act of walking or climbing stairs in detail, fragmenting the banal act by a series of shots from a great variety of angles, often fragmenting the body of the victim with ECUs of "foot on the stair," "hand on the banister," combined with extreme long shots which momentarily reintegrate the body. Intercut into the series are shots of the victim's face and, usually, point-of-view (POV) shots from the victim's eyes of the empty staircase. No monster is visible, but the scene is overlaid with menace because of the elaborate visual treatment devoted to an ordinary act that would usually be without interest. The classic form of this figure is probably given in *Psycho* when Arbogast (Martin Balsam) ascends the staircase of the terrible house. (In Hitchcock's scene, the presence of the monster can be inferred from the "god's-eye" shot from high over the stairwell; it is not strictly taken from Norman Bates' POV but upper regions of the house have already been associated with him.) The majority of the so-called slasher films repeat this figure as a preliminary to the attack.

American Werewolf in London (1981) inserts a fast-moving dolly shot over the moors of Northern England into a scene in which the protagonist, David Kessler, is confined to a hospital bed in London. No monster or human is visible in the shot, but it apparently represents the vision of something or someone. The monster is present, momentarily, only as a point of view. Although David considers the insert to

Curse of the Demon *(aka* Night of the Demon*), 1957. The sight of the monster obscured. Still courtesy of Jerry Ohlinger's Movie Material Store.*

be only a disturbing fragment of a "dream," the viewer is cued by the title of the film to take the shot as evidence that the American has already (mentally) been transformed into the werewolf.

The third figural category is the most intriguing. Here, the viewer *knows* that the monster is not physically on the scene, may not even be near it, but the position or movement of the camera seems to contradict this knowledge, overlaying the scene with a "sense" of the monstrous. Toward the beginning of the 1983 TV movie *The Demon Murder Case*, *before* the demon invades the film, a couple are conversing in their house. Although the sound is recorded as though the viewer/auditor were with them in the room, the shot is an extreme long shot of the exterior of the house, the camera gradually tracking from left to right. Instances of these motivated camera movements abound in the contemporary terror film, although this refusal to give even a partial vision of an innocent interpersonal scene is rare. In the changing visual codes of the horror film, the prowling or creeping camera has become associated with the vision of a monster preparing to attack. It is interpreted as a POV shot. Here (and in other films), no monster lurks on the scene, but since the movement has come to "speak" a threatening presence, a monstrous overtone contaminates an ordinary, more or less meaningless scene. Another common instance of the third category occurs when a character, usually seated, is performing an everyday act such as reading, talking on the phone, and so on.

Little of significance is happening or being spoken. Rather than offering a clear or full view of the subject, the camera is placed at an "unnatural" distance behind objects of decor which intrude into the frame in the foreground, creating either a visual barrier or, at the least, a distraction between the viewer and the person viewed. In this figure the camera sometimes looks from and through an area of darkness into an illuminated scene or, still viewing from a distance, performs unmotivated creeping movements around the static or sedentary subject. Again, the imagery carries a threatening overtone. In the opening scenes of *The Exorcist*, the Ellen Burstyn character is filmed in her living room through several variations of this figure.

PART 3

The creeping camera, the distant, partial, or blocked vision, the frame within the frame: in each of these instances of the third figure the viewer seems to be invited to look less at *what* is seen than at *how* it is seen. As Steven Heath writes, in another context, "What counts is as much the representation as the represented, is as much the production as the product."[14]

The means of representation—the manner or mode of viewing—is foregrounded, even fetishized. In effect, I believe that each of the figures (in all three categories) involves the viewer in a structure of fetishism. Indeed, a fetishistic structure may be more central to the horror genre than to cinema as a whole due to the greater need of horror cinema to defend the viewer against his or her own desire for full vision.

Film theory has made extensive use of the psychoanalytic description of fetishism as a key toward understanding the sexual positioning of the viewer which is invited by the visual text. Recently, I have begun to wonder if we haven't accorded too much respect to the letter of Freudian and Lacanian law while neglecting some of the more profound implications of Freud's attempt to deal with arrested vision, blocked and diverted desire, and the structure of disavowal. If, like Mulvey in "Visual Pleasure," we take the fetish as a memorial or monument to male castration anxiety, all kinds of problems are raised. In the classical view, invoked by Mulvey and others, the fetish is formed when the male child perceives that the female lacks a penis. He *has* a penis; therefore, she has been castrated. The vision proves that castration is possible. The boy fears that he too will meet the same fate, so he disavows the perception. He cannot totally refute the perception of absence. He "knows very well" that the woman does not have a penis, but cannot abide the knowledge, so he finds or "creates" a substitute for the female genital in order to avoid encountering the vision of absence.[15]

The fetishistic look in cinema cannot, according to Mulvey, take pleasure in looking at woman as an erotic object but must transform her into a spectacle satisfying in itself, as in the cinema of Von Sternberg. Dietrich is not to be penetrated or possessed, but looked at, admired. Once she has been reconstructed into an image, the female no longer threatens the male. To the fetishistic look, Mulvey opposed the "active" look of voyeurism, which seeks to penetrate, control, subdue the woman. Both forms of visual pleasure are essentially male, reflecting male control over the means of representation in our society, including the cinema.[16] As Mulvey admits in a later article on *Duel in the Sun* (1946), this theory offers little to explain transsexual identification in the viewing experience. When the female viewer identifies with the male position in the film, is she denying some "essential" femininity, or transforming that femininity from a passive to an active positioning?[17] Or is every viewer more or less bisexual when forming identifications during the viewing experience? I would provisionally argue the latter, but insofar as the characters/personae offered by Hollywood for identification are traditionally male—active, masculine identity comes to be confused with action/aggression and the feminine with passion, suffering, and the masochistic position. Description of sexual sites and roles in film theory is not only contaminated by the sexual "assignments" given by traditional culture, but with the political assumption that activity is preferable to passivity in cinema, as in life.

A second problem with theories of fetishism in cinema involves taking the penis too literally—too physically—as the male sexual organ. Fetishism is capable of being extended outside of its strict sense of a psychotic sexual perversion only if we substitute the term *phallus* for penis. Phallus is cultural, rather than physical, representing all the symbolic values attached to the penis—connotations of potency, penetration, invasion, aggression.

A strict clinical view of fetishism would also run aground when confronted with sadomasochistic cinemas of display like hard-core pornography and (sometimes) the horror film. There is no question that pornography is voyeuristic, that it is an erotically charged cinema that wishes to control the woman, but it also wishes to look at her at leisure, to put her on display. Yet Mulvey claims that the voyeuristic look is opposed to the fetishistic.[18] Second, the pornographic gaze finds pleasure, not horror, in the spectacle of the castrated, naked vagina. It delights in the absence of the penis, in part because the woman's lack affirms the male's potency. He has it, she doesn't—which recognition justifies the humiliation of the woman.[19]

I believe it is more useful, particularly when dealing with horror cinema, to broaden the sense of fetishism, while still remaining within a psychoanalytic framework. Let us set the question of sexual difference aside, momentarily, and see fetishism as an arrested or blocked vision which has recoiled from, or fears to approach *any* image of horror (not necessarily the horror of the castrated woman). The Freudian notion of fetishism involves a substitution of signifiers: the fetish both *re*-presents and hides what the subject really *wants* to see but it is also the symptom of fear of looking. The fetishistic act is the means by which the subject protects himself/herself against a horrible spectacle, and gains pleasure from a vision which stops short of this spectacle. It is essentially a defensive vision, but one which is enjoyed by the spectator precisely *because* it lurks on the threshold, because it refuses to fully see.

When my friend at Northwestern held her hands over her eyes to prevent full vision of the image of horrible excess upon the screen, she was gaining a pleasure similar to that of the fetishist. (Sometimes she peeked through her fingers to achieve a partial vision in place of a completely blocked one.) In any case, she defended herself against the image. But through its figures of blocked, partial, and delayed vision horror cinema *itself* defends the viewer from the vision of the monstrous that we know lurks somewhere beyond the substitute images we see before us on the screen. The horror is screened, but in the scenes I have mentioned it is also screened off. In other words, horror is screened in the process of screening it off.

In fetishism, one disavows an absence, relocates it in an *other* scene, and treats it as a presence. Not wanting to see the absence, the fetishist-as-viewer imposes a presence upon a neutral object or scene and invests (cathects) it with the desired, fantasmatic qualities which give the promise of pleasure. Now this is complex and approximate, but what I rightly or wrongly call the "figures" of horror cinema seem to presume that the viewer wants a full vision of horror and simultaneously does *not* want to see it screened. This is somewhat different from the strict view of fetishism, since, in the case of horror cinema, a *long* look at the object of terror tends to rob this object of its traumatic qualities. The viewer "knows" that the more he/she stares, the more the terror will dissipate—to the extent that the image of full horror will be revealed (unveiled) as more constructed, more artificial, more a fantasy, more a *fiction* than the fiction which prepares and exhibits it. To look the horror in the face for very long robs it of its power.

I suggest that the viewer does not want, or *should* not want, to doubt the terror of the terrible. So through this figural *seepage* from another, absent scene, the film overlays horror into scenes of apparent nonhorror in order to: (a) *protect* the viewer from the excess of the traumatic vision; (b) *inoculate* the viewer to accept the full vision, when, long delayed, it is screened; and (c) *protect itself against the viewer* by delaying or withholding the full vision of horror and by permitting the horror to bleed through the figures into empty scenes; it obtains a capital gain—pleasure for the viewer, profit for the industry—by refusing the viewer's scopophilia while yet allowing the drive to *almost* see—to almost find its object.

Seeing through not seeing; vision refused through vision given. To me, the most fascinating aspect of "everyday" cinema is the way in which it denies the pleasures it promises, while delivering them through the back door. This defensive strategy of pleasure, in which the viewer collaborates, is not confined to horror cinema. But because this is a genre that promises excess—trauma—the figures of defense are more obvious here.

AFTERWORD

In this short analysis of some of the ways in which horror cinema defends viewers against their own desire, I do not pretend to give a complete account of the conventions and codes of the genre. Like the theorists of scopophilia, I have dealt only with visual communication. Sound plays a crucial role in horror film by filling in the relatively empty visuals with suggestions of menace. Often, sound works to reinforce or intensify the threat of the visual figure. In other cases, the presence of the monster is given entirely through the soundtrack, as when heavy breathing or the unresolved repetitive motifs of suspense music are overlaid onto an apparently innocent scene. In the latter strategy, sound functions not to cue the viewer/auditor how to interpret the visuals but, like the visual figures outlined here, communicates an *other* scene while yet withholding it from full presence. The text invites the viewer simultaneously to respond to two contradictory "realities" of discourse, while allowing either message to be disavowed as *more* fictional than the other "track" of the fiction.

NOTES

1. This condensed account of contemporary reception theory leans heavily on the work of Wolfgang Iser, *The Act of Reading: A Theory of Aesthetic Response* (Baltimore, Md.: Johns Hopkins University Press, 1978). See also Susan R. Suleiman, "Introduction: Varieties of Audience-Oriented Criticism," in *The Reader in the Text,* ed. Suleiman and Inge Crosman (Princeton, N.J.: Princeton University Press, 1980), for a broad account of the issues involved.

2. "Realization" translates Roman Ingarden's term *Konkretisation*—the process by which individual readers, listeners, or viewers engage and activate the text.

3. In his 1975 "Histoire/discours," Christian Metz proposed that the vision of the viewer (as voyeur) is "the seeing of an outlaw, of an *Id* unrelated to any *Ego*." Trans. as "Story/discourse. A Note on Two Kinds of Voyeurism," in *The Imaginary Signifier,* ed. Metz (Bloomington: Indiana University Press, 1982), 97. My emphasis here is on the limits, not the omnipotence, of viewing.

4. J. B. Pontalis, "Dream as Object," *International Review of Psycho-Analysis*, 1 (London, 1974): 132.

5. When the dream becomes a nightmare, dreamers sometimes utilize the protective shield of "the dream screen" to ward off its content in place of the usual defense of waking up. My assumption here is that although the feature film is more analogous to the daydream than to the dream, the producers of the fantasy (Hollywood—the industry) do not want the viewer to "wake up" during the film. When pleasure threatens to move over the edge into unpleasure, discomfort, Hollywood provides some approximation of the dream screen in order that the viewer will not repudiate the excess of the promise—reject the film or leave the theatre. Hollywood promotes easy pleasures even when it promotes the spectacle of pain verging on sadomasochism, but, at the last minute, withholding it. Cf. Bertram Lewin, "Sleep, the Mouth, and the Dream Screen," *Psychoanalytic Quarterly* 15 (1946): 419–34, on the psychoanalytic concept.

6. Cf. M. Masud R. Khan, "The Changing Use of Dreams in Psychoanalytical Practice," *International Journal of Psychoanalysis* 57 (1976): 324–30.

7. Metz, *The Imaginary Signifier*, Chaps. 3 and 4, and "Story/Discourse"; Stephen Heath, "Narrative Space" and "Body, Voice," in *Questions of Cinema* (Bloomington: Indiana University Press, 1981); Jean-Louis Baudry, "The Apparatus," *camera obscura*, no. 1 (1976): 104–26; and Laura Mulvey, "Visual Pleasure and Narrative Cinema," *Screen* 16, no. 3 (1975): 6–18.

8. Khan, "The Changing Use of Dreams."

9. Jean Laplanche and J. B. Pontalis, *The Language of Psycho-Analysis* (New York: Norton, 1973), 314–18; Daniel Lagache, "Fantasy, Reality and Truth," *International Journal of Psychoanalysis* 45 (1964): 180–89.

10. Stephen King, *Danse Macabre* (New York: Everest House, 1981).

11. Jean Francois Lyotard, "The Psychoanalytical Approach," in *Main Trends in Aesthetics and the Sciences of Art,* ed. Mikel Dufrenne (New York: Holmes & Meier, 1979), 134–50.

12. Cf. Lotte Eisner, *The Haunted Screen* (Berkeley: University of California Press, 1973), 199–206.

13. Tobe Hooper is the director of record, but *Poltergeist* is clearly controlled by Steven Spielberg. The "spectral light" motif was first introduced in *Close Encounters of the Third Kind* (1977) to render the alien presence more wondrous. In *Poltergeist*, the light both threatens and attracts.

14. Heath, "Negative Space," in *Questions of Cinema*, 51.

15. The best accounts of fetishism within the framework of classical psychoanalysis are Sigmund Freud, "Fetishism," in *The Standard Edition of the Complete Psychological Works of Sigmund Freud*, trans. and ed. James Strachey, vol. 21 (London: Hogarth Press and the Institute of Psychoanalysis, 1961): 147–57; and Z. Alexander Aarons, "Fetish, Fact and Fantasy: A Clinical Study of the Problems of Fetishism," *International Review of Psychoanalysis*, vol. 2 (1972): 199–203.

16. Mulvey, "Visual Pleasure and Narrative Cinema," 13–18.

17. Mulvey, "Afterthoughts on 'Visual Pleasure and Narrative Cinema' Inspired by *Duel in the Sun*," *Framework*, nos. 15–17 (1981), 12–15. Mulvey rejects the idea "that a hidden, as yet undiscovered femininity exists," but argues that "Hollywood genre films structured around masculine pleasure, offering an identification with the *active* point of view, allow a woman spectator to rediscover that lost aspect of her sexual identity, the never fully repressed bedrock of feminine neurosis" (p. 13).

18. Mulvey, "Visual Pleasure and Narrative Cinema."

19. Cf. Dennis Giles, "Pornographic Space: The Other Place," *1977 Film Studies Annual*, Part 2 (Pleasantville, N.Y.: Redgrave, 1977), 52–66.

4

The Aesthetics of Fright

Morris Dickstein

The release of Stanley Kubrick's *The Shining* (1980)—three years and $18 million in the making—provided a roaring climax to a whole decade of horror films, but it seems unlikely to have the enormous impact that *2001: A Space Odyssey* had in kicking off the science fiction revival. *The Shining* is less a horror film than a meticulous, enthralling academic imitation of one, just as Werner Herzog's *Nosferatu* (1979) is a ravishingly beautiful meditation on the whole genre, in the form of a tribute, scene by scene, to one of its enduring classics. Kubrick is a very cerebral filmmaker, and every shot in *The Shining* seems too perfect, too calculated; like John Carpenter in *The Fog* (1979) and George Romero in *Dawn of the Dead* (1978), he appears to have forgotten that the main point of a horror film is to frighten us, or rather to play on our fears. Given enough money, the successful genre director is quickly smitten with art, which can hinder the visceral, manipulative interchange between filmmaker and spectator. Kubrick, in any case, is hardly a director with an easy instinct for the temper of the audience.

It's less difficult to understand why people make horror films than why they go to them, or why these films prosper during certain periods. Popular film genres usually run in cycles, depending mainly on how much money they're making. But fright and terror have never really been out of style, not since the classic chillers like *The Cabinet of Dr. Caligari* (1919), which shows us life through the eyes of a madman;

Murnau's original *Nosferatu* (1922), based on Bram Stoker's *Dracula* (1897), which partly naturalized the genre and took it out of doors; and the famous Lon Chaney version of *The Phantom of the Opera* (1925). The appetite for horror seems almost timeless in its persistence, but such films thrive in periods of low-level social anxiety, such as Weimar Germany, the Depression, and the Cold War. Their surge of popularity in America during the '70s suggested currents of disquiet that were not always visible on the surface of our national life.

A gory cult film like Tobe Hooper's *The Texas Chainsaw Massacre* (1974), for example, clearly belonged to the last phase of the Vietnam War, when a great deal of violence was projected onto less taboo subjects, such as the West in *The Wild Bunch* (1969), the urban jungle in *Dirty Harry* (1972), World War II and Korea in *Patton* (1970) and *M*A*S*H* (1970). Like the Broadway musical *Sweeney Todd*, *Chainsaw* emphasizes a whole technology and economy of death, full of black-comic exaggeration, with stress on physical mutilation, severed limbs, and the victimization of the young. This is truly a film to get sick at.

In *Chainsaw* at least the threat retains a human form, however demented; the berserk butchers even make up a nuclear family, with their own little intimate rituals. But in more recent horror films like *Alien* (1979), the monster is a disgusting but almost invincible bloblike organism, and the stress is on the victim's essential powerlessness. This seems roughly to reflect a post-Vietnam sense of impotence and futility before a vast array of insoluble problems, from inflation, jobs, and urban crime to America's deteriorating world position. None of our current films are "about" these dilemmas, but they seem to breathe the same atmosphere.

Another feature of the new wave of horror is a hardcore pornography of violence made possible by the virtual elimination of censorship: the portrayal of explicit sex and of graphic violence developed in tandem. Horror films, apart from the ways they may mirror the social mood, have deep psychological sources that often involve a sexuality displaced into aggression: the sensual bite of Dracula, the long knife plunging into the female victims in Hitchcock's *Psycho* (1960) and John Carpenter's *Halloween* (1978). These last two films particularly exploit the voyeurism inherent in all cinema. The murderer is a voyeur enraged by his own excitement, and the camera appeals to our complicity by putting us repeatedly in his position, seeing what he sees, tempted to feel what he feels.

Films with a great deal of gore in them play to our voyeurism in another way. They shatter taboos, perhaps the last taboos we still have now that every sort of sex can be freely shown. As John Carpenter himself has pointed out, "The reason that these films are popular is that audiences want to see something that's forbidden. All these films toy with the rage and anger we have within us. That's the tantalizing aspect of such films as *Night of the Living Dead* (1968) and *The Texas Chainsaw Massacre* (1974), which are like spending a night in a charnel house. They do touch some awful nerve. And the more forbidden, the more alluring."[1]

Filmmakers realized early on that the darkened theater and the flickering images created a kind of dream space. The technology of film also made it possible for these images to be stylized and manipulated in a way that brought them beyond simple vision—the recording of how things look—and toward subjective awareness, the movement of our minds. As the art historian Erwin Panofsky wrote in a famous essay, "The movies have the power, entirely denied to the theatre, to convey psychological experiences by directly projecting their content to the screen, substituting, as it were, the eye of the beholder for the consciousness of the character."[2] Films have always thrived on wish-fulfillment fantasies, escapist fables in which the knotty dilemmas of real life yield happily to will and desire; but many other films have been grisly nightmares that touch on the basic fears that make us all vulnerable.

Today it seems that more people are paying money to be frightened than to be amused. Hardly a week passes without the release of some cheaply made shocker. Hitchcock's *Psycho* was already an attempt to go one up on these cheap thrillers, and it had an enormous influence on those that followed. George Romero's *Night of the Living Dead* (1968) not only found a new midnight teenage audience but also signaled a return to the classic ghoulish simplicities of the genre. It also made an enormous amount of money on a minimal investment, as have recent movies like *Halloween*, *When a Stranger Calls* (1979), *Silent Scream* (1980), and *Friday the 13th* (1980). Such films in turn spawn more extravagant productions that also make money, like Romero's half-satiric sequel, *Dawn of the Dead* (1978), and Ridley Scott's expensive *Alien*, a combination of sci-fi and horror directed at the anxious underside of the *Star Wars* (1977) audience.

These much-touted examples, quite impervious to bad reviews, tell only part of the story of our obsession with horror. Most horror films are never even written up: they are staples of the drive-ins and exploitation houses, where they rub shoulders with sex pictures and macho action flicks. The "art" of the horror film is a ludicrous notion since horror, even at its most commercially exploitative, is genuinely subcultural, like the wild child that can never be tamed, or the half-human mutant who appeals to our secret fascination with deformity and the grotesque. Horror and pornography are the most truly schlocky of all film types, the ones most likely to be betrayed by artistic treatment and lavish production values. Horror films are the ultimate B-movies, crude, cheap, and basic—the specialty of back street studios and plucky independents. The most typical examples are the movies which Jacques Tourneur, Robert Wise, and Mark Robson directed for Val Lewton at RKO in the early 1940s, such as *Cat People* (1942), or Roger Corman's tacky versions of Poe in the early 1960s, like *The Tomb of Ligeia* (1964).

Fear and desire are our most primitive impulses, both ridiculously easy to arouse—few props are necessary to draw us in. Science fiction is much more conceptual: its kind of expensive hardware could only hamper the way horror or sex films work, and dilute their impact. Why people pay to be aroused is no mystery, but it's much harder to guess why they willingly let themselves be terrified, and why they're doing so in increasing numbers these days.

To go to a horror film, as everyone realizes, is to submit to an *experience*, to court a certain danger, to risk being disturbed, shaken up, assaulted. Much of popular culture, like so much that happens to us in the larger world, washes over us without really reaching us. Many people keep their television sets on all day as a shadowy background to their regular lives, perhaps as a defense against loneliness or conversation; but even the soap operas they avidly follow scarcely engross half their attention. But my friends were either envious or aghast when I told them how many horror films I was seeing in preparation for this article. Even distributors were dubious when I arranged to see more than one at a time, as if I might disintegrate under the shock of all that emotional manipulation, as John Cassavetes simply explodes, like an oversize firecracker, at the end of Brian De Palma's brilliant firecracker of a movie, *The Fury* (1978).

Poor Cassavetes, who plays an insidiously good villain, is blown apart and sent to hell by a young girl who has telekinetic "powers": when she touches people's hands, she can read the story of their lives; when this upsets her—and she is easily upset—she holds on more

tightly, and they begin to bleed at every orifice. This is a kind of parable for the way horror works. These films have a short-term power over
us that few other stories can match; with their instinct for our deepest
anxieties, they seem to be able to read our minds; and if they grip us
too tightly, we imagine we might come unhinged, or blow up, or be
"scared to death."

The fear of death is the ultimate attraction of all horror films. Those
who submit to them are generally young, and they go seeking the kinds
of thrills that can only be had through risk and danger. In *Beyond the
Pleasure Principle*, an inquiry into the negative dimensions of our fantasy lives, including our nightmares and death wishes, Freud described
how children create games around the very things they most fear, as a
way of subduing those fears and gaining control.[3] Horror films are a
safe, routinized way of playing with death, like going on the roller
coaster or parachute jump at an amusement park. There is always *some*
chance, however remote, that the car will jump the tracks—otherwise
the thrill would be gone—but this death trip is essentially vicarious.

Going to horror films is a way of neutralizing anxiety by putting an
aesthetic bracket around it. Even the most terrifying nightmare must
come to an end; although it may trouble the mind for days afterward,
it must be followed by a sense of relief: "Thank God it was only a
dream!" Sleep research and psychiatry have both shown that dreams
are vital to the psychic economy. (Repeated interruptions can bring on
the symptoms of psychosis.) Horror films have some of the same
cathartic or purgative effect. They lance and probe our encapsulated
fears, and drain off feelings we didn't even know we had.

This is why horror films work best when they remain simple and
fundamental, like *Halloween* and *Night of the Living Dead*, which have
the timeless aura of the early classics of the genre. A dark street, a
deserted house, a creaking door, an escaped madman, a throng of
ghouls and zombies ("pure motorized instinct")—these seem to me far
more effective than the spaceship setting of *Alien*, the antisuburban satire of *Dawn of the Dead* (set in a shopping center), or the excessive
gore of *The Texas Chainsaw Massacre*. It's easy to enumerate the elemental fears that horror films uncover, stir up, and temporarily allay:
fear of the dark, fear of being alone, fear of enclosure, fear of the supernatural, fear of human blood, fear of corpses and cemeteries, fear of the
unquiet spirits of the dead, and so on.

Many of these fears occur more commonly in anthropological
accounts of primitive tribes than in contemporary stories. Civilized

man, as he grows out of childhood and adolescence, is taught to subdue his fears and superstitions and to accept the notion that society will protect him. We are told that if we behave with rational self-restraint others will do likewise. But on some level we never really believe this.

People throughout history have told each other ghost stories as a way of both terrifying and reassuring themselves by making their fears explicit. (John Carpenter's film *The Fog* begins with an elaborate ghost story, told to children with macabre glee by a hammy John Houseman.) Unlike our amorphous insecurities, stories are dramatic and offer release, for they have clear-cut conflicts, villains, turning points, and resolutions. Primitive man rehearsed myths and fables that gave form and dimension to the unknown—made it more human, more comprehensible. The endless permutations of the Dracula and Frankenstein stories suggest that these are some modern counterparts to ancient myths.

The decline of religion and the increasing secularization of society have given more and more mythical resonance to popular culture, which provides us with binding and common experiences and satisfies some primitive needs. The subcultural material in horror films is one form of this return of the repressed. Once, as children, we may actually have believed that on Halloween the bogeyman would come to get us; in *Halloween* that fear comes out again, and we gasp and laugh at the same time (a typically uneasy reaction of horror movie audiences). The psychological impact is transient but intense as these elemental fears rise up and evaporate almost as soon as they appear. Like all vicarious experiences, going to horror films is a repetition compulsion, a movie mogul's dream. We are "scared to death" but rarely end up dead. After all, it was only a movie, only a bad dream.

I'm not trying to be subtle about these movies, and certainly I don't want to intellectualize them. They aren't allegories, and at their best they aren't even that complicated, although we like it when they find new wrinkles for the old simple pattern. The purest horror is gothic, but we don't want to see the same haunted house again and again, not even in Transylvania. Turn it into an out-of-the-way motel in *Psycho*, a piece of small-town America in *Halloween*, or even a spaceship in *Alien*, and the creaking doors and unburied corpses gain a new lease on life (i.e., death).

Alien is the kind of film that throws away so much money on sets and special effects that it looks almost cheap, but not in the familiar schlocky way. Like *The Shining*, which tries hard for a cheap, grainy look in its opening scenes, *Alien* pretends to be badly made, full of dim images and indistinct, mumbled dialogue, which the director hoped would prove disorienting but is merely annoying. Far too self-conscious for its own good, *Alien* plays with mythical images of birth and parturition, as Kubrick plays with time and recurrence. We hear about the "umbilicus" of the "mother ship," along with literary allusions to Conrad and Melville. (Kubrick evokes the world of Scott Fitzgerald.)

In the tradition of *2001: A Space Odyssey* (1968), *Alien* makes little effort to humanize the crew of the spaceship, except for the Ishmael figure, the lone survivor, played by Sigourney Weaver. One of the characters, the "science officer," even turns out to be a robot—a neat twist in the long tradition of mad or inhuman scientists who tamper with nature for the sake of forbidden knowledge or power. It is he who brings the alien organism aboard, on the orders of the "company" that owns the ship and the computer that runs it, at the cost of the lives of nearly all the crew. All the technology of the movie is there to be wasted: it's quite useless against the "perfect organism" that the twin evils of science and capitalism are determined to bring back to Earth.

What makes this film disturbing, more disquieting than cathartic, is the claustral quality of the ship, which is heightened by the mysterious growth and mutation of the monster inside. Before I saw it, a friend told me it was a film about cancer, and I can see his point. We react viscerally to the insuperable power of the monster, its implacable irrationality and otherness. Many recent genre films have this fatalistic and paranoid quality; the monsters are totally inhuman creatures of motiveless malignity, and the films give their "heroes" little chance of defeating them. Such films deliberately play havoc with the expectations we bring from previous films. Sometimes these bitter and ironic endings work, as in *Night of the Living Dead*, where the lone survivor in a houseful of victims—a black man whose cool resourcefulness had given the film its only measure of hope—is shot by a lawman who takes him for one of the zombies.

The point of this ending is that the rescuers, who supposedly represent civilization, turn out to be as dangerous as the monsters, and the victims are hard to tell from the human-seeming ghouls who prey on them. The same kind of reversal occurs in Fred Walton's *When a Stranger Calls* when Charles Durning, a former detective hired to track down an escaped psychopath, sets out to kill him instead of bringing him back. The killer, once little more than a vicious animal, has been treated for years with drugs and psychotherapy, and he approaches people now with a pathetic need for affection and human contact. In one scene we see him cowering, naked and alone, in a public toilet, trying to find the person behind the face in the mirror. The escaped killer has become the victim, the former lawman has become a kind of avenging monster, and our natural sympathies are confused and dispersed.

Hitchcock, with his suavely ingratiating villains and subtly guilty victims, is a master of this principle of exchange, through which melodramatic plots can take on a surprising moral and emotional complexity. Recent horror films like *Alien* avoid giving the monster any redeeming qualities, but this was certainly not true of the classic horror films of the 1930s, such as *Frankenstein* (1931), or *King Kong* (1933), or the misunderstood creatures played by Claude Rains in *The Invisible Man* (1933) and the remake of *The Phantom of the Opera* (1943). When my son was four or five, he cried through the ending of *King Kong* on television as the beast, already brought down by love, is attacked by planes—actually piloted by the two directors!—and falls to his death from the Empire State Building. Many of the other classic monsters also have their warm, furry side and their own poignant predicaments. As Stuart Kaminsky has noted, "The true villains of many horror films are not the monsters, but the people who created them."[4]

These films are true to the conception of Mary Shelley's original *Frankenstein* novel of 1818. Mrs. Shelley shared her husband's radical conviction that the source of evil was in our social relationships, not in original sin or innate aggressiveness. Her monster is the botched work of an obsessed experimenter who toys with life but then abandons his own offspring. At first the creature, far from wanting to kill, seeks only warmth, affection, and community, but because of his misshapen appearance he gets them only from a blind man. He is utterly isolated from human fellowship, for everyone judges him by what he looks like. Finally, their cruelty and rejection turn him into the very thing he appears to be, and he begins to take revenge on the family of his creator. James Whale's movie versions, especially the wonderful sequel, *The Bride of Frankenstein* (1935), preserve a good deal of the sympathetic side of Mrs. Shelley's vision. This misbegotten fellow isn't really so bad, he's just misunderstood, and his tormentors seem more genuinely malicious than he is.

In the next great horror period, the 1950s, there are still some manlike creatures that haunt films like *The Thing* (1951) and *Creature from the Black Lagoon* (1954), sometimes done up with very good special effects. But usually the danger is far more pervasive and impalpable:

something from outer space, or a biological mutation, or something within the people themselves. As the old pre-war monsters become comedy characters, material for Abbott and Costello, a new paranoia, a doomsday psychology, enters the horror-sci-fi field. This is often attributed to Cold War anxieties and to fear of nuclear war. Interplanetary invaders can serve as transparent stand-ins for the Russians, and the films usually blame monstrous mutations on the radiation from nuclear tests.

But the most revealing films of the period are those that deal with the monster within. In *Forbidden Planet* (1956), an ingeniously Freudian adaptation of Shakespeare's *The Tempest*, the Caliban-like creature is a destructive electromagnetic field, which is an unwitting projection of the repressed wishes of the benign scientist himself. (This Prospero has the darker shadings people usually miss in the original play.) And in Don Siegel's celebrated *Invasion of the Body Snatchers* (1956), the alien presence is not the pods but a growing army of friends and family who have been transformed by them—turned not into ghouls with visible fangs but into eerie versions of themselves, tranquilized creatures without anxiety or affect.

The politics of this film are exceptionally ambiguous. In one sense these look-alikes embody an anti-Communist vision of an invisible fifth column undermining the American way of life, a belief that They are gradually taking over. But in their emotionless normality and self-content, the Pod People are surely a warning about conformity and the loss of identity in a monolithic society. The monsters in this ordinary town are no more than our ordinary, timid, complacent selves. In a gradual reversal, the few who hold out against them, the dissenters who cling to their individuality, become the objects of a witch-hunt pursued by the kind of wolf pack that once went out after Frankenstein.

The intriguing principle of exchange in this film is that people "turn" just by letting go, falling asleep—they can be caught napping as their freedom ebbs away—yet still look exactly like their former selves. Good characters turn in the same way in *Night of the Living Dead*. At first, in the old paranoid manner, the film portrays the ghouls as a wholly alien and unstoppable force. But eventually director Romero hits on the trick that even the besieged victims can turn into predators and join the legion of zombies within minutes after "dying," although they can be killed permanently, by a blow or a bullet to the brain. This creates more of a balance of forces, with less feeling of utter helplessness, but it also heightens the personal tension inside the beleaguered enclave: the enemy is also within. (Romero spoils this device and milks it for comedy in *Dawn of the Dead* by turning the zombies into doll-like figures in a shooting gallery, who must all be methodically rekilled after being "killed.")

Except for *When a Stranger Calls*, most of our recent horror films, like *The Omen* (1976) and *Halloween*, avoid these ambiguous links between monster and victim and treat the danger as a completely alien threat, "pure evil" (says Donald Pleasence in *Halloween*), a surrogate for the Devil—even when the creature is actually inside us, as in *The Exorcist* (1973), or seems to be our own flesh and blood, as in *The Omen* and *Damien–Omen II* (1978). The obscene rasping voice of Mercedes McCambridge is not really a *part* of poor Linda Blair in *The Exorcist* (1973): she's merely dubbing her dialogue. And the snakelike creature that bursts out of the chest of one of the crewmen in *Alien* is certainly giving a new and more literal twist to the idea of the monster within. This is the film's scariest and most effective moment, but unlike Dr. Morbius in *Forbidden Planet*, this man's unconscious is in no way implicated, only his digestion. Futuristic advances in biology have evidently made psychoanalysis irrelevant, since inwardness is obsolete.

The many incarnations of the Devil since *Rosemary's Baby* (1968) have an especially ominous ideological ring, though they make for ingeniously decadent horror, full of pseudo-religious overtones. The Blakean innocence of the flower child in '60s mythology has given way to the absolute evil of these possessed children, who must either be eradicated or violently wrenched free of their inner selves. This sort of evil refutes all visions of social progress, all Shelleyan or Rousseauian conceptions of human nature, for it can't be reasoned with, can't be educated, can't be reformed—it can only be exorcised. At the end of *The Omen*, Gregory Peck loses his life for hesitating to drive a stake through the heart of the beautiful child he has raised as his own son. This is an apology for hardheartedness worthy of Milton Friedman, an assault on sentimentality that would warm the heart of a neoconservative. It is '70s-style backlash—and apocalyptic pessimism—with a vengeance.

In *The Shining*, Kubrick reverses this pernicious grouping and makes the father the agent of the Devil—a good Faustian posture for a would-be writer—with the psychic child, the waiflike '60s wife, and the kindly (but dispensable) black man as his available victims. He substitutes a real family for the false families in *The Omen* and *Damien—Omen II* (1978). But like many horror films, *The Shining*, for all its brilliance of execution, comes to grief on the problem of motivation. Kubrick de-emphasizes the theme of the "evil house" which linked Stephen King's novel to the gothic tradition. Instead, *The Shining* becomes the first horror film that blames it all on writer's block, beyond which it simply relies on madness, as so many cheap horror films do, as an explanation for all kinky and violent behavior. This is a scenarist's cop-out which makes inordinate demands on Jack Nicholson's mobile face and leering satanic grin as a substitute for motivation.

Yet Kubrick complicates the picture by showing the gradual (if less drastic) derangement of the wife and child as well. (The boy, like Tony Perkins in *Psycho*, withdraws increasingly into his alter ego, while the wife actually strikes the first blows with a baseball bat and a kitchen knife.) Perhaps with resonances from Kubrick's own life, the film shows how family dynamics go awry under the pressure of isolation, especially when one member assumes the prerogatives of genius: Do Not Disturb ("All work and no play . . ."). At its most convincing, *The Shining* is not a portrait of a madman or of a haunted house but, as Kubrick himself told an interviewer, the story of one man's family quietly going insane together.[5]

The Shining, 1980. Jack Torrance (Jack Nicholson) chats with the phantom bartender Lloyd (Joe Turkel). From the editors' collection.

Horror films remain exceptionally lovely to look at even when their point of view is gloomy and their material sordid. They often have a stunning visual quality that seems quintessentially cinematic, and they attract neurotic but visually oriented directors who are still captivated by sharply etched childhood memories. The Universal films of the 1930s, with their great shadowy compositions, were among the first to reflect the visual influence of the German expressionist cinema of the 1920s, whose stylized symbolism and morbidity had seemed quite alien to the spirit of Hollywood. Some of the new horror films were shot by the great German cinematographer Karl Freund, who had worked with Fritz Lang on *Metropolis* (1926) and later directed *The Mummy* (1932) and MGM's *Mad Love* (1935). (These films even affected the look of *Citizen Kane* [1941], whose gothic touches put the tycoon in direct line of the great '30s monsters.)

More recently, Brian De Palma's films, with their brilliant technique and spectacular camera work, use trashy *Grand Guignol* material as occasions for exquisite exercises in style. De Palma is probably the best director to work in this new wave of horror, followed at some distance by Carpenter, Romero, and, perhaps, Hooper. Their films, shot mainly in color, work best when they have their own visual signature: a mass of figures looking like death camp inmates, seen from a low angle, surging forward hypnotically in *Night of the Living Dead*; a jack-o'-lantern in *Halloween*, reproduced on a larger scale in shots of suburban houses at night, isolated pools of light surrounded by darkness; low tracking shots down long empty corridors in *The Shining*; the murderers in whiteface in *Halloween* and *Chainsaw*, the one breathing heavily behind his impersonal, implacable mask, the other whirling around dementedly with his smoking tool in the air; drowned mariners in *The Fog*; an amazing variety of shots of blood, including menstrual blood, in De Palma's *Carrie* (1976) and *The Fury*, films that, like *Halloween*, express a powerful ambivalence about female sexuality.

The extraordinary thing about these images is not simply their beauty but their suggestiveness, the unconscious reverberations they have for us. The best horror films avoid overwhelming us with gore and violence, which can easily turn comical when overdone, or be pointlessly punishing to the audience. Both Carpenter and De Palma work more by suggestion, like their acknowledged master, Hitchcock, and like some erotic filmmakers who eschew hard-core sex for being too literal and unimaginative: organ-grinding rather than fantasy. As Carpenter observed in a recent interview, "You've got to put them on edge. And you can't gross them out. Because you'll lose them. . . . Don't show the meat when the knife goes in, don't cut to the blood going everywhere, then all of them will stay with you. If you suggest it, they'll do it right up here, in their heads. This idea, of the audience projecting their fantasy, is to me the secret of movies. And the secret for me is that I get emotionally involved."[6]

Getting caught up emotionally, walking out drained and satisfied, waking up relieved to deal with more workaday problems—this is the secret of all horror films. When I asked my students why they subjected themselves to such pulverizing experiences, one girl answered, dialectically, "Well, life is so boring, so routine"; another said, "It makes the blood boil"; a third boasted with some relish (and a look of bravery) that *Halloween* was the scariest movie she'd ever seen. It would seem that ordinary life today, even for the young, is out of touch with some of our most potent energies and anxieties. Perhaps liberalism and secularism have exorcised too much of our sense of evil. Perhaps the real legacy of advanced industrial society in the '70s was boredom. Horror films, which excavate archaic fears and taboos and explore deeply buried wishes, have undoubtedly come along to help redress the balance.

NOTES

1. Quoted by Aljean Harmetz, "Cheap and Profitable, Horror Films Are Multiplying," *New York Times* (October 24, 1979), C21.

2. Erwin Panofsky, "Style and Medium in the Motion Pictures," in *Film Theory and Criticism: Introductory Readings*, ed. Gerald Mast and Marshall Cohen (New York: Oxford University Press, 1974), 156.

3. Sigmund Freud, *Beyond the Pleasure Principle*, trans. James Strachey (New York: Bantam Books, 1959), 32–38.

4. Stuart Kaminsky, *American Film Genres* (Bowling Green, Ohio: Popular Press, 1974), 107.

5. For a similar view, see Michel Ciment, *Kubrick*, trans. Gilbert Adair (New York: Holt, Rinehart and Winston, 1983), 144.

6. John Carpenter, interviewed by Todd McCarthy, "Trick and Treat," *Film Comment* 16, no. 1 (January–February 1980): 23.

5

The Witch in Film: Myth and Reality

Sharon Russell

Women and witches: both words have mythic associations and many times both partake of the same myth. Women have been persecuted as witches because they were women, and women now use the term *witch* as a means of revenge against persecution. But beyond myth lies reality, and the concept of the witch is a negative myth derived from a false interpretation of reality. If the image of the witch in films is a product of a myth, this myth must be explored. Any filmic representation of the witch must be considered in the light of the myth and its reality.

The mythic use of the concept of the witch is bifacial. Men have used it as a means of confirming deeply held suspicions as to the true nature of women, a product of the misogyny inherent in the Judeo-Christian tradition. Women see the myth as a means of male suppression, especially of the residual powers of matriarchal societies that survived into the Middle Ages. There is a duality in the manifestations of the myth as well, a division between religious and folkloric expressions of witchcraft. On one side the witch is a person, usually female, who is responsible for maleficium, evil acts, expressed through charms, potents, curses, the midwife who kills or delivers deliberately deformed children, the jealous woman who makes former lovers impotent. On the other side, the witch is the participant in Satanic rites, inversions of

orthodox Christian practice or extension of it into areas considered
nonhuman, such as cannibalism or copulation with the Devil at great
sabbats that are reached by flying through the air on broomsticks. It is
the union of these two aspects that occasioned the great witch hunts of
the Middle Ages, and it is also in this area that there is the greatest
distance between popular belief and the reality of the events as they
occurred. Until very recently most people, while discounting the more
extreme aspects of the various confessions forced from so-called
witches, felt that there must be some underlying truth in the accounts
of witches' sabbats and the worship of horned gods and other manifestations of the Devil.

Jules Michelet, in *Satanism and Witchcraft*, written during the aftermath of the French Revolution, saw in the cults an expression of peas-
ant revolt, a response to their oppression.[1] Margaret Murray, a British
anthropologist, is largely responsible for the widely held belief that the
cults represented the last manifestations of old religions such as the
matriarchal, which had survived the encroachment of Christianity, and
that the witch hunts represented the church's attempt to finally repress
these anti-Christian rites. It is this latter approach that has been
accepted by many feminists and has been the reason for the high
esteem given to witches and work that deals with them among some
feminist critics. Many scholars have long felt uneasy with Murray's
approach. One of these, R. E. L. Masters in *Eros and Evil*, logically
argues that the reports of the painfulness of intercourse with demons
suggests a Christian sense of guilt rather than the kind of sexual pleasure associated with earlier orgiastic rites.[2] But until recently scholars
were still left with an uneasy sense that there remained a certain factual
level to the accounts of these rites cited by Michelet and Murray. In his
book *Europe's Inner Demons*, Norman Cohen carefully destroys all
suggestions of documentary proof that any rites took place.[3] He shows
that there is no factual basis for any accounts of witches' sabbats, and
that instead these reports are either forgeries or the result of stories
originated by the church and other authorities as a means of first persecuting nonorthodox groups such as the Vaudois or of destroying the
power of such organizations as the Knights Templar. The stories used
to justify these persecutions were identical to those used to persecute
early Christians and which were also used by Christians to attack Jews.
But such an approach can only influence present and future attitudes
towards witchcraft. The myths must die, but the past cannot be judged
by facts only recently available. Films made yesterday cannot be judged
in terms of a reality discovered only today.

But can the myth in any form be seen in feminist terms? It is a myth that still posits at its core a male deity who forces his attentions, sexual or otherwise, on his female devotees. The rites themselves promote the concept of female promiscuity and female lust. Masters points out that both the myth of the insatiable woman and the myth of the chaste and pure woman, which occurred as a reaction to the excesses of the great witch hunts, are essentially male creations designed to excuse the possibility of masculine inadequacy (in men's minds) arising from the differences in male and female physiology. (The tumescence-detumescence mechanism that limits male sexual activity endows the male with a permanent sense of sexual inadequacy.) Thus belief in the myth of the witch's sabbat, demonic rites, inversions of the Mass are not liberating feminist positions, but, in actuality, reinforce male myths even to the retention of a male as the central figure in the myth. At the same time, the witch, a male creation, has historically been seen as a threat to men and male domination. The very need to create a myth is a recognition of the potency of the fears that force it into existence. In understanding its use it is also important to distinguish between a male use of a masculine myth and a female attempt to transform it.

An understanding of the history of the myth is important because the witch as a figure holds an interesting position relative to other monster figures in popular culture. Although there are many novels and films that deal with female monster figures, there are few serious treatments of witches as figures of terror or power. Many treatments of Satanic cults focus on the male as the center of the cult rather than the female. Most monster figures emerged from the Gothic tradition in which women were most often victims or—what is a tamer version of the witch—the *femme fatale* or the *belle dame sans merci*. The *femme fatale* leading men to their doom is entirely a sexual image deriving from the siren and the vampire, mysterious but not threatening figures for the Romantics. Old women as witches practically disappear during this period, and the evil enchantress holds none of the power of the witches of the Middle Ages as folklore or fairytale figures of fear. As Mario Praz indicates in *The Romantic Agony*, the rise of the Byronic superman precludes strong females.[4] Carmen as a Romantic heroine is not a real sorceress; imprisonment for brawling is substituted for death by burning. Real fears of witches are diffused, and those female monsters which become, in the twentieth century, the subject of films are mainly extensions of the vampire myth, a myth that posed a popular rather than an official fear and which had male as well as female manifestations. (There is no church document on vampirism comparable to the *Mallus Maleficiarum*, a treatise on witchcraft written in 1486.)

The use of the witch in film does not follow the usual pattern of other characters in the horror genre. The number and distribution of witches films point to some interesting differences between films about witches and horror films in general. Although there are relatively few silent horror films (and most of these concern monsters), witch films form a large portion of the early explorations of the trickfilm, the film concerned with the use of special effects. In these films it is the maleficium attributed to witches, the spells and charms that they cast, that interest the filmmaker because these acts provide an excuse for various trick occurrences. In the Méliès film *The Enchanted Well*, the witch's curse is the impetus for the various tricks that the well performs. The actions of witches, sorcerers, demons, and devils provide the rationale for displays of virtuosity on the part of the filmmaker. It is true that in some of these films witches do ride on broomsticks or perform other actions associated with sabbats, but it is the way that the action is performed, the filmmaking "magic" required to present the illusion, which is the focus of the film.

Benjamin Christensen's *Häxan (Witchcraft through the Ages)*, made in 1921, is one of the first films to treat the question of witches seriously. While many of the early trickfilms were comedies, this film takes what purports to be a documentary approach to the subject. Throughout the early silent era there were also several adaptations of the Joan of Arc story, the most famous being Carl Dreyer's *La Passion de Jeanne d'Arc* (1928). The pivotal problem in this story is the attempt to discover whether Joan is inspired by God or by the Devil. She is finally burned as a witch. The early nonhumorous manifestations of the myth treat it from a historical perspective not usually associated with the horror genre. Whereas the monster may be at the center of these other films, it is witchcraft itself which is often the focal point of early explorations of the theme.

In the 1930s, when the Universal Studio cycle of horror films began to appear, witchcraft was not treated at all. Of the few films that deal with the subject in any capacity, one, *The Wizard of Oz* (1939), presents it within the larger context of a fantasy, an adaptation of a children's book into a musical format (not the usual method of exposition for a horror film even though it certainly has terrifying moments). The other two major films of this period continue the historical approach to the subject begun in the '20s. And it is not until the '40s that the first recognizable uses of this theme (the aim being to create fear in the audience rather than a calm exploration of the subject) in the horror genre appear with *The Seventh Victim* (1943) and *Weird Woman* (1944). But the historical and comic approaches which began with the silents still continued in the Victor Fleming version of *Joan of Arc* (1948) and the René Clair comedy, *I Married a Witch* (1942). More witch films appeared in the '50s, but several of these still dealt with the historical (Joan or the Salem witches) or the comic (*Bell, Book and Candle*, 1958). It is not until the '60s that the witch becomes another creature in the gallery of available horror film figures.

Many horror figures have their origins in folklore which is transformed into literature and then to film. Others begin as literary creations. When these figures are taken over by film they retain characteristics that make them easily identifiable. They act in predictable ways and retain established characteristics throughout subsequent portrayals. Their characters may deepen, motivation for their actions may be clearer, but the iconic traits acquired by a horror figure become standardized. Monsters that are created through some kind of human intervention work out of a relationship to their creator (serve him or rebel against his control). Females seldom create monsters or control them (except perhaps as a variant of the mother/son relationship, as in *Trog* [1970], or through the act of giving birth to a monster). There are, of course, female horror figures. Most common among these are those falling under the category of the undead—vampires, zombies, women buried alive. And women can make themselves into monsters in the Dr. Jekyll/Mr. Hyde tradition. But these figures seldom operate independently. Female vampires are usually controlled either by Dracula or by a Dracula-like figure.

Witches in literature and folklore generally operate independently. It is only in their filmic representations that male control enters as a central theme. In recent years, when there has been an upsurge in the number of witch films, these often contain a male as the dominant, controlling the witch either as a Satan figure or in the hidden structure of the film as its focus. *Burn, Witch, Burn* (1961) would seem to be about the wife/witch of the title, but the actual focal point is the husband, who is most important for the development of the plot. The iconic characteristics developed by witches in film often run counter to those manifestations in myth and folklore. Even when the witch is central to the plot, it is the ramifications of witchcraft, the hunting and burning of witches, rather than the power inherent in the figure that are developed. The general movement from exploration to exploitation of the myth that has occurred recently still fails to give full emphasis to the symbolic power of the witch.

Even two major films which seem to be explorations of the power of witchcraft and therefore feminist expositions of this theme can, on closer examination, be seen as not too distant from popular exploitations of it. In *Day of Wrath* (1943) Dreyer certainly presents one of the most balanced, humane, and terrifying portrayals of those conflicts that produce witches and witch trials. And in *A Very Curious Girl* (1969) Nelly Kaplan attempts a feminist expression of the myth, a fable of a witch's revenge. Each of these films represents one aspect of the development of the witch film.

Dreyer's film is both an extension of his interest in the supernatural, begun with such films as *Vampyr* (1932) and continuing to later films (*Ordet*, 1954), and an examination of the historical implication of witchcraft begun with *La Passion de Jeanne d'Arc*. In *Day of Wrath* the story is set in a historical period, that of the witch hunts in Denmark. It begins with the pursuit of Marthe, an old woman who has been accused as a witch. She attempts to take refuge with Anne, the young wife of the parson, Absolon. Absolon's mother also lives with them in the rectory. Marthe is discovered and taken to be tortured until she confesses. Martin, Absolon's son from a previous marriage, returns home, and he and Anne gradually fall in love. During the course of Marthe's inquisition, Anne learns that her mother was a witch who had been saved from burning by Absolon because he wanted to marry Anne. Anne becomes convinced of her powers. When Absolon dies from an apparent heart attack during a quarrel, she is convinced that she has inherited her mother's abilities. At Absolon's funeral his mother accuses her of witchcraft, and when Martin deserts her she acknowledges the truth of the accusation. The final images of the film are a shot of her face and then a shot of the cross.

Dreyer's world is a world in flux. Women become examples of challenges to the status quo: they must embody power in order to become the viable force necessary for the conflicts in his films to reach the tragic proportions that he is constantly trying to find. Tragedy is always possible in his world because the oppositions which he establishes are denials of absolutes and recognitions of possibilities which are prevented from being fulfilled. Many critics have noted the sympathy in Dreyer's films for older people (often women) in the context of a more general conflict between youth and age. Absolon's evil is miti-

Witch burning in Day of Wrath, *1943. Still courtesy of
Jerry Ohlinger's Movie Material Store.*

gated by his realization of his errors as he sits in front of the fire in a
scene that is intercut with Martin and Anne's walk in the moonlight.
Male/female dichotomies are blurred by the constant presence of the
choir of young boys—boys who will grow up to be like the fathers
portrayed in the burning sequence, but who, for the present, sing like
women. Even the traditional method of depicting the conflict between
good and evil as an opposition of light and darkness is obliterated. Few
faces are ever fully lit. The strongest love scenes between Martin and
Anne take place at night, the daytime boat ride only foreshadowing the
ultimate destruction of their love.

The ambiguities in the presentation of Anne are inherent in Dreyer's
worldview. He belongs to that strange kinship of Scandinavians whose
attitudes toward women are reflections of larger concerns, from Strind-
berg's misogyny and Bergman's neurotics, to Stiller, Sjostrom, and
Ibsen's women, who are used to counter the strong Lutheranism of
their society. Dreyer's work is balanced between a portrayal of the joy
of life and a search for real tragedy, a return to the Greeks. Except for

those few films with happy endings, Dreyer's women, like Electra and Antigone, are impelled towards a destiny of their destruction and often the destruction of those whose lives they touch.

In *A Very Curious Girl* Marie's mother is also considered a witch by the villagers. With her mother's death Marie assumes her powers. She lures the village men to a strange funeral ritual where she gets them drunk and has them bury her mother. When Marie puts on makeup before the funeral she begins the transformation into witch/*femme fatale,* which will enable her to gain her revenge on the village that has mistreated both her and her mother. The killing of her pet ram (among other associations, it represents the horned god of the Devil) strengthens her resolve. She turns to prostitution as a means of getting both money and information. Much of the money she spends on items that are later discarded, but she also purchases a tape recorder. At the end of the film, she plays in church the recordings of confidential revelations made by the men of the village, returns home, burns the consumer products she has amassed and takes off down the road.

A Very Curious Girl develops its message through the reversal of usual expectations: the woman triumphs, the witch does the burning rather than is burned, the prostitute doesn't repent yet is happy at the end, sex is a means of oppressing men rather than being oppressed by them. The objections to the use of a witch as a liberating figure have already been presented, and many writers have discussed the problems in Kaplan's approach to the economic and social aspects of prostitution. But by associating Marie with both witchcraft and seduction, Kaplan defuses any of the power that the myth would have (even if the historical problems in its use were discounted). While Anne in *Day of Wrath* is really more closely tied in maleficia (curses, etc.) than to participation in demonic ritual, Marie's maleficia are accomplished through the exploitation of her body. She may revolt against the village, but she really conforms to most male expectations from Circe to *la belle dame sans merci.* Revenge and expressions of anger are certainly positive forces, but in *A Very Curious Girl* they become part of the traditional male view of female betrayal. The use of the witch in this film then becomes a double negative (which does not cancel itself and thereby become a positive image). A male-created myth is used as the basis for the creation of a masculine image of woman. The real reversal would be a portrayal and recognition of the terrifying power inherent in the popular image of the witch.

Perhaps one of the reasons that the witch has never gained extended popularity as a horror figure is that she embodies fears that men would rather forget. Universal, in the '30s, ignored witches in its horror cycle. Hammer, in the '50s and '60s, dealt with them only briefly, and then often concentrated on the witch hunt or the presence of the Devil (a male domination figure). Because witches are believed to have the power to cause impotence, they are the ultimate expressions of male fears of castration, and as such they cannot be confronted too often on the screen. The very real terror that this threat conveys is far beyond the fears usually portrayed in horror films. In any case these other horrors are usually perpetrated on women rather than by them (the vampire as rapist, the monster as lover of the beautiful woman).

Even though it has been shown that the myth of the witch is essentially a male creation, a product of male fears, the only valid reversal of it would be to have it, as the proverbial monster, turn on its creator, and force a confrontation with these fears. Neither Dreyer nor Kaplan forces this confrontation. They instead opt for the weaker version of the myth diluted by the addition of woman as temptress leading men to their doom. This may be a way to achieve tragedy or revenge, but it is not the road to liberation.

NOTES

1. Jules Michelet, *Satanism and Witchcraft* (Secaucus, N.J.: Citadel, 1960).

2. R. E. L. Masters, *Eros and Evil: The Sexual Psychopathology of Witchcraft* (New York: AMS Press, 1962).

3. Norman Cohen, *Europe's Inner Demons* (New York: New American Library, 1977).

4. Mario Praz, *The Romantic Agony*, trans. Angus Davidson (New York: Oxford University Press, 1970).

6

Daughters of Darkness: The Lesbian Vampire on Film

Bonnie Zimmerman

> . . . they all know she's there.
> and no one goes out after dark.
> they tuck their daughters into bed, and lock their doors.
> they say, we should have killed her back then,
> when we first knew.
>
>
> and their daughters lie awake in their beds,
> and smile.

—Karen Lindsey, "Vampire"[1]

The return of the Vampire—tall, dark, and irresistibly male—has not yet revived interest in a surprising phenomenon of the 1960s and early '70s: the lesbian vampire film. Although the archetypal vampire in this culture is Dracula, often accompanied by submissive brides and female followers, lesbian vampires have a long and worthy history in literature, legend, and film. Two sources for the lesbian vampire myth have been used extensively by filmmakers. One is the Countess Elizabeth Bathory, a sixteenth-century Hungarian noblewoman who was reputed to have tortured 650 virgins, bathing in their blood in order to preserve her youth. The second source is Joseph Sheridan LeFanu's *Carmilla* (1871), an intensely erotic novella recounting the story of the Countess Millarca Karnstein, who lives through the centuries by vampirizing young girls.

One of the earliest classic vampire films, Carl Dreyer's *Vampyr* (1932), is a very free adaptation of *Carmilla*, purged of all suggestions of lesbian sexuality. *Dracula's Daughter* (1936) includes a muted lesbian encounter between a reluctant vampire-woman and a servant girl, suggesting an important class dynamic to the lesbian vampire myth. When the seducer is another woman, she must derive her power from her class position rather than her sex. *Blood of Dracula* (American International, 1957) combines this class element with the classic stereotype of the schoolgirl/teacher lesbian relationship: the socially dominant teacher (who herself is not a vampire), through scientific experiment, turns her powerless student into a blood-sucking monster.

Several other films prior to 1970—*La Danza Macabra* (1963), *La Meschera del Demonio* (also called *Black Sunday*, 1969), and *I Vampiri* (1957)—also feature female vampires who exhibit greater or lesser degrees of interest in their own sex. Two films based on *Carmilla*— Roger Vadim's *Et Mourir de Plaisir* (*Blood and Roses*, 1960) and *La Maldición de los Karnstein* (*Terror in the Crypt*, 1963)—exploit particularly well such conventions of the gothic horror genre as historical settings, mysterious castles, and aristocratic characters, as well as the dream sequences of surrealism, to draw us into their fantasy landscapes.

Although, like all vampire films, these pre-1970 examples express a nostalgia for death and a subtle "juxtaposition of erotic and macabre imagery,"[2] after 1970 filmmakers began to explore the explicit connections between sex and violence, not only in a heterosexual context but in a lesbian one as well. One impetus for these films was certainly the desire to capitalize on the market for pornography, since the lesbian vampire genre can allow nudity, blood, and sexual titillation in a "safe" fantasy structure. The English company Hammer Films (responsible for the Christopher Lee Dracula series as well) based its exploitation trilogy—*The Vampire Lovers* (1970), *Lust for a Vampire* (1971), and *Twins of Evil* (1971)—on the ubiquitous *Carmilla*. These Hammer films connect the proven conventions of the genre—a gothic girls school, black magic, moonlit lakes, and period costumes—with modern expectations of sex and blood. A final *Carmilla* of the period was *La Novia Ensangrentada* (1972).

On the other hand, *Countess Dracula* (1971), *La Noche de Walpurgis* (1970), and *Blood Ceremony* (1973) were each inspired by the legend of the Countess Bathory. *Countess Dracula*, another Hammer film, is particularly interesting in that the vampire countess attempts to consume the personality and body of her own daughter, a suggestive parallel to the version of mother–daughter relationships popularized by Nancy Friday (*My Mother, My Self*) and Ingmar Bergman (*Autumn Sonata*, 1978).

Finally, a number of films developed lesbian themes independent of either *Carmilla* or the Countess Bathory. American-International graduate Stephanie Rothman is moderately sympathetic to lesbianism in *The Velvet Vampire* (1971), although she stops short of allowing her women full expression of their attraction.[3] She also introduces a feminist twist: the vampire halts in her pursuit of the female victim to attack a rapist. Jean Rollin's *La Frisson des Vampires* (1970), on the other hand, is a striking articulation of the male fantasy of the "butch" lesbian, complete with metal chains and black leather boots. He also makes explicit a theme that is implicit in most of these films and in our culture as a whole: that lesbians and homosexuals are narcissists capable of making love only to images of themselves. Hammer's vampires seduce young women who are strikingly similar to themselves; Rollin's lesbian is finally reduced to sucking the blood from her own veins.

This brief filmography suggests that lesbian vampire films use many of the stereotypes that have been attached to lesbianism at least since the nineteenth century: lesbianism is sterile and morbid; lesbians are rich, decadent women who seduce the young and powerless. But the fact that the lesbian vampire myth returned with such force and popularity in the films of the early 1970s suggests to me that an additional factor may have been added by the specific historical developments of the '60s and '70s: feminism and public awareness of lesbianism.

The lesbian vampire, besides being a gothic fantasy archetype, can be used to express a fundamental male fear that woman-bonding will exclude men and threaten male supremacy. Lesbianism—love between women—must be vampirism; elements of violence, compulsion, hypnosis, paralysis, and the supernatural must be present. One woman must be a vampire, draining the life of the other woman, yet holding her in a bond stronger than the grave. Pirie, excusing the negative stereotype of the female vampire (which he notes appears at exactly the time women were challenging such degrading images), argues that "the function of the vampire movie is precisely to incarnate the most hostile aspects of sexuality in a concrete form."[4] But it is necessary to ask why and in what form hostile sexuality gets incarnated in the lesbian vampire film.

The male vampire has been used to suggest that heterosexuality is sometimes indistinguishable from rape: the recent Frank Langella *Dracula* (1979) crudely overemphasizes this identification. The function of the lesbian vampire is to contain attraction between women within the same boundaries of sexual violence, to force it into a particular model of sexuality. By showing the lesbian as a vampire-rapist who violates and destroys her victim, men alleviate their fears that lesbian love could create an alternate model, that two women without coercion or morbidity might prefer one another to a man.

Although direct parallels between social forces and popular culture are risky at best, the popularity of the lesbian vampire film in the early 1970s may be related to the beginnings of an international feminist movement, as a result of which women began both to challenge male domination and to bond strongly with each other.[5] Since feminism between 1970 and 1973 was not yet perceived as a fundamental threat, men could enjoy the sexual thrill provided by images of lesbian vampires stealing women and sometimes destroying men in the process. The creators of those images—like the pornographic filmmakers who appeal to male fantasies with scenes of lesbianism—must have felt secure enough in their power and that of their primary male audience to flirt with lesbianism and female violence against men. It is suggestive that lesbian vampires no longer populate the screen (not even to relay the myth's normative message to women: if you value your neck, stick with your man). Today men do not want to see themselves the victims, but the perpetrators of sexual violence; they want to see women subdued and violated by men, not other women. The explicitly male sexual threat of Dracula is the message for the '80s.

The myth of the lesbian vampire, however, carries in it the potentiality for a feminist revision of meaning. The Karen Lindsey poem that prefaces this chapter tells us that sexual attraction between women can threaten the authority of the male-dominated society. The lesbian vampire film can lend itself to an even more extreme reading: that in turning to each other, women triumph over and destroy men themselves.

One film that is considerably ambiguous about the lesbian vampire

and thus lends itself particularly well to a feminist interpretation, is
Daughters of Darkness (*La Rouge aux Levres*, 1970), a Belgian film
directed by Harry Kumel. I saw this film shortly after its release in this
country; the audience consisted of aficionados of soft porn, followers
of the new wave intrigued by the presence of Delphine Seyrig, and a
large contingent of lesbians curious about the film's advertised display
of lesbianism. My analysis of *Daughters of Darkness* is intended to
raise some questions about the meaning of the archetype and the possibilities of interpreting hostile images from a feminist perspective. It is
certainly limited by the fact that these lesbian vampire films are simply
not around any longer and available for careful study. But I hope that
my ideas stir some discussion and a revival of interest in this lost genre.

    Daughters of Darkness opens in Ostend, off-season, where a newly-
wed couple—immaculate, handsome, a veritable Barbie-and-Ken—
have stopped on their way to England to break the news of their
marriage to his family. They epitomize the perfect heterosexual couple,
except that he turns out to be a sexual sadist and his "mother" is really
an aging homosexual lover. The others visitors at the hotel are a beautiful countess who appears only at night and her devoted female companion. She is, of course, the Countess Bathory (Delphine Seyrig),
who after a thirty-year absence has returned to the Ostend hotel as
young and fresh as ever (diet and lots of sleep, she explains, have prolonged her youth). While her assistant distracts the newlywed husband,
the countess seduces his willing bride. (She is fed up with her husband's overt sadism, preferring the subtleties of a bite on the neck.)
The vampire assistant is killed—it is not clear how—by the husband,
who then confronts his bride and the countess. In the midst of their
altercation, the two women conveniently shatter a crystal bowl over his
hands, exchange a look which is equally erotic and hungry, then
quickly clamp their lips to his wrists. *La rouge aux levres*—blood on
the lips. The new lovers drive off into the sunrise, only to end in a fiery
automobile crash which, in accordance with traditional vampire lore,
ends the countess's reign by impaling her on a tree branch. But the
countess's spirit immediately transmigrates into the body of the young
bride, who then returns to the hotel to seduce another willing victim.[6]

    Kumel places *Daughters of Darkness* solidly within the gothic hor-
ror tradition through his use of the empty hotel (equivalent in effect to
the mysterious castle), aristocratic characters, and an evocative use of
color: the countess, with her bleached white hair and silver lamé
gowns, suggests the glamour of death, the assistant in solid black

*Daughters of Darkness, 1970. The Countess (Delphine Seyrig)
seducing her victims. From the editors' collection.*

reminds us of night terrors, the blood-red of violent sexuality marks
the dissolves between scenes. At the same time that the film evokes the
atmosphere of the vampire genre and carries its message that woman-
bonding is unnatural and dangerous, it also, as critics have noted, suggests the radical potential of the myth.

Pirie notes that "the overall framework of ideas [in the film] is not
just sexual but political," limiting its political stance, however, to that
of a class analysis of bourgeois decadence and alienation.[7] I think, however, that *Daughters of Darkness* can be given a feminist reading that
uncovers a "lucidly anti-male" as well as anti-bourgeois political
stance.[8] The "anti-male" bias inherent in the lesbian vampire myth can
be expressed and seen as a justification for women's suppression, but
it also can be interpreted by feminists as a justified attack on male
power, a revenge fantasy, and a desire for separation from the male
world. The following analysis of *Daughters of Darkness* further
explains these ideas.

The lesbian vampire myth, to begin with, is a variation of the classic
triangle: man and female vampire battling for possession of a woman.

Pirie notes that lesbian vampire films such as *Daughters of Darkness* often incorporate the motif of the honeymoon (the honeymoon also appears in some heterosexual vampire films, and in satires of the horror genre, such as *The Rocky Horror Picture Show* [1975]). I would suggest that this is because the honeymoon, traditionally, is a transitional period during which the husband asserts his power and control over his bride, winning or forcing her into institutionalized heterosexuality. For the husband, then, the honeymoon period provides fear and anxiety: will he prove potent enough, both sexually and socially, to "bind" his bride to himself and the marriage structure? Bondage and discipline in *Daughters of Darkness* is used as a highly appropriate symbol of the husband's fledgling power over his bride (while in *La Frisson des Vampires*, male power is mocked by the lesbian vampire's chains). The virgin-bride, linked to the institution of heterosexuality by socialization rather than by experience, is particularly vulnerable to the blandishments of a sinister sexual force. Women must be forced into marriage, into "normal" womanhood, since, left to their own designs, they might be as easily attracted to a "perverse" form of sexuality, whether extramarital, diabolical (possession by the devil), or lesbian.

It is essential that in a film that explores this male fear of heterosexual inadequacy the point of view be firmly and unambiguously male. The male viewer or reader must be able to step in imaginatively to take over when the situation has reached the appropriate level of sexual arousal, thus potentially spiraling out of control. The heterosexual context of the film must be very clear; lesbianism must be presented as an aberration. This is the function of the lesbian interlude in a pornographic film: the male viewer, excited by the promise of stepping in to separate two women and thus prove his superior prowess, is able to affirm both his sexual potency and his masculine superiority at the same time.

When the lesbian is also a vampire, he has an added explanation for the attraction one woman might have for another. It is not he who is inadequate; he is competing with supernatural powers. A man who offers his woman life through his sexual potency (symbolized by sperm) cannot compete with the vampire who sucks away her life (symbolized by blood). Instead, he must destroy the vampire—the lesbian—who threatens male power through sexual attacks on women. For, in fact, whether the woman vampire is lesbian or heterosexual, her real object of attack is always the male.

This is the message contained within the fantasy structures of the lesbian vampire genre. But in *Daughters of Darkness*, heterosexuality is of a decidedly ambiguous character. The only male in the film is unsympathetic and hardly a character men might care to identify with, since he is himself sexually aberrant, the kept man of an elderly transvestite. Furthermore, because of his own homosexuality, he is particularly vulnerable in relation to his bride, and thus abuses his male "privilege" of establishing control over his woman. His sadism and murderousness are outside the conventions of gothic fantasy since he himself is not a vampire: he is a simple killer. And he is an ineffective one as well, since he ends up the victim of the vampires, one of whom is his own bride. Although the purpose of the lesbian vampire myth is to provide a way for men to soothe their sexual anxieties, *Daughters of Darkness* accentuates that anxiety instead.

Furthermore, Delphine Seyrig is a very atypical lesbian vampire. She is a mature woman, unlike many other lesbian vampires who appear young and themselves vulnerable. This, in addition to her off-screen celebrity, gives her an aura of authority. She is never shown nude and is thus not vulnerable to male prurience as most lesbian vampires are. In the film she is the sexual and political equal of, if not superior to, the male character. She is never shown actually attacking the young bride; there are no bites on the neck, no bared fangs.

Instead, we see Seyrig sitting with a distracted look on her face, her hand gently stroking the hair of her original assistant. Or we see her hand wander slowly toward the bride, more to protect her from her husband than to threaten her. She is portrayed as being a sophisticated, intelligent, motherly, and fascinating woman. If there were any lingering doubts as to her benignity, Seyrig inclines toward a camp interpretation that dissipates some of the gothic atmosphere. Altogether, we might be tempted to doubt that any supernatural means were necessary to entice the young woman, were we not shown the two vampires sucking the husband's blood. In this rivalry between man and vampire for possession of the bride's body and soul, the vampire's power seems both superior to and more desirable than the man's.

Finally, the ending of the film emphasizes the power of woman and the attractiveness of lesbianism. The spirit of the countess immediately occupies a new body once it is deprived of the old, suggesting that lesbianism is eternal, passing effortlessly from one woman to another. No attempt of man or god can prevent the lesbian from passing on her "curse." The effect of this transference is not at all horrifying, but rather amusing, almost charming, especially to a lesbian viewer. The stiff-faced beauty queen, whom we have seen as innocent bride, passive masochist, and fascinated victim, is now the powerful, immortal lesbian vampire. Any woman, this suggests, can be lucky enough to be a lesbian.

I am not arguing that *Daughters of Darkness* in itself is a feminist film, although Kumel seems to be manipulating our expectations of the genre. As an academic and film historian, he must certainly have been aware of his effects, especially since it is reported that he would not have made the film without Seyrig, because of whom many of the negative aspects of the lesbian vampire are mitigated. But it is when the viewer is herself a lesbian and feminist that the film takes on a kaleidoscope of meaning. It shows lesbianism as attractive and heterosexuality as abnormal and ineffectual. It carries a subtle message justifying man-hating that casts in a political light the traditional fear-of-woman theme inherent in vampire mythology. It gives the last laugh to Countess Bathory and not to the vampire hunters. It is filmed with style and humor, not with horror and violence. It suggests that women have good reasons for turning away from sadistic men to other women and even justifies, to a limited extent, the elimination of men.

It suggests finally that the lesbian vampire theme—although originally misogynistic and anti-lesbian—can be revised and reinterpreted, thus opening it to use by feminists.[9] The myth has been used to attack female autonomy and bonding, and to express male fear of women. A feminist reading of *Daughters of Darkness* suggests that feminists can transform this myth (as we are transforming the patriarchal myth of witchcraft, for example). The many daughters of Carmilla and the Countess Bathory still lie awake in their beds smiling, waiting for the kiss of the revitalized lesbian vampire.

NOTES

1. Karen Lindsey, "Vampire," first appeared in *The Second Wave* 2, no. 2 (1972): 36.

2. David Pirie, *The Vampire Cinema* (New York: Crescent Books, 1977), 100.

3. Dannis Peary, "Stephanie Rothman: R-Rated Feminist," in *Women and the Cinema*, ed. Karyn Kay and Gerald Peary (New York: E. P. Dutton, 1977), 179–92. I have not seen Rothman's films, but, on the surface, Peary's argument for Rothman as a feminist seems to me to be overstated.

4. Pirie, *The Vampire Cinema*, 100.

5. Sharon Russell, in private correspondence, suggests also that "there is some increase in [the] number of films dealing with witches during periods when women's roles increase in importance." These relationships need further study. See Russell's work in *Film Reader* 3, 80–90. Reprinted in this volume.

6. Werner Herzog, in his recent *Nosferatu* (1979), uses the same transference device: after the original vampire dies, his victim immediately takes on the same physical characteristics.

7. Pirie, *The Vampire Cinema,* 113.

8. Parker Tyler, *Screening the Sexes* (New York: Holt, Rinehart and Winston, 1972), 115. As is typical of this book, Tyler's observation is brilliant and totally undeveloped.

9. Another delightful revision of the vampire image is Sue Fink's and Joelyn Grippo's "Leaping," as sung by Meg Christian on *Face the Music.*

7

"Canyons of Nightmare": The Jewish Horror Film

Lester D. Friedman

What it showed was always the same—
A vertical panel with him on it,
Being a horrible bit of movement
At the edge of knowledge, overhanging
The canyons of nightmare . . .

—"The Night Mirror" by John Holland

INTRODUCTION

During the late summer and early fall of 1978, *Film Comment* published two strikingly original articles on the horror film by critic Robin Wood. Wood's first essay expands on the common analogy between dreams and films by providing a fresh insight that unites psychology, politics, and sociology, arguing that movies are both "the personal dreams of their makers and the collective dreams of their audiences—a fusion made possible by the shared structures of a common ideology." Given this supposition, Wood offers a basic formula for the horror film: "normality is threatened by the monster." Such a simple and general formula gives us three variables: normality, the monster, and the relationship between the two. "It is the third variable," says Wood, "that constitutes the essential subject of the horror film."[1]

Because Wood's premises fuse psychology, politics, and sociology, they open up some fertile areas of examination within this genre. He discusses horror pictures as manifestations of repressed sexual energy, citing Robert Florey's *Murders in the Rue Morgue* (1932) as a classic example. Finally, he analyzes the connection between family and horror—a theme prevalent in such contemporary pictures as *Rosemary's Baby* (1968), *Night of the Living Dead* (1968), *Sisters* (1973), and *Carrie* (1976)—and concludes that these films show examples of "the sense of civilization condemning itself through its popular culture." But Wood's ideas need not be restricted to the realms of Freudian psychology, sexual politics, and familiar sociology. Indeed, his formula provides an important way to analyze a particular kind of horror movie: the Jewish horror film.

Often horror films tend to avoid including specifically ethnic characters because they want a kind of universal appeal. *Dracula* (1931) and *Frankenstein* (1931), to cite two obvious examples, contain no recognizable ethnic characters. Even the countries in which their action occurs are not identified: both are set in vague, mythical foreign locales, with topographies that owe more to Universal's back lot than to natural geography. Most horror film characters, therefore, are types rather than individuals, and the situations are symbolic rather than particular. So, when the man and/or monsters are clearly identified either ethnically or racially the horror film becomes immediately more complex and more purposeful. If, for example, Count Dracula were a Jew or Baron Frankenstein were black, we would instantly become aware of new levels of meaning.[2] The horror takes on political, social, and sexual connotations linked with its characters' ethnic or racial identifications.

These imaginary transformations illustrate Wood's sociological concerns, particularly his repeated emphasis on the importance of the relationships between normality and the monster. Why normal society ostracizes the monster suddenly becomes as important as what the monster does to alienate society. Why the monster attacks normality quickly receives equal attention with what normality does to repel the monster. Thus, rooting the men and/or monsters in an ethnic tradition forces us to pay careful attention to the film's racial particulars as well as to its universal implications, for the characters now embody a specific history of social issues and concerns.

Furthermore, horror films with clearly defined ethnic characters either implicitly or explicitly deal with issues involving racism and

xenophobia; their seemingly innocuous genre icons and stock situations reflect and sometimes criticize complicated racial problems. Horror films may contain powerful social attacks that "serious" films
cannot hope to duplicate, and deliver their message to an audience not
usually inclined to watch "morally uplifting" social dramas. At the
very least, such pictures present examples of a period's prevailing ethnic prejudices and social mores. A good example of how the inclusion
of ethnic characters necessarily raises social issues within the horror
film is Paul Wegener's 1920 classic, *The Golem: How He Came into the
World*.

THE JEW AS MONSTER

Lotte Eisner calls *The Golem* "one of the greatest films of its period."
Richard Taylor says it "foreshadows the psychological and spiritual
obsessions that were to preoccupy the German cinema," and Paul
Monaco notes how the film contains many of the thematic strands that
tie Weimar Republic pictures together.[3] These and most other critics of
this film focus on the elements that make it an outstanding example of
German Expressionist filmmaking: the twisted sets designed by the
great architect Hans Pölzig, the lighting style strongly influenced by
Max Reinhardt, the mysterious special effects created by Carl Boese,
the dream quality of the exquisite *mise-en-scène,* and the supernatural
plot elements. Some writers have noted how both *Frankenstein* director James Whale and actor Boris Karloff were influenced by Wegener's
direction and performance (he played the Golem), much as Mary Shelley—who devoured German ghost stories—was no doubt herself
influenced by versions of the Golem legend.[4] But none of these commentators considers the social ramifications of this film in terms of the
conflicts between its Jewish and gentile characters. To understand the
historical importance of this legend, how Wegener's alteration of the
Golem story is particularly significant, and what message the film gives
audiences about Jews, we must first go back to the tales of the Golem
so prevalent in Jewish legends.
   The word *golem* comes from the Hebrew and means "matter without shape" or "a yet unformed thing" (Psalms, 139:16). Jewish literature contains several tales in which learned men create living beings out
of clay. In fact, the Talmud claims Adam went through such a stage
when he was "a still unformed mass." The first manmade golem story

concerns Enoch, son of Seth and grandson of Adam, who formed a figure out of earth that was brought to life by the archangel of evil, Samael. Later golem stories came down to us from the fourth (B.C.), fourth, eleventh, twelfth, sixteenth, and eighteenth centuries. Christian writers, like Samuel Brenz (1614), Johann Wulfer (1674), Christopher Arnold (1674), Gustav Meyrink (1916), and Jorge Luis Borges (1958), have also commented on these strange creatures created by Jews. Even America's favorite hero, the Man of Steel, confronted this monster in the comic *Superman Meets the Galactic Golem* (1972).

The men who called these "unformed masses" to life, usually so-called miracle working rebbes, are very important figures in Hasidic folklore, a movement that stresses belief in mystical happenings and supernatural events.[5] But such tales have become part of Jewish secular as well as religious life. For example, the Weizmann Institute in Rehovot, Israel, has a computer called Golem No. 1. In 1927 Yiddish poet H. Leivick wrote *The Golem: A Dramatic Poem in Eight Scenes*, and in 1970 novelist Abraham Rothberg wrote *The Sword of the Golem*. A humorous version of the tale appears in Avram Davidson's "The Golem," written in 1955 and included in *The Jewish Caravan* (1965). In addition, the golem legends have become children's stories: Sulamith Ish-Kishor, *The Master of Miracle: A Novel of the Golem* (1971); Beverly Brodsky McDermott, *The Golem* (1976); and Peter Rugell, *The Return of the Golem: A Chanukah Story* (1979).[6] Even a modern Jewish poet like John Hollander writes about "my ancestor, the Rabbi Loew of Prague,/He made the Golem . . . /And quickened him with a Name that has been/ Hidden behind all names that one could know."[7]

The tale of the golem made by Hollander's "ancestor," Rabbi Loew of Prague, has emerged over the years as the most famous of these legends, and indeed, is the clear source of Wegener's three films on the subject: *The Golem* (1914); *The Golem and the Dancer* (1917), and *The Golem: How He Came into the World*. Carlos Clarens hypothesizes that Wegener first came into direct contact with the golem stories during his filming of *The Student of Prague* (1913).[8] There the German director encountered the impressive statue of the miracle-working Rabbi Loew in front of Prague's City Hall, and at the entrance to the old Jewish section of the city he found an even more inspiring sculpture: a brooding, yet eloquent, stone depiction of the rabbi's golem. Wegener's fascination with these two statues motivated him to learn all he could about the magical rabbi and his fantastic creation. *The Golem* provides ample evidence that he eventually became quite familiar with

the Loew/golem legends that intrigued him all his life, for it follows
the general outline of the story supposedly written by R. Yitzchak ben
Shimshon Katz, Loew's son-in-law, and popularized in 1909 by R.
Yudel Rosenberg.[9]

Two altered aspects of the legend Wegener knew so well prove
important in understanding the film's Jewish/gentile interaction. Wegener obviously knew the basic motivation for the golem's creation:
Rabbi Loew sought to protect the Jewish community from Christian
oppression. For centuries Jews had been accused of blood-libel, the
Christian claim that Jews murdered non-Jews so their blood could be
used during the Passover seder. In a famous 1572 meeting, Rabbi Loew
debated Cardinal John Sylvester on this and other religious topics, and
he so impressed Emperor Rudolf II of Hapsburg that the monarch
thereafter protected his Jewish subjects from false charges. But Loew
was forced to create the golem to protect his community from the
nefarious plots of Father Thaddeus, a renegade priest dedicated to
destroying all Jews.

In Wegener's film, however, it is not a fanatical priest who threatens
the Jews; rather, the Emperor decides to expel the Jews for three specific reasons: (a) despising Christian ceremonies, (b) endangering the
lives and property of their fellow men, and (c) practicing black magic.
Ironically, the film shows men guilty of at least the last two charges
and hints that they may be guilty of the first as well. Magic and mystery dominate the lives of the film's alien Jews who scuttle about Wegener's expressionistic ghetto. All his Jewish characters wear wizard-like
hats and inhabit cavelike dwellings. Wegener's use of Reinhardt's striking lighting effects and Pölzig's angled sets combine to give the ghetto's
mise-en-scène a dark and dangerous look, emphasizing the superstitions and sorcery that rule the lives of its bizarre inhabitants. The end-
lessly twisting staircases; narrow, crowded streets; dimly illuminated
rooms; and sinister below-lit figures encourage us to believe the
emperor is correct: these people do practice black magic and are a
threat.

Finally, of course, Rabbi Loew does actually employ black magic in
his creation of the golem, an impressive scene in which he summons
up the dreaded spirit of Astaroth to reveal the word that will bring life
to his creature of clay. Given these circumstances, one comes to agree
that the Jews should be expelled before they do real damage to the
body politic. We even get a hint of their destructive potential when
Loew commands the golem to destroy the emperor's palace. So,

instead of calling up a spirit to protect an unjustly accused group of defenseless people, as was evident in all the Loew/golem legends Wegener encountered in Prague, the celluloid golem Wegener creates represents a distinct danger to the film's gentiles posed by a potentially powerful group of outsiders, the Jews.

Even more telling in raising gentile fears about Jews is Wegener's alteration of the golem's eventual destruction. All the various golem stories conclude with Jews destroying their own creations, sometimes at the urgings of the monsters themselves. Ben Sir's fourth century (B.C.E.) golem, for example, requests that his maker destroy him "lest the world submit to idolatry." One thousand years later, Rabbi Zera orders another golem demolished, saying "You are a creature of magic; return to your dust." In the sixteenth century, Elliyahy of Chelm eliminated his creature when "he became afraid that the golem might cause havoc and destruction." The Katz/Rosenberg story offers Rabbi Loew's explanation for obliterating his golem:

> I have decided that it is time to return Yossele [the name Loew gives his creation]. He has served us well. We created him because of the blood accusations. Now, thank God, they have ceased. Before making this decision, I have waited a whole year to ascertain whether the accusations have ceased permanently. I am confident that they have terminated. Therefore, I feel that the golem must be destroyed. His mission is accomplished. If we keep him longer than necessary, we may fall into the danger of misusing sacred property.[10]

To do this, Loew orders Yossele to sleep in the temple attic, the rabbi and his disciples reverse the original process of creation, the golem returns to a lump of earth shaped like a man, the men cover the lifeless hunk with books, and the rabbi forbids anyone to enter the attic ever again. The important point here, then, is that these miracle-working Jews, like Loew, always used their powers wisely; they realized that moral responsibility begins, not ends, with creation, and they destroyed their creatures when they threatened to roam beyond their makers' control.

Wegener offers no such morally responsible Jews in *The Golem*. Though Rabbi Loew finally removes the written word which animates the creature from the amulet around its neck, he rushes out to bask in the praise of his fellow Jews before breaking the lifeless mass of clay into harmless pieces. Jealous of the rabbi's daughter Miriam's affair with Florian, a gentile knight, the rabbi's servant reactivates the golem and instructs it to kill the intruder. It does so, flinging the hapless knight from a high rooftop, and then goes on a rampage, kidnapping Miriam, setting fire to homes, and battering down the massive ghetto door. Finally, the havoc ends when the golem lifts up a lovely little girl who innocently removes the written word from its amulet and freezes the monster into clay once again.

Wegener's visual imagery conveys important information here, as do his implicit social messages. The rabbi's inability to destroy his creation before it goes berserk, and his preference for glory over responsibility, show him as a shallow figure who utterly fails to recognize the enormity of the power he has unleashed. Florian's death, a seeming punishment for his interracial romance, puts audience sympathy on the side of the gentiles rather than the Jews, particularly since Wegener's high-angle shot shows the mangled knight in a Christlike pose. The fact that Florian is the film's gentile figure may, however inadvertently, raise the issue of Jews as Christ killers.

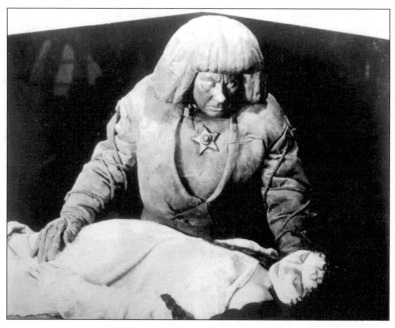

Director Paul Wegener as The Golem, *1920. Still courtesy of Jerry Ohlinger's Movie Material Store.*

The golem's end is equally revealing. Since the children he confronts are playing outside the huge door and foreboding walls that enclose the Jewish ghetto, and since their Aryan blondness contrasts sharply to the swarthiness of the film's Jewish characters, we can assume Wegener means us to interpret them as gentiles. Thus a clear social message, however unintentional, emerges: the non-Jew must protect his community from Jewish evil. In this case, the golem embodies the Jewish threat which, if unchecked, would destroy the Christian community. The emperor was right all along. These Jews and their black magic are a real threat to the "lives and property of their fellow men." The beautiful blonde child who vanquishes the Jewish menace becomes an innocent defender of her faith as well as her people.

This Aryan sensibility is only slightly removed from overt anti-Semitism where the evil is more openly defined as Jewish and the cure more drastic. If 1920 seems too early to see signs of Nazism in German thinking, remember that on February 29, 1920, Hitler addressed a highly publicized mass meeting at the Hofbrauhaus. Here he delivered a venomous denunciation of the Jews, recited the party's twenty-five-point program, and concluded his presentation with another attack on the Jews. Point four of his announced program read: "Only those who are our fellow countrymen can become citizens. Only those who have German blood, regardless of creed, can be our countrymen. Hence no Jew can be a countryman."[11]

My point here is not that Wegener was an early Nazi, but it should be noted that during the reign of the Third Reich he did not flee his homeland like so many other German artists. Instead, he made several propaganda films, among them *Ein Mann will nach Deutschland* (*A Man Must Go to Germany*, 1934) and *Starker als die Liebe* (*Stronger than Love*, 1938), acted in others, such as *Hans Westmar* (1933) and *Der grosse König* (*The Great King*, 1942), and was eventually named Actor of the State. Such fears about Jews were as intrinsic a part of Wegener's heritage as was his intense fascination with the mysterious and the supernatural.[12] Both beliefs manifested themselves in conscious and unconscious ways that the director, himself, was powerless to control and may not have even recognized. A sensitivity to the role of Jewish characters in a film like *The Golem* awakens a viewer to the social realities that inform its historical material, visual images, and thematic issues.

Most critics interpret the film from a contemporary viewpoint, without fully considering its impact on a 1920s German audience. Wegener's depiction of Jews could not help but influence 1920s Germans in their perception of contemporary Jews in the streets of Dresden and the shops of Berlin, in the same way as Griffith's *Birth of a Nation* (1915) affected race relations in the America of its time. To dismiss off-handedly Wegener's use of Jews as personifications of "magic and mysticism" is to blind oneself to the film's crucial social and political implications. An ethnic character brings with him a historical tradition that must have, at the very least, an implicit impact within the film and be recognized as having reverberations beyond the limits of the frame.

Earlier I argued that the inclusion of ethnic characters within the horror movie format should force us to consider political and sociological contexts, for these figures necessarily inject ethnic issues into any film. This is almost always the case outside the frame, since viewers from one racial group inevitably watch films containing different racial group members. But one possible exception, at least inside the frame, does exist: a picture completely populated by members of the same racial group. Such a film, however, should be a world unto itself, with no mention of outside forces that represent the dominance of other cultures. For Jews, this situation occurred in the 1930s and 1940s during the heyday of the Yiddish Cinema, and the best representative of the supernatural in these films is *The Dybbuck* (1938).

Judith N. Goldberg, author of the only book-length treatment of Yiddish films, calls *The Dybbuck* "a glorious celebration of the traditional past. . . . The most widely known and celebrated of all Polish Yiddish films . . . [and] probably the most successful Yiddish film ever made"; while Parker Tyler labels it "a beautiful anachronism . . . the most solemn attestation to the mystic power of the spirit the imagination has ever purveyed to the film reel . . . [a film] of dark, bewitching, passionate beauty."[13] Like the golem stories, accounts of people possessed by spirits are sprinkled throughout Jewish legends and folktales, although they are prevalent in gentile tales as well. Some biblical scholars argue that it was Samael, the evil archangel, who took over the body of Eden's serpent and lured Eve to taste the forbidden fruit; others claim King Saul's body was inhabited by another evil spirit and that David's music was a type of exorcism. King Solomon was reputed to have a remedy for removing evil spirits, as was Rabbi Eliezar in the first century. Several Talmudic discussions detail examples of this supernatural phenomenon. Though many more examples of possession abound in Jewish culture, the actual word *dybbuck* (from the Hebrew for "holding fast") did not appear in writings until the eighteenth century, and it was popularized by the emergence of S. Anski's 1916 play of that title.

Anski, a Russian Jew who devoted the majority of his time to the Socialist-Revolutionary cause, began writing Yiddish folk legends late in his life. Gershon Winkler theorizes that Anski found the sources for his play in the *Maaseh Buch* (*Book of Stories*), a 1602 account of supernatural occurrences that was widely circulated in both Hebrew and Yiddish, although other scholars feel Anski's travels through Ukranian hasidic settlements on behalf of the Historic-Ethnographic Society of St. Petersberg inspired his work.[14] Whatever his sources, Anski tapped a receptive vein in the Jewish psyche. His play proved extremely popular and was performed all over the world. It metamorphosed into an opera in 1936, as well as Polish (1938) and Israeli (1968) movies, the earlier film remaining the most famous.

This earlier version of Anski's play is an almost literal adaptation of its dramatic source. It chronicles the fortunes of Sender (M. Libman) and Nisson (G. Lamberger), two ardent disciples of the Hasidic Rebbe of Miropol (A. Morewski). The men's wives are both pregnant, and they pledge that if one has a son and the other a daughter their children will marry, even though a mysterious stranger warns them that "the lives of the unborn should not be pledged." Over the next eighteen years, the men lose track of each other and forget their oath. Sender becomes a wealthy merchant and his precious daughter, Leah (Lili Liliana), a great beauty. Nisson drowns, and his son, Channon (L. Leibgold), one day appears in Sender's village on his way to study at the Yeshiva. Slowly, Leah and Channon begin to fall in love, although her father has no idea the boy is his long-lost friend's son. Because he cannot afford to marry Leah, Channon uses his occult power to obtain wealth, and dies in the process. His spirit then takes over Leah's body, becoming a dybbuck, a wandering soul which inhabits the flesh of one it once loved. Finally, a distraught Sender arranges for the wonder-working Rebbe to exorcise the dybbuck, setting it free for a peaceful life beyond the grave.

The Dybbuck functions as an interesting precurser of *The Exorcist* (1973), although without all the special effects pyrotechnics that set heads spinning, beds twirling, and obscenities flying. Both films use the possession-of-children motif—as do other horror films like *Village of the Damned* (1970), *The Omen* (1976), and *Carrie*—which is a particularly painful situation. In effect, these children become zombies, powerless figures who do the bidding of forces lodged deep within themselves. *The Dybbuck*, however, differs significantly from these other films in that the spirit that possesses the innocent's body is not viewed as totally unsympathetic. Channon takes over another's flesh out of love for her; in fact, at one point Leah even invites him to do so, saying "two souls may inhabit one body." The scene where Channon's spirit does exit Leah's body is particularly bittersweet, and Tyler calls it "one of the most moving things I know in the poetry of the theater."[15] Even the film's written prologue tells us that when two souls fuse into one, they burn "like an everlasting light/Never to be extinguished."

THE JEW AS VICTIM

The Golem and *The Dybbuck* are examples of films that, whatever their artistic pretensions, clearly fall within the overall genre of horror /supernatural movies. But gloomy castles, frightening monsters, and mad scientists are not prerequisites for horror films. "A work need not provide shocks of horror," observes S. S. Prawer; "the uncanny may be diffused over the whole as an atmosphere." D. L. White agrees, noting that the force at work in a horror film is "the triggering of our basic fear of the unknown. . . . It is not necessary to go beyond conventional situations to find ingredients of horror."[16] Indeed, the "monster" who threatens normality in Wood's basic formula does not necessarily have to possess supernatural powers or appear in outlandish situations; instead, he may be a human being whose actions and philosophy remove him from what respectable society deems normal, so that his very existence comes to represent a threat. Quiet, well-mannered Norman Bates, for example, is far more frightening than an exotic, Transylvanian vampire; hence *Psycho* (1960) is far more horrifying than *Dracula* (1931) because the threat comes from the human personality and exists as part of everyday life.

Any character far enough removed from acceptable society's vision of right and wrong almost automatically becomes a monster that threatens normality. The civilized world received its most vivid examples of socially deviant malevolence in the form of Hitler and his Nazis, devilish incarnations who plunged the world into a hellish nightmare. A director's reel images could not be more frightening, more terrible, than newsreel pictures of row after row of goose-stepping soldiers transformed into unfeeling zombie warriors by a lunatic dictator.

Baron Frankenstein's probes of human life pall before reports of Dr. Mengele's perverse "medical experiments." No movie monster is more horrible than the black-uniformed S. S. trooper, his external dress revealing the deep darkness of his psyche. Photographs and films taken in concentration camps grasp the strikingly sad resemblance between the tortured inmates and the walking dead of so many vampire movies. What demonic power could match Hitler's feat of turning members of the most humane professions into murderers and supporters of a totally immoral regime? Hitler and his followers transformed the world into a vast and terrifying horror movie in which good and evil battled to the death for mankind's soul. These real-world German monsters loomed on American movie screens as evil incarnate, a presence so powerful that beside them the depravity of a Shylock or a Fagin was rendered almost inconsequential. No horror film character could produce the fear and loathing Nazi figures drew from audiences in the 1940s—and still do today. Because they were the primary and immediate target of these modern monsters, Jews began to symbolize everyone threatened by the new demons. Thus, the war years saw the celluloid Jew go through a startling transformation: in effect, the Jew moved from monster to victim of the monster, the traditional role with which audience members most identify in horror films. Two such films, *The Mortal Storm* (1940) and *Address Unknown* (1944), are representative examples of the Nazi horror pictures.

Before the United States entered World War II, one of the few films to deal with the Nazi/Jew situation was director Frank Borzage's *The Mortal Storm*, although today its contrived melodrama makes it far less powerful than it was in 1940. Historically, the film remains important because it represents Hollywood's first attempt to depict Nazi Germany. Although the persecuted Doctor Viktor Roth (Frank Morgan) is identified only as a non-Aryan, the film makes it clear that he is a Jew, by having the Nazis force him to wear an armband with a "J" on it. Interestingly, Borzage uses situations familiar to horror film lovers to condemn the Nazi menace, particularly the monster's ability to alter everyday life. Bosley Crowther noted Borzage's strategy, calling the film "one of the most harrowing and inflammatory fictions ever placed on the screen. . . . It strikes out powerfully with both hands at the unmitigated brutality of a system which could turn a small university community into a hotbed of hatred and mortal vengeance."[17]

Set in January 1933, on the eve of Hitler's appointment as chancellor, *The Mortal Storm*, like many of Borzage's other films, involves two lovers separated by outside forces. The prologue, heard against a visual background of clouds that gather speed and move across the sky, speaks of "the mortal storm in which man finds himself today" and the "evil elements" within man. After an establishing longshot of the picturesque mountains surrounding the small German town, the story focuses on the beloved patriarch, Professor Roth, and his family: wife (Irene Rich), daughter Freya (Margaret Sullavan), and stepsons Otto (Robert Stack) and Erich (William Orr). At the school's celebration of the professor's birthday, his two favorite students clarify their concerns: Fritz Marberg (Robert Young) talks of love for the fatherland and Martin Breitner (James Stewart) about personal love and affection. The professor's own speech stresses honor and loyalty above either patriotism or love. At home in the midst of a private birthday celebration, a maid breaks up the party with an excited announcement of Hitler's appointment. Fritz and the stepsons rush off to hear details on the radio; Martin, the professor, his wife, and Freya remain at the half-deserted table, the scene symbolically portraying Hitler's destruction of normal German family life.

As the film progresses, Hitler's policies disrupt many other once-normal aspects of German life. For example, when an old school-teacher (Thomas Ross) refuses to return the "Heil Hitler" salute, he is attacked and only barely saved by Martin's spirited defense. Moreover, Roth's once worshipful students have metamorphosed into vehement Nazis; friendly puppies have now become predatory werewolves. When the professor claims that chemical analysis shows no difference between the blood of Aryans and that of non-Aryans, Fritz and the others boycott his classes. Later, the old professor sadly watches the burning of books by Einstein and Heine, among others, in a ceremony that ironically contrasts his own birthday celebration. Finally, the government bars Roth from teaching. Taken into custody, he is sent to a concentration camp, where he finally dies. His fleeing family is stopped at the border and accused of "blasphemy" for attempting to smuggle Roth's final book out of the country. Martin, however, bravely attempts to save Freya, only to see her shot and die in his arms as they escape to freedom across the mountains seen in the film's opening shots.

In addition, an analysis of Fritz Marber's attitude toward Freya as compared to his notion of politics yields some interesting cross-associations. Throughout the picture Fritz treats her as if she has neither intelligence nor ideas of her own. "I'll do the thinking for both of us," he tells her, echoing Hitler's paternalistic attitude toward the German people. Fritz's dictatorial attitude contrasts directly with the Jewish professor who prizes "tolerance and a sense of humor." Service to the Third Reich, the film implies, turns thinking men into blindly obedient animals willing to turn on their friends and families. Hitler has become Dr. Moreau, and all who follow him are lost souls trapped on an island of hate and ignorance.

The Mortal Storm was Hollywood's fledgling attempt to confront the Nazi menace, using "non-Aryans" as threatened "everymen." Borzage's portrayal of Hitler's disruption of traditional German life stamps Hitler as an evil force that needs to be defeated so that order may once again reign. The interracial love symbolized by Freya and Martin, a truly American approach to practical political differences, dominates such films during the decade. Thus, *The Mortal Storm* confronts the German monster on a personal rather than a political scale. It assumes that all large-scale issues can ultimately be reduced to much smaller concerns. For Hollywood at this point, love can defeat this monster.

Address Unknown (1944) traces the relationship between two families caught up in the world of politics and war. The opening shots, as in *The Mortal Storm*, show the world of normal relations before the advent of the monster. Here director William Cameron Menzies depicts the friendship and respect between two partners in the art business. Martin Schultz (Paul Lukas) returns to Germany and sends back artifacts, while Max Einstein (Morris Carnovsky) stays in San Francisco and sells them. Martin's son, Heinrich (Peter Van Eyck), resides with Max, while Max's daughter, Grisella (K. T. Stevens), goes to Germany for an acting job before she is to marry Heinrich. Because of his need for personal aggrandizement and his weak personality, Martin becomes hypnotized by Nazi propaganda, forgetting his ties to Max and totally forsaking Grisella when she needs him the most.

Menzies's handling of the Jewish elements in the film is both intriguing and contrived. Early in the film Max calls Jew-baiting a "minor activity" in a voice-over letter to Martin, while the camera shows a German merchant gloating as his Jewish rival's store is burned to the ground. The effects of Nazi perversion of traditional values become clear when Martin's activities culminate in Grisella's death. When the Germans order her to remove some offensive lines from a play ("Blessed are the meek for they shall inherit the earth; blessed are the peasants for they shall be called the children of God"), she refuses and causes a riot. The audience hoots her off the stage with cries of "Judin! Judin!" After she asks if calling "a man a Jew robs him of his humanity," the crazed mob storms the stage and chases her from the theater. Martin refuses her sanctuary, and Grisella is tracked down and murdered, another sacrificial victim of the ravenous monster. As for Martin, his actions prove that once one sides with the monster against normal values, he must necessarily betray his former friends. In selling his soul to the devil, Martin destroys the best part of his own nature, his compassionate humanity.

After the war, and continuing up to the present day, Hollywood filmmakers have continued to use Nazis as symbols of monstrous evil and Jews as their "everyman" victims. Like Dracula and Frankenstein's monster, celluloid Nazis keep reappearing on American movie screens, no matter how many symbolic stakes are driven into their hearts. *Marathon Man* (1976), for instance, features a sadistic ex-Nazi dentist who tortures a Jewish graduate student to obtain information the boy does not possess. Eventually the Jew escapes this Kafkaesque situation, forcing his German tormentor to suffer some of the pain he caused others. *Voyage of the Damned* (1979) sets its story back in 1939, as Jewish immigrants become pathetic pawns in Hitler's elaborate propaganda exercise. *The Pawnbroker* (1965) shows a desperate man's battle to confront the death camp horrors that have made him part of the "walking dead." *The Boys from Brazil* (1979) portrays the Nazis as monsters who justify their atrocities by claiming a higher purpose, and *The Man in the Glass Booth* (1975) presents the difficulty of assigning total guilt and innocence in a world of complex realities.

THE JEW AS COMIC CHARACTER IN
HORROR/SUPERNATURAL FILMS

Sig Altman in *The Comic Image of the Jew* concludes that the "Jew is the comic figure par excellence in films," "that the very word 'Jewish' has become laden with humorous overtones," and that "Jewish identity is itself a kind of automatic comic device projected at an audience 'programmed' to receive it."[18] Altman's book presents a notable attempt to trace the role of comedy throughout Jewish history and art, and to place contemporary Jewish humor (and humorists) in a historical perspective. Several of his points, briefly summarized below, contribute to an understanding of the films under discussion. First, the role of the jester has for centuries been an important one in Jewish culture. The *badken* or *marshallik* was a sort of Lear's fool allowed the privilege of caustic humor and social criticism without fear of reprisal. Second, Jewish self-deprecating and self-ironic humor has been the constant companion of a people forced for so long to live under someone else's rules. This adaptation of the "Stepin' Fetchit" demeanor to ward off possible aggression and to make Jews seem as inoffensive as possible was a necessary tactic in a hostile world. An "I'll-say-it-about-myself-before-you-do" attitude represents a defense mechanism strengthened by years of persecution, powerlessness, and paranoia. Third, Jewish humor has been a crucial part of Jewish writing from Sholem Aleichem to Isaac Bashevis Singer to Philip Roth to Woody Allen. An expression of both self-love and self-hatred, such humor in early films springs directly from a vaudeville ethos where ethnic stereotypes like the drunken Irishman and the dumb Swede were commonplaces that raised few eyebrows and even fewer consciousnesses. Finally, even though the comic images of Jews presented in films were often created, acted, and fostered by Jews themselves, the interpretation of such urges as hostile, demeaning outlets for latent anti-Semitic feelings cannot be totally dismissed.

Laughter is the Jew's shield, his protection against an oppressive world. At its best, however, such humor goes even further. Isaac Rosenfield's observation about Sholem Aleichem, that his comedy is built on "the incongruity between man's ambitions and his impotence to achieve them,"[19] defines tragedy as well as comedy, and therein lies the essence of the best Jewish humor's delicate mixture of the serious and the comic. The Jewish screen persona is often admired for his dreams while he is simultaneously mocked for his failures. Novelist Saul Bellow writes in his introduction to *Great Jewish Short Stories* (1963) that in much Jewish literature, "laughter and trembling are so curiously mingled that it is not easy to determine the relations between the two. At times the laughter seems simply to restore the equilibrium of sanity; at times the figures of the story, or parable, appear to invite or encourage the trembling with the secret aim of overcoming it by means of laughter."[20] Jewish comedy mixes laughter and trembling, pain and pleasure, into a unified organic whole. One film that blends laughter and trembling in a gentle manner as it unites a Jewish protagonist with the supernatural is *The Angel Levine* (1970).

Based on a short story in Bernard Malamud's *The Magic Barrel* (1958), and directed by Czechoslovakian-born Jan Kadar, the film partakes of the old Jewish mystical tradition that critic Irving Malin says occurs when "the supernatural and the trivial jostle each other."[21] Certainly Morris Mishkin (Zero Mostel) needs a miracle. His only daughter has run off with a "nogoodnik," his beloved wife, Fanny (Ida Kaminska), is dying day-by-day before his eyes, and his back is so sore it keeps him from working at his sewing machine to earn a living. The kindly neighborhood doctor (Milo O'Shea), who represents the limits of rational thought and scientific accomplishment in the face of death, can do little to help Fanny recover, although he assures the old man she will. Mishkin's miracle arrives in the form of a black man (Harry Belafonte) who claims to be not only a Jew but also an angel. Sent from heaven, he must get Mishkin to believe in him within twenty-four hours or lose his powers. Only when Mishkin believes can his miracle occur. His early suspicions about this black man's claims turn to complete disbelief when the angel's very earthy girl friend (Gloria Foster) shows up, insisting that he marry her in light of their four-year courtship. Eventually the white Jew who needs to believe in miracles and the black angel who needs someone to believe in him sit and argue over inconsequentials, as the clock ticks away. Only in the terrible twenty-fifth hour does Mishkin come to accept that the black man is an angel, but by then it is too late to save Fanny.

The Little Shop of Horrors (1960) provides an even stranger mixture of Jewish comedy and horror. Like its predecessor, *A Bucket of Blood* (1959)—which was also directed by Roger Corman and written by Charles B. Griffith—it focuses on the conflict between a Jewish schnook and the gentile world that oppresses him. The film's protagonist is Seymour (Mel Welles), a Lower East Side florist. Seymour loves Mushnik's dizzy daughter, Audrey (Jackie Joseph), who pays no attention to him. Early in the picture, Seymour becomes very disturbed over the droopy condition of a strange plant in Mushnik's shop. When he accidentally cuts his hand and some blood drips onto the plant's leaves, Seymour makes the startling discovery that the plant's natural food is human blood. The more blood it receives, the more the plant blooms— and the more blood it needs to keep it growing. "Feeeed me! I'm hunn- nnngry!" it screams at Seymour, who dutifully goes out to locate new sources of nourishment for his newfound dependent. He finds it in the veins of his oppressive gentile neighbors, whom he feeds to the demanding plant. As the plant grows larger and larger, a horticulture magazine decides to do a feature story on the exotic specimen and the man who has made it thrive. But when its gigantic petals open during the interview, they reveal the faces of Seymour's hapless victims. Finally, after a wild chase, Seymour tumbles into the plant and becomes the last scrap of food for its carnivorous appetite.

Corman shot *The Little Shop of Horrors* in two days on an unused backlot set, and it looks like it. Certainly, it scares no one over the age of three. Horror is not Corman's point, and any fears quickly disappear beneath the film's dominant tone of Jewish humor. But some social commentary remains. Seymour, the modern descendant of generations of Jewish schlemiels, becomes a coarse precursor of the persona Woody Allen will adopt in the next decade, although Allen uses the role with far greater effectiveness and meaning. In *The Little Shop of Horrors*, the schlemiel takes out his frustrations in a deadly manner, resorting to murder in order to attain and then keep his social status, as well as to capture the affections of the girl he desires.

It has been suggested that Corman's film is "a satire of Jewish social climbing of the most ruthless sort," an observation supported by the film.[22] But the argument that the plant becomes a "surrogate Jewish mother" misses the point completely. It is Seymour who becomes the mother-figure in the film; the plant is the whining, parasitic, spoiled child. Seymour basks in the reflected glory of his "offspring," and he kills to fulfill his "child's" demands. As such, the film becomes a parable of black humor that emphasizes the disastrousness of giving all to a child, of defining oneself by the achievements of others, and of losing any sense of moral values in a blindly desperate attempt to provide for a child's wishes. Such a course of action can lead only to one end: destruction by the very thing the parent has created, a monstrous dependant whose appetite remains forever unsatiated.

Two vampire spoofs containing Jewish characters also parody serious horror film situations. *The Fearless Vampire Killers* (1967), a film eventually disowned by its director, Roman Polanski, after disputes with MGM,[23] contains a strange Jewish vampire, Yoine Shagal (Alfie Bass). After he is bitten by Count von Krolock (Ferdy Mayne) and turned into a vampire, the lusty Shagal heads straight for the voluptuous blonde, Magda (Fiona Lewis), who has rejected him in life. When Magda tries to defend herself with a crucifix, Shagal gleefully exclaims, "Oy! Have you got the wrong vampire!" Though the character of the licentious Jewish vampire provides much of the film's humor, Polanski injects a few social comments on the class hierarchy present among the undead. For example, Shagal remains an outsider even in vampire society, much as he was in his former fife. The count and his ghoulish aristocracy ostracize him, and his coarse, wooden coffin is dragged out to the barn, segregated from the other vampires' resting places. The cleverness of the Jew, however, apparently extends into the world of the living dead, as Shagal whittles his way into the coffin of the count's son and sleeps obediently at his feet.

Of the horror films in which Jews appear during the 1970s, one moviemaker uses the element of Jewish humor to add to the genre's appeal, much as it did earlier in *The Little Shop of Horrors* and *The Fearless Vampire Killers*. The decade's best example of this tendency is director Stan Dragoti's fetching parody of the vampire film, *Love at First Bite* (1979). Among the humorous touches, such as swinging modern girls who think Dracula's (George Hamilton) bite is just another kinky sexual activity, Dragoti includes Richard Benjamin as psychiatrist Jeffrey Rosenberg, a Jewish descendant of Dr. Van Helsing, Dracula's archenemy. Rosenberg persists in confusing the various means of vampiricide. In one memorable moment, he reaches underneath his shirt to extract an amulet to ward off Dracula's advances. The audience, as well as the count, assumes a cross will be forthcoming; instead, Rosenberg brings forth a Star of David, a symbol that has no effect on the bemused Dracula. So unlike his illustrious and successful ancestor, Rosenberg cannot defeat his sharp-fanged opponent, who escapes at the film's conclusion with his willing bride (Susan St. James).

JEWISH HORROR FILMS WITHOUT JEWISH CHARACTERS

Most of this article has been concerned with films containing Jewish characters within the frame, the image of the Jews on the screen taking precedence over the imprint of the man behind the camera. Any approach which concentrates on who is and who is not Jewish, and what the fact has to do with an artist's work, gets tangled up in very thorny problems. In film analysis, confusion inevitably springs from replacing actual pictorial representations with intuited attitudes. How do we identify specifically Jewish humor as opposed to gentile humor? If an artist comes from a Jewish home is he automatically endowed with so-called Jewish wit and pathos? Can a Jewish filmmaker consciously or unconsciously avoid including ethnic issues in his works? However one answers these questions, no large scale agreement exists among any given group of people, Jews or non-Jews. Even with these problems, two films—both directed by Jewish comic auteurs—deserve at least brief mention here, for they inject a Jewish sensibility into the horror film genre: Woody Allen's *Everything You Always Wanted to Know about Sex (But Were Afraid to Ask)* (1972) and Mel Brooks' *Young Frankenstein* (1974).[24]

Maurice Yacowar has correctly observed that Allen's movie "is not a film about sex, but a film about films about sex. Moreover, it demonstrates the tensions that have led Western culture to develop cinematic and television programming that is at once obsessed with sex and too inhibited to deal with the subject openly."[25] This is precisely the case in the section of the film that parodies horror films, "Are the Findings of Doctors and Clinics Who Do Sexual Research Accurate?" Actually, Allen burlesques two familiar horror film plots and their characters in this section. In the figure of the insane Dr. Bernardo (John Carradine) and his deformed assistant (Ref Sanchez), he makes fun of the stereotypical mad scientist and his hunchbacked servant; in the sequence with the escaped, forty-foot-high breast, he ridicules the out-of-control creature feature. Allen, at one point, even resorts to a familiar defense to protect himself against the "very clever tit": he holds up a small wooden cross which proves totally ineffective. Given Allen's other films, it is difficult to refrain from a Freudian analysis of this larger-than-life breast segment. Allen's continual problem with women, ranging from mothers to aunts to girlfriends to lovers, is by now a familiar part of his screen persona. Allen's creation of a towering mammary represents both his sexual anxieties, as well as American culture's neurotic fixation on the female breast.[26]

In a serious moment, Allen told interviewer Frank Rich that "life is like a concentration camp. You're stuck here and there's no way out. You can only rage impotently against your persecutors."[27] For Allen, these rages take the form of an unceasing stream of half-comic/half-serious jokes that speak to our fears and uncertainties while they poke fun at our inadequacies. Through his unique blend of laughter and trembling, of horror and humor, Allen has become the comic conscience of our time, a master of satiric humor that places him in the same company as Jonathan Swift and Laurence Sterne.

Like Allen, director/writer Mel Brooks's humor emanates from his Jewish roots. "He has vaudeville in his blood and chicken fat in his head," says James Monaco.[28] Brooks himself seems to concur and locates the roots of his own comedy in Jewish pain:

Look at Jewish history. Unrelieved, lamenting would be intolerable. So, for every ten Jews beating their breasts, God designated one to be crazy and amuse the breast-beaters. By the time I was five I knew I was that one. . . . You want to know where my comedy comes from? It comes from not being kissed by a girl until you're sixteen. It comes from the feeling that, as a Jew and as a person, you don't fit into the mainstream of American society. It comes from the realization that even though you're better and smarter, you'll never belong.[29]

Brooks's revealing remarks provide further evidence of the mixture of pain and pleasure that characterizes much Jewish comedy.

Brooks's comments about his sense of never belonging, of never quite fitting into America's mainstream, allow him to view the horror film genre from a particularly sensitive angle: the alienation of the monster. In *Young Frankenstein*, his parody of the mad-scientist-try-ing-to-be-God pictures, Brooks's sympathies are clearly with his crea-ture (Peter Boyle). The pathetic monster is so driven to fit in, to belong, that he is willing to don white tie and tails and join his maker (Gene Wilder) in a duet of "Puttin' On the Ritz." Robin Wood observes that "few horror films have totally unsympathetic monsters . . . [since] the monster is the embodiment of all that our culture represses."[30] Cer-tainly, Brooks carries this tendency to its ultimate lengths. Brooks's monster eventually does gain acceptance, due to his master's foresight in making his sexual organs proportional to the rest of his huge body, but not before middle-class society almost destroys his fragile spirit. Though no specific Jewish characters appear in *Young Frankenstein*, the picture reverberates with a Jewish sense of comic alienation that leads Brooks to focus his attention on the problems of society's out-casts, its deviants. Since Jewish artists like Brooks and Allen laugh at themselves, if they see themselves as monsters, their monster movies must be funny.

CONCLUSION

Some of the films I have examined are lamps that help extinguish the darkness of ignorance. Others simply mirror long-held prejudices. But all these horror films with Jewish characters should make us more aware of racial issues. As sensitive viewers, we must ask ourselves why a director, scriptwriter, and/or producer has included Jewish figures in his horror film. What important elements does such a character bring to the work? Would the film be the same if the ethnic characters were identified? How sensitive is the filmmaker to minority stereotyping? Why would the film be less (or more) satisfying, less (or more) involving, without such an ethnic figure?

Even more important, we must recognize that all works of art blend conscious and unconscious ideas and feelings. Once a work is completed, its creator becomes a commentator on it; his version of what his creation means is no more accurate or right than any other critic's interpretation. A creative artist, therefore, can tell us only what he intended his work to be, not what it is. We need not feel constrained by the boundaries of his limited understanding. Shakespeare, to cite an obvious example, never studied Freud, but *Hamlet* presents a powerful depiction of the Oedipus complex. To discuss only what a sixteenth-century Englishman meant his play to be about (assuming we could discover what that was) would drastically simplify the drama, perhaps limiting its value to that of historical artifact. But by discussing *Hamlet* in terms that Shakespeare could never have used, modern critics have helped make the play more understandable to a generation obsessed with psychological analysis. Thus, every age "discovers" what in a work of art relates most to its own needs and desires, even if the artist himself was not consciously aware of all he created. Such is the case in the cinema, as well as in the other arts, so it should not surprise us when filmmakers seem unaware of their movies' implications.

As thinking people, it behooves us to remember that many of our deepest feelings about minorities are created and nurtured by the visual media that permeate our lives. In particular, films and television reveal, reflect, and redefine the ever-changing roles of minorities in American society by shaping—some would also say, distorting—a group's historical movements into a series of powerful and evocative images. Though many movies with ethnic characters are valuable aesthetic objects of worth and beauty, almost all remain interesting as historical artifacts that help chart the history of minority groups in the United States. Whether they explain or exploit ethnic characters, these films either implicitly or explicitly show how they affect a cultural context and how that context influences them. Such movies dynamically depict both the minority group's profound impact on American society and that society's perception of the ethnic groups within its midst. It is a two-way process inherent in the first horror films as well as the latest.[31]

NOTES

1. Robin Wood, "Return of the Repressed," *Film Comment* 14, no. 4 (July–August, 1978), 25–32, and "Gods and Monsters," *Film Comment* 14, no. 5 (September–October, 1978), 19–25. All quotes from Wood refer to these two articles. These pieces were revised and incorporated into Wood's "Introduction to the American Horror Film," included in this volume.

2. Actually, a few films did have a black vampire. The first, *Blacula* (1972), starred William Marshall in the title role. Later, he appeared in *Scream Blacula Scream* (1973). Also, there was a 1972 film called *Blackenstein*.

3. Introduction to John Kobal, *Great Film Stills of the German Silent Era* (New York: Dover Publications, 1981), v; Richard Taylor, *Film Propaganda: Soviet Russia and Nazi Germany* (New York: Barnes and Noble, 1979), 139; Paul Monaco, *Cinema and Society* (New York Elsevier Scientific Publishing Company, 1976), 118, 124, 136, 138, 144, 146. Throughout this analysis, I refer mainly to the 1920 Wegener film, which most critics regard as the greatest movie version of the golem story. The director, however, did make two others, one in 1914 and another in 1917. In addition, there are two French versions (1936, 1960), two Czechoslovakian versions (1951, 1960), two British versions (1960, 1972), and a Polish version (1980).

4. S. S. Prawer, *Caligari's Children: The Film as Tale of Terror* (New York: Oxford University Press, 1980), 28–29; Gershon Winkler, *The Golem of Prague* (New York: The Judaica Press, 1980), 19–20.

5. For a brief discussion of Hasidic beliefs, see Raphael Patai, *Gates to the Old City* (New York: Avon Books, 1980), 667–69.

6. An excellent recapitulation and analysis of the various permutations of the golem tales is contained in Arnold Goldsmith, *The Golem Remembered, 1901–1980* (Detroit: Wayne State University Press, 1981).

7. John Hollander, *The Night Mirror* (New York: Atheneum, 1971), 37–39. For more on the golem legends, see Gershon Scholem, *Major Trends in Jewish Mysticism* (New York: Schocken Books, 1941); Joachim Neugroschel, ed., *Yenne Velt*, vol. 1 (New York: The Stonehill Publishing Company, 1976); and Louis Ginzberg, *The Legends of the Jews* (Philadelphia: The Jewish Publication Society of America, 1939).

8. Carlos Clarens, *Horror Movies* (London: Secker and Warburg, 1967), 25. For more on Wegener, see Lotte Eisner, *The Haunted Screen* (Berkeley: University of California Press, 1969), 33–40; Siegfried Kracauer, *From Caligari to Hitler: A Psychological History of the German Film* (Princeton: Princeton University Press, 1947), 28–32; H. H. Wollenberg, *Fifty Years of German Film* (London: The Falcon Press, 1948), 10–22; John D. Barlow, *German Expressionist Film* (Boston: Twayne Publishers, 1982), 67–69.

9. There is considerable controversy over the authenticity of the Rosenberg book. Some scholars, like Joachim Neugroschel (351), dismiss it as a story

Rosenberg wrote himself and passed off as Katz's to authenticate it. Others, like Gershon Winkler (1980), defend the document as accurate, literal, and factual (518). Goldsmith (38–50) seems less concerned with the authenticity of the stories than with Rosenberg's resurrection of a new folk hero.

10. Winkler, 276–77.

11. Robert Payne, *The Life and Death of Adolf Hitler* (New York: Praeger, 1973), 142–48.

12. Prawer argues that "a student of German culture cannot but be struck by the prominent part which weird fantasies have played in German art (109)." He goes on to note this tendency in the works of Tieck, Kleist, Eichendorff, Hoffmann, Heine, Mann, Kafka, von Hofmannsthal, Musil, Schiller, Goethe, Wagner, Bocklin, Kubin, Weber, and Marschner.

13. Judith N. Goldberg, *Laughter through Tears: The Yiddish Cinema* (Rutherford, N.J.: Fairleigh Dickinson University Press, 1983), 25, 112, 113; Parker Tyler, *Classics of the Foreign Film* (New York: Citadel Press, 1962), 120.

14. I am indebted to Gershon Winkler's book, *Dybbuck* (New York: The Judaica Press, 1982), 123, for this background information on the dybbuck in Jewish history.

15. Tyler, *Classics of the Foreign Film,* 121.

16. Prawer, 111; D. L. White, "The Poetics of Horror: More than Meets the Eye," in Barry Grant, ed., *Film Genre: Theory and Criticism* (Metuchen, N.J.: Scarecrow Press, 1977), 132.

17. Bosley Crowther, *New York Times* (June 21, 1940).

18. Sig Altman, *The Comic Image of the Jew* (Rutherford, N.J.: Fairleigh Dickinson University Press, 1971), 11, 49, 50.

19. Theodore Solotaroff, ed., *Age of Enormity* (Cleveland: The World Publishing Company, 1962), 34.

20. Saul Bellow, ed., *Great Jewish Short Stories* (New York: Dell, 1973), 12.

21. Irving Malin, *Jews and Americans* (Carbondale: Southern Illinois University Press, 1965), 156.

22. Chris Morris, "Roger Corman: The Schlemiel as Outlaw," in Todd McCarthy and Charles Flynn, eds., *Kings of the Bs* (New York: Dutton, 1975), 67.

23. Polanski asked that his name be removed from the credits when, prior to its American release, MGM's Martin Ransohoff made several drastic changes, including cutting and redubbing the picture. The film as Polanski originally fashioned it was seen worldwide outside the United States.

24. For more on Allen's and Brooks's specifically Jewish films, see Lester D. Friedman, *Hollywood's Image of the Jew* (New York: Frederick Ungar, 1982).

25. Maurice Yacowar, *Loser Take All: The Comic Art of Woody Allen* (New York: Frederick Ungar, 1979), 137–38.

26. Yacowar, 148.

27. Frank Rich, "Woody Allen Wipes the Smile off His Face," *Esquire* (May 1977), 76.

Chapter 7

28. James Monaco, *American Film Now* (New York: Oxford University Press, 1979), 236.

29. Paul D. Zimmerman, "The Mad Mad Mel Brooks," *Newsweek* (February 17, 1975), 57.

30. Wood, "Return of the Repressed," 27.

31. I would like to thank Sharon Rivo, director of the National Center of Jewish Film, for loaning me a print of *The Dybbuck*, and Phil Serling, president, Syracuse Cinephile Society, for loaning me a print of *The Golem*.

8

An Introduction to the American Horror Film

Robin Wood

REPRESSION, THE OTHER, THE MONSTER

The most significant development—in film criticism, and in progressive ideas generally—of the last few decades has clearly been the increasing confluence of Marx and Freud, or more precisely of the traditions of thought arising from them: the recognition that social revolution and sexual revolution are inseparably linked and necessary to each other. From Marx we derive our awareness of the dominant ideology—the ideology of bourgeois capitalism—as an insidious all-pervasive force capable of concealment behind the most protean disguises, and the necessity of exposing its operation whenever and wherever possible. It is psychoanalytic theory that has provided (without Freud's awareness of the full revolutionary potential of what he was unleashing) the most effective means of examining the ways in which that ideology is transmitted and perpetuated, centrally through the institutionalization of the patriarchal nuclear family. The battle for liberation, the battle against oppression (whether economic, legal, or ideological), gains enormous extra significance through the addition of that term *patriarchal,* since patriarchy long *precedes* and far *exceeds* what we call capitalism. It is here, through the medium of psychoanalytic theory, that Feminism and Gay Liberation join forces with Marxism in their progress toward a common aim, the overthrow of patriarchal capitalist ideology and the structures and institutions that sustain it and are sustained by it.

Psychoanalytic theory, like Marxism, now provides various models, inflecting basic premises in significantly different ways. It is not certain that the Lacanian model prompted by (among others) *Screen* magazine is the most satisfactory.[1]

On the evidence so far it seems certainly not the most potentially effective, leading either to paralysis or to a new academicism perhaps more sterile than the old, and driving its students into monastic cells rather than the streets. I want to indicate briefly a possible alternative model, developed out of Freud by Marcuse and given definitive formulation in a recent book by Gad Horowitz, *Repression*:[2] a model that enables us to connect theory closely with the ways we actually think and feel and conduct our lives—those daily practicalities from which the theorizing of *Screen* seems often so remote. The book's subtitle is "Basic and Surplus Repression in Psychoanalytic Theory: Freud, Reich, Marcuse." It is the crucial distinction between basic and surplus repression that is so useful in relation to direct political militancy and so suggestive in relation to the reading of our cultural artifacts (among them our horror films), and through them, our culture itself. Horowitz had devoted a dense, often difficult and closely argued book on the subject; in the space at my disposal I can offer only a bald and simplified account.

Basic repression is universal, necessary, and inescapable. It is what makes possible our development from an uncoordinated animal capable of little beyond screaming and convulsions into a human being; it is bound up with the ability to accept the postponement of gratification, with the development of our thought and memory processes, of our capacity for self-control, of our recognition of and consideration for other people. Surplus repression, on the other hand, is specific to a particular culture and is the process whereby people are conditioned from earliest infancy to take on predetermined roles within that culture. In terms of our own culture, then, *basic* repression makes us distinctively human, capable of directing our own lives and co-existing with others, while *surplus* repression makes us (if it works) into monogamous, heterosexual, bourgeois, patriarchal capitalists ("bourgeois" even if we are born into the proletariat, for we are talking here of ideological norms rather than material status). *If* it works; if it doesn't, the result is either a neurotic or a revolutionary (or both), and if revolutionaries account for a very small proportion of the population, neurotics account for a very large one. Hardly surprising. All known existing societies are to some degree surplus-repressive, but the degree varies enormously, from the trivial to the overwhelming. Freud saw long ago that our own civilization had reached a point where the burden of repression was becoming all-but-insupportable, an insight Horowitz (following Marcuse) brilliantly relates to Marx's theory of alienated labor: the most immediately obvious characteristics of life in our culture are frustration, dissatisfaction, anxiety, greed, possessiveness, jealousy, neuroticism: no more than what psychoanalytic theory shows to be the logical product of patriarchal capitalism. What needs to be stressed is that the kind of challenges now being made to the system—and the kind of perceptions and recognitions that structure those challenges and give them impetus—become possible (become in the literal sense *thinkable*) only in the circumstances of the system's imminent disintegration. While the system retained sufficient conviction, credibility, and show of coherence to suppress them, it did so. The struggle for liberation is not utopian, but a practical necessity.

Given that our culture offers an extreme example of surplus repressiveness, one can ask what, exactly, in the interests of alienated labor and the patriarchal family, is repressed. One needs here both to distinguish between the concepts of *re*pression and *op*pression, and to suggest the continuity between them. In psychoanalytic terms, what is *re*pressed is not accessible to the conscious mind (except through analysis or, if one can penetrate their disguises, in dreams). We may also not be conscious of ways in which we are *op*pressed, but it is much easier to become so: we are oppressed by something "out there." One might perhaps define repression as fully internalized oppression (while reminding ourselves that all the groundwork of repression is laid in infancy), thereby suggesting both the difference and the connection. A specific example may make this clearer: our social structure demands the *re*pression of the bisexuality that psychoanalysis shows to be the natural heritage of every human individual, and the *op*pression of homosexuals: obviously, the two phenomena are not identical, but equally obviously they are closely connected. What escapes *re*pression has to be dealt with by *op*pression.

What, then, is repressed in our culture? First, sexual energy itself, together with its possible successful sublimation into nonsexual creativity—sexuality being the source of creative energy in general. The "ideal" inhabitant of our culture will be the individual whose sexuality is sufficiently fulfilled by the monogamous heterosexual union necessary for the reproduction of future ideal inhabitants and whose sublimated sexuality (creativity) is sufficiently fulfilled in the totally noncreative and nonfulfilling labor (whether in factory or office) to which our society dooms the overwhelming majority of its members. The "ideal," in other words, is as close as possible to an automaton in whom both sexual and intellectual energy have been reduced to a minimum. Otherwise, the "ideal" is a contradiction in terms and a logical impossibility; hence the necessary frustration, anxiety, and neuroticism of our culture.

Second, bisexuality—which should be understood both literally (in terms of possible sexual orientation and practice) and in a more general sense. Bisexuality represents the most obvious and direct affront to the principle of monogamy and its supportive romantic myth of "the one right person"; the homosexual impulse in both men and women represents the most obvious threat to the "norm" of sexuality as reproductive and restricted by the "ideal" of family. But more generally we confront here the whole edifice of clear-cut sexual differentiation that bourgeois-capitalist ideology erects on the flimsy and dubious foundations of biological difference: the social norms of masculinity and femininity, the social definitions of manliness and womanliness, the whole vast apparatus of oppressive male/female myths, the systematic repression from infancy ("blue for a boy . . . ") of the man's "femininity" and the woman's "masculinity" in the interests of forming human beings for specific predetermined social roles.

Third, the particularly severe repression of female sexuality/creativity; the attribution to the female of passivity, her preparation for her subordinate and dependent role in our culture. Clearly, a crucial aspect of the repression of bisexuality is the denial to women of drives culturally associated with masculinity: activeness, aggression, self-assertion, organizational power, creativity itself.

Fourth—and fundamental—the repression of the sexuality of children, taking different forms from infancy, through "latency" and puberty, and into adolescence—the process moving, indeed, from *re*pression to *op*pression, from the denial of the infant's nature as sexual being to the veto on the expression of sexuality before marriage.

None of these forms of repression is necessary for the existence of civilization in some form (i.e., none is "basic"), for the development of our human-ness. Indeed, they impose limitations and restrictions on that development, stunting human potential. All are the outcome of the requirements of the particular, surplus-repressive civilization in which we live.

Closely linked to the concept of repression—indeed, truly inseparable from it—is another concept necessary to an understanding of ideology on which psychoanalysis throws much light, the concept of "the Other": that which bourgeois ideology cannot recognize or accept but must deal with (as Barthes suggests in *Mythologies*[3]) in one of two ways: either by rejecting and if possible annihilating it, or by rendering it safe and assimilating it, converting it as far as possible into a replica of itself. The concept of Otherness can be theorized in many ways and on many levels. Its psychoanalytic significance resides in the fact that it functions not simply as something external to the culture or to the self, but also as what is repressed (but never destroyed) in the self and projected outward in order to be hated and disowned. A particularly vivid example—and one that throws light on a great many classical Westerns—is the relationship of the Puritan settlers to the Indians in the early days of America. The Puritans rejected any perception that the Indians had a culture, a civilization, of their own; they perceived them not merely as savage but, literally, as devils or the spawn of the Devil; and, since the Devil and sexuality are inextricably linked in the Puritan consciousness, they perceived them as sexually promiscuous, creatures of unbridled libido. The connection between this view of the Indian and Puritan repression is obvious: a classic and extreme case of the projection onto the Other of what is repressed within the Self, in order that it can be discredited, disowned, and, if possible, annihilated. It is repression, in other words, that makes impossible the healthy alternative: the full recognition and acceptance of the Other's autonomy and right to exist.

Some versions, then, of the figure of the Other as it operates within our culture, of its relation to repression and oppression, and of how it is characteristically dealt with:

Quite simply, other people. It is logical and probable that under capitalism all human relations will be characterized by power, dominance, possessiveness, manipulation: the extension into relationships of the property principle. Given the subordinate and dependent position of women, this is especially true of the culture's central relationship, the male/female, and explains why marriage as we have it is characteristically a kind of mutual imperialism/colonization, an exchange of different forms of possession and independence, both economic and emotional. In theory, relations between people of the same sex stand more chance of evading this contamination, but in practice most gay and lesbian relationships tend to rely on heterosexual models. The "otherness," the autonomy, of the partner, her/his right to freedom and independence of being, is perceived as a threat to the possession/dependence principle and denied.

Woman. In a male-dominated culture, where power, money, law, social institutions are controlled by past, present, and future patriarchs, woman as the Other assumes particular significance. The dominant images of women in our culture are entirely male-created and male-controlled. Woman's autonomy and independence are denied; on to women men project their own innate, repressed femininity in order to disown it as inferior (to be called "unmanly"—i.e., like a woman—is the supreme insult).

The proletariat. Insofar as it still has any autonomous existence, escaping its colonization by bourgeois ideology. It remains, at least, a conveniently available object for projection: the bourgeois obsession with cleanliness, which psychoanalysis shows to be closely associated, as outward symptom, with sexual repression, and bourgeois sexual repression itself, find their inverse reflections in the myths of working-class squalor and sexuality.

Other cultures. If they are sufficiently remote, no problem: they can be simultaneously deprived of their true character and exoticized (e.g., Polynesian cultures as embodied by Dorothy Lamour). If they are inconveniently close, we already have the example of the American Indian: the procedure is very precisely represented in Ford's *Drums along the Mohawk* (1939), with its double vision of the Indians as "sons of Belial" fit only for extermination, or the Christian, domesticated, servile, and (hopefully) comic Blueback.

Ethnic groups within the culture. Again, an easily available projection-object (myths of black sexuality, "animality," etc.). Acceptable in either of two ways: either they keep to their ghettoes and don't trouble us with their "otherness," or they behave as we do and become replicas of the good bourgeois, their otherness reduced to the one unfortunate difference of color. We are more likely to invite a Pakistani to dinner if he dresses in a business suit.

Alternative ideologies or political systems. The exemplary case is of course Marxism, the strategy that of parody. Still almost totally repressed within our preuniversity education system (despite the key importance of Marx—whatever way you look at it—in the development of twentieth-century thought). Marxism exists generally in our culture only in the form of bourgeois myth that renders it indistinguishable from Stalinism (rather like confusing the teachings of Christ with the Spanish Inquisition).

Deviations from ideological sexual norms. Notably bisexuality and homosexuality. One of the clearest instances of the operation of the repression/projection mechanism: homophobia (the irrational hatred and fear of homosexuals) is only explicable as the outcome of the unsuccessful repression of bisexual tendencies: what is hated in others is what is rejected (but nonetheless continues to exist) within the self.

Children. When we have worked our way through all the other liberation movements, we may discover that children are the most oppressed section of the population (unfortunately, we cannot expect to liberate our children until we have successfully liberated ourselves). Most clearly of all, the "otherness" of children (see Freudian theories of infantile sexuality) is that which is repressed within ourselves, its expression therefore hated in others: what the previous generation repressed in us, and what we, in turn, repress in our children, seeking to mold them into replicas of ourselves, perpetuators of a discredited tradition.

All this may seem to have taken us rather far from our immediate subject. In fact, I have been laying the foundations, stone by stone, for a theory of the American horror film which (without being exhaustive) should provide us with a means of approaching the films seriously and responsibly. One could, I think, approach any of the genres from the same starting point; but it is the horror film that responds in the most clear-cut and direct way, because central to it is the actual dramatization of the dual concept, the repressed/the other, in the figure of the Monster. One might say that the true subject of the horror genre is the struggle for recognition of all that our civilization represses or oppresses: its re-emergence dramatized, as in our nightmares, as an object of horror, a matter for terror, the "happy ending" (when it exists) typically signifying the restoration of repression.

I think my analysis of what is repressed, combined with my account of the Other as it functions within our culture, will be found to offer a comprehensive survey of horror film monsters from German Expressionism on. It is possible to produce "monstrous" embodiments of virtually every item in the list. Let me preface this by saying that the general sexual content of the horror film has long been recognized, and the list of monsters representing a generalized sexual threat would be interminable; also, the generalized concept of "otherness" offered by the first item on my list cannot be represented by specific films.

Female sexuality

Earlier examples are the panther woman of *Island of Lost Souls* (1932) and the heroine of the 1942 *Cat People* (the association of women with cats runs right through and beyond the Hollywood cinema, cutting across periods and genres from *Bringing Up Baby* [1938] to *Alien* [1979]); but the definitive Feminist horror film is clearly De Palma's *Sisters* (1972), co-scripted by the director and Louisa Rose, among the most complete and rigorous analyses of the oppression of women under patriarchal culture in the whole popular cinema.

The proletariat

I would claim here Whale's *Frankenstein* (1931), partly on the strength of its pervasive class references, more on the strength of Karloff's costume: Frankenstein *could* have dressed his creature in top hat, white tie and tails, but in fact chose laborer's clothes. Less disputable, in recent years we have *The Texas Chainsaw Massacre* (1974), with its monstrous family of retired, but still practicing, slaughterhouse workers; the underprivileged devil worshippers of *Race with the Devil* (1975); and the revolutionary army of *Assault on Precinct 13* (1976).

Other cultures

In the '30s the monster was almost invariably foreign; the rebellious animal-humans of *Island of Lost Souls* (although created by the white man's science) on one level clearly signify a "savage," unsuccessfully colonized culture. Recently, one horror film, *The Manitou* (1977), identified the monster with the American Indian (*Prophecy* [1979] plays tantalizingly with this possibility—also linking it to urban blacks—before opting for the altogether safer and less interesting explanation of industrial pollution).

Ethnic groups

The Possession of Joel Delaney (1972) links diabolic possession with Puerto Ricans; blacks (and a leader clad as an Indian) are prominent, again, in *Assault on Precinct 13*'s monstrous army.

Alternative ideologies

The '50s science-fiction cycle of invasion movies are generally regarded as being concerned with the Communist threat.

Homosexuality and bisexuality

Both Murnau's *Nosferatu* (1922) and Whale's *Frankenstein* (1931) can be claimed as implicitly (on certain levels) identifying their monsters with repressed homosexuality. Recent, less arguable, instances are Dr. Frank 'n' Furter of *The Rocky Horror Picture Show* (1975) (he, not his creature, is clearly the film's real monster) and, more impressive, the bisexual god of Larry Cohen's *God Told Me To (Demon*, 1977).

Children

Since *Rosemary's Baby* (1968) children have figured prominently in horror films as the monster or its medium: *The Exorcist* (1973), *The Omen* (1976), and so on. Cohen's two *It's Alive* films (1974, 1978) again offer perhaps the most interesting and impressive example. There is also the Michael of *Halloween's* (1978) remarkable opening.

This offers us no more than a beginning, from which one might proceed to interpret specific horror films in detail as well as further exploring the genre's social significance, the insights it offers into our culture. I shall add here simply that these notions of repression and the Other afford us not merely a means of access but a rudimentary categorization of horror films in social/political terms, distinguishing the progressive from the reactionary; the criterion being the way in which the monster is presented and defined.

RETURN OF THE REPRESSED

I want first to offer a series of general propositions about the American horror film, then attempt to define the particular nature of its evolution in the '60s and '70s.

Popularity and Disreputability

The horror film has consistently been one of the most popular and, at the same time, the most disreputable of Hollywood genres. The popularity itself has a peculiar characteristic that sets the horror film apart from other genres: it is restricted to aficionados and complemented by total rejection, people tending to go to horror films either obsessively or not at all. They are dismissed with contempt by the majority of

reviewer-critics, or simply ignored. (The situation has changed somewhat since *Psycho* [1960], which conferred on the horror film something of the dignity that *Stagecoach* [1939] conferred on the Western,
but the disdain still largely continues. I have read no serious or illuminating accounts of, for example, *Raw Meat* [*Deathline*, 1972], *It's
Alive*, or *The Hills Have Eyes* [1977]). The popularity, however, also
continues. Most horror films make money; the ones that don't are
those with overt intellectual pretensions, obviously "difficult" works
like *God Told Me To (Demon)* and *Exorcist II: The Heretic* (1977).
Another psychologically interesting aspect of this popularity is that
many people who go regularly to horror films profess to ridicule them
and go in order to laugh—which is not true, generally speaking, of the
Western or the gangster movie.

Dreams and Nightmares

The analogy frequently invoked between films and dreams is usually
concerned with the experience of the audience. The spectator sits in
darkness, and the sort of involvement the entertainment film invites
necessitates a certain switching off of consciousness, a losing of oneself
in a fantasy-experience. But the analogy is also useful from the point
of view of the filmmakers. Dreams—the embodiment of repressed
desires, tensions, fears that our conscious mind rejects—become possible when the "censor" that guards our subconscious relaxes in sleep,
although even then the desires can only emerge in disguise, as fantasies
that are "innocent" or apparently meaningless.

One of the functions of the concept of "entertainment"—by definition, that which we don't take seriously, or think about much ("It's
only entertainment")—is to act as a kind of partial sleep of consciousness. For the filmmakers as well as for the audience, full awareness
stops at the level of plot, action, and character, in which the most dangerous and subversive implications can disguise themselves and escape
detection. This is why seemingly innocuous genre movies can be far
more radical and fundamentally undermining than works of conscious
social criticism, which must always concern themselves with the possibility of reforming aspects of a social system whose basic rightness
must not be challenged. The old tendency to dismiss the Hollywood
cinema as escapist always defined escape merely negatively, as escape
from, but escape logically must also be escape *to*. Dreams are also
escapes, from the unresolved tensions of our lives into fantasies. Yet the

fantasies are not meaningless; they can represent attempts to resolve those tensions in more radical ways than our consciousness can countenance.

Popular films, then, respond to interpretation as at once the personal dreams of their makers and the collective dreams of their audiences—the fusion made possible by the shared structures of a common ideology. It becomes easy, if this is granted, to offer a simple definition of horror films: they are our collective nightmares. The conditions under which a dream becomes a nightmare are: (a) that the repressed wish is, from the point of view of consciousness, so terrible that it must be repudiated as loathsome; and (b) that it is so strong and powerful as to constitute a serious threat. The disreputability noted above—the general agreement that horror films are not to be taken seriously—works clearly for the genre viewed from this position. The censor (in both the common and the Freudian sense) is lulled into sleep and relaxes vigilance.

The Surrealists

It is worth nothing here that one group of intellectuals did take American horror movies very seriously indeed: the writers, painters, and filmmakers of the Surrealist movement. Luis Buñuel numbers *The Beast with Five Fingers* (1946) among his favorite films and paid homage to it in *The Exterminating Angel* (1962); and Georges Franju, an heir of the Surrealists, numbers *The Fly* (1958) among *his*. The association is highly significant, given the commitment of the Surrealists to Freud, the unconscious, dreams, and the overthrow of repression.

Basic Formula

At this stage it is necessary to offer a simple and obvious basic formula for the horror film: normality is threatened by the Monster. I use "normality" here in a strictly nonevaluative sense, to mean simply "conformity to the dominant social norms"; one must firmly resist the common tendency to treat the word as if it were more or less synonymous with "health." The very simplicity of this formula has a number of advantages:

1. It covers the entire range of horror films, being applicable whether the Monster is a vampire, a giant gorilla, an extraterres-

trial invader, an amorphous gooey mass, or a child possessed by the Devil, and this makes it possible to connect the most seemingly heterogeneous movies.

2. It suggests the possibility of extension to other genres: substitute for "Monster" the term *Indians,* for example, and one has a formula for a large number of classical Westerns.

3. Although so simple, the formula provides three variables: normality, the Monster, and, crucially, the relationship between the two. The definition of normality in horror films is in general boringly constant: the heterosexual monogamous couple, the family, and the social institutions (police, church, armed forces) that support and defend them. The Monster is, of course, much more protean, changing from period to period as society's basic fears clothe themselves in fashionable or immediately accessible garments—rather as dreams use material from recent memory to express conflicts or desires that may go back to early childhood.

It is the third variable, the relationship between normality and the Monster, that constitutes the essential subject of the horror film. It, too, changes and develops, the development taking the form of a long process of clarification or revelation. The relationship has one privileged form: the figure of the doppelganger, alter ego, or double, a figure that has recurred constantly in Western culture, especially during the past hundred years. The *locus classicus* is Stevenson's *Dr. Jekyll and Mr. Hyde,* where normality and Monster are two aspects of the same person. The figure recurs throughout two major sources of the American horror film, German Expressionist cinema (the two Marias of *Metropolis* [1926], the presentation of protagonist and vampire as mirror reflections in *Nosferatu* [1922], the very title of F. W. Murnau's lost Jekyll-and-Hyde film, *Der Januskopf* [1920]), and the tales of Poe. Variants can be traced in such oppositions as Ahab/the white whale in *Moby Dick* and Ethan/Scar in *The Searchers* (1956). The Westerns of Anthony Mann are rich in doubles, often contained within families or family patterns; *Man of the West* (1958), a film that relates very suggestively to the horror genre, represents the fullest elaboration.

I shall limit myself for the moment to one example from the horror film, choosing it partly because it is so central, partly because the motif is there less obvious, partially disguised, and partly because it points forward to Larry Cohen and *It's Alive:* the relationship of Monster to creator in the *Frankenstein* films. Their identity is made explicit in *Son of Frankenstein* (1939), the most intelligent of the Universal series, near the start of which the title figure (Basil Rathbone) complains bitterly that everyone believes "Frankenstein" to be the name of the monster. (We discover subsequently that the town has also come to be called Frankenstein, the symbiosis of Monster and creator spreading over the entire environment.) But we should be alerted to the relationship's true significance from the moment in the James Whale original where Frankenstein's decision to create his monster is juxtaposed very precisely with his decision to become engaged. The doppelganger motif reveals the Monster as normality's shadow.

Ambivalence

The principle of ambivalence is most eloquently elaborated in A. P. Rossiter's *Angel with Horns*, among the most brilliant of all books on Shakespeare. Rossiter first expounds it with reference to *Richard III*. Richard, the "angel with horns," both horrifies us with his evil and delights us with his intellect, his art, his audacity; while our moral sense is appalled by his outrages, another part of us gleefully identifies with him.[4] The application of this to the horror film is clear. Few horror films have totally unsympathetic Monsters (*The Thing* [1951] is a significant exception); in many (notably the *Frankenstein* films) the Monster is clearly the emotional center, and much more human than the cardboard representatives of normality. The Frankenstein monster suffers, weeps, responds to music, longs to relate to people; Henry and Elizabeth merely declaim histrionically. Even in *Son of Frankenstein*—the film in which the restructured monster is explicitly designated evil and superhuman—the monster's emotional commitment to Ygor and grief over his death carries far greater weight than any of the other relationships in the film.

But the principle goes far beyond the Monster's being sympathetic. Ambivalence extends to our attitude to normality. Central to the effect and fascination of horror films is their fulfillment of our nightmare wish to smash the norms that oppress us and which our moral conditioning teaches us to revere. The overwhelming commercial success of *The Omen* cannot possibly be explained in terms of a simple, unequivocal *horror* at the Devil's progress.

Freudian Theses

Finally, one can simply state the two elementary (and closely interconnected) Freudian theses that structure this chapter: that in a society built on monogamy and family there will be an enormous surplus of sexual energy that will have to be repressed; and that what is repressed must always strive to return.

Before considering how the horror film has developed in the past decade, I want to test the validity of the above ideas by applying them to a classical horror film. I have chosen Robert Florey's *Murders in the Rue Morgue* (1932) because it is a highly distinguished example, and generally neglected; because its images suggest Surrealism as much as Expressionism; and because it occupies a particularly interesting place in the genre's evolution, linking two of the most famous, though most disparate, horror films ever made. On the one hand it looks back very clearly to *The Cabinet of Dr. Caligari* (1919): the Expressionist sets and lighting, with Karl Freund as cinematographer; the fairground that provides the starting point for the action; the figure of the diabolical doctor, who shows off his exhibit and later sends it to kidnap the heroine; the flight over the rooftops. On the other hand it looks forward, equally clearly, to *King Kong* (1933): instead of *Caligari*'s sleepwalker, a gorilla, which falls in love with the heroine, abducts her at night and is shot down from a roof. It is as important to notice the basic motifs that recur obstinately throughout the evolution of the horror film in Western culture as it is to be aware of the detailed particularities of individual films. *Murders in the Rue Morgue* responds well to the application of my formula.

Normality. The film is quite obsessive about its heterosexual couples. At the opening, we have two couples responding to the various spectacles of the fairground; there is a scene in the middle where numerous carefree couples disport themselves picturesquely amid nature. Crucial to the film, however, is Pierre's love-speech to Camille on her balcony, with its exaggerated emphasis on purity: she is both a "flower" and a "star"; she is told not to be curious about what goes on in the houses of the city around them ("Better not to know"); she is also prevented from obtaining knowledge of the nature of Pierre's activities in the morgue (a "horrid old place"). Even the usual gay stereotype, Pierre's plump and effeminate friend, fits very well into the pattern. He is provided with a girlfriend, to recuperate him into the heterosexual coupling of normality. His relationship with Pierre (they share an apartment, he wears an apron, cooks the dinner, and fusses) is a parody of bourgeois marriage, the incongruity underlining the relationship's repressive sexlessness. And he underlines the attempts at separating "pure" normality from the pervasive contamination of outside forces by complaining that Pierre "brings the morgue into their home."

The Monster. *Murders in the Rue Morgue* has a divided Monster, a phenomenon not uncommon in the horror film. (In *The Cabinet of Dr. Caligari*, the Monster is both Caligari and Cesar; in *Island of Lost Souls*, both Dr. Moreau and his creatures). Here the division is tripartite: Dr. Mirakle (Bela Lugosi), his servant-assistant, and Erik, "the beast with a human soul." The servant's role is small, but important because of his appearance: half-human, half-animal, he bridges the gap between Mirakle and Erik. Scientist and ape are linked, however, in another way: Mirakle himself lusts after Camille, and Erik (the animal extension of himself) represents the instrument for the satisfaction of that lust. Together, they combine the two great, apparently contradictory, dreads of American culture as expressed in its cinema: intellectuality and eroticism.

Relationship. The film's superficial project is to insist that purity-normality can be separated from contaminating eroticism-degradation; its deeper project is to demonstrate the impossibility of such a separation. In the opening sequence, the couples view a series of fairground acts as spectacles (the separation of stage from audience seeming to guarantee safety): an erotic dance by "Arabian" girls, a Wild Red Indian show, and finally Erik the ape. The association of the three is suggestive of the link between the horror film and the Western—the link of horror, Indians, and released libido. In each case the separation of show and audience is shown to be precarious: Pierre's sidekick asks his girl if she "could learn to do that dance" for him; two spectators adopt the name "apache" to apply to the savages of Paris; the audience enters the third booth between the legs of an enormous painted ape, where its phallus would be. Dr. Mirakle's introduction uses evolutionary theory to deny separation: Erik is "the darkness at the dawn of Man." His subsequent experiments are carried out to prove that Erik's blood can be "mixed with the blood of man"—and as the experiments all involve women, the sexual connotations are plain.

Although not obvious, the "double" motif subtly structures the film. It comes nearest to explicitness in the effeminate friend's remark that Pierre is becoming fanatical, "like that Dr. Mirakle." But Pierre and Mirakle are paralleled repeatedly, both in the construction of the scenario and through the *mise-en-scène*. At the end of the balcony love scene Florey cuts from the lovers' kiss to Mirakle and Erik watching from their carriage. Later, the juxtaposition is reversed, the camera panning from Mirakle-Erik lurking in the shadows to Pierre-Camille embracing on the balcony; it is as if the Monster were waiting to be released by the kiss. Mirakle sends Camille a bonnet; she assumes it is from Pierre. After Pierre leaves her at night, there is a knock at her door. She assumes it is Pierre come back and opens; it is Mirakle. Bearing in mind that Mirakle and Erik are not really distinct from one another, one must see Pierre and this composite Monster paralleled throughout as rival mates for Camille, like Jonathan and Nosferatu, or like David Ladd and the underworld man of *Raw Meat*. (The motif's recurrence across different periods and different continents testifies to its importance.) At the climax, Pierre and Erik confront each other like mirror images on the rooftop, and Erik is shot down by Pierre: the hero's drive is to destroy the doppelganger who embodies his repressed self.

Murders in the Rue Morgue is fascinating for its unresolved self-contradiction. In the fairground, Mirakle is denounced as a heretic, in the name of the Biblical/Christian tradition of God's creation of man; the whole notion of purity/normality clearly associates with this—explicitly, in the very prominent, carefully lit crucifix above Camille's bed. Yet Mirakle's Darwinian theories are also obviously meant to be correct. Erik and humanity are *not* separable; the ape exists in all of us; the "morgue" cannot be excluded from the "home."

The horror film since the 1960s has been dominated by five recurrent motifs. The list of examples offered in each case begins with what I take to be the decisive source-film of each trend—not necessarily the first, but the film that, because of its distinction or popularity, can be thought of as responsible for the ensuing cycle. I have included a few British films that seem to me American-derived (*Raw Meat*, arguably the finest British horror film, was directed by an American, Gary Sherman); they lie outside the main British tradition represented by Hammer Productions, a tradition very intelligently treated in David Pirie's book, *A Heritage of Horror*. The lists are not, of course, meant to be exhaustive.

The Monster as human psychotic or schizophrenic: *Psycho*; *Homicidal* (1961), *Repulsion* (1965), *Sisters*, *Schizo* (1976).
The revenge of Nature: *The Birds* (1963); *Frogs* (1972), *Night of the Lepus* (1972), *Day of the Animals* (1977), *Squirm* (1976).
Satanism, diabolic possession, the Antichrist: *Rosemary's Baby*; *The Exorcist*, *The Omen*, *The Possession of Joel Delaney*, *The Car*

(1977), *God Told Me To (Demon)*, and *Race with the Devil*, which, along with *High Plains Drifter* (1973), interestingly connects this motif with the Western.

The Terrible Child (often closely connected to the above). To the first three films in the above add: *Night of the Living Dead* (1968), *Hands of the Ripper* (1971), *It's Alive, Cathy's Curse* (1976); also, although here the "children" are older, *Carrie* (1976) and *The Fury* (1978).

Cannibalism: *Night of the Living Dead*; *Raw Meat, Frightmare* (1974), *The Texas Chainsaw Massacre, The Hills Have Eyes*.

These apparently heterogeneous motifs are drawn deeper together by a single unifying master-figure: the Family. The connection is most tenuous and intermittent in what has proved, on the whole, the least interesting and productive of these concurrent cycles, the "revenge of Nature" films; but even there, in the more distinguished examples (outstandingly, of course, *The Birds*, but also in *Squirm*), the attacks are linked to, or seem triggered by, familial or sexual tensions. Elsewhere, the connection of the family to horror has become overwhelmingly consistent: the psychotic/schizophrenic, the Antichrist and the child-monster are all shown as products of the family, whether the family itself is regarded as guilty (the "psychotic" films) or innocent (*The Omen*).

The "cannibalism" motif functions in two ways. Occasionally members of a family devour each other (*Night of the Living Dead*; and *Psycho*'s Mrs. Bates is a metaphorical cannibal who swallows up her son). More frequently, cannibalism is the family's means of sustaining or nourishing itself (*The Texas Chainsaw Massacre, The Hills Have Eyes*). Pete Walker's revoltingly gruesome and ugly British horror film, *Frightmare*, deserves a note here, its central figure being a sweet and gentle old mother who has the one unfortunate flaw that she can't survive without eating human flesh, a craving guiltily indulged by her devoted husband.

If we see the evolution of the horror film in terms of an inexorable "return of the repressed," we will not be surprised by this final emergence of the genre's real significance—together with a sense that it is currently the most important of all American genres and perhaps the most progressive, even in its overt nihilism—in a period of extreme cultural crisis and disintegration, which alone offers the possibility of radical change and rebuilding. To do justice to the lengthy process of that emergence would involve a dual investigation too complex for the framework of this article: into the evolution of the horror film, and into the changing treatment of the family in the Hollywood cinema. I shall content myself here with a few further propositions.

1. The family (or marital) comedy in which the 1930s and '40s are so rich turns sour in the '50s (*Father of the Bride* [1950], *The Long, Long Trailer* [1954]) and peters out; the family horror film starts (not, of course, without precedents) with *Psycho* in 1960, and gains impetus with *Rosemary's Baby* and *Night of the Living Dead* toward the end of the decade.

2. As the horror film enters into its apocalyptic phase, so does the Western. *The Wild Bunch* appeared in 1969, the year after *Rosemary's Baby*. And *High Plains Drifter* fused their basic elements in a Western in which the Hero from the Wilderness turns out to be the Devil (or his emissary) and burns the town (American civilization) to the ground after revealing it as fundamentally corrupt and renaming it Hell.

3. The family comedies that seemed so innocent and celebratory in the '30s and '40s appear much less so in retrospect from the '70s. In my book *Personal Views*[5] I pointed to the remarkable anticipation in *Meet Me in St. Louis* (1944) of the Terrible Child of the '70s horror film, especially in the two scenes (Halloween and the destruction of the snow people) in which Margaret O'Brien symbolically kills parent-figures. What is symbolic in 1944 becomes literal in *Night of the Living Dead*, where a little girl kills and devours her parents—just as the implications of another anticipatory family film of the early '40s, *Shadow of a Doubt* (1943), becomes literally enacted in *It's Alive* (the monster as product of the family).

4. The process whereby horror becomes associated with its true milieu, the family, is reflected in its steady *geographical* progress toward America:

   a. In the 1930s, horror is always foreign. The films are set in Paris (*Murders in the Rue Morgue*), Middle Europe (*Frankenstein*, *Dracula*) or on uncharted islands (*Island of Lost Souls*, *King Kong*); it is always external to Americans, who may be attacked by it physically but remain (superficially, that is) uncontaminated by it morally. The designation of horror as foreign stands even when the "normal" characters are Europeans. In *Murders in the Rue Morgue*, for example, the young couples, though nominally French, are to all intents and purposes nice clean-living Americans (with American accents); the foreignness of the horror characters is strongly underlined, both by Lugosi's accent and by the fact that nobody knows where he comes from. The foreignness of horror in the '30s can be interpreted in two ways: simply, as a means of disavowal (horror exists, but is un-American), and more interesting and unconscious, as a means of locating horror as a "country of the mind," as a psychological state: the films set on uncharted (and usually nameless) islands lend themselves particularly to interpretation of this kind.

b. The Val Lewton films of the '40s are in some ways outside the mainstream development of the horror film. They seem to have had little direct influence on its evolution (certain occasional haunted-house movies like *The Uninvited* [1944] and *The Haunting* [1963] may owe something to them), though they strikingly anticipate, by at least two decades, some of the features of the modern horror film. *Cat People* is centered on the repression of female sexuality, in a period where the Monster is almost invariably male and phallic. (Other rare exceptions are the panther-woman of *Island of Lost Souls* and, presumably, *Dracula's Daughter* [1936], which I have not seen.) *The Seventh Victim* (1943) has strong undertones of sibling envy and sexual jealousy (the structure and editing of the last scene suggesting that Jacqueline's suicide is willed by her "nice" husband and sister rather than by the "evil" devil-worshippers), as well as containing striking anticipations of *Psycho* and *Rosemary's Baby*; it is also set firmly in America, with no attempt to disown evil as foreign.

Above all, *I Walked with a Zombie* (1943) explicitly locates horror at the heart of the family, identifying it with sexual repressiveness in the cause of preserving family unity. *The Seventh Victim* apart, horror is still associated with foreignness; Irena in *Cat People* is from Serbia, *Zombie* is set in the West Indies, *The Leopard Man* (1943) in Mexico, and so on. Yet the best of the series are concerned with the undermining of such distinctions—with the idea that no one escapes contamination. Accordingly, the concept of the Monster becomes diffused through the film (closely linked to the celebrated

Lewton emphasis on atmosphere, rather than overt shock), no longer identified with a single figure.

Zombie, one of the finest of all American horror films, carries this furthest. It is built on an elaborate set of apparently clear-cut structural oppositions—Canada-West Indies, white-black, light-darkness, life-death, science-black magic, Christianity-Voodoo, conscious-unconscious, and so on—and it proceeds systematically to blur all of them. Jessica is both living and dead; Mrs. Rand mixes medicine, Christianity, and voodoo; the figurehead is both St. Sebastian and a black slave; the black–white opposition is poetically undercut in a complex patterning of dresses and voodoo patches; the motivation of *all* the characters is called into question; the messenger-zombie Carrefour can't be kept out of the white domain.

c. The 1950s science fiction cycles project horror onto either extraterrestrial invaders or mutations from the insect world, but they are usually set in America; even when they are not (*The Thing*), the human characters are American. The films, apparently simple, prove on inspection often very difficult to "read." The basic narrative patterns of the horror film repeat themselves obstinately and continue to carry their traditional meanings, but they are encrusted with layers of more transient, topical material. *Them!* (1954), for example, seems to offer three layers of meaning. Explicitly, it sets out to cope with the fear of nuclear energy and atomic experiment: the giant ants are mutants produced by the radioactive aftermath of a bomb explosion; they are eventually destroyed under the guidance of a humane and benevolent science embodied in the comfortingly paternal figure of Edmund Gwenn. The fear of Communist infiltration also seems present, in the emphasis on the ants as a subversive subterranean army and on their elaborate communications system. Yet the film continues to respond convincingly to the application of my basic formula and its Freudian implications. The ants rise up from underground (the unconscious); they kill by holding their victims and injecting into them huge (excessive) quantities of formic acid (the release of repressed phallic energy); and both the opening and final climax of the film are centered on the destruction (respectively actual and potential) of family groups.

Since *Psycho*, the Hollywood cinema has implicitly recognized horror as both American and familial. I want to conclude this section by briefly examining two key works of recent years that offer particularly illuminating and suggestive contrasts and comparisons: *The Omen* and *The Texas Chainsaw Massacre*. One can partly define the nature of each by means of a chart of oppositions:

The Omen	The Texas Chainsaw Massacre
big-budget	low-budget
glossy production values	raw, unpolished
stars	unknown actors
bourgeois entertainment	nonbourgeois "exploitation"
good taste	bad taste
"good" family	"bad" family
the Monster imported from Europe	the Monster indigenously American
child destroys parent-figures	parents destroy "children"
traditional values reaffirmed	traditional values negated

I don't wish to make any claims for *The Omen* as a work of art: the most one could say is that it achieves a sufficient level of impersonal professional efficiency to ensure that the "kicks" inherent in its scenario are not dulled. I would add here that my description of *Massacre* as "raw, unpolished" refers to the overall effect of the film, as it seems to be generally experienced. Its *mise-en-scène* is, without question, everywhere more intelligent, more inventive, more cinematically educated and sophisticated, than that of *The Omen*. Hooper's cinematic intelligence, indeed, becomes more apparent on every viewing, as one gets over the initial traumatizing impact and learns to respect the pervasive felicities of camera placement and movement.

In obvious ways *The Omen* is old-fashioned, traditional, reactionary: the "goodness" of the family unit isn't questioned, "horror" is disowned by having the devil-child a product of the Old World, unwittingly *adopted* into the American family, the devil-child and his independent-female guardian (loosely interpretable in "mythic" terms as representing child liberation and women's liberation) are regarded as purely evil (oh for a cinematic Blake to reverse all the terms).

Yet the film remains of great interest. It is about the end of the world, but the "world" the film envisages ending is very particularly defined

I Walked with a Zombie, *1943. The zombie Carrefour (Darby Jones) enters the white domain of Francis Dee. From the editors' collection.*

within it: the bourgeois, capitalist, patriarchal Establishment. Here "normality" is not merely threatened by the monster, but totally annihilated: the state, the church, the family. The principle of ambivalence must once again be invoked: with a film so shrewdly calculated for box-office response, it is legitimate to ask what general satisfaction it offers its audience.

Superficially, the satisfaction of finding traditional values reaffirmed (even if "our" world is ending, it was still the good, right, true one); more deeply, and far more powerfully, under cover of this, the satisfaction of the ruthless logic with which the premise is carried through—the supreme satisfaction (masquerading as the final horror) being the revelation, as the camera cranes down in the last shot, that the Devil has been adopted by the president and first lady of the United States. The translation of the film into Blakean terms is not, in fact, that difficult: the devil-child is its implicit hero, whose systematic destruction of the bourgeois Establishment the audience follows with a secret relish. *The Omen* would make no sense in a society that was not prepared to enjoy and surreptitiously condone the working out of its own destruction.

As Andrew Britton pointed out to me, *The Omen* and *The Texas Chainsaw Massacre* (together with numerous other recent horror films) have one premise disturbingly in common: the annihilation is inevitable, humanity is now completely powerless, there is nothing anyone can do to arrest the process. (Ideology, that is, can encompass despair, but not the imagining of constructive radical alternatives.) *The Omen* invokes ancient prophecy and shows it inexorably fulfilling itself despite all efforts at intervention; we infer near the opening of *Massacre* that the Age of Aquarius, whose advent was so recently celebrated in *Hair* (1979), has already passed, giving way to the Age of Saturn and universal malevolence. Uncontrol is emphasized throughout the film: not only have the five young victims no control over their destiny, their slaughterers (variously psychotic and degenerate) keep losing control of themselves and each other.

This is partly (in conjunction with the film's relentless and unremitting intensity) what gives *Massacre*, to such a degree (beyond any other film in my experience), the authentic quality of nightmare. I have had since childhood a recurring nightmare whose pattern seems to be shared by a very large number of people within our culture: I am running away from some vaguely terrible oppressors who are going to do dreadful things to me; I run to a house or a car, and so on, for help; I discover its occupants to be precisely the people I am fleeing. This pattern is repeated twice in *Massacre*, where Sally "escapes" from Leatherface, first to his own home, then to the service station run by his father.

The application of my formula to *Massacre* produces interesting results: the pattern is still there, as is the significant relationship between the terms, but the definitions of "normality" and "Monster" have become partly reversed. Here "normality" is clearly represented by the quasi-liberated, permissive young (though still forming two couples and a brother/sister family unit, hence reproducing the patterns of the past); the monster is the family, one of the great composite monsters of the American cinema, incorporating four characters and three generations, and imagined with an intensity and audacity that far transcend the connotations of the term "exploitation movie." It has a number of important aspects:

1. The image of the "Terrible House" stems from a long tradition in America (and Western capitalist) culture.[6] Traditionally, it rep-

resents an extension or "objectification" of the personalities of the inhabitants. *Massacre* offers two complementary "terrible houses": the once imposing, now totally decayed house of Franklin's and Sally's parents (where we keep *expecting* something appalling to happen), and the more modest, outwardly spruce, inwardly macabre villa of the monstrous family wherein every item of decor is an expression of the characters' degeneracy. The borderline between home and slaughterhouse (between work and leisure) has disappeared—the slaughterhouse has invaded the home, humanity has begun literally to "prey upon itself, like monsters of the deep." Finally, what the "terrible house" (whether in Poe's "Fall of the House of Usher," in *Psycho*, in *Mandingo* [1975], or here) signifies is the dead weight of the past crushing the life of the younger generation, the future—an idea beautifully realized in the shot that starts on the ominous grey, decayed Franklin house and tilts down to show Kirk and Pam, dwarfed in longshot, playing and laughing as they run to the swimming hole, and to their doom.

2. The contrast between the two houses underlines the distinction the film makes between the affluent young and the psychotic family, representatives of an exploited and degraded proletariat. Sally's father used to send his cattle to the slaughterhouse of which the family are products.

3. The all-male family (the grandmother exists only as a decomposing corpse) also derives from a long American tradition, with notable antecedents in Ford's Westerns (the Clantons of *My Darling Clementine* [1946], the Cleggses of *Wagon Master* [1950]) and in *Man of the West*. The absence of woman (conceived of as a civilizing, humanizing influence) deprives the family of its social sense and social meaning while leaving its strength of primitive loyalties largely untouched. In *Massacre*, woman becomes the ultimate object of the characters' animus (and, I think, the film's, since the sadistic torments visited on Sally go far beyond what is necessary to the narrative).

4. The release of sexuality in the horror film is always presented as perverted, monstrous, and excessive (whether it takes the form of vampires, giant ants, or Mrs. Bates), both the perversion and the excess being the logical outcome of repression. Nowhere is this carried further than in *Massacre*. Here sexuality is totally perverted from its functions, into sadism, violence, and cannibalism.

It is striking that there is no suggestion anywhere that Sally is the object of an overtly sexual threat: she is to be tormented, killed, dismembered, eaten, but not raped. Ultimately, the most terrifying thing about the film is its total negativity; the repressed energies—represented most unforgettably by Leatherface and his continuously whirring phallic chainsaw—are presented as irredeemably debased and distorted. It is no accident that the four most intense horror films of the 1970s at "exploitation" level (*Night of the Living Dead*, *Raw Meat*, and *The Hills Have Eyes* are the other three) are all centered on cannibalism, and on the specific notion of present and future (the younger generation) being devoured by the past. Cannibalism represents the ultimate in possessiveness, hence the logical end of human relations under capitalism. The implication is that "liberation" and "permissiveness," as defined within our culture, are at once inadequate and too late—too feeble, too unaware, too undirected to withstand the legacy of long repression.

5. This connects closely with the recurrence of the "double" motif in *Massacre*. The young people are, on the whole, uncharacterized and undifferentiated (the film's energies are mainly with its monsters—as usual in the horror film, the characteristic here surviving the reversal of definitions), but in their midst is Franklin, who is as grotesque, and almost as psychotic, as his nemesis Leatherface. (The film's refusal to sentimentalize the fact that he is crippled may remind one of the blind beggars of Buñuel.) Franklin associates himself with the slaughterers by imitating the actions of Leatherface's brother, the hitchhiker: wondering whether he, too, could slice open his own hand, and toying with the idea of actually doing so. (Kirk remarks, "You're as crazy as he is.") Insofar as the other young people are characterized, it is in terms of a pervasive petty malice. Just before Kirk enters the house to meet his death, he teases Pam by dropping into her hand a human tooth he has found on the doorstep; later, Jerry torments Franklin to the verge of hysteria by playing on his fears that the hitchhiker will pursue and kill him. Franklin resents being neglected by the others, Sally resents being burdened with him on her vacation. The monstrous cruelties of the slaughterhouse family have their more pallid reflection within "normality." (The reflection pattern here is more fully worked out in *The Hills Have Eyes*, with its stranded "normal" family besieged by its dark mirror

image, the terrible shadow-family from the hills, who want to kill the men, rape the women, and eat the baby.)

6. Despite the family's monstrousness, a degree of ambivalence is still present in the response they evoke. Partly, this is rooted in our sense of them as a *family*. They are held together—and torn apart—by bonds and tensions with which we are all familiar, with which, indeed, we are likely to have grown up. We cannot cleanly dissociate ourselves from them. Then there is the sense that *they* are victims, too—of the slaughterhouse environment, of capitalism—*our* victims, in fact. Finally, they manifest a degraded but impressive creativity. The news reporter at the start describes the tableau of decomposing corpses in the graveyard (presumably the work of the hitchhiker, and perhaps a homage to his grandparents: a female corpse is posed in the lap of a male corpse in a hideous parody of domesticity) as "a grisly work of art." The phrase, apt for the film itself, also describes the artworks among which the family live, some of which achieve a kind of hideous aesthetic beauty: the light bulb held up by a human hand, the sofa constructed out of human and animal bones, surmounted by ornamental skulls, the hanging lamp over the dining table that appears to be a shrunken human head. The film's monsters do not lack that characteristically human quality, an aesthetic sense, however perverted its form; also, they waste nothing, a lesson we are all taught as children.

7. Central to the film—and centered on its monstrous family—is the sense of grotesque comedy, which in no way diminishes (rather, it intensifies) its nightmare horrors: Leatherface chasing Sally with the chainsaw, unable to stop and turn, skidding, wheeling, like an animated character in a cartoon; the father's response to Leatherface's devastations, which by that time include four murders and the prolonged terrorization of the heroine ("Look what your brother did to that door"); Leatherface dressed up in jacket and tie and fresh black wig for formal dinner with Grandpa; the macabre farce of Grandpa's repeated failures to kill Sally with the hammer. The film's sense of fundamental horror is closely allied to a sense of the fundamentally absurd. The family, after all, only carries to its logical conclusion the basic (though unstated) tenet of capitalism, that people have the right to live off other people. In twentieth-century art, the sense of the absurd is always closely linked to total despair (Beckett, Ionesco . . .). The fusion of night-

mare and absurdity is carried even further in *Death Trap* (*Eaten Alive*, 1976), a film that confirms that the creative impulse in Hooper's work is centered in his monsters (here, the grotesque and pathetic Neville Brand) and is essentially nihilistic.

The Texas Chainsaw Massacre, unlike *The Omen*, achieves the force of authentic art, profoundly disturbing, intensely personal, yet at the same time far more than personal, as the general response it has evoked demonstrates. As a "collective nightmare" it brings to a focus a spirit of negativity, an undifferentiated lust for destruction that seems to lie not far below the surface of the modern collective consciousness. Watching it recently with a large, half-stoned youth audience who cheered and applauded every one of Leatherface's outrages against their representatives on the screen, was a terrifying experience. It must not be seen as an isolated phenomenon: it expresses, with unique force and intensity, at least one important aspect of what the horror film has come to signify, the sense of a civilization condemning itself, through its popular culture, to ultimate disintegration, and ambivalently (with the simultaneous horror/wish-fulfillment of nightmare) celebrating the fact. We must not, of course, see that as the last word.

THE REACTIONARY WING

I suggested earlier that the theory of repression offers us a means towards a political categorization of horror movies. Such a categorization, however, can never be rigid or clear-cut. While I have stressed the genre's progressive or radical elements, its potential for the subversion of bourgeois patriarchal norms, it is obvious enough that this potential is never free from ambiguity. The genre carries within itself the capability of reactionary inflection, and perhaps no horror film is entirely immune from its operations. It need not surprise us that there is a powerful reactionary tradition to be acknowledged—so powerful that it may at times appear the dominant one. Its characteristics are, in extreme cases, very strongly marked.

Before noting them, however, it is important to make one major distinction, between the reactionary horror film and the "apocalyptic" horror film. The latter expresses, obviously, despair and negativity, yet its very negation can be claimed as progressive: the "apocalypse," even when presented in metaphysical terms (the end of the world), is generally reinterpretable in social/political ones (the end of the highly spe-cific world of patriarchal capitalism). The majority of the most distinguished American horror films (especially in the '70s) are con-cerned with this particular apocalypse; they are progressive insofar as their negativity is not recuperable into the dominant ideology, but constitutes (on the contrary) the recognition of that ideology's disinte-gration, its untenability, as all it has repressed explodes and blows it apart. *The Texas Chainsaw Massacre, Sisters, Demon* are all apocalyptic in this sense; so are Romero's two *Living Dead* movies. (Having said that, it must be added that important distinctions remain to be made among these works.) Some of the characteristics, then, that have con-tributed to the genre's reactionary wing:

1. The designation of the monster as simply evil. Insofar as horror films are typical manifestations of our culture, the *dominant* des-ignation of the monster must necessarily be "evil": what is repressed (in the individual, in the culture) must always return as a threat, perceived by the consciousness as ugly, terrible, obscene. Horror films, it might be said, are progressive precisely to the degree that they refuse to be satisfied with this simple designa-tion—to the degree that, whether explicitly or implicitly, con-sciously or unconsciously, they modify, question, challenge, seek to invert it. All monsters are by definition destructive, but their destructiveness is capable of being variously explained, excused and justified. To identify what is repressed with "evil incarnate" (a metaphysical, rather than a social, definition) is automatically to suggest that there is nothing to be done but strive to *keep* it repressed. Films in which the "monster" is identified as the devil clearly occupy a privileged place in this group; although even the devil can be presented with varying degrees of (deliberate or inad-vertent) sympathy and fascination—*The Omen* should not sim-ply be bracketed with *The Sentinel* (1976) for consignment to merited oblivion.

2. The presence of Christianity (insofar as it is given weight or pre-sented as a positive force) is in general a portent of reaction. This is a comment less on Christianity itself than on what it signifies within the Hollywood cinema and the dominant ideology). *The Exorcist* is an instructive instance: its validity is in direct propor-tion to its failure convincingly to impose its theology.

3. The presentation of the monster as totally nonhuman. The "pro-

gressiveness" of the horror film depends partly on the monster's capacity to arouse sympathy; one can feel little for a mass of viscous black slime. The political (McCarthyite) level of '50s science-fiction films—the myth of Communism as total dehumanization—accounts for the prevalence of this kind of monster in that period.

4. The confusion (in terms of what the film wishes to regard as "monstrous") of *repressed* sexuality with sexuality itself. The distinction is not always clear-cut; perhaps it never can be, in a culture whose attitudes to sexuality remain largely negative and where a fear of sex is implanted from infancy. One can, however, isolate a few extreme examples where the sense of horror is motivated by sexual disgust.

A very common generic pattern plays on the ambiguity of the monster as the "return of the repressed" and the monster as punishment for sexual promiscuity (or, in the more extreme puritanical cases, for any sexual expression whatever: two teenagers kiss; enter, immediately, the Blob). Both the *Jaws* films ([1975, 1978] their sources in both '50s McCarthyite science fiction and all those beach party/monster movies that disappeared with the B feature) are obvious recent examples, Spielberg's film being somewhat more complex, less blatant, than Szwarc's, though the difference is chiefly one of ideological sophistication.

I want to examine briefly here some examples of the "reactionary" horror film in the '70s, of widely differing distinction but considerable interest in clarifying these tendencies.

David Cronenberg's *Shivers* (1975, formerly *The Parasite Murders*) is, indeed, of very special interest here, as it is a film single-mindedly about sexual liberation, a prospect it views with unmitigated horror. The entire film is premised on and motivated by sexual disgust. The release of sexuality is linked inseparably with the spreading of venereal disease, the scientist responsible for the experiments having seen fit (for reasons never made clear) to include a VD component in his aphrodisiac parasite. The parasites themselves are modeled very obviously on phalluses, but with strong excremental overtones (their color) and continual associations with blood; the point is underlined when one enters the Barbara Steele character through her vagina. If the film presents sexuality in general as the object of loathing, it has a very special animus reserved for female sexuality (a theme repeated, if scarcely developed, in Cronenberg's subsequent *Rabid* [1976]). The parasites are spread initially by a young girl (the original subject of the scientist's experiments), the film's Pandora whose released eroticism precipitates general cataclysm; throughout, sexually aroused preying women are presented with a particular intensity of horror and disgust. *Shivers* systematically chronicles the breaking of every sexual-social taboo— promiscuity, lesbianism, homosexuality, age difference, and finally, incest—but each step is presented as merely one more addition to the accumulation of horrors. At the same time, the film shows absolutely no feeling for traditional relationships (or for human beings, for that matter): with its unremitting ugliness and crudity, it is very rare in its achievement of *total* negation.

The Brood (1979), again, is thematically central to the concept of the horror film proposed here (its subject being the transmission of neurosis through the family structure), and the precise antithesis of the genre's progressive potential. It carries over all the major structural components of its two predecessors (as an auteur, Cronenberg is nothing if not consistent): the figure of the scientist (here psychotherapist) who, attempting to promote social progress, precipitates disaster; the expression of unqualified horror at the idea of releasing what has been repressed; the projection of horror and evil onto women and their sexuality, the ultimate dread being of women usurping the active, aggressive role that patriarchal ideology assigns to the male. The film is remarkable for its literal enactment, at its climax, of the Freudian perception that, under patriarchy, the child becomes the woman's penis-substitute—Samantha Eggar's latest offspring representing, unmistakably, a monstrous phallus. The film is laboriously explicit about its meaning: the terrible children are the physical embodiments of the woman's rage. But that rage is never seen as the logical product of woman's situation within patriarchal culture; it is blamed entirely on the woman's mother (the father being culpable only in his weakness and ineffectuality). The film is useful for offering an extremely instructive comparison with *Sisters* on the one hand and *It's Alive* on the other.

In turning from Cronenberg's films to *Halloween* I do not want to suggest that I *am* bracketing them together. John Carpenter's films reveal in many ways an engaging artistic personality: they communicate, at the very least, a delight in skill and craftsmanship, a pleasure in play with the medium, that is one of the essential expressions of true creativity. Yet the film-buff innocence that accounts for much of the charm of *Dark Star* (1974) can go on to combine (in *Assault on Precinct 13*) *Rio Bravo* (1959) and *Night of the Living Dead* without any apparent awareness of the ideological consequences of converting Hawks' fascists (or Romero's ghouls, for that matter) into an army of revolutionaries. The film buff is very much to the fore again in *Halloween*, covering the film's confusions, its lack of real *thinking*, with a formal/ stylistic inventiveness that is initially irresistible. If nothing in the film is new, everything testifies to Carpenter's powers of assimilation (as opposed to mere imitation): as a resourceful amalgam of *Psycho*, *The Texas Chainsaw Massacre*, *The Exorcist*, and *Black Christmas* (1975), *Halloween* is cunning in the extreme.

The confusions, however, are present at its very foundation, in the conception of the monster. The opening is quite stunning both in its virtuosity and its resonances. The long killer's-point-of-view tracking shot with which the film begins establishes the basis for the first murder as sexual repression: the girl is killed because she arouses in the voyeur-murderer feelings he has simultaneously to deny and enact in the form of violent assault. The second shot reveals the murderer as the victim's bewildered six-year-old brother. Crammed into those first two shots (in which *Psycho* unites with the Halloween sequence of *Meet Me in St. Louis*) are the implications for the definitive family horror film: the child-monster, product of the nuclear family and the small-town environment; the sexual repression of children; the incest taboo that denies sexual feeling precisely where the proximities of family life most encourage it. Not only are those implications not realized in the succeeding film, their trace is obscured and all but obliterated. The film identifies the killer with "the Bogeyman," as the embodiment of an eternal and unchanging evil which, by definition, can't be understood; and with the Devil ("those eyes . . . the Devil's eyes"), by none other than his own psychoanalyst (Donald Pleasence)—surely the most extreme instance of Hollywood's perversion of psychoanalysis into an instrument of repression.

The film proceeds to lay itself wide open to the reading offered by Jonathan Rosenbaum:[7] the killer's victims are all sexually promiscuous, the one survivor a virgin; the monster becomes (in the tradition of all those beach-party monster movies of the late '50s to early '60s) simply the instrument of Puritan vengeance and repression rather than the embodiment of what Puritanism repressed.

Halloween is more interesting than that—if only because it is more confused. The basic premise of the action is that Laurie is the killer's real quarry throughout (the other girls merely distractions *en route*), because she is for him the reincarnation of the sister he murdered as a child (he first sees her in relation to a little boy who resembles him as he was then, and becomes fixated on her from that moment). This compulsion to reenact the childhood crime keeps Michael tied at least to the *possibility* of psychoanalytical explanation, thereby suggesting that Donald Pleasence may be wrong. If we accept that, then one tantalizing unresolved detail becomes crucial: the question of how Michael learned to drive a car. There are only two possible explanations: either he *is* the devil, possessed of supernatural powers; or he has *not* spent the last nine years (as Pleasence would have us believe) sitting staring blankly at a wall meditating further horrors. (It is to Carpenter's credit that the issue is raised in the dialogue, not glossed over as an unfortunate plot necessity we aren't supposed to notice; but he appears to use it merely as another tease, a bit of meaningless mystification). The possibility this opens up is that of reading the whole film against the Pleasence character: Michael's "evil" is what his analyst has been projecting onto him for the past nine years. Unfortunately, this remains merely a possibility in the material that Carpenter chose not to take up: it does not constitute a legitimate (let alone a coherent) reading of the actual film. Carpenter's interviews suggest that he strongly resists examining the connotative level of his own work; it remains to be seen how long this very talented filmmaker can preserve this false innocence.

At first glance, *Alien* seems little more than *Halloween*-in-outerspace: more expensive, less personal, but made with similar professional skill and flair for manipulating its audiences. Yet it has several distinctive features that give it a limited interest in its own right: it clearly wants to be taken, on a fairly simple level, as a "progressive" movie, notably in its depiction of women. What it offers on this level amounts in fact to no more than a "pop" feminism that reduces the whole involved question of sexual difference and thousands of years of patriarchal oppression to the bright suggestion that a woman can do anything a man can do (almost). This masks (not very effectively) its fundamentally reactionary nature.

Besides its resemblance to *Halloween* in general narrative pattern and suspense strategies (Where is the monster hiding? Who will be killed next? When? How? and so on), *Alien* has more precise parallels with *The Thing*. There is the enclosed space, cut off from outside help; the definition of the monster as both non- and super-human; the fact that it feeds on human beings; its apparent indestructibility. Most clearly of all, the relationship of Ash, the robot science officer, to the alien is very close to that of Professor Carrington to the Thing; in both films, science regards the alien as a superior form of life to which human life must therefore be subordinate; in both films, science is initially responsible for bringing the monster into the community and thereby endangering the latter's existence.

What strikingly distinguishes *Alien* from both *Halloween* and *The Thing* (and virtually every other horror movie) is the apparently total absence of sexuality. Although there are two women among the spaceship's crew of seven, there is no "love-interest," not even any sexual banter—in fact, with the characters restricted exclusively to the use of surnames, no recognition anywhere of sexual difference (unless we see Parker's ironic resentment of Ripley's domineeringness as motivated partly by the fact that she is a woman; but he reacts like that to all displays of authority in the film, and his actual phrase for her is "son-of-a-bitch"). Only at the end of the film, after all the men have been killed, is female sexuality allowed to become a presence (as Ripley undresses, not knowing that the alien is still alive and in the compartment). The film constructs a new "normality" in which sexual differentiation ceases to have effective existence—on condition that sexuality be obliterated altogether.

The term *son-of-a-bitch* is applied (by Ripley herself) to one other character in the film: the alien. The cinematic confrontation of its two "sons of bitches" is the film's logical culmination. Its resolution of ideological contradictions is clear in the presentation of Ripley herself: she is a "safe threat," set against the real threat of the alien. On the one hand, she is the film's myth of the "emancipated woman": "masculine," aggressive, self-assertive, she takes over the ship after the deaths of Kane and Dallas, rebelling against and dethroning both "Mother" (the computer) and father (Ash, the robot). On the other hand, the film is careful to supply her with "feminine," quasi-maternal characteristics (her care for Jones, the cat) and gives her, *vis-à-vis* the alien, the most reactionary position of the entire crew (it is she who is opposed to letting it on board, even to save Kane's life). She is, of course, in the film's terms, quite right, but that merely confirms the ideologically reactionary nature of the film, in its attitude to the Other.

If male and female are superficially and trendily united in Ripley, they are completely fused in the alien (whose most striking characteristic is its ability to transform itself). The sexuality so rigorously repressed in the film returns grotesquely and terrifying in its monster (the more extreme the repression, the more excessive the monster). At first associated with femaleness (it begins as an egg in a vast womb), it attaches itself to the most "feminine" of the crew's males (John Hurt, most famous for his portrayal of Quentin Crisp) and enters him through the mouth as a preliminary to being "born" out of his stomach. The alien's phallic identity is strongly marked (the long reptilian neck); but so is its large, expandable mouth, armed with tiers of sharp metallic teeth. As a composite image of archetypal sexual dreads it could scarcely be bettered: the monstrous phallus combined with *vagina dentata*. Throughout the film, the alien and the cat are repeatedly paralleled or juxtaposed, an association that may remind us of the panther/domestic cat opposition in *Cat People* (the cats even have the same surname, the John Paul Jones of Tourneur's movie reduced here to a mere "Jones" or "Jonesy"). The film creates its image of the emancipated woman only to subject her to massive terrorization (the use of flashing lights throughout *Alien*'s climactic scenes strikingly recalls the finale of *Looking for Mr. Goodbar* [1977]) and enlist her in the battle for patriarchal repression. Having destroyed the alien, Ripley can become completely "feminine"—soft and passive, her domesticated pussy safely asleep.

It is not surprising, although it is disturbing and sad, that at present it is the reactionary horror film that dominates the genre. This is entirely in keeping with the overall movement of Hollywood in the past five years. Vietnam, Nixon, and Watergate produced a crisis in ideological confidence, which the Carter administration has temporarily resolved; *Rocky* (1976), *Star Wars* (1977), *Heaven Can Wait* (1978), all overwhelming popular successes, are but the echoes of a national sigh of relief. *Sisters*, *Demon*, *Night of the Living Dead*, *The Texas Chainsaw Massacre*, in their various ways reflect ideological disintegration and lay bare the possibility of social revolution; *Halloween* and *Alien*, while deliberately evoking maximum terror and panic, variously seal it over again.

NOTES

1. Andrew Britton, "The Ideology of *Screen*," *Movie*, no. 26 (Winter 1978/79): 2–29.

2. Gad Horowitz, *Repression: Basic and Surplus Repression in Psychoanalytic Theory* (Toronto: University of Toronto Press, 1977).

3. Roland Barthes, *Mythologies*, trans. Annette Lavers (New York: Hill and Wang, 1977).

4. A. P. Rossiter, *Angel with Horns* (London: Longmans, 1961).

5. Robin Wood, *Personal Views: Explorations in Film* (London: G. Fraser, 1976).

6. For a fuller treatment of this, see Andrew Britton, "*Mandingo*," *Movie*, no. 22 (Spring 1976): 122.

7. Jonathan Rosenbaum, "*Halloween*," *Take One* 7, no. 2 (January 1979): 8–9.

9

Eros and Syphilization: The Contemporary Horror Film

Dana B. Polan

In the 1950s film *It, The Terror from Beyond Space* (1958), everything conspires to assert the Otherness of the monster—its complete and irrevocable difference from everything that the film upholds as the decent everyday world, the world of ostensibly average men and women. Sneaking aboard a spacecraft returning to Earth, the monster stands as a force of pure and complete menace, an irrationality that attacks without motivation and even without goal (other than simply to realize the sheer desire to attack). The film draws a moral bar between two ways of life—its images of a normal way of life versus a destructive, malevolent one—and it consequently suggests that this bar is of necessity inevitable, eternal, and unbreakable.

Even the title suggests the difference of the monster by turning it

---

In this chapter, I make little or no distinction between horror and monster films, finding in both forms versions of the formula that, as Robin Wood argues, underlies narratives of menace: "Normality is threatened by the Monster." See Wood's introduction to *The American Nightmare: Essays on the Horror Film* (Toronto: Festival of Festivals, 1979), 14 and passim and reprinted in this volume as chapter 8. As I hope my analysis will suggest, a quick separation of films into airtight genres may miss the filiations, interchanges, and resonances between genres.

into a mere thing, an "It." Not accidentally, many '50s monster titles imply the monster's membership in a community of the nonhuman: *The Blob* (1958), *Them!* (1954), *The Creature from the Black Lagoon* (1954), *The Thing* (1951). The extreme threat of the monster here allows no possibility of communication with it, of mediation between the two worlds; consequently, the films suggest that the only way to deal with that which is monstrous is through reactive forces of high violence (in order: rifles, grenades, high voltage, atomic radiation). Rare exceptions, early in the '50s, would be films like *The Day the Earth Stood Still* (1951) and *Red Planet Mars* (1952), but even the latter film tells of the benevolence of Martians only to still find monstros-ity—in this case, in the Soviet regime and in fugitive Nazis. Generally, the '50s monster film argues that the desire to deal with the monster through anything other than violence is a sign of misguided (i.e., in the films' terms, liberal) weakness, a woefully inadequate and self-dooming gesture. In many '50s monster films (e.g., *War of the Worlds*, 1953) there is a character, often a priest, whose attitude toward the monsters is, "Let us try to reason with them." Several seconds later that charac-ter will be a smoldering pile of ashes in consequence of his belief that monsters share anything, such as rationality and humanism, with human beings.

Part of the significance of recent horror films lies in the way they reject or problematize this simple moral binary opposition to suggest that horror is not something from out there, something strange, mar-ginal, ex-centric, the mark of a force from elsewhere, the in-human. With an unrelenting insistence, horror films now suggest that the hor-ror is not merely among us, but rather part of us, caused by us. These films do often continue the older concern with monstrosity as a realm of incommunicability, of dangerous silences, but the films see the fail-ure to communicate as an inherent *part of the human realm itself*, not something that assails humanity from an elsewhere. The films look at current modes of everyday life and see that life itself as a source and embodiment of the monstrous; the breakup of older forms of social relations seems to incite attack, seems to direct a virtually inward-directed wrath. Already dissolute, the quotidian world brings about its own further dissolution.

In *The Howling* (1980), for example, a husband and wife have trou-ble with their sex life ("We're just out of sync," the wife complains), and several seconds later the husband slips out to turn into a werewolf and rut with a female werewolf; the succession of the scenes sets up a logic of implication and causation that suggests that the problem of the marriage somehow encourages the unleashing of beastly elements (and the husband is reading *You Can't Go Home Again* just before the transformation). In *Halloween* (1978) and *Slumber Party Massacre* (1982), boys and girls who play around get murdered by the maniac while the virginal heroine survives—evidently because she refuses what the films picture as a kind of moral decadence. Even as seemingly classical a monster film as *Alligator* (1980), which echoes the '50s film *Them!* and its images of mutant creatures living in the L.A. sewers, implies our own responsibility for the monstrous. A freak of industrial waste (like the mutant in *Prophecy* [1979] or the monster-family in *The Hills Have Eyes* [1977]), the alligator stands for a kind of return of the repressed as society's destructive forces turn against the engendering society itself (and with a melodramatic sense of justice, the monster's greatest attack is directed against a lawn party of the man whose chemical company caused the mutation in the first place). As close as *Alligator* may be to the '50s film, it is also not that far from a new-era horror film like *It's Alive* (1974), that completes the metaphoric use of the L.A. sewers by turning the classical horror film into a modern "family romance."

Here, the sewer becomes the place for the father's recognition and acceptance of his mutant baby. Here, the sewer is no longer some mysterious, other place but literally a sign of the repressed (the sewer is where you cast off things you don't want), also a sign therefore of the act of repression. Here we might invoke a distinction that Robin Wood makes between "oppression" and "repression": where oppression enacts the crushing of alien elements, of that which is ostensibly different, repression involves the crushing of internal qualities, of those aspects of the self (whether individual or social) that one would like to banish or disavow.[1] In this sense, the '50s film deals with oppression—monsters as pure exteriority outside the realm of the human—while the new horror films seem to feel that oppression may finally be only another guise for repression: that is, that the very act of constituting another is ultimately a refusal to recognize something about the self. In this sense, if the tanks and machine guns and jets of *Them!*, blasting away at ant holes and sewer hide-outs, seem to indicate a full-scale war with full-scale enemies (war, that is, as oppression), in contrast, the images of helmeted policemen (coupled with the fact that they are policemen–civil servants—and not military personnel) in *It's Alive* can serve as a sign of domestic warfare, an attempted repression. For exam-

The mutant baby in It's Alive, *1974. From the editors' collection.*

ple, a scene of police storming an L.A. bungalow where the baby has been reported seems iconographically quite reminiscent of the (in)famous S.W.A.T. team attack on, and destruction of, a Symbionese Liberation Army hideout in Los Angeles. Similarly, the opening of *Dawn of the Dead* (1978) maps the horror film onto images of inner-city rebellion as S.W.A.T. members have to battle a ghetto community so organically bound together that it refuses to give up its relatives even though they have turned into zombies. Such images of an everyday life run through by urban and suburban violence seem a fitting commentary on dissent in the '60s and '70s, showing how an earlier mythology of consensus (for example, Daniel Bell's declaration at the end of the '50s that America had reached an End of Ideology, so that disagreement could only be aberrant or un-American)[2] could sustain itself only by a conscious self-ignorance, the election of some regions as monstrous turning out by the '70s to be the dominant system's grappling with its own monstrosity.

The new films argue that in some sense we partake of the monstrous, that in some way our lives are leading to the breakdown of traditional society. A few of the films, such as *Wolfen* (1981), view this breakdown as a progressive necessity; with its opening scene of an attack on a rich politician, *Wolfen*'s story of killer wolves menacing Manhattan from the concrete jungle of the South Bronx is an explicit comment on, and critique of, the very kind of ghettoizing and marginalizing that occurs when the dominant ideology equates same/different with good/monstrous. This is not to imply, though, that a film like *Wolfen* is progressive; indeed, its answer to the problems of class seems to be no less problematic—a set of appeals to romanticized visions of a new communal work coupled, without any sense of the inappropriateness on the film's part of such a coupling, to a mystique of the lone brooderhero (Albert Finney as *angst*-ridden cop) and a simultaneous affirmation of the heterosexual couple as basic social unit.

With a nostalgia that in some films can fuel a conservatism (as in *Poltergeist*'s [1982] invocation of the good, old family as haven in a heartless world), many of the new films suggest that in our devotion to the now, to the modern, we have created an agonistic and antagonistic culture of narcissism and have lost something that held us together, something that gave our lives a sustaining cohesion and "value." The flip-side of nostalgia will show up in such films as a discontent with, a suspicion of, the new as decadent, malevolent, morally inadequate. For example, *The Howling* begins with a reporter discovering a man (who is actually a werewolf) in a sex shop, and so suggests a connection between moral decadence and monstrosity—the man's werewolf transformation occurring as a porno film plays in the background. Even more extreme in its fear of, and recoil from, the lifestyles of today, *Shivers* (*They Came from Within*, 1975) views our world as doomed because of its internal libidinal energies. Chronicling the attack of sluglike parasites on an apartment complex, *Shivers* constantly shifts its attention from the menace the parasites cause to attacks by the people who have the parasites within them: the shifts imply ultimately that the people themselves, in their very lifestyles, are already parasitic, and that the parasite creatures are themselves no more than enabling devices that bring to the surface a latent condition of the modern human being. To put it bluntly (as a scientist in the film does when he refers to the parasites as "combination aphrodisiac and venereal disease"), the parasites are the outbreak of libido, of the Id as destructive desire against all the restraints of established order and propriety. The parasites strengthen sexual drives, and the film views this process with revulsion, picturing female desire, incest, homosexuality, rape, and adultery as equivalent forms of evil, of what the film imagines as a fundamental challenge to the very security of human life.

With an opening credit sequence that shows a publicity film for the apartment complex and emphasizes the pleasures of the place, *Shivers* implies that the new hedonistic society, the "me" generation attitude, is responsible for the decline of the West. It is this hedonism that is monstrous; the attack of the parasites does no more than speed up an inevitable process. Where an earlier film like the first version of *Invasion of the Body Snatchers* (1956) saw sleep, lifelessness, and the lack of emotion as the evils that endanger modern society, the new horror films view emotion, energy, and especially libidinal vitality, as the sources of social breakdown (significantly, the remake of *Invasion* [1978] keeps the original motif of sleep but maps it onto images of maladjustment, problems in relationships, romantic alienation). Emotion, rather than its absence, becomes something that one must steel one's self against, through a disciplining of the body (both personal and social). The hero-doctor in *Shivers* seems to hang on as long as he does because of his basic coldness, an absolutely blasé professionalism that shows up even in the eyebrows that never arch, even when the situation would seem to have reached an extreme of horror.

The new horror films vary from each other in a number of details but the majority seem to rely on a concept of an evil apocalypse that grows from within the social order, the threat of our own potential monstrosity as an ultimate challenge to, and test of, the stuff of which society is made. The politics of each film relates in a large degree to the ways—both in terms of its *mise-en-scène* and generic elements—it reacts to this apocalypse and to the possibilities of salvation. A great number of the films, for example, seem to work under the pressure of a nihilism, a hopelessness. For instance, in *The Howling*, there is no way finally to stop the onslaught of werewolves; the last scene shows how the werewolves are no longer marginalized to the woods (where they could only prey on rich narcissists out for therapy) but now have invaded the city (and a working-class bar), a city too benumbed by the media to react. In *The Texas Chainsaw Massacre* (1974), there is nothing rational or calculated that the young bourgeois woman, Sally, can do to escape the onslaught of the chainsaw-toting Leatherface; when she does escape, it is by pure accident, and so the film suggests that one's defense against horror is finally subject to the forces of an arbitrary fate.

Especially when the monster is explicitly shown to be an inevitable part of everyday life or human nature does such hopelessness reign. In this respect, it is interesting to note what happens in the recent films to those figures that the '50s horror film used as signs of power and efficacy—doctors and scientists. In the most optimistic of these films, the doctor or scientist is literally the source of solutions to monstrous ills as he (and the use of the male pronoun tends to be accurate here) calmly and rationally plugs away at a cure or ultimate weapon in the sanctity of his laboratory. Even films that show the scientist to be the cause of monstrosity (for example, *I Was a Teenage Werewolf* [1957], where it is a mad doctor's injections that turn the teenager into a were-wolf) suggest that it is not science that is at fault, but only an unfortu-nate misuse of science. Many films, such as *I Was a Teenage Werewolf*, give the mad scientist a sane, protesting partner, as if to suggest how the mad scientist could equally have made the choice to use his talents for good. In contrast, the newer films suggest that if horror has all-too-human origins, the physical sciences can have little diagnostic or curative power; they are quite simply out of their league. New horror films either eliminate the scientist figure altogether or they emphasize his inconsequentiality. For example, ecology monster films like *Proph-ecy* might seem like the '50s films about monsters unleashed by radia-tion, but they remove the sources of horror from the specificity of the scientific laboratory or the barren wasteland (for example, the North Pole of *The Beast from 20,000 Fathoms*, [1953]) to suggest that horror now can break out anywhere and everywhere: mutations can occur in the Canadian woods (*Prophecy*) or in the L.A. sewers (*Alligator*) or in an L.A. hospital (*It's Alive*). Some films show the scientist causing the monster but, in contrast to the '50s film, with no intention to do so; unlike the mad scientist of *I Was a Teenage Werewolf*, the young chemi-cal researcher of *Alligator* doesn't know that his chemical wastes are causing mutations. Significantly, even social scientists, especially psy-chologists, are shown ineffective in their attempts to gain control of an elusive horror. Thus, for example, the psychiatrist-therapists of *The Howling* and *The Brood* (1979) fail in their attempts to normalize mon-sters and so are killed off. Science is no longer a potential knowledge, an accomplishment, a savior; it has become a mere irrelevance or even a positive danger. Significantly, the heroes of the new horror films are rarely doctors or scientists (and even the hero of *Shivers* does little *as doctor* once the parasites start attacking) but professionals of public order: soldiers (*The Crazies*, 1973), government agents (*The Fury* [1978] and *Swamp Thing* [1982], with its karate-chopping intelligence agent heroine), or, most often, cops (*Wolfen, Alligator, Q* [1982], *Dawn of the Dead, The Car* [1977]). Representative in this respect is *Jaws'* (1975) demonstration of the intellectual marine biologist's ultimate worthlessness (and even, perhaps, cowardice) against the ordinary cop's efficiency with a simple tool, a rifle (and, as if to strengthen the image of the ordinary law enforcer's worth, the film eliminates the novel's affair between the biologist and the cop's wife).

In those cases where the horror film narrative refuses complete nihilism and draws back from an attitude of pure cynicism to suggest a way out, the position it retreats to is often that of militarism or fascism or aggressive professionalism (for which the cop is the "ideal" hero). The solution of violent counter-attack to the horror of apocalypse would seem to derive from the fear of the modern horror film of modernity's fall, of society's corruption of itself through eros, through an ostensible dissociation of sensibility that is also, in these films' terms, a dissociation of an older, organic society. See, for example, the scene in *The Texas Chainsaw Massacre* where the brother and sister, Sally and Franklin, face each other in filial anger and disgust across the width of the screen—the distance suggesting the alienation in the heart of family relations—just before Leatherface goes at them with the chainsaw. The solution that the film narratives seem to promote, then, is a kind of *forced* organicism, a strong professional group forming itself to come in and remove the apocalyptic threat. In *Night of the Living Dead* (1968), deer hunters become zombie hunters, and gleefully and professionally wipe out the living dead (and, by accident, the hero); this celebration of violent might and right becomes even more orgiastic in *Dawn of the Dead*, where the zombie-infested shopping mall receives a counterattack by a S.W.A.T. team which happily knocks off the zombies (and a motorcycle gang) as if it were all a game. As Tony Williams' analysis of *Assault on Precinct 13* (1976) suggests, the distance from the Hawksian adventure of male camaraderie, to the almost vigilante-like violence of the new crime film, to the new horror film is not that great.[3]

To be sure, the '50s monster film seems to deal with a growth of organic society; indeed, many of the plots revolve around the ways that the monstrous attack makes the hero and heroine fall in love (see, for example, *It, the Terror from beyond Space*; *Them!*; and *War of the Worlds*).[4] But the difference lies precisely in that emphasis in the '50s film on love as the cause of organicism; with few exceptions (e.g., *Alligator*), even those modern horror films that would seem closest to the '50s films in their plot of an inhuman menace attacking the human way

of life nonetheless start with already-formed couples and then chronicle the tensions and internalized aggression that attack by the monster
causes in the heterosexual unit (see, for example, the couples in *Dawn
of the Dead, The Howling, The Brood, Invasion of the Body Snatchers*).
Good relationships will either turn bad or their very goodness will
seem to invite destruction; thus, many films show the tragic death of
one member of the couple, as in *American Werewolf in London* (1981)
or *The Crazies*. Another option (which begins, perhaps, with the team-
ing up of Lila Crane and Sam Loomis in *Psycho*) is to show male and
female meeting arbitrarily because of the attack but forming no alliance
of love, which is the situation of the protagonists in both *Night of the
Living Dead* and *Scanners* (1980), for example. In all these cases, there
seems to be a disavowal or even refusal of a mythology of love's
redemptive powers, of what Raymond Bellour has called the Oedipal
trajectory of classic American cinema.[5]

All too often, though, the films disavow an ideology of romance
only to substitute an equally problematic ideology of discipline and
denial, a faith in cold pragmatism as the only way of life able to survive
in the modern world. If the monsters are symptomatic expressions of
libido and uncontrol, the answer—or so the force of reaction
implies—is to make violence, the ruthless obliteration of the monsters,
erotic in its own right, thereby stealing from the monsters the very
energy that sustains them. In *Dawn of the Dead*, for example, the consuming power of the monsters (who ravenously eat flesh) becomes
analogous to their earlier power as commodity consumers (one of the
S.W.A.T. team members suggests that the zombies return to the shopping mall because of what it meant to them once); in response, the protagonists become consumers in their own right and meet the
consumptive destruction of the zombies with a destruction that is of
an equally intense sort. Robin Wood's observation, watching *The Texas
Chainsaw Massacre* "with a large, half-stoned youth audience who
cheered and applauded every one of Leatherface's outrages against
their representatives on the screen, was a terrifying experience,"[6] has
its contrasting complement in the audiences for *Dawn of the Dead*,
who cheer each triumph of the forces of authority against the forces of
destruction. The gunshot explosions of heads, shoulders, torsos, and
so on, outdo the zombie attack in terms of engrossing spectacle.[7]

This creation and exploitation of a thrill of violence to ends supportive of violent authority suggest that any nomination of the horror film
as a progressive genre, simply because it depicts certain limitations of
dominant society, would be wrong in missing the ways a critique of

certain aspects of domination may itself derive from other equally dominating aspects of that same society. (For example, in the 1960s, a critique of racism often came from a position of imputed male power, as in Eldridge Cleaver's infamous declaration that black power could be achieved through the rape of white women. Even the nihilism that Robin Wood so correctly finds in the horror film[8] is not always progressive; one must examine what the historical options are for where the nihilism can lead. Echoing Andrew Britton's declaration in *The American Nightmare*, that "the return of the repressed isn't clearly distinguished from the return of repression,"[9] we might suggest that, as a disdain for the conditions of the present, nihilism can easily fuel desires for regression as well as progress. Indeed, history would seem to suggest that nihilism is an attitude that can lead in opposing directions in different historical contexts; cultural despair has often made those who despair desirous of a force like fascism as a drastic but disciplined and disciplining promise of solution to cultural ills.[10]

At their political worst, the horror films can serve as justification for vigilante violence. At their best, they can serve as a critique of the very ideological justifications by which contemporary society sustains itself. What is revealing in this respect about the end of, say, *Alligator*, is the way it brings together these conflicting impulses. Fired from the police to consequently become that sort of lone hero so central to American mythology, the main character rejects authority's ineffectual ways of dealing with the monster. Against a romantic myth embodied by the big-game hunter the authorities hire to shoot down the alligator, the hero shows that, à la *Jaws*, the ordinary shnook can make a go of it, can prove his own worth. He blows the alligator to bits with dynamite and the film ends. But at least two excesses remain. First, to blow up the alligator, the hero must also blow up an entire city street (and almost blow up an innocent bystander in the process); the destruction of disorder may have to make a necessary detour through a destruction of order. Second, the film ends with a track into the sewer to show another alligator—a baby about to be mutated by industrial waste—and thereby once again show the inevitable problems of a society based on contradictions.

NOTES

1. Robin Wood, "An Introduction to the American Horror Film," *The American Nightmare: Essays on the Horror Film*, ed. Robin Wood and Richard Lippe (Toronto: Festival of Festivals, 1979), 8 and passim.

2. Daniel Bell, *The End of Ideology: On the Exhaustion of Political Ideas in the Fifties* (Glencoe, Ill.: The Free Press, 1960).

3. Tony Williams, "*Assault on Precinct 13*: The Mechanics of Repression," in *The American Nightmare*, 67–73.

4. On the centrality of the love story to the '50s horror/monster film, see Margaret Tarratt, "Monsters from the Id," in *Film Genre Reader III,* ed. Barry K. Grant (Austin: University of Texas Press, 2003), 346–65.

5. See especially "Alternation, Segmentation, Hypnosis: Interview with Janet Bergstrom," *camera obscura*, nos. 3–4 (Summer 1979): 87–100.

6. Wood, "An Introduction," 22.

7. When I went to see *Dawn,* three white youths, who had obviously seen the film before, stood around in the men's room before the start of the film talking with gleeful anticipation of "that scene where the S.W.A.T. guy blows the nigger's head off."

8. Wood, "An Introduction," passim.

9. Andrew Britton, "The Devil, Probably: The Symbolism of Evil," in *The American Nightmare*, 41.

10. For an analysis of the ties between despair and conservatism, see Fritz Stern, *The Politics of Cultural Despair: A Study in the Rise of Germanic Ideology* (Berkeley: University of California Press, 1961).

10

Rich and Strange: The Yuppie Horror Film

Barry Keith Grant

In this chapter, I shall discuss a group of recent American movies that presents a distinct variation of the horror film we might call "yuppie horror." This group includes, among others, *After Hours* (1985), *Desperately Seeking Susan* (1985), *Something Wild* (1986), *Fatal Attraction* (1987), *Bad Influence* (1991), *Pacific Heights* (1990), *The Hand that Rocks the Cradle* (1992), *Poison Ivy* (1992), *Single White Female* (1992), and *The Temp* (1993). Some of these films, to be sure, reveal affinities to other genres: both *Something Wild* and *Desperately Seeking Susan*, for example, possess elements of screwball comedy—a genre, it is worth noting, that shares with horror the irruption of the irrational into the workaday world. Yet, to a significant extent, all these films retain much of the style and syntax of the horror genre, while substituting a new set of semantic elements, what Rick Altman defines as a genre's "building blocks."[1] And although it may be argued that some of these movies exhibit only minimal relation to the horror film, together they form a distinct generic cycle that, instead of expressing the repression and contradictions of bourgeois society generally, as many critics agree is central to the ideology of the genre,[2] specifically addresses the anxieties of an affluent culture in an era of prolonged recession.

The term *yuppie* was coined in 1983 to describe an emergent and seemingly distinct class of young urban professionals, transcending categories of both race and gender, that embraced values of conspicuous consumption and technology as unambiguously positive.[3] Yuppiedom thus combined the "me-generation" philosophy of the Carter era with Reaganomics, becoming a convenient icon of the era's *zeitgeist*.

More precisely, according to Marisa Piesman and Marilee Hartley in *The Yuppie Handbook*, the term would include a person of either gender who meets the following criteria: "(1) resides in or near one of the major cities; (2) claims to be between the ages of 25 and 45; and (3) lives on aspirations of glory, prestige, recognition, fame, social status, power, money or any and all combinations of the above. . . ."[4] These values coalesced into a lifestyle, a veritable *weltanschauung*, that embraced what one observer has called a "religion of Transcendental Acquisitions."[5] The yuppie philosophy is nicely expressed in *Bad Influence* when the yuppie Michael, asked whether he *needs* his elaborate new video system, replies, "That's not the point." Michael Douglas' Gordon Gekko in *Wall Street* (1987), with his hair slicked back and braces on his trousers, has become the perfect icon of the high-powered businessman, and the patron saint for yuppies, for whom "greed is good" because "money means choices."[6] The word *yuppie* caught hold of the popular imagination, generating much media hype and spawning a gaggle of other demographic acronyms. In short order there were, among others, DINKS (Double Income No Kids), WOOFS (Well Off Older Folks), and SWELLS (Single Women Earning Lots and Lots).[7] The trend is nicely satirized in the instant group identified in Whit Stillman's comedy of manners, *Metropolitan* (1990): the indelicate and cumbersome UHBs, or Urban Haute Bourgeoisie, a term that by the end of the film shows signs of catching on despite its apparent awkwardness.

Commercial cinema, with its antennae sharply attuned to popular taste, mobilized the tested appeal and contemporary popularity of the horror film in the late 1970s and early '80s to address this new cultural force with money to spend in the '90s. Further, yuppies had infiltrated the movie industry itself, which beckoned with the lure of high-powered deals. "You can work on your screenplay/I'll update my *C.V.*," David Frishberg sings in his satiric song "Quality Time." Indeed, both *The Player* (1992) and *Swimming with Sharks* (1994) showed yuppie monsters as Hollywood producers. With typical self-absorption, yuppie moviemakers may have assumed that their own preoccupations were generically marketable. Thus the fears and anxieties of the yuppie subculture, which has been estimated to include anywhere from four million to twenty million people,[8] encourage the transformation of "evil" in these movies from the classic horror film's otherworldly supernatural to the material and economic pressures of this world that is too much with us. This change strikes me as marking a generic shift as profound as, say, the shifting antinomies of the contemporary Western.

DEFINING YUPPIE HORROR

Yuppie horror is a subgenre that employs—but modifies—the codes and conventions of the classic horror film. "A good horror film," notes Bruce Kawin, "takes you down into the depths and shows you something about the landscape; it might be compared to Charon, and the horror experience to a visit to the land of the dead. . . ."[9] In *After Hours*, Paul's taxi ride to the different, Bohemian world of Soho in *lower* Manhattan is shot in fast motion—a joke about New York cabdrivers, to be sure, but also a suggestion of crossing over into another place, like Jonathan Harker's coach ride through the Borgo Pass in Murnau's classic *Nosferatu* (1922). Other instances of the use of this narrative convention of the genre include Michael's descent into the underground bar in *Bad Influence*, site of alternative sexual practices (the passwords include "gay white male" and "fun loving couple"), and the movement in *Desperately Seeking Susan* from the rational materialism of Fort Lee, New Jersey, to the dark and magical world of Manhattan, as if New York were across the river Styx rather than the more mundane (but perhaps equally dead) Hudson.

In an economy characterized by increasing economic polarization and spreading poverty, these scenes of crossing into the nether world of urban decay "exude the Manichaean, middle-class paranoia . . . that once you leave bourgeois life, you're immediately prey to crime, madness, squalor, poverty."[10] Hence in *Bonfire of the Vanities* (1990) wannabe Gecko Sherman McCoy quickly plummets from being a self-described "master of the universe" with a "6 million dollar apartment" to the dark underpass of a highway ramp in the Fort Apache wilderness of the South Bronx. So, too, in *Pacific Heights* the reddish lightbulbs of the "Loan" sign behind Patty Parker flash as if in warning to abandon all hope ye who enter here.

This fear informs the premise of the descent by middle-class characters into the hell of the inner city, as in both *Trespass* and *Judgment
Night* (both 1993)—the latter employing the metaphor of the mobile
home as lack of bourgeois stability, an idea earlier used by the supernatural horror film *Race with the Devil* (1975). Like the return of the
oppressed, this nightmarish world threatens always to erupt, as in
Grand Canyon (1992), when Steve Martin's yuppie entrepreneur is
hospitalized after a mugger takes his Rolex. To use the terms of another
of these movies, one must always be on guard against the temp who
aspires to become permanent.

Within this dark underworld of bankruptcy and property divesti-
ture, several of the films offer upscale variations on the horror film's
old dark house, what Robin Wood calls the terrible house and Carol J.
Clover the terrible place, making them into gothic, horrifying "work-
spaces" or "living spaces."[11] Indeed, the eponymous upscale high rise
in *Sliver* (1993) is explicitly referred to several times by some of its
inhabitants as a "haunted house." The New York apartment building
in which the two women live in *Single White Female* is visually reminiscent of the spooky Dakota in *Rosemary's Baby* (1968)—a deliberately resonant reference, as Polanski's film may be seen as an early
instance of yuppie horror in which Satan's manifestation functions as
the unrepressed return of Guy's real desire to further his career over
commitment to raising a family.[12] In *Unlawful Entry* (1992) the instal-
lation of the warning system and the periodic spotlight from the police
car put the white family in the position of South Central L.A. blacks,
making their home seem more like a prison, a horrifying vision of the
couple's anxiety about whether they can afford their house. Michael's
place in *Bad Influence* becomes frightening mostly after Alex has
stripped it clean of all the yuppie toys—an ironic inversion of the conventionally cluttered Gothic mansion.

This seeming oxymoron of the terrible luxury home is explicitly the
subject of *Pacific Heights*. The plot concerns a couple's efforts to gen-
trify an old Victorian house, a popular yuppie pastime.[13] Initially, the
yuppie couple, Patty Parker and Drake Goodman, conceive of their
home as little more than a profitable investment, as a financial arrangement not unlike their cohabitational agreement. But the home soaks up
renovation money like an insatiable sponge, a money pit—a scenario
presented in a manner not like the blithe spirit of *Mr. Blandings Builds
His Dream House* (1948) but with the ominous foreboding of *Amity-
ville Horror* (1979), perhaps the first real estate horror film. (Stephen

King perceptively described this film as the generic "horror movie as economic nightmare.")[14] Drake and Patty inexorably fall from the beatific heights of potential profit to the depths of looming insolvency.

An essential visual difference between horror and science fiction films is one of vision. In science fiction, vision—of the characters, the text, and the spectator—is characteristically bright and directed upward and out, while in horror, oppositely, it is directed down and inward, darkened and obscured.[15] A similar visual design tends to inform yuppie horror films. In *Poison Ivy,* for example, both the mother and the deadly outsider contemplate plummeting downward into the big sleep of reason, creating a vertiginous gloom that pervades the entire film from the opening giddy bird's-eye shots of Drew Barrymore swinging out over a steep cliff. The sleek black car driven by Carter Hayes in *Pacific Heights* appears ominously over the crests of hilly San Francisco streets as if surfacing from the underworld. Carter, Peyton in *The Hand That Rocks the Cradle,* and the deadly roommate Ellen in *Single White Female* are all associated with the basement and darkness. *Pacific Heights* uses a swirling 360-degree camera movement at crucial moments in Patty and Drake's crumbling finances, both to visualize their sinking deeper and deeper into debt and to lend their descent into the maelstrom metaphysical weight, as if their very worldview had been pulled out from under them, à la *Vertigo* (1958). Not coincidentally, this Hitchcock film is one among several referred to diegetically on the television in the smartly intertextual *Single White Female.*

MONSTROUS OTHERS
AND MATERIAL FEARS

An essential element of the horror film is the presence of a monster. In yuppie horror films the villains are commonly coded as such. Alex's face in *Bad Influence* is frequently streaked by the noirish shadows of trendy Levelor blinds, and the killer's face in *Desperately Seeking Susan* is often bathed in a hellish red light. When Carter Hayes successfully installs himself in the apartment of the yuppie couple's home, he is said by their lawyer to have "taken possession"; in the climax, Carter is impaled, a fitting demise for a blood-sucking vampire, financially speaking. In the climaxes of *Fatal Attraction* and *Something Wild,* both Alex and Ray seem implausibly unstoppable, like their supernatural counterparts Jason, Michael Meyers, and Freddie Kreuger. And in *The Hand That Rocks the Cradle*, the tension established between the seeming girlish innocence of the evil nanny Peyton (Rebecca De Mornay) and her fiendish malevolence is firmly rooted in the tradition of such "possessed child" horror films as *The Exorcist* (1973) and *The Omen* (1976), and further back, *The Bad Seed* (1956).

Furthermore, much like the traditional monsters, the evil characters in yuppie horror movies function as the Other, as an external, disavowed projection of something repressed or denied within the individual psyche or collective culture. These films tend to depict the monstrous Other as the protagonist's doppelganger or double, a convention Wood calls "the privileged form" of the horror film.[16] Roland Barthes writes that "The petit-bourgeois is a man unable to imagine the Other" and so makes him over into the image of himself, a point that would seem especially true for yuppies, who, according to sociologist Jerry Savells, "*assume* control of their lives and their fate, without question."[17] Pam Cook has suggested, for example, that Max Cady in Scorsese's remake of *Cape Fear* (1992) offers a "distorted picture" of the Bowden family's "own rage and pain, and of their desire for revenge," called forth from within the family by the daughter, Danielle; Cook argues that the film has to be understood as Danielle's subjective vision, what Kawin would call her "mindscreen," because it is marked by her voice-over in the form of recollection.[18]

Cook's reading may be applied equally to several other of these films, among them *Pacific Heights*, *Bad Influence*, and *Poison Ivy*. In the latter, for example, the bad girl who seduces the father is clearly the incarnation of the rebellious daughter who considers herself to be unfeminine and unloved. The film's narrative, as in *Cape Fear*, is framed by the daughter's voice-over recollection. In Michael Cimino's remake of *The Desperate Hours* (1991), the fleeing criminal Michael Bosworth, threatening the upscale family he has taken hostage in their home, suggests that he represents a "reproach" to what he refers to as the "mendacity" of the family patriarch, who is having an extra-marital affair, as if he were the return of the man's repressed self—the Father confronted by Tennessee Williams's Big Daddy, as it were—a relation wholly absent from the original version.

Similarly, in *Something Wild*, Charlie begins as what Lulu calls a "closet rebel," but the "something wild" within him is brought out by his passion for Lulu/Audrey and his struggle against Ray Sinclair. During the climax, Charlie and Ray seem to embrace even as they fight, like twin Stanley Kowalskis in their T-shirts. Lulu says to Charlie in the end, "What are you going to do now that you've seen how the other half lives . . . the other half of you?" A similar reading is invited by *Desperately Seeking Susan*, in which the bland Roberta learns to be more assured sexually, like the extroverted Susan whom she encounters, significantly, through the personal want ads. In *Single White Female*, in a way the inverse of *Poison Ivy,* Ellen is the plain Other of Allie, the *un*attractive woman whose career would proceed unimpeded by sexual entanglements. The shots of the two women in mirrors, posed in positions reminiscent of the famous mirror shot in Bergman's *Persona* (1966), makes their psychological interdependence clear. In *Pacific Heights*, an updating of Hitchcock's *Strangers on a Train* (1951), Drake Goodman grows increasingly violent in response to the "bad influence" of Carter Hayes. At first glibly willing to commit white collar crime by, as he says, "fudging the numbers a bit," Drake later viciously beats Carter and is about to strike him a murderous blow with a tire iron when he is finally restrained by Patty's screaming plea. But like Nathaniel Hawthorne's Goodman before him, Drake has glimpsed the underlying moral ambiguity of human nature.

In *Bad Influence*, Alex is the incarnation of what Michael calls the "voice that tells you what to do some time," a therapeutic materialization of Michael's much-needed assertiveness training. Like Bruno Antony to Guy Haines in Hitchcock's film, Alex is Michael's unrestrained Id, the embodiment of Michelob's yuppie admonition, "You can have it all." As Alex shows Michael how to be more competitive and assertive, Michael's hair, like his personality, becomes increasingly Gekko-like. In the end, before going over the edge himself, Michael shoots Alex, who falls heavily from a pier, the water closing over him as he sinks back into the murky depths from which he had emerged, the creature from the black lagoon of Michael's mind now vanquished.

Even *Fatal Attraction*, which has almost uniformly been condemned for its scapegoating of the professional female, may be read in this way. It is possible to view the narrative as Dan Gallagher's horrifying mindscreen or psychodrama, wherein the results of his affair with Alex Forrest is, on one level, the return of his repressed dissatisfaction with his marriage.[19] Dan feels trapped by domesticity, his discontent imaged forth in the family's cramped apartment. He is clearly disappointed about the evening's prospects when he returns from walking the dog to find their daughter sleeping in his bed with his wife, Beth. So he fantasizes a relationship with no distracting responsibilities in the form of Alex. But when this networking party turns into a nightmare, to assuage his guilt Dan projects the blame onto her—at one point he calls her "sick"—making her a monstrous Other because she does not recognize what he calls "the rules" for such affairs. Alex will not be "reasonable," will not be treated like the sides of beef that hang outside her apartment building. She refuses to allow the removal of her voice, an ideological operation of the text that feminist critics such as Kaja Silverman and Mary Ann Doane have argued happens so often in Hollywood film. Alex telephones Dan insistently and leaves an audiocassette in his car that questions his masculinity—both instances of an assertive female voice that seems beyond his masculine control. Indeed, it is not Alex but Dan who is silenced, as her adamant refusal to have an abortion leaves him, as he admits, "no say."

Many commentators on yuppiedom have noted that yuppies are always threatened by the looming specter of "burnout" because they are "workaholic[s] whose main identity and sense of self-worth is often supplied by [professional] success. . . ."[20] Burnout is thus a fearful possibility that, like the portrait of Dorian Gray, haunts the yuppie's prized public image. It is no coincidence that Michael in *Bad Influence*,

Fatal Attraction, *1987. Alex Forrest (Glenn Close) invades the domestic space of Dan and Beth Gallagher (Michael Douglas and Anne Archer).*

Drake Goodman in *Pacific Heights*, and Allie in *Single White Female* all show clear evidence of work-related stress. As one commentator puts it, "You can, after all, stay on the fast track only so long, even in a $125 pair of running shoes."[21] The important distinction is that the visage of Dorian Gray in yuppie horror films is handsome rather than grotesque. Here the craggy ugliness of a Rondo Hatton is replaced by the smooth charm of a Rob Lowe, for the ethical horrors of cupidity supersede the physical revulsion of the classic horror film. The fact that so many of these characters are at once ethically monstrous and physically attractive befits an age in which, as someone observes in *The Temp*, "They still stab you in the back as much as in the '80s, only now they smile when they do it."

Indeed, it is exactly this view that animates the worldly narrative of *Ghost* (1990), a film that, while marginal as horror, is nevertheless strongly informed by yuppie angst, and Brett Easton Ellis's remarkable 1991 novel *American Psycho*, a book that perhaps stands in relation to yuppie horror as *Psycho* (1960)—to which its title obviously refers—does to the modern horror film. The book is a first-person chronicle by a handsome Wall Street mass murderer, Patrick Bateman. If yuppie consciousness and values fetishize appearances—"Surface surface surface was all anyone found meaning in," Bateman observes[22]—then yuppie horror films show how frightening such surfaces can really be. "I have a knife with a serrated blade in the pocket of my Valentino jacket," Bateman matter-of-factly observes at one point,[23] like that sage observer in *The Temp*. It is perhaps no accident that Ellis' narrator often describes his perceptions in terms of movie techniques such as pans, dissolves, and slow motion.[24] Narrated with the same kind of dark humor as pervades *Psycho,* it is as if Norman has grown up and moved from a remote place off the main highway to the fast lane in the big city. Master Bates has become BateMAN—but ironically the onanism (a handy image of yuppiedom's self-possession) only suggested in the Hitchcock film is chillingly literal in the novel.

Because of the valorization of conspicuous wealth in the yuppie worldview (and one of the great jokes of Ellis's style in *American Psycho*), the monsters in yuppie horror films tend to threaten materiality more than mortality. For yuppies, in the words of the portrait in *Newsweek*, "the perfection of their possessions enables them to rise above the messy turmoil of their emotional lives."[25] Thus, yuppie horror films exploit the subculture's aspiration for material comfort, and the material success the characters so covet becomes frighteningly vulnerable and fragile, like the scale model of Patty and Drake's home in *Pacific Heights* that is shown smashing in close-up.

The vindictive Cady sums it up well in *Cape Fear* when he says, "That house, that car, that wife and kid, they mean nothing to you now." In these films, the Puritanlike material emblems of election come to seem suddenly damned. The appurtenances of an expensive lifestyle often turn deadly, like Claire's greenhouse in *The Hand that Rocks the Cradle* which becomes an elaborate weapon hailing lethal shards on her best friend, Marlene. The husband in *Unlawful Entry*, fetching a golf club to ward off a possible intruder in their home, jokes to his wife that if it turns out to be dangerous he'll come back for his driver. This yuppie joke is realized in *Something Wild* when Audrey uses one of Charlie's clubs to whack the attacking Ray, and in *Bad Influence*, where one of Michael's clubs (he owns a set, although, of course, he doesn't play) serves as the murder weapon for Alex. *The Hand that Rocks the Cradle* devotes much of its time to chronicling objects that become "unruly." In an upscale yuppie home fitted with, as Elayne Rapping notes, tasteful "houseware 'touches' out of L. L. Bean and Bloomingdale's,"[26] Peyton is like a yuppie gremlin, relocating material icons of yuppie status, such as a gold cigarette lighter, and thus encouraging a "misreading" of their subcultural signification.

Perhaps, then, the quintessential moment of fright in the yuppie horror film is the image in *After Hours*—emphasized by Scorsese in slow motion—of aspiring yuppie Paul's lone $20 bill flying out of the cab window. In yuppie horror films, it would seem that to be underfunded is more frightening than being undead. So Charlie desperately clutches at his wallet in *Something Wild*, whereas he allows himself to be handcuffed to the bed by Lulu, whom he has just met, with barely a protest. Because yuppies are already "possessed," these films suggest, they are more frightened by the sight of acid eating into the smooth finish of Dan's Volvo in *Fatal Attraction* than by, say, Uncle Ira no longer quite being Uncle Ira in *Invasion of the Body Snatchers* (1956).

Breakdown (1997) tells the story of a married couple (Kurt Russell, Kathleen Quinlan) traveling across the country because the husband is taking a new job. Somewhere in the southwest their vehicle breaks down; a passing trucker volunteers to take the wife to a telephone booth down the road apiece to call for assistance while the husband stays with the vehicle. But the wife disappears without a trace (echoes of *The Vanishing*, 1988 and 1993). The trucker and his helpers, who had secretly sabotaged the couple's vehicle earlier at a gas station, force the husband to withdraw his savings from a local bank in return for his wife, but all along they have planned to kill them, as they have many others before. The husband must outwit them on his own and save his wife's life as well, which of course he does. *Breakdown* dispenses almost completely with character development. Here the mechanics of the horror thriller are tied to the mechanism of the automobile, and of the road movie. We don't know anything about the protagonist's old or new job, his dissatisfactions with them or aspirations regarding them. All we find out is that the couple is concerned about their finances, and that they have used all their savings to finance this trip, which is thus an investment in their future. The villains are monsters who seek to ruin the couple's already weak portfolio.

The film's most important "character" is their vehicle, a Jeep Grand Cherokee. The Jeep is a yuppie vehicle of choice, and SUVs are consequently one of the prime icons of the yuppie horror film. SUVs provide practicality, survivalist appeal, and durability. More expensive than most makes of automobiles, they are an indication of class status and economic privilege, literally rising above the common crowd of cars. With the four-wheel drive capability of going "off-road," people with enough money to buy one have the luxury of getting far from the madding crowd. One of the only expository details given about the couple in the film is that they have spent most of their savings on this new Jeep. And one of the horrors of the film is watching the Jeep reduced to mere jetsam as it floats away down a river.

IDEOLOGY OF YUPPIE HORROR

While this yuppie cycle tends to rely primarily on the visual and narrative conventions of the classic horror film, on occasion their very discursive structure is also similar, employing what Tzvetan Todorov has called the "fantastic," which critics have found to inform traditional horror films.[27] According to Todorov, the fantastic is characterized by a "hesitation" that eludes either a realist explanation (the "uncanny") or a supernatural one (the "marvelous").

Such hesitation is found in those yuppie horror films that can be read as mindscreens, as already discussed, and perhaps the most interesting of the films in this regard is *The Temp*. Narrated from the viewpoint of the male protagonist, the film begins with him finishing a therapy session, and we soon learn that he has suffered from paranoid delusions in the past. He seems to have recovered, for he is successful and competent in his high-powered executive position; but when an ambitious new secretary begins working for him, perceived rivals start dying in curious circumstances. Since we never see the secretary actually do anything ominous until the end, we can't be sure whether the protagonist's dark interpretation of events is correct or whether the woman is merely a terrific secretary and the deaths and other mishaps are merely a series of unhappy coincidences. This intriguing ambiguity is clearly resolved in the climax, though, where the patriarchal power of the narrator/male boss is forcefully reinstated with the defeat of the infernal secretary who has refused to stay in her allotted place on the corporate ladder. But until the film reaches for such predictable generic and ideological closure, it insistently questions patriarchal assumptions.

Fredric Jameson's observation that *Something Wild* is about patriarchy applies to many of these movies, which on another level, as my reading of *Fatal Attraction* suggests, are about masculinity in crisis.[28] This is hardly surprising, given that yuppie horror films necessarily question (by expressing an unease about) capitalist ideology. Indeed, to the very substantial extent to which yuppie horror films are about masculine panic, they are simply the most overt articulation of a theme that dominates contemporary Hollywood cinema, most obviously in the contemporaneous trend of hyperbolic action movies, with their excessive display of masculine "hardbodies."

This is not to suggest, however, that all yuppie horror movies in the end endorse the ideological status quo. For if we were to examine them according to Wood's "basic formula for the horror film"—the way the texts define normality, the monster, and the relation between these two terms[29]—we would find they range from the reactionary to the progressive, as with any genre. In *Pacific Heights*, for example, all's well that ends well: Patty reconciles with Drake, sells the house for a tidy profit, and defeats Carter Hayes while adding to her income—tax-free yet. The film thus endorses yuppie capitalist values and neutralizes any potential threat in the fact that Patty, as Carter says, has "crossed the line" of acceptable behavior.

By contrast, the ending of *Fatal Attraction* may be seen as more subversive. It is Beth who kills Alex, after which she and Dan embrace, reunited because she has submitted to the patriarchal imaginary—only then can marriage be "happy." The final shot is thus heavy with Sirkian irony, worthy of the famous ending of *Magnificent Obsession* (1953): the camera pans to the fireplace mantle, the hearth of the family home, showing a photograph of the married couple—a still image—and a pair of bronzed baby shoes. Both objects undercut the notion that anything has changed in Dan and Beth's marriage; rather, the objects connote immobility and stasis, and offer a comment on their embrace of traditional values. Similar is the ending of *After Hours*, when Paul returns from the nether world and arrives at the entrance to his midtown office. Now the iron gates of life open of their own accord and, transformed by the golden light of dawn, seem to beckon Paul into the comfy heaven of his low-level executive job.

In their articulation of lurking dread, even the most conservative of these films is more interesting than bland yuppie movies like *Rain Man* (1988), wherein the yuppie is humanized and learns that there are more important things in life than imported sports cars, or *Grand Canyon*, in which the economic gap is dwarfed by the geographical one.[30] Jameson is right to call *Something Wild* and other such movies modern gothic tales, although he incorrectly, I think, chooses to stress their reliance on nostalgia, for these movies are emphatically about *now*.[31]

Certainly the fact that mainstream cinema has turned more to horror and the thriller than to, say, comedy and the musical, as it did in the past, to address fears about America's affluent but struggling economy as well as the very nature of contemporary relationships, tells us how deeply these anxieties are rooted. Indeed, these films tend to locate these larger cultural concerns at a more basic, personal level, within the dynamic of intimate personal relationships—the perfect adaptation of the horror genre to the troubled narcissism of the post me-generation. In yuppie horror films, monsters do not roam the countryside, killing indiscriminately; instead, we find ourselves sleeping with the enemy, often literally.

In the earlier yuppie horror films, the nightmarish situations were as often as not the result of recklessness rather than fiendishness. But as the recession has deepened, the monsters have tended to become increasingly malevolent: the Big Chill has become a wind from hell. (One might view the cycle of films based on old TV series—*The Addams Family* (1992), *The Beverly Hillbillies* (1993), *The Flintstones* (1994), and *Car 54, Where Are You?* (1994)—as the flipside of yuppie anxiety. Truly based on nostalgic appeal, they recall both the historical "better time" of the affluent 1960s, when the shows where first broadcast, and the ahistorical once-upon-a-time fantasy world of TV-land.)

Certainly, as I've suggested, there are earlier horror films, such as *Rosemary's Baby* and *Race with the Devil*, that anticipate the yuppie cycle. *The Exorcist* is similar to Polanski's film in that it suggests that the demonic possession of the daughter is the result of the mother's putting her career before family. But of the several movies that one might cite as precursors of this modern horror cycle, only *Strangers on a Train*, in typical Hitchcock fashion, steadfastly refuses to locate or "explain" the monstrous as supernatural. And while there are earlier movies that we might identify as examples of Stephen King's notion of economic horror, the yuppie horror cycle truly begins to appear around the time of the publication in 1985 of an article titled "Second Thoughts on Having It All" in *New York* magazine, described by one observer as an "epochal event."[32] Whether the yuppie protagonists are contained within their space in the movies of besiegement (*Fatal Attraction*, *Pacific Heights*, *The Hand that Rocks the Cradle*) or removed from it in the "road movies" (*Something Wild*, *After Hours*), they share a frightening sense of alienation from a comfortable, privileged routine. Films that combine elements of both subclassifications (*Trespass*, *Judgment Night*) emphatically demonstrate that you can't take it with you, even if you have yuppie buying power.

Significantly, yuppie horror films exhibit minimal interest in gore and splatter effects. They avoid the kind of body horror characteristic of, say, George Romero or David Cronenberg, even though, as one writer puts it, "the body is the yuppie's most prized possession."[33] In these movies, as I've suggested, it is less life than "lifestyle" that is threatened. *Disclosure* (1994) is filled with trendy dialogue about the dilemmas of contemporary sexual politics, and it suggests throughout a fear of the body that culminates, in the climactic scene where Michael Douglas is pursued by a virtual reality Demi Moore, in its rejection altogether. The greater concern with lifestyle in yuppie horror movies is perhaps nowhere more clear than in such movies as *The Firm* and *The Fugitive* (both 1993): the former is an upscale variation on such demonic cult horror films as Lewton's *The Seventh Victim* (1943); the latter little more than the hoary mechanics of the chase, situated within a yuppie context. Graphic body horror, by contrast, has become increasingly characteristic of the more mainstream horror film and movies in which the body literally becomes a thing, as in *Robocop* (1987), *The Terminator* (1984), and such less distinguished clones as *Universal Soldier* (1992).

For similar reasons, fear of racial difference is not particularly

important in yuppie horror movies. As in yuppie ideology, race is sub-
sumed by economic difference. Hence, *Judgment Night* is careful to
include an African American among the group of four suburban men
who carelessly venture, in a state-of-the-art mobile home, into the
monstrous violence of inner-city Detroit. By contrast, race had been
an issue (albeit an infrequent one) in such earlier horror films as *White
Zombie* (1932) and *I Walked with a Zombie* (1943), and has returned
more recently in such mainstream horror movies as *The People under
the Stairs* (1991), *Candyman* (1992), and *Candyman II* (1995). But
whether the monstrous Other in yuppie horror films is seemingly aristocratic (as in *Bad Influence*) or strictly blue collar (as in *Poison Ivy*),
the fear exploited may be understood as the nightmarish result of the
yuppie's typical narcissistic self-absorption.

CONCLUSION

If, as some would argue, yuppies are nothing more than a "media
mirage,"[34] an imaginative creation of the culture industry, they nevertheless have had a powerful effect on advertising and marketing. Moreover, since yuppies come from the baby boomer generation that
constituted the teenagers to whom horror films became increasingly
addressed in the 1950s and '60s, they share an already established bond
with the genre. Thus it is not surprising that Hollywood would seek to
incorporate into its rhetoric these viewers who, in the words of one
advertising executive, are themselves "like a Hollywood movie, not real
life."[35]

Curiously, Rick Altman does not include horror in his examples of
durable genres that have established a particularly coherent syntax,
although the genre has been around since almost the beginning of cinema and, of course, before that in literature and folklore.[36] Surely, the
yuppie horror film is a particularly vivid contemporary instance of a
genre's semantic modification within its existing syntax to accommo-
date a newly defined potential audience. Indeed, horror is a rather
flexible genre—"extremely limber, extremely adaptable, extremely
useful," in the words of Stephen King.[37] In fact, the yuppie horror film
would seem a vivid demonstration of Altman's thesis that the "relationship between the semantic and syntactic constitutes the very site of
negotiation between Hollywood and its audience."[38] And if this cycle
of the horror film demonstrates the protean adaptability of genre, it

also reveals the inevitable anxiety generated by the biggest monster of all, late capitalism.

NOTES

1. Rick Altman, "A Semantic/Syntactic Approach to Film Genre," in *Film Genre Reader II,* ed. Barry Keith Grant (Austin: University of Texas Press, 1996), 30.

2. See, for example, Robin Wood, *Hollywood from Vietnam to Reagan* (New York: Columbia University Press, 1986), chaps. 5 and 6; Carol J. Clover, *Men, Women and Chain Saws: Gender in the Modern Horror Film* (Princeton, N.J.: Princeton University Press, 1992); and several of the essays in this volume.

3. Jerry Adler et al., "The Year of the Yuppie," *Newsweek* (December 31, 1984), 14; and John L. Hammond, "Yuppies," *Public Opinion Quarterly* 50 (Winter 1986): 496.

4. Marissa Piesman and Marilee Hartley, *The Yuppie Handbook: The State of the Art Manual for Young Urban Professionals* (New York: Long Shadow Books, 1984), 12.

5. Adler et al., "The Year of the Yuppie," 19.

6. Jerry Savells, "Who are the 'Yuppies'? A Popular View," *International Journal of Comparative Sociology* 27, nos. 3–4 (1986): 235.

7. Susan Kastner, "So . . . Where Have All the Yuppies Gone?," Toronto *Star* (April 17, 1991), A4.

8. Savells, "Who are the 'Yuppies'?" 234.

9. Bruce Kawin, "Children of the Light," in *Film Genre Reader II*, ed. Grant, 309.

10. John Powers, "Bleak Chic," *American Film* 12, no. 5 (March 1987): 51.

11. Wood, *Hollywood from Vietnam to Reagan*, 90; Clover, *Men, Women and Chain Saws*, 30.

12. The importance of Ira Levin's fiction, including *Rosemary's Baby*, *The Stepford Wives*, and *Sliver*, to yuppie horror is significant and certainly a subject inviting further research.

13. Carol M. Ward, "The Hollywood Yuppie: 1980–88," in *Beyond the Stars: Stock Characters in American Popular Film*, ed. Paul Loukides and Linda K. Fuller (Bowling Green, Ohio: Bowling Green University Popular Press, 1990), 97.

14. Stephen King, *Danse Macabre* (New York: Everest House, 1981), 138.

15. Barry Keith Grant, "'Sensuous Elaboration': Reason and the Visible in the Science Fiction Film," in *Alien Zone II: The Spaces of Science-Fiction Cinema*, ed. Annette Kuhn (London and New York: Verso, 1999), 16–20.

16. Wood, *Hollywood from Vietnam to Reagan*, 79.

17. Roland Barthes, "Myth Today," *Mythologies*, ed. and trans. Annette

Lavers (New York: Hill and Wang, 1977), 151; Savells, "Who are the 'Yuppies'?" 235.

18. Pam Cook, "Scorsese's Masquerade," *Sight and Sound* 1, no. 12 (April 1992): 15. *Mindscreen* is the term used by Bruce Kawin to describe sequences of subjective vision in his book *Mindscreen: Bergman, Godard and First-Person Film* (Princeton, N.J.: Princeton University Press, 1978).

19. It is worth noting that the action in Adrian Lyne's next film, *Jacob's Ladder* (1990), is revealed explicitly at the end to have occurred entirely in the mind of the protagonist in the moment of his death. The only other similar reading of *Fatal Attraction* of which I am aware is N. A. Morris, "In Defense of *Fatal Attraction*," *Movie* 33 (Winter 1989): 53–55.

20. Ward, "The Hollywood Yuppie," 106.

21. Adler et al., "The Year of the Yuppie," 24.

22. Brett Easton Ellis, *American Psycho* (New York: Vintage, 1991), 375.

23. Ellis, *American Psycho*, 52.

24. Ellis, *American Psycho*, 5, 8, 114.

25. Adler et al., "The Year of the Yuppie," 19.

26. Elayne Rapping, "*The Hand that Rocks the Cradle*," *Cineaste* 19, nos. 2–3 (December 1992): 65.

27. Tsvetan Todorov, *The Fantastic: A Structural Approach to a Literary Genre*, trans. Richard Howard (Ithaca: Cornell University Press, 1975). For an application of Todorov's ideas to the horror film, see, for example, Tom Gunning, "'Like unto a Leopard': Figurative Discourse in *Cat People* and Todorov's *The Fantastic*," *Wide Angle* 10, no. 3 (1988): 30–39.

28. Fredric Jameson, *Postmodernism, or, the Cultural Logic of Late Capitalism* (Durham, N.C.: Duke University Press, 1992), 291.

29. Wood, *Hollywood from Vietnam to Reagan*, 78.

30. In the context of romantic comedy, Steve Neale argues that the end of *Something Wild* "manoeuvres its couple . . . into an 'old-fashioned,' 'traditional' and ideologically conventional position." "The Big Romance or Something Wild?: Romantic Comedy Today," *Screen* 33, no. 3 (Autumn 1992): 297.

31. Jameson, *Postmodernism, or, the Cultural Logic of Late Capitalism*, 289–90.

32. George F. Will, "Reality Says You Can't Have It All," *Newsweek* (February 3, 1986), 78. "Second Thoughts on Having It All" appeared with no byline in *New York* 18 (July 15, 1985), 32–50ff.

33. Adler et al., "The Year of the Yuppie," 14.

34. Hammond, "Yuppies," 496.

35. Kastner, "So . . . Where Have All the Yuppies Gone?," A4.

36. Altman, "A Semantic/Syntactic Approach," 35.

37. King, *Danse Macabre*, 138.

38. Altman, "A Semantic/Syntactic Approach," 35.

2

FILMS AND FILMMAKERS

11

Enunciation and the Production of Horror in *White Zombie*

Edward Lowry and Richard deCordova

The horror film has typically served as an ideal site for the examination of the classical film text as symptom. A genre predicated on the production of fear in the viewer, it depends upon a variety of filmic and narrative techniques that call forth certain "disturbing" unconscious associations. The extension of these associations to the realm of ideology (viewed as a socio-cultural unconscious) has served as a primary means of analyzing the genre—from Siegfried Kracauer's "psychological study" of the German film in the 1920s[1] to Robin Wood's more explicitly psychoanalytic discussion of American horror movies in the 1970s.[2]

Similarly, the overdetermination of psychoanalytic terms in the horror film, which seems inherent in the genre's emphasis on the viewer's unconscious fears, has made it a fertile ground for the application of psychoanalytic methods to classical film texts. The attempt to cross generic and psychoanalytic considerations is perhaps exemplified at its most extreme in Roger Dadoun's discussion of certain "clinical" symptoms of fetishism in the vampire film.[3] Yet specific horror films have served again and again as subjects for the application of psychoanalytic methods in pursuit of larger generalizations about the classical film. Thierry Kuntzel, for example, chose *The Most Dangerous Game*

(1932) to demonstrate the analogies between the work of the classical
film and the Freudian conception of the dream work;[4] and Raymond
Bellour's examinations of filmic enunciation have repeatedly focused
on the "horrific" suspense films of Alfred Hitchcock.[5]

Still, the horror film has proved one of the most difficult genres to
define, at least in purely structural terms. Thomas Schatz's *Hollywood
Genres*, for example, omits discussion of the genre altogether; and it is
indeed difficult to imagine how the horror movie—which encompasses
in its popular definition stories of psychological aberration and supernatural transformation, of possession by irrational forces and the rational creation of monsters, of internalized psychosis and externalized
terror—might be forced to conform as a whole either to Schatz's
"genres of order" or to his "genres of integration."[6] Certainly, a large
number of horror films (e.g., *Alien* ([1979], *Night of the Living Dead*
[1968], either version of *The Thing* [1951, 1982]) function within an
ideologically contested space where the conflict is externalized in violence, in much the same manner as the Westerns, gangster movies, and
detective films, which Schatz defines as "genres of order." Yet it is just
as easy to think of horror films (e.g., *The Exorcist* [1973], *White Zombie* [1932], any version of *Dr. Jekyll and Mr. Hyde*) that function
largely within the civilized, "familial" space, where conflict (although
often violent) is motivated or strongly linked to internalized, emotional factors, and where the ultimate goal of the social group
(although often thwarted) is the restoration of the aberrant character
to the social milieu. Such films would then be classifiable amongst
Schatz's "genres of integration," which include the musical, the screwball comedy, and the family melodrama. (In this respect, note, for
example, the ease with which the family melodrama and the horror
film are blended in a film like *Bigger Than Life* [1956] or a TV soap
like *Dark Shadows*.)

If we first acknowledge the horror genre's propensity toward certain
subjects, it may then prove more productive to examine it in terms of
its enunciative techniques—those filmic and narrative devices by which
the classical film attempts to produce horror. At the same time, it is
essential, of course, to remain aware of the psychological determina-
tions implicit in these techniques, since it would be reductive if not
impossible to define the horror film entirely in formal terms (although
a film like Dario Argento's *Suspiria* [1979] might pose an interesting
challenge to this notion).

The classical film is at least partially defined by a model in which desires embodied in the characters are in some way linked to (or conversely, distinguished from) the desires of the "ideal viewer," whom the text attempts to center by means of certain conventional techniques. These desires (via the characters) motivate certain actions within a complex but rigidly defined framework—the diegetic boundaries of the fictional "cosmos" of the film, the hermeneutic code of classical narrative requiring resolution of conflict, the filmic conventions of classical cinema, and so on. To this extent, the production of fear in the viewer depends on the text's success in situating the viewer (in inscribing the viewer position) in a disturbing relationship to the enunciation of desire and the system within which it operates.

On the level of the narrative, this is frequently figured in terms of an excessive desire that threatens systematic order (the law), a model that emerges in a variety of generic clichés: the mad scientist who challenges the life-creating power of the deity, the repressed individual whose sado-erotic desires find expression in lycanthropy or a chemical transformation from man to beast, the psychotic whose desires are realized in murder and mutilation, the character possessed with supernatural powers enabling him/her to possess another character. In each of these cases, the viewer's desires may be aligned with the excessive, monstrous desires of the "mad" character, even as they are tempered by a dependence on the narrative, filmic, legal, and cosmic systems to restrict and punish those desires.[7] The classical horror film thus places the viewer in a position to enjoy and share the sadistic, excessive desire, even while s/he is threatened by that desire, which is figured as fearsome and "undesirable" (and the enjoyment of which is masochistic).

It is this dialectic of desire and law in the narrative which produces this duality in the viewer; and it is the ultimate systematization of the classical film and the distance engendered by its recognition as an "aesthetic object" which allows the playing out of forbidden desires in a "safe" context. Certainly, the dialectic of desire and law functions throughout the classic film; but the horror film (and the horrific moment within any film) is characterized by excess, by the very threat implicit in the possibility that excessive desire may overcome the systematic restrictions of the text. This may occur, for example, when the excessiveness of "gore" violates the expected limits set by convention or by legal or moral restraint. It is certainly most evident when horror is carried out of the theater to structure the viewer's post-filmic experience, engendering a fear of ghouls, monsters, or psycho killers.

In the classical film, desire and its relationship to the ideal viewer

position is figured in terms of a fairly strict system of filmic enunciation. Thus, in the horror film, the excessiveness of desire is not only
echoed by the enunciation, but to a large extent determined by it. The
placement of the camera in the subjective position of the psychotic
killer (to cite one very obvious and, since *Halloween* [1978], conven-
tionalized enunciative instance in the horror film) situates the viewer
in a sadistic position in relation to the violence depicted (through the
camera, the viewer participates in murder and/or mutilation), yet
inscribes the potential for the viewer to assume a masochistic distance
from the image (which is precisely the space of horror), to reject the
position as untenable (the viewer's desire not to participate, most
clearly manifested in the covering of the eyes).

The 1932 American horror film *White Zombie* provides a provocative text for examining the role of enunciation in the horror film. First,
it contains a variety of enunciative techniques (superimpositions, dissolves, split screens, intercutting) which, although each a part of the
classical film lexicon, are especially highlighted and given explicitly
systematized functions in the text. In view of a model of classical cinema that posits a "transparency" resulting from the effacement of the
marks of enunciation, *White Zombie* attests to the first and most obvious objection to be raised: the classical cinema is not nearly so homog-
enous as the model would suggest. Yet the very excessiveness in the
enunciative markings of *White Zombie* is still rigidly systematized,
illustrating Stephen Heath's assertion that "the classical cinema does
not efface the signs of production, it contains them."[8]

Second, from a historical perspective, we may approach the enunciative techniques of *White Zombie* as the product of the first cycle of
American sound horror films (produced as it was the year after Universal's *Dracula* and *Frankenstein* [both 1931] and the same year as
RKO's *The Most Dangerous Game*). The difference between the enunciative techniques of *White Zombie* and other films of the period may
thus be related to a kind of experimentation characteristic of the early
films within a generic cycle. This notion is further enhanced by two
factors that suggest possible explanations for the film's dissimilarity to
certain conventions of Hollywood production and the horror genre.
First, *White Zombie* is an independent production made outside the
studio system on "poverty row" means, which nevertheless received
distribution by United Artists.[9] Second, it marks the first film in the
subgenre of the "zombie" film.[10]

Finally, in regard to an analysis of the means by which the classical text produces horror, *White Zombie* offers a formative example of the narrative/filmic figuration of desire in terms of possession. Not only is the paradigm of possessor/possessed (which provides a consistent structural basis for the subgenre that *White Zombie* initiated)[11] figured narratively among the characters of the film, it is also figured in the enunciative devices employed to situate the viewer on *both* sides of the paradigm at different points. The position of the viewer as possessor of the image and as possessed by the image speaks to some of the central issues raised regarding the filmic apparatus. As Christian Metz has shown, the situation of the viewer in the cinema bears strong resemblance to the dynamic of possessor/possessed which functions in the relation of subject and object inherent in "clinical" voyeurism and fetishism.[12] Bellour has demonstrated the possessor/possessed dynamic even more explicitly in his comparison of the cinematic apparatus and hypnosis, in which he turns to specifically "horrific" sequences in *Dr. Mabuse* (1922) and *Schatten* (*Warning Shadows,* 1923).[13]

White Zombie is exemplary in its production of two different types of space: one, the so-called transparent, realistic, sutured space; the other, a "fantastic" space in which the marks of punctuation are foregrounded. As will be shown, this division/opposition serves a definite textual function, but it does not necessarily translate into a useful theoretical distinction. What is more crucial is the larger enunciative strategy that articulates these two types of space as a difference and works to contain them in the fiction.

What is evident in the two conspicuously "nonclassical" scenes we will examine is the extreme systematization of the enunciation, even when the enunciative markings appear most aberrant and "excessive." This systematization proceeds both through the formal figures of the classical film (alternation, point-of-view shots, etc.) and, in a slightly different way, through a limited set of thematic paradigms which structure this particular film.

The paradigm "possessor/possessed" sets the central problematic of the fiction and provides the terms for the circulation of characters within it. It is a paradigm marked by its instability and reversibility. The Haitian plantation owner Beaumont (Robert Frazer) possesses Madeline (Madge Bellamy), the pure American ingenue who becomes the "white zombie," but then loses her as he is himself possessed by the zombie-master Legendre (Bela Lugosi). This drama of possession is, of course, central to the subgenre; the zombie film enacts quite literally what in other films is represented only by implication: the link between character alliances and property relations.

It is not surprising, then, that this paradigm is imbricated with another, more stable one: the difference of the sexes. It is the woman Madeline who is to be possessed: by her fiancé, Neil (John Harron), then by Beaumont, then by Legendre, and finally again by Neil. Neil's possession of Madeline is the guarantee of the film's circularity, and thus, of its resolution: the correct couple is reunited.[14]

Enunciation in *White Zombie* presents itself in terms of these paradigms and works to position the spectator in relation to them through its mode of address. This is especially evident in the enunciative symbolization of possessor/possessed. In the scenes we will examine, Legendre possesses not only the zombies, but also, ostensibly, the enunciation itself. The shots follow the trajectory of his desire; thus, he possesses the spectator's vision as well. At the most dramatic points of the film, the spectator is placed in the uncomfortable position of the zombie, the one possessed.

THE FANTASTIC SPACE

The first appearance of the fantastic space in *White Zombie* occurs in the opening sequence of the film, marking the introduction of Legendre in the narrative. After stopping briefly to observe a funeral taking place in the middle of the road (a "dissonant" locale explained narratively as the safest place, since the traffic discourages grave-robbing), the coach carrying Madeline and Neil proceeds toward Beaumont's mansion. Framed in longshot, the coach approaches the camera/spectator surrounded by almost total darkness.

Suddenly, two enormous eyes are superimposed across the frame, staring directly at the spectator. The shot of the coach (1) fades out, leaving only the eyes against a black background (shot 2). Almost immediately, another longshot of the coach proceeding toward the camera begins to fade in; but this time Legendre stands in the midground at the center of the frame, next to the road, facing the carriage, with his back toward the camera (shots 2 and 3). The enormous eyes still fill the frame, but as soon as the new shot has faded in completely, the eyes shrink and move toward Legendre. When they reach the back of his head, they fade out completely, disappearing into him. He then stops the coach, and a strange, silent meeting between him and the couple takes place (shot 3).

This segment is composed of three shots linked by two dissolves.

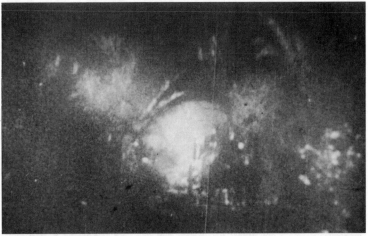

Shot 1

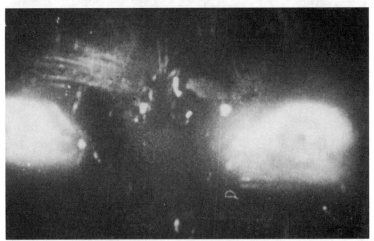

Shot 2

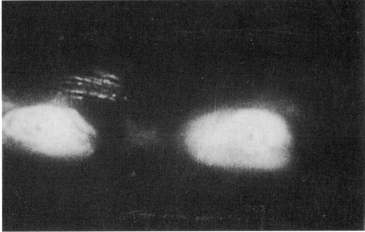

Shot 3

Five frame enlargements from White Zombie, *shots 1–5.*

Shot 4

Shot 5

But these dissolves are not employed in the simple manner of linking different times or places. In fact, they function as superimpositions, condensing one shot with the next and producing a single progression of five distinct shots.

Shot 1 is read as a continuation of the space represented in the opening shots of the film—a "realistic" space, though one which is distorted after the conventions of the horror film. Shot 2 marks a rupture of this space insofar as it condenses two spaces in a third which has no "realistic" relation to the first shot; that is, the narrative diegesis does not account for a pair of gigantic eyes hovering over the road, occupying the same space as the coach, and thus visible to Madeline, Neil, and the driver. In diegetic terms, these eyes are not *really* there; yet in terms of enunciation, they are the dominant marking of the segment. They mark shot 1 as *seen* from another space outside the diegetic space; not only by the spectator in front of the screen, but by another spectator *within* the film, yet *outside* the "realistic" space. The eyes both see the action and dominate it; they are situated in a position which cannot *logically* ("realistically") exist. Diegetically, the eyes must be read as *super*natural; and in their rupture of the "natural" space, they are marked as the enunciator of the scene itself.

Shot 3 finds the eyes alone in the frame, without reference to the realist, "natural" space of the coach. This shot demonstrates the entirely fantastic[15] realm of *White Zombie*'s diegesis, a realm that will reassert itself on several occasions to mark a supernatural domination of the "natural" space. Later, similar shots will be marked as Madeline's point of view under this domination. Here they represent no one's point of view; furthermore, they are presented as completely anonymous, cut from any reference to a body or a character. Denied, for the moment, an access to *what* the eyes see, the spectator is left to contemplate the eyes themselves, staring at the camera with the same dominating gaze which will later place certain characters under hypnotic control. Thus, shot 3 finds the eyes inscribed in their most powerful enunciative position: they see everything, while the spectator sees only the eyes. The presentation of the unknown and potentially threatening enunciator in shot 3 provides a clue to the way in which *White Zombie* will work to produce horror.

Shot 4 returns the disembodied eyes to a relation with the space of the narrative, inscribing them in the character of Legendre. As they recede and dissolve into his head, the "supernatural" space is condensed into the "natural," and the unknown threat is linked to a single character. It is as though Legendre calls in his all-seeing eyes from the supernatural realm to reconstitute himself for an encounter in the "natural" world (much as Dracula transforms himself from bat to human form). Curiously, in the dissolve of shot 4, the eyes are reduced to a size corresponding with that of Legendre; yet they dissolve into the *back* of his head, as he faces away from the camera and (like the spectator) toward the oncoming coach. The combination of these two looks (with and toward the camera) literally accounts for a 360-degree field of vision. Even more important is that the eyes, which momentarily "threaten" the spectator with their direct glare (violating the convention of the indirect look slightly offscreen), are inscribed in a character facing the same direction as the spectator, thereby linking the threatening, all-seeing *vision* to the spectator's point of view and to the enunciation itself.

Eyes represent the single most pervasive symbolic constellation in *White Zombie*, marked both within the diegesis and by the enunciation as the term of possession. The disembodied eyes, which recur in two other instances (at the point of Madeline's possession and at the moment when Legendre orders her to murder Neil), enunciate horror in terms of violation (of the sutured space; of the code of the look; of the autonomous character by means of hypnosis). On several other occasions, Legendre's direct gaze into the camera reasserts this violation without the direct enunciation of the fantastic space: when he silently orders his zombies to rob Madeline's grave; just before the out-of-focus point-of-view shot in which Beaumont's servant is paralyzed; in the final shot of the sequence in which he possesses Madeline. Legendre's eyes are figured as the symbolic opposite of Madeline's once she is possessed. As a zombie, Madeline looks at nothing, sees nothing, and her gaze is often directed toward a point slightly above the camera (as differentiated from the "normal" characters who follow the conventional code of looking offscreen left or right; and from Legendre's direct stare). Under the control of Legendre's direct, violating, possessing gaze, Madeline's are the empty eyes of the woman-object and become themselves objects of horror: "I can't stand those empty, staring eyes," Beaumont confesses, horrified at the reduction of Madeline to a fetish object, for which he is responsible.[16]

The eyes that appear over the road first gaze directly at us, then follow the movement of our vision into the dissolve and disappear into Legendre himself. Thus, we possess Legendre's (the possessor's) vision; but at the same time, we are possessed *by* it (and its enunciative power).

The spectator, then, is placed in a contradictory position with regard to the paradigm of possessor/possessed. It is perhaps not surprising that it is at this moment that the fantastic merges most manifestly with the phantasmic. Two aspects of psychoanalytic theory relating to the phantasm are pertinent here.

The first concerns the importance of the frame, the window, and the door in the primal scene, which for Freud serves as the prototypical phantasm. "It is through a window that the first spectacle is seen. The signification of this window lies not on the side of the spectacle seen but rather on the side of the look itself."[17] In the opening sequence of *White Zombie* it is the spectator's act of seeing that is foregrounded. What is important is the way in which the enunciative apparatus (and thereby the spectator's position of seeing) is diegeticized and accorded a place in the fiction. The eyes above the road have little to do with the diegetic fiction, except insofar as the spectator's vision is itself implicated in the struggle. It is in this way that the enunciation positions the spectator in relation to the paradigm possessor/possessed.

The second pertinent aspect of the phantasm is the instability of the subject's position within it. Laplanche and Pontalis discuss this in relation to the phantasm of seduction: "A father seduces a child: this would be the typical formulation of the phantasm of seduction. . . . [This structure] is a scenario with multiple entries, within which nothing says that the subject will find its place right away in the term child. The subject can fix itself just as easily to the term father, or even in the verb seduces."[18]

As we have shown, the appearance of the eyes across the road in *White Zombie* places the spectator in a contradictory position. Before Legendre appears, the spectator possesses a view of Madeline through (significantly enough) the window of the coach. Five shots after the eyes appear, however, the spectator assumes the position of Madeline's point of view. These two instances, condensed across the appearance of the fantastic eyes which posit vision *per se* and domination, leave the spectator to waver between the two positions they represent.[19] If the dominant phantasm of the film may be posed as "Someone (some man) possesses a woman," it is evident that here the spectator is both situated as the object possessed and inscribed, at the same time, in the most extreme performance of a man's possession of a woman. Here, one might recall Thierry Kuntzel's observation that the success of *The Most Dangerous Game* "is to render all of the positions within the 'phantasy' acceptable."[20]

White Zombie works to reinforce the spectator's position at the site of this "someone," of the male possessor. At the end of the film, we see Madeline's vision return only from the point of view of the male(s). The ideological trajectory of the film, however, is to reinstate the *correct* "someone," that being Neil, in the position of possessor. In fact, Neil's position in the film is virtually empty, except in his fulfillment of this function. He is "correct" only in terms of the law and of the "natural" as it is posed by the film. In these terms, both Legendre and Beaumont are situated against the law, on the side of the perverse. It is this relationship to the law which differentiates the three male characters—characters whose desires are, in fact, very much the same.

THE CONDENSATION OF SPACES

Legendre's position as the film's enunciator is most clearly revealed in the sequence in which he transforms Madeline into a zombie. The sequence is structured in terms of an alternation between a scene on the exterior of Beaumont's house, where Legendre performs the voodoo ritual, and the interior, at the wedding dinner of Neil and Madeline, where Legendre's magic begins to take effect. Given the supernatural premise of the film's fiction and the conventional filmic technique of cross-cutting, the action of this sequence in no way *requires* the activation of a fantastic space. Convention allows the potential for an action represented in one place to have an effect (even supernatural) on the action in another; cross-cutting enables the linking of shots in such cases according to the logic of cause and effect, preserving an imaginary unity between the fictional locales. In fact, the sequence of Madeline's possession begins to unfold in exactly this fashion; but as the cross-cutting quickens (accelerating the drama), the exterior and interior spaces established by the sequence begin to meld with one another in the creation of a fantastic space linked to the eyes hovering above the road. An analysis of this sequence not only reveals the work of the enunciation in producing this space, but also the ways in which the conventions of classical cinema, especially the code of the look, contribute to its production.

The sequence of Madeline's possession is clearly set aside from those that surround it. It is immediately preceded by the wedding of Madeline and Neil, and immediately followed by Madeline's funeral. The words of the wedding ceremony, which lead into the scene, and those of the funeral, which lead out of it, are in both cases spoken by the missionary Dr. Bruner, who does not appear in the sequence of the possession. In addition, a musical theme runs throughout the sequence, linking the shots and separating the whole from the sequences around it.

The sequence to be analyzed contains twenty-nine shots, alternating between the exterior and interior locales according to a pattern of "tightening" by which the shots in either place become fewer and fewer each time. At shot 27, however, the spaces "meld" in the fantastic space, after which the alternation continues briefly, but only with the significant marking of the subsequent shots. The following breakdown provides a scheme for this pattern of alternation:

Exterior	Interior
Shots 1–11	Shots 12–19
Shots 20–21	Shots 22–23
Shots 24–25	Shot 26
Shot 27	Shot 28
Shot 29	

The position of Legendre in shot 1, once again facing away from the camera and in the same direction as the spectator, recalls the earlier scene of the eyes above the roadway, and thus his omnipotent position as the enunciator of the scene to follow. His glances offscreen left in shots 2, 3, and 4 establish the object of his actions as outside the frame. Shot 5 clearly establishes Beaumont's house as the object of Legendre's gaze, separating the two terms (Legendre and Beaumont's house) presented together in shot 1, and creating the basis for the alternation that will structure the sequence.

Shots 4 through 10 compose a carefully articulated symbolic circuit that precisely situates the terms brought into play by the voodoo ritual. Shot 4 begins as a close-up of Legendre's hands as they produce the "magic" with an ensemble of objects: a candle, Madeline's scarf, and a knife (shot 4a). This "magic" involves the fashioning of a fetish (central to voodoo): a *representation* of Madeline, created from the candle by the aggression of Legendre's knife, combined with a *fragment* of Madeline, an object stolen from her, her scarf. Pulled from her neck by Legendre during their first encounter, the scarf reiterates another aggression; as described by Madeline, "It felt like hands clutching me."

Shot 1

Shot 2

Shot 3

Thirty-eight frame enlargements from White Zombie, *shots 1–29b.*

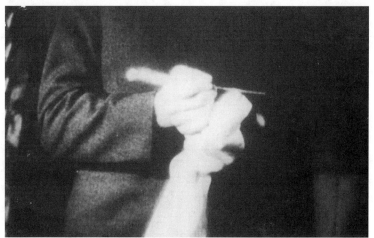

Shot 4a

Shot 4b

Shot 5

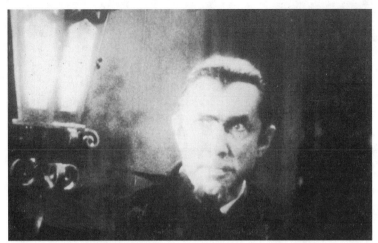

Shot 6a

Shot 6b

Shot 7

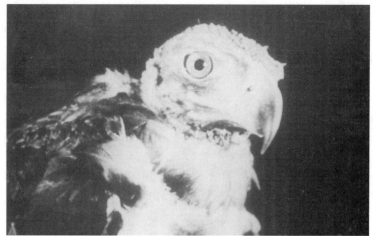

Shot 8

Shot 9

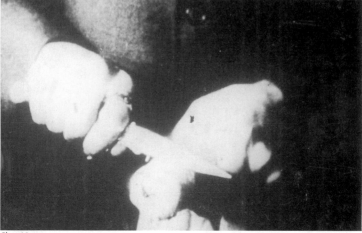

Shot 10

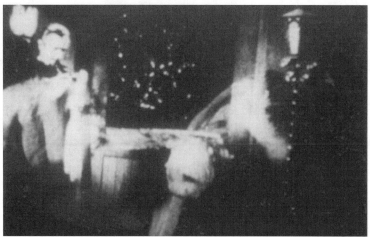

Shot 10/11

Shot 11

Shot 12

Shot 13a

Shot 13b

Shot 13c

Shot 13d

Shot 14

Shot 15

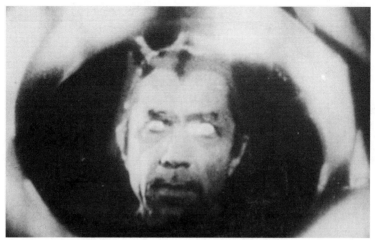

Shot 16

Shot 17

Shot 18

Shot 19

Shot 20

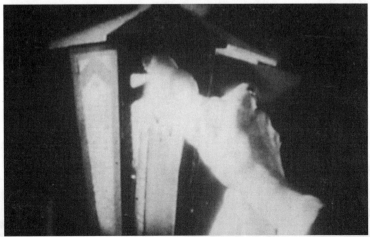

Shot 21

Shot 22a

Shot 22b

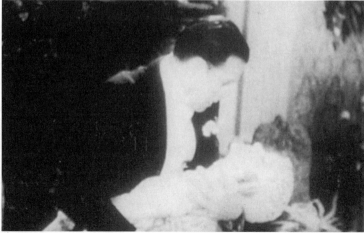

Shot 23

Shot 24

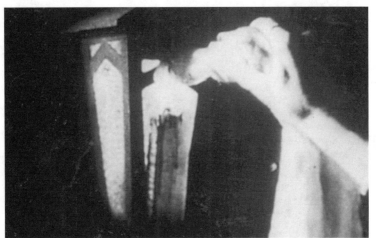

Shot 25

Shot 26

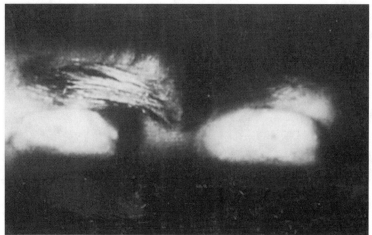

Shot 27

Shot 28a

Shot 28b

Shot 29a

Shot 29b

The tilt up from Legendre's hands to his face (shot 4b) provides a strong link between the aggression of the knife and stolen object, and the aggression of his dominating gaze offscreen.

Shot 5, the point-of-view shot of Beaumont's house, introduces the second term of the ensemble: the object of Legendre's gaze and aggression. Bracketed by his offscreen glances in shots 4 and 6, the house becomes a term which Legendre's gaze enunciates and links directly to the fetish. Yet the object of his look is more than the house; it is as well Madeline, who is within. Shot 5 insists, however, that it is the exterior of the house which stands before Legendre, thus preserving the "realist" space of the exterior. Legendre's glances throughout the sequence nevertheless assert that he sees something more, a hypothesis clearly within diegetic possibility, given his ability to see all; but it is a vision which the spectator is not yet allowed to share.

The cry of the vulture heard over shot 6 introduces the third term of the ensemble, but it is again Legendre's glance (shot 6a) which enunciates the camera movement toward the bird: a tilt up, which follows the direction of his look (shot 6b). The vulture appears as a purely symbolic term, with no function in the action whatsoever. Appearing here for the first time, it will return on three other occasions: on the rocks outside Legendre's castle; at the window of the castle during the scene of Beaumont's possession; and in the final scene in which Legendre dies. As a carrion bird that feeds on the bodies of the dead, the vulture is a metaphor for Legendre, who lives off the labor of zombies. This metaphoric relationship is so strong that the bird follows Legendre off the cliff when he plunges to his death.

Shots 7 and 9, close-ups of Legendre that bracket shot 8, the close-up of the vulture, accomplish a metaphoric substitution of one term for the other, since shot 8 cannot, in "realistic" spatial terms, be a point-of-view shot. Legendre could not possibly be looking at the bird behind his back, even though his glance up introduces shot 8; he can only see the bird to the extent that he is all-seeing. His wry smile in shots 7 and 9 emphasizes his complicity with this nonhuman symbol of death. Yet the cry of the vulture first occurs over shot 6, the final term of the seeing/seen alternation between Legendre and the house, and as such, seems at first to emanate from the house itself. Thus the vulture's cry might also be related to the object of Legendre's look, to the scream of his victim, condensed with the scream of aggression.

Legendre's glance from the vulture to the fetish in shot 9 completes the (potentially infinite) symbolic circuit: fetish, house (Madeline), vulture, fetish, and so on. The circuit is enclosed around Legendre as enunciator, and shot 9 insists on the centrality of his look, which makes the final link (vulture to fetish) between two offscreen terms.

Shots 4 through 10 make up a pause in the progression of the scene, a hesitation in the action. The pause assumes the import of a ritual where certain terms are placed in a significant relation, a linkage of terms which the enunciation substitutes for the unrepresentable magic of voodoo. The dissolve between shots 10 and 11 is employed according to common convention to indicate a short passage of time. What is omitted by the dissolve is Legendre's work in carving the candle. What is emphasized in its place is the *destruction* of the carving, the action that justifies the cross-cutting and eventually "produces" the fantastic space.

Only in shot 11 is the spectator allowed to see the completed carving, and only then in medium longshot. Clearly the carving represents a naked woman, and the logic of the narrative (reasserted by Legendre's offscreen looks) indicates that the woman is Madeline. Codes of censorship prohibit a close-up of the fetish and, to an extent, underline its "obscenity." In the same way, the creation of this naked effigy is a violation of Madeline's chastity, insofar as it is a sexualization of her body. The implicitly phallic candle is explicitly sexualized by its transformation into a fetish. Further, the naked representation made by Legendre emphasizes that his all-seeing power allows him to see not only into the house, but through Madeline's clothes as well. Thus the fetish is the product of Madeline's violation by Legendre's look.

The direct cut between shots 11 and 12 indicates (again according to convention) a simultaneity of actions. For the first time in the sequence, we see what Legendre *seems* to be seeing from the exterior: the wedding dinner of Madeline and Neil. The musical theme, which begins in shot 1 and continues through shot 11, is suddenly lowered in volume at the beginning of shot 12. Its continuation links the exterior and interior scenes, but suggests that the source of, and/or impetus for, the music is centered outside with Legendre. At this point, then, the music provides the single mark of continuation between the scenes outside and inside.

The tightening of the frame in shot 13, to a medium shot excluding all but one character, demonstrates an enunciative technique employed repeatedly in *White Zombie* to isolate characters even when they are in diegetic proximity. Shot 13 employs a pan to link the characters, even as they are framed individually, resulting in their looks always being directed offscreen. Thus, the spectator sees only a single character's gestures without seeing their interaction. The central interaction in this scene will, in fact, take place between Madeline and Legendre, in another space; they are to be linked by editing, even as the characters at the table are separated by framing. The series of shots begins with Beaumont (shot 13a), who *believes* himself to be the enunciator of the scene (he has given Madeline the zombie potion; he assumes Legendre's magic is done at his behest), and therefore initiates a toast to a bride he ironically intends to take for himself. Yet the camera refuses to follow his look offscreen left, panning instead toward Neil on the right (shot 13b), and only then moving left toward Madeline. This movement displaces Beaumont, who has seated himself between the couple, and links the hands of Madeline and Neil (as they exchange the glass) across Beaumont's face (shot 13c). Not only is the final displacement of Beaumont by the couple prefigured in this shot, but so is his displacement by Legendre, since shot 13 is echoed in the later, climactic scene in which Beaumont sits helpless at a table while Legendre (to one side of him) orders Madeline (to his other side) to kill Neil. Shot 13 concludes with Madeline (shot 13d), the object indicated initially by Beaumont's look offscreen, but inscribed by the camera movement as the object of Neil's look as well. The final framing of Madeline insists she is the key point of the triangle. The frivolous game of fortune-telling that follows (shots 14 and 15)—utterly false in terms of actual predictions and an indication of Madeline's lack of seriousness regarding the supernatural—becomes quite somber when she actually does see an omen in the glass.

Shot 16 represents the invasion of the interior scene by Legendre, who is still "physically" on the exterior. The loud music cue that accompanies the appearance of Legendre's face in Madeline's glass reasserts the musical theme, providing a direct link to the ritual taking place outside. Here, Legendre's power, not only to see inside the house but to appear there as well, is asserted from a position visible only to Madeline and the spectator, who shares her point of view in shot 16. His hypnotic stare is directed at her, directed into the camera; it is the moment of violation.

Legendre's direct stare from Madeline's glass recalls the threatening enunciative mark of his eyes above the road. Once again, he stares at the spectator, but here (in contrast to the earlier scene), the spectator's position is inscribed in an identification—Madeline's point of view. His stare once again appears in a fantastic space; there is no way to relate the apparition of Legendre to his simultaneous location outside. His face is afloat in darkness and his eyes are lit to emphasize his stare. Yet here the fantastic space is inscribed as the vision or hallucination of Madeline, and it clearly occurs *within* the "natural" space of Beaumont's house, located very specifically in Madeline's glass.

Legendre is clearly the enunciator of this apparition; it is he who enters the house and who takes hypnotic control of Madeline. Yet Madeline is allowed to see what no one else can: an apparition which asserts the supernatural at the very point she mocked it with her playful predictions of happiness and love. At the moment of her possession, she shares with Legendre a privileged access to the fantastic space.

Shot 16 inscribes Madeline as the object of still a third look, beyond those of Beaumont and Neil—that of Legendre. As the crux of their collective gaze, she is asserted as the object of their conflict. Legendre's superiority as enunciator allows him a look visible only to Madeline (and the spectator), powerful enough to hypnotize and possess her, and unrestricted by "natural" space. This guarantees his initial triumph over both Beaumont and Neil.

With shot 17, Madeline is already in Legendre's power. Her empty stare, later referred to by Beaumont as a signifier of her soullessness, is the indication that she is no longer Madeline, but only an object of the desires of men. She has lost her power to *return* the look of anyone. Later, Beaumont's dissatisfaction with "his" possession of Madeline centers on the fact that he cannot "possess" her look as an indication of her desire. He wants the life brought back to her eyes, but only to the extent that it would allow her to reciprocate his look. Both Legendre and Beaumont are thus situated on the side of the perverse since they want to possess Madeline, but have no access to this signifier of Madeline's reciprocal desire.

Shot 18 reprises the framing of shot 14, the last moment of normalcy at the wedding dinner. As such, it reasserts the spatial unity to emphasize the disruption that has taken place. Neil moves toward Madeline, who stares blankly into space; Beaumont is left alone in the center with nothing to do but to watch the scene he has instigated. It is the first figuration of his main role for the rest of the film: the helpless observer of the intrigue his desires have set in motion.

Shot 19 presents the first framing of the couple in the sequence. It is therefore ironic that Madeline is represented as no longer being Madeline, depriving the couple of its wholeness (restoration of which will be the narrative project of the remainder of the film). Neil's insistent gaze at Madeline in this shot reaffirms her position as object, since she is unable to return his look. Henceforth, until the final scene, Madeline will regard *no one*, or rather no one in the "natural" space.

The destruction of the fetish is the violation on the exterior which corresponds to the possession of Madeline on the interior. In shot 20, Legendre inserts the candle into the lamp, an image with symbolic sexual overtones made even clearer in light of Freud's identification of the fetish as a substitute phallus. The ritual destruction of the candle inaugurates an exchange of sorts. Madeline replaces the fetish.

Shot 21 is inscribed as what Legendre sees, much as was the house in shot 5. He no longer looks toward the house to "see" Madeline; he now watches her as the fetish in the lamp. Legendre's point of view of Madeline's violation (shot 21) can thus be read as a kind of reverse shot of Madeline's point of view in shot 16. Just as the intrusion of the supernatural allows her to see Legendre where he is not (in her glass), Legendre's powers allow him (but not the spectator) to see Madeline where she is not (in the candle fetish). Therefore, if Legendre sees Madeline from her glass, it is possible to speculate that she is seeing him from the position of the fetish, that she has taken the place of the fetish to the extent that its burning causes her death, that the eyes staring up from her glass are those which are gazing at the burning candle. Madeline reacts to the burning of the candle not as though she is on fire, but as though she sees something horrifying, something she must push away (shot 22a). It is clear, then, that she is not seeing "nothing" (as her blank stare suggests), but a real threat that is invisible in the "natural" space that Neil and Beaumont occupy.

The pan at the end of shot 22 framing Beaumont (shot 22b) defines him as the spectator of the scene—a scene performed for him, at his request. His look of horror indicates a repulsion engendered by his "perverse" desire for Madeline, by his exclusion from the drama taking place between the newlyweds and between Madeline and Legendre.

Shot 23 reframes the beginning of shot 22 exactly, now inscribed as the scene viewed by Beaumont. Neil's look toward him is unsuspecting—not accusing, but pleading. The camera, however, is not directed by Neil's look this time; it remains fixed, emphasizing his isolation and helplessness. For both Beaumont and Neil, the scene is out of control.

From shot 20, the first return to the exterior scene, the alternation between exterior and interior progresses in pairs of shots representing each locale: shots 20–21, exterior; shots 22–23, interior; shots 24–25, exterior. Shot 26 stands alone, the final shot before the introduction of the purely fantastic space of shot 27, which is a repetition of the shot of the eyes that was superimposed over the road in the film's opening sequence (shot 3 from the five-shot sequence earlier in the chapter, figure 11a). As such, it represents Legendre's domination as all-seeing enunciator at the very moment of his triumph over Madeline. But here there is no superimposition, as over the road.

The appearance of the eyes at this crucial point in the ever-quickening cross-cutting between exterior and interior is both a rupture of the alternating pattern and a condensation of both spaces. The eyes are neither outside with Legendre, who is involved in the voodoo ritual, nor inside with Madeline, even to the extent that the apparition of Legendre's face within her glass occurred inside the house. As of shot 26, Madeline is unconscious, looking at nothing, since her eyes are closed; therefore, the eyes cannot be related to the space of the room, even as an hallucination. Yet they might be read as Madeline's point of view *while* unconscious. At the same time, they represent the supernatural Legendre *outside* of spatial reference, as in the opening scene, before the eyes dissolved into his body. The space of the supernatural, the space of the unconscious: as the culmination of a tightening pattern of cross-cutting and the condensation of interior and exterior scenes in still a third locale, it is the space of horror.

The two shots which follow return to a differentiation of exterior and interior spaces, though the pattern of alternation is reversed; yet both remain problematic in terms of locale as they are significantly marked as *different* from the alternating shots which preceded them. Shot 28 offers a kind of ritualized restatement of the sequence's conclusion, presenting again the death of Madeline. We have already seen her collapse and realize, from the dialogue, that Neil believes her to be dead (from shot 23). But shot 28 reframes her, isolating her from Neil, in whose arms she is resting, and virtually proposes a new diegesis. Madeline's eyes are open again (shot 28a), only to close slowly, one at a time. Her empty stare, which opens shot 28, now suggests that shot 27 may be her point of view, although still one without reference to the space in which she is located. As if to reassert the separation of Madeline from the interior space, she is marked in this shot by the passing of strange shadows over her (shot 28b), without any conceivable diegetic motivation. It is no longer a matter of whether or not Madeline hallucinates. These shadows are more closely related to another vision, perhaps even the point of view of the disembodied eyes in shot 27 viewing Madeline in a kind of fantastic distortion of the interior space.

Shot 29, clearly in the exterior where the ritual was performed, nevertheless departs from the preceding exterior shots significantly. Legendre, no longer involved in the ritual, and no longer directing his attention to objects onscreen or off, looks directly into the camera (shot 29a) and walks menacingly toward it (shot 29b). As in the scenes employing the fantastic space, he violates the code of the indirect look; yet here, he is in what is (or was) a "natural" space. Following shot 28, his stare might be read as a fantastic reverse shot from Madeline's closed eyes, though in that case, we must assume that Madeline can actually see Legendre on the exterior, where previously she had seen him only in a kind of hallucination. We must assume that, by her death and/or possession, she now shares his all-seeing powers. But we can accept shot 29 as Madeline's point of view only if we are willing to grant that her position is represented by the position which was held by the camera in the exterior shots throughout the sequence.

Thus, it is only with the greatest difficulty that we can explain shot 29 within the classical patterns of alternation and point of view, even granting the intervention of a separate, fantastic space. The overriding sense of shot 29 is that it is no longer the spectator sharing the point of view of Madeline, but the viewer of the film as represented by the camera who is the object of Legendre's menacing glare. There are simply no characters spatially situated in such a way as to allow the displacement of the point-of-view shot onto them. It is the camera lens into which Legendre stares, the camera lens which he approaches, the camera lens which he finally engulfs with his body. The shot seems to function as a direct marking by which Legendre identifies himself as enunciator of the action by violating the conventions of enunciation and asserting the power of his position over that of the spectator. Thus the shot condenses Legendre's manipulation of the intrigue via the supernatural and his manipulation of the enunciation.

The fear (and excitement) of violation may be the key to the experience of the horror film. *White Zombie* employs a variety of classic codes to situate the spectator within the drama of possession. Yet on the level of enunciation, it poses still another "threat" to the spectator, one which emerges from a violation of what is conceived as the classical spectator position itself. Horror is thus produced by the disruption of conventional space, by the intervention of another space commandeered by an "evil" enunciator whose tyranny reaches its peak as he returns the spectator's stare and devours the camera with his shadow.

THE RECUPERATION OF
"NATURAL" SPACE

The dissolve that links/separates the beginning of the possession sequence from the wedding scene that precedes it (apparently signifying a short passage of time) also provides an enunciation of the symbolic association between Legendre and the patriarchal, "lovably" awkward minister Dr. Bruner. The final shot of the wedding shows Bruner standing in the center of the frame with his back toward the camera, facing the couple he is marrying. The dissolve to the exterior of Beaumont's house (shot 1) finds Legendre in the same position, facing the same direction, so that the figure of Bruner is virtually transformed *into* that of Legendre. Thus, the enunciation marks the usurpation of the Christian wedding by the voodoo ritual, linking it to the transformation of the "good" symbolic father into the "bad."

Dr. Bruner's many titles in *White Zombie* point to a certain ambiguity which stems from the diverse functions he must fulfill in the structuration of the narrative. On the one hand, he is a minister, the representative of Western religion in opposition to Haitian superstition. On the other, his title "Doctor" (assuming it is an academic honor) refers to Bruner's position in relation to knowledge and marks the conflation of the two contradictory discourses he articulates: the (Western) religious and the rational. (The prototype for such a character might be Van Helsing in the *Dracula* films.) On the journey to Legendre's castle, Bruner also acts as a medical doctor, although it is a witch doctor who actually diagnoses Neil's jungle fever. Bruner's religious and rational functions are also conflated with his function as articulator of the law. The three are virtually inseparable throughout most of the film, as in the wedding scene when his legal and religious functions completely overlap. In a later scene, where Bruner consults the Haitian law books in order to assure Neil that Madeline may still be alive, he stresses the fact that there is necessarily a rational explanation behind her disappearance, and thus poses the terms of the hermeneutic: "I've been trying to get to the bottom of this for years."

Therefore, one might assume that the truth of "zombie" is forthcoming. However, the hermeneutic as posed is finally displaced onto another "truth": that of the couple. Bruner's part in the articulation of the law, in fact, far exceeds the legal *per se*. It is intricately involved in reinstating a normality to the fiction within which the couple emerges as a socially sanctioned truth. Two points seem important in this regard. First, Bruner never appears in any of the scenes involving the fantastic space; he is associated with the "natural," realist space which is the space of the law. Second, Bruner is the only main character in the film who remains consistently outside the circuit of desire. He is a necessary counterpart to Neil, who has desire but who is helpless in his complete lack of knowledge.

The symbolic struggle between good and evil constitutes one of the least coherent aspects of *White Zombie*. Obviously, the enunciation must be taken away from Legendre and resituated on the side of the law. The accomplishment of this is enunciated comically by the last line of the film: the doctor's habitual "Have you got a match?" which in this case refers rather directly (though inadvertently) to the reunited couple. This shift in control involves a number of condensations which are not accounted for logically at the level of the story itself. The shift follows another sort of logic. Dr. Bruner's line guarantees the final restoration of the law. In many ways, one might expect an open struggle between good and evil in a conclusive duel between Bruner and Legendre. However, the doctor's position outside the circuit of desire renders him insufficient in terms of the symbolic struggle for Madeline. Therefore, the film will posit the struggle in the supernatural space, giving Neil and Madeline access to its enunciation by means, one supposes, of their "true" love.

This aspect of the supernatural first appears in the cafe where Neil is drinking shortly after Madeline's apparent death. The scene is crosscut with the stealing of Madeline's body by Legendre and his zombies. Suddenly, Madeline appears in her wedding gown, superimposed, first, on Neil's table, and then, amongst the shadows of dancers on the wall behind him. She calls out to him, then disappears. Neil looks offscreen and runs off toward the camera. This shot is linked by the next, which returns to Madeline's tomb (Neil's destination), by the sound of a dog barking, an enunciative mark associated with the doctor (heard over his initial entrance in the film). It is thus opposed to the vulture cry, which is the mark of Legendre.

This scene is crucial in that it constitutes the first moment in which Legendre is not all-seeing, all-knowing, and all-powerful. He is caught by surprise by Neil's approach and must flee. It is as though his enunciative control is contested by the power of "love," a force which has allowed Madeline access to the supernatural in order to appear to Neil after her death. It is also significant that this force is imbricated by a mark of Bruner's presence, even though (as we have noted) he himself never appears within the supernatural space.

The second assignment of a supernatural space to the couple occurs in another sequence of cross-cutting. Upstairs in Legendre's castle, Madeline is being prepared for a zombie marriage to Legendre. Seemingly asserting her own will (something zombies are supposed to have lost), she walks to a window and stares out. Neil, who is below at a distant campsite recovering from his fever, suddenly awakes and responds to Madeline's gaze by calling her name. The two terms of this alternation are then joined by an elaborate series of wipes motivated ostensibly by the closeness of the lovers' souls. This "communication" passes entirely without Legendre's knowledge, and it is only after Neil enters the castle that Legendre discovers him. This discovery, of course, reinstitutes Legendre's control over the couple to the extent that he is able to force Madeline to the point of killing Neil. It is only the intervention of the doctor's hand (knocking the knife from Madeline's hand) that saves Neil.

With this intervention (entirely within the "natural" space), Bruner virtually replaces Legendre in the symbolization of the enunciation. This is accomplished through three substitutions that cross the bar of the paradigm previously separating the two characters. First, Bruner's *hand* enters the frame, foiling Legendre's hands, pressed together in a recurrent gesture by which he is able to control others. (Hands form a second symbolic constellation in the film, less pervasive than that of eyes.) Second, the sound cue accompanying Bruner's action is the one that earlier marked the appearance of Legendre's face in Madeline's glass, and thus her death and possession. Finally, Bruner has changed into black clothing, breaching the conventional system (consistent until this moment) within which good and evil are symbolized by white and black, respectively.

However excessive in the moments of intervention by the fantastic space, Legendre's control over the enunciation in *White Zombie* is situated in a meaning produced, a fictional movement which ascribes the enunciation to particular characters only in order to recuperate it as a term in a purely diegetic struggle for possession and control. The horror-producing method of *White Zombie* works by assigning to the character of Legendre an excessive, *other* space which seemingly threatens the proper coherence and the systematic restrictions of the classical text. Thus, the spectator's position in the dialectic of desire and the law is played out through opposing enunciative forms. Of course, as we have shown, it is precisely the codes of classical cinema which allow for the production of this other, "fantastic" space: alternation, the code of the look, the sutured space of Hollywood representation.

Thus, the opposition between the two types of space should not be seen in terms of a classical and a nonclassical style, but instead in terms of its role in articulating desire and the law within the fiction, and the spectator's relationship to that fiction. At the end of *White Zombie*, the law restores everything to its "natural" state (the couple, Bruner's position presiding over their desire, and so on). Concomitantly, the enunciation returns to the "classical" space, which *represents* the "natural," demonstrating its capacity to contain the many discourses that constitute it.

NOTES

1. Siegfried Kracauer, *From Caligari to Hitler: A Psychological History of the German Film* (Princeton, N.J.: Princeton University Press, 1947).

2. Robin Wood, "Introduction to the American Horror Film," in *The American Nightmare*, ed. Robin Wood and Richard Lippe (Toronto: Festival of Festivals, 1979), 7–28. Reprinted in this volume.

3. Roger Dadoun, "Fetishism in the Horror Film," *Enclitic* 1, no. 2 (Fall 1977): 39–63; originally in *Nouvelle Review de Psychanalyse*, no. 2 (Automne 1970): 227–47.

4. Thierry Kuntzel, "The Film Work, 2," *camera obscura*, no. 5 (Spring 1980): 7–68; originally in *Communications*, no. 23 (1975): 136–89.

5. See, for example, the following articles by Raymond Bellour: "*Les Oiseaux*: description d'une sequence," *Cahiers du cinéma*, no. 216 (Octobre 1969): 24–38 (on *The Birds*); "Le blocage symbolique," *Communications*, no. 23 (1975): 235–350 (on *North by Northwest*); "Hitchcock: The Enunciator," *camera obscura*, no. 2 (Fall 1977): 69–91 (mostly on *Marnie*), "Psychosis, Neurosis, Perversion," *camera obscura*, nos. 3/4 (Summer 1979): 105–32 (on *Psycho*).

6. Thomas Schatz, *Hollywood Genres* (New York: Random House, 1981); see esp. chap. 2.

7. Robin Wood notes this duality in viewer allegiance, which he terms *ambivalence*. Wood, "Introduction," 14–15.

8. Stephen Heath, "Narrative Space," *Screen* 17, no. 3 (Autumn 1976): 97.

9. *White Zombie* was produced by Edward Halperin and directed by his brother Victor Halperin for Halperin Productions. "The brothers, who came from Chicago in the early twenties and set up their own production company, were continually theorizing and experimenting to find a scientific approach to moviemaking. They made graphs analyzing successful films in an effort to establish foolproof structural formulae. By the time they embarked on *White*

Zombie, they were in their mid-thirties and had made some thirty features. Having thoroughly studied available talking pictures, they reached the accurate conclusion that most contained too much talk and not enough action. They decided to hold the dialogue to fifteen per cent—only what was necessary to advance the story. Just as a good artist will follow through with a planned design, the Halperins stuck with their decision, even though it meant they must prune pages from the script." George E. Turner and Michael H. Price, *Forgotten Horrors: Early Talkie Chillers from Poverty Row* (S. Brunswick: A. S. Barnes & Co., 1979), 56.

10. "The word *zombie* was introduced to the American reading public in 1929 in William B. Seabrook's book on Haitian voodoo, *The Magic Island,* and to the dramatic stage in Kenneth Webb's New York play, *Zombie,* which opened in February of 1932. In March of that year Webb brought suit against movie producers Edward and Victor Hugo Halperin, who had announced their intention of making a movie entitled *White Zombie.* The Halperin brothers won the case and completed their movie for summer release, thereby introducing the zombie to motion pictures." Turner and Price, *Forgotten Horrors,* 57.

11. Val Lewton's *I Walked with a Zombie* (1943) is clearly the most renowned example of the subgenre; but zombies remain a staple of the horror film to this day. Not all zombie films, however, are structured according to the possessor/possessed paradigm. Those that are frequently remain close to the Haitian legend from which the subgenre sprang (although the Halperins' sequel, *Revolt of the Zombies* [1936], was moved to a Cambodian setting). The motivations of "possessors" vary from film to film. In *White Zombie, The Voodoo Man* (1944), and *Voodoo Woman* (1956), women are possessed for implicitly sexual reasons. Zombies are used to labor for their masters in a sugar mill in *White Zombie,* and in a mine in *Plague of the Zombies* (1966). In *King of the Zombies* (1941), *Revenge of the Zombies* (1943), and *Shock Waves* (1977), zombies are enlisted to aid the Nazi cause. During the 1950s, the theme of possession by an "other" is frequently transferred to narratives about extraterrestrials; such films as Don Siegel's *Invasion of the Body Snatchers* and Roger Corman's *It Conquered the World* (both 1956) are clearly related to the zombie film on this basis. Significant exceptions to the possessor/possessed structuration in the subgenre are George A. Romero's *Night of the Living Dead* (1968) and *Dawn of the Dead* (1978), where zombies are possessed by no one, but as a group constitute themselves as an "other."

12. Christian Metz, *The Imaginary Signifier* (Bloomington: Indiana University Press, 1982), 58–78, 91–97.

13. Janet Bergstrom, "Alternation, Segmentation, Hypnosis: An Interview with Raymond Bellour," *camera obscura,* nos. 3/4 (Summer 1979): 100–03.

14. We have benefited here from Thierry Kuntzel's analysis of *The Most Dangerous Game,* a film that bears certain similarities to *White Zombie.* Kunt-

zel points to the importance of the stability of the paradigm of sexual difference in *The Most Dangerous Game*, where the woman is situated more or less
outside (as the prize) of the struggle initiated through the other major paradigm of the film, that of "hunter/hunted." Kuntzel, "The Film Work, 2."

15. Our use of the term *fantastic* in this context is related to the definition
offered by Tzvetan Todorov in *The Fantastic: A Structural Approach to a Literary Genre*, trans. Richard Howard (Ithaca, N.Y.: Cornell University Press,
1975), 25: "In a world which is indeed our world, the one we know, a world
without devils, sylphides, or vampires, there occurs an event which cannot be
explained by the laws of this same familiar world. The person who experiences
the event must opt for one of two possible solutions: either he is the victim of
an illusion of the senses, or a product of the imagination—and laws of the
world remain what they are; or else the event has really taken place, it is an
integral part of reality—but then this reality is controlled by laws unknown to
us. Either the devil is an illusion, an imaginary being; or else he really exists,
precisely like other living beings—with this reservation, that we encounter him
infrequently. The fantastic occupies the duration of this uncertainty. . . . The
fantastic is that hesitation experienced by a person who knows only the laws
of nature, confronting an apparently supernatural event."

16. Cf. Roger Dadoun's discussion of the imagery of emptiness and "the
void" in the horror film (and especially the vampire subgenre, which is related
to the zombie film by a variation of the paradigm "possessor/possessed") and
its relationship to fetishism as described by Freud. Dadoun, "Fetishism."

17. Catherine Clement, "De la Méconnaissance: Fantasme, Texte, Scene,"
Langages, no. 17, 41 (our translation).

18. Jean Laplanche and J. B. Pontalis, "Fantasme originaire, fantasmes des
origines, origine du fantasme," *Les Temps Modernes* 19, no. 215 (April 1964):
1861 (our translation).

19. For a discussion in psychoanalytic terms of the multiple identificatory
positions available to the spectator, especially in relation to Freud's essay "A
Child Is Being Beaten," see D. N. Rodowick, "The Difficulty of Difference,"
Wide Angle 5, no. 1 (1982): 4–15.

20. Kuntzel, "The Film Work," *Communications*, 23, 150 (our translation).

12

King Kong: Ape and Essence

Noël Carroll

Because its basic subject matter is fear, the horror film is a popular-genre vehicle that is prone to manifesting the specific anxieties that dominate the cultural context in which it was made. For example, horror films of the late 1970s and early '80s—e.g., *Alien* (1979), *The Thing* (1982), *Dawn of the Dead* (1978), *Halloween* and *Halloween II* (1978, 1982), the *Friday the 13th* series, *The Evil Dead* (1983), and so on—emphasize the recurring theme of survival at a time in American history when economic circumstances have transformed the mere "bottom-line" commendation that "he/she is a survivor" into the highest badge of achievement that one can hope for. Likewise, the 1930s theme of the unjustly alienated monster, such as Frankenstein's progeny, signaled the depression anxiety of being cast out of civil society due to impoverishment; the 1950s invasion obsession reflected internal politics and the apprehension engendered there; and the early 1970s' infatuation with possession and telekinesis announced a complex fantasy of powerlessness combined with infantile delusions of impotence during a period when it was a common experience to be enraged at being at the utter mercy of the seemingly unpredictable shifts in the national and international economy. The purpose of this article is to examine the social anxieties submerged in the classic horror film *King Kong* (1933) which, interestingly enough, literalizes survival metaphors that bear a noteworthy relation to those found in contemporary tales of terror.

King Kong is one of the miracles of cinema, beguiling audiences of all ages and every intellectual pretension. It is a film that abounds with interpretations. These come in many shapes and sizes—Kong as Christ, Kong as Black, Kong as commodity, Kong as rapist, Kong enraptured by *l'amour fou*, Kong as Third World, Kong as dream, Kong as myth, Kong according to Freud, according to Jung, and even according to Lacan. The 1976 version of *King Kong* selects a few of these interpretations—notably Kong as Third World, Kong as commodity and *l'amour fou*—and makes them explicit; the helicopters seem to sweep in from the Mekong Delta and the swooning heroine suggests that Kong is not always alone in his madness. Yet the remake seems so much the worse for its clarification. For certainly part of the fascination of the original was its openness to interpretive play.

What I wish to explore here is an aspect of *Kong* that has been given scant attention heretofore—what I call its evolutionary theme. I am not offering this theme in order to reject previous interpretations but because it seems to me that this theme can be used to answer certain questions about *Kong*. Some of these concern the incessant repetition of visual and narrative motifs, especially in the second half of the film. Some examples of these repetitions include: the sacrifice of Darrow on a platform with her arms splayed/the visually similar "crucifixion" of Kong in New York; Kong fights a snakelike reptile/he attacks a subway; Kong climbs to the summit of Skull Mountain/Kong climbs the Empire State Building; Kong fights a pterodactyl/Kong fights the rickety bi-planes. There are more of these repetitions and I will discuss them later. Even the 1976 remake of *Kong* acknowledges them, although characteristically in an all-too-conspicuous way when, in a flashback, we catch on to Kong's interest in the World Trade Center. The repetitions in the original function to equate the island with Manhattan and this raises questions not only about why the equation is forged but also about what significance it could have for its audience. I will try to answer both these by reference to an implicit theme of evolution in *Kong*. Specifically, *Kong* can be seen as a popular illustration of Social Darwinist metaphors which, in turn, were and to some extent still are generally held articles of faith of the American *weltanschauung*, shared by every class. In this light, the equation of the city with the jungle is perfectly fitting—almost "natural." What seems like an incongruous, surrealist metaphor is really a literalization of a banal but persuasive American belief about the nature of society.

To appreciate the basic elements of the evolutionary theme in *Kong*, it is helpful to examine its sources. One might think that this is a monumental task, requiring us to go back to the earliest tales of heroes and dragons. But this is not the case. For although *Kong* is packed with dinosaurs and dinosaurs appear to be our best cues for identifying the subgenre that *Kong* inhabits, *Kong* is not even peripherally a dragon story. The reason is simple; dinosaurs do not belong to the same symbolic species as dragons. Dragons, from Egypt onward, are fusion figures, condensing metaphysical forces such as earth, air, fire, and water into one composite entity. The recent *Dragonslayer* (1981), for example, carries on this tradition; its dragon walks, crawls, and lives underground (earth), it flies (sky), belches flame (fire), and sleeps underwater, as well as compounding biological parts of different genera, a tendency most pronounced in the dragonelles, which look like bulldog-lizards. Dinosaurs, on the other hand, are not composite creatures and the ideas we associate with them are inextricably bound up with our ideas of the prehistoric. Thus, as symbols, dinosaurs and their fictional lost world are rather modern, in other words, as modern as our concept of prehistory.

There is no ancient literature concerning dinosaurs because our knowledge of dinosaurs is only two centuries old. Fossils, mostly imprints of sea life, were familiar in the Middle Ages but few persons, save da Vinci, had any glimmering of what they were; many thought that they were the residues of abortive trial runs that God had made at creation before he succeeded. The first significant fossil find of a dinosaur occurred in 1780 in a gravel pit at Pietersberg, near Maestricht in Holland. The skeleton was shipped in 1794 as a trophy of war to Paris where it was analyzed by Georges Cuvier who, on the basis of this find plus his analyses of the American mastodon, a Siberian mammoth and a small Bavarian pterodactyl, declared that the earth had once been populated by creatures now extinct.

The name *dinosaur* (*deinos*—"terrifying"; *sauros*—"lizard") was coined in 1842 by Sir Richard Owen, a man who was quite instrumental in implanting the creatures in the popular imagination. In 1852, Joseph Paxton's Crystal Palace was dismantled and reconstructed in Sydenham, where it was to be a permanent display for the achievements of art and science. Owen, at the suggestion of Prince Albert, was asked to decorate the grounds with life-size models of his dinosaurs. Here we find the popular prototypes of all those lumbering movie monsters. The models were executed by Benjamin Waterhouse Hawkins in 1853 and they are referred to in Dickens' *Bleak House*. The next

fifty years witnessed a lively and at times extremely competitive proliferation of models and paintings of dinosaurs, many produced for
museums and universities. Working under Willis O'Brien, Marcel Del-
gado used such paintings by Charles R. Knight from the American
Museum of Natural History in New York as models for the creatures
in *The Lost World* (1925). By that time the visage of the dinosaur and
the "look" of the prehistoric world—including dinosaurs locked in an
archetypal clash for survival—had been etched graphically in the popular mind.

There could be no fiction of the prehistoric world variety until the
scientific conception of it had taken root. The earliest significant
appearance of dinosaurs in literature occurs in chapter 33 of Jules
Verne's *Journey to the Center of the Earth* (1864). Prof. Lidenbrock
and his nephew watch from afar as two sea monsters struggle. They are
not victims of the beasts but rather observers, which is much in keeping with the rest of the book—Verne's work is not presented as allegor-
ically satiric in the manner of forerunners such as Ludwig Holberg's *A
Journey to the World Underground* (1742) and the anonymous *A Voyage to the World in the Center of the Earth* (1755); instead, Verne's is a
heuristic device for propagating the most recent science.[1]

In *Journey to the Center of the Earth*, adventure is less important
than detail and description; if you ever need to know about the equipment you'll need to explore caves, read this book. Verne's characters
catalogue the stratas of the earth and even spy a human leading a mastodon in the distance. But unlike later exercises in this genre, to which
King Kong is indebted, *Journey to the Center of the Earth* is written
from a pre-Darwinian point of view and its heroes steer clear of direct
confrontation with these prehistoric creatures.

The prehistoric world genre was most popular from the 1880s to the
1930s. At first, the Earth's poles were favored locations for lost worlds,
but Southeast Asia also was a draftable locale, perhaps as a result of the
growing dissemination of information about the discovery of Angkor
Thom.

In some cases, the prehistoric motif was conjoined with the Atlantean, as in Cutcliffe Hyne's *The Lost Continent* (1900). Such novels
continued to be written after World War I: Karl zu Eulenburg's *Die
Brunnen der Grossen Tiefe* (1926) and Owen Rutter's *The Monster of
Mu* (1932) are two examples. The subgenre of the missing link, which
is relevant to *King Kong* since the anthropomorphized gorilla may be
seen as one, was also active at this time and included entries like Gouv-

erneur Morris's *The Pagan's Progress* (1904), Carl Edward's *Two-Legs* (1906), and F. Britten Austin's *When Mankind Was Young* (1926). Throughout this period a number of plot elements—which are essential to *Kong*—as well as their cultural associations were in the process of being established.

The best known and probably the best written—at least the wittiest—prehistoric creature story is Sir Arthur Conan Doyle's *The Lost World* (1912). It begins with a rollicking satire of academics and proceeds to a plateau in South America that is swarming with dinosaurs. Among other adventures, Prof. Challenger and his confreres help the savage humans of the lost world to overcome their more ape-like foes. Since Challenger is mistaken by the ape types as one of their own, it seems fair to say that Doyle is turning something that could be treated as intraspecies tribal warfare into interspecies warfare for territorial dominance. The prehistoric world is presented under the metaphor of war at the same time that war is cast as interspecies competition. It is hard to resist seeing *The Lost World* as an apology for colonialism. Anglo-Saxons arrive with their superior technology and know-how and aid the "human" population to gain its rightful place by defeating its subhuman competitors. This is achieved against a backdrop of clashing dinosaurs—the paradigm or associated picture in the popular imagination of, indeed the icon for, "the survival of the fittest."

The combination of dinosaurs with the biologically charged characterization of battling nation/tribes (in which the "humans" are aided by Europeans) is a recurring motif in prehistoric tales; it registers the application of intrinsically nondramatic biological concepts like "competition" and "survival" to social contexts where the biological concepts become particularized, dramatized, and literalized. Fictional interracial warfare replete with a background of battling dinosaurs is not really so far removed from political polemics like the American Rev. Josiah Strong's *Our Country: Its Possible Future and Its Present Crisis*, wherein the confrontation of Anglo-Saxon ideals with other races is envisioned in terms of the survival of the fittest. This tendency to translate the terms of pure biological theory into vivid, combat-oriented metaphors for picturing society was rife at the turn of the century and prehistoric tales may, therefore, be seen in conjunction with the currency of Social Darwinism.

The man who was most responsible for crystallizing the motifs of the prehistoric world adventure—undoubtedly because he wrote so many stories in this genre—was Edgar Rice Burroughs. Burroughs' lost world, Caspak, is elaborated in three novels: *The Land that Time Forgot, The People that Time Forgot,* and *Out of the Abyss,* all copyrighted in 1918.[2] Caspak is located somewhere in the South Pacific, near the Antarctic; it is uncharted; its towering cliffs make it impenetrable. Also, the layout of Caspak recapitulates Burroughs' idea of evolution. One end of the island is completely prehistoric. As one progresses inland, life reaches higher and higher grades on the evolutionary scale. Most of the fully human people of Caspak, the Galu, have undergone complete primate evolution during their own lifetime. They are "cor sva jo," or "from the beginning," which means they were spawned as apes at the far end of the island; each day they wade in revivifying puddles; and at times some of them hear the call, and walk to the next stage of evolution, biologically transformed. One day you're an ape-man, an Alu, and suddenly you are changed and you travel to the next, more human, niche in evolution; you join the tribe of the club-men, the Bo-lu. Next you become a Sto-lu (hatchet man), a Band-lu (spear-man), a Kro-lu (bow-man), and so on. These are not just tribe/nations but tribes that are also differentiated as distinct species. Where Verne depicted the spatial concept of the earth's stratification by means of time, in other words, a journey that is somewhat like a tour, Burroughs visualizes the temporal concept of evolution through space—the map of Caspak is a fictional evolutionary time line.

All of Caspak is at war; the modern visitors arrive only to be immediately attacked by dinosaurs. The Darwinian struggle for survival, complete with giant reptiles, begins as soon as their submarine surfaces. Caspak is an almost Hobbesian state of nature: "It is the way in Caspak. If you do not kill, we shall be killed, therefore it is wise to kill first whomever does not belong to one's tribe," To-mar tells Tom Billings in *The People that Time Forgot.* To be caught outside one's tribal/species territory is certain death, even though all the primates are at least dimly aware that they are connected through Caspak's strange biological design. Caspak is not only a microcosm of evolution but a microcosm of social relations as seen through a Social Darwinian optic, a jungle where the law of every living thing is strife.

The smartest species on Caspak is not exactly human. Called Weiroos, they are all male and winged. They kidnap Galu women in order to propagate their species. It is understood in Caspak that whichever intelligent species is first to procreate viviparously will dominate Caspak. Two themes of evolution—breeding and dominance—are thus conjoined in a rough, symbolic, popular mechanics sort of imagery that also gives an added significance to Burroughs' favorite plot device, the abduction of human women by nonhumans.[3]

Burroughs was an extremely repetitive writer, which probably accounts for the massive number of novels he produced in such a short time. Certain formulas are repeated with unnerving frequency—heroes are often described as never-being-what-you'd-call-a-ladies'-man just before romantic scenes, and the hero's prowess in this or that kind of collegiate athletics is adduced just before the performance of some incredible physical feat. Certain plot situations also appear almost mandatory in the Caspak series, and in the vastly similar Pellucidar series—for example, the escape from the enemy capital. Indeed, the overall plot structures of these books are strikingly similar. In each of the Caspak books, the male protagonist, in the course of the adventure, falls in love with a woman and the plot unravels as the hero and heroine are separated—often the female is abducted by a nonhuman—and then rejoined. Each of the novels climaxes with the final reunion of the lovers. In the first two Pellucidar novels, David seems to make a habit of rescuing Dian the Beautiful from Phutra, the Mahar capital. Burroughs undoubtedly uses this structure because it is an easy way to generate scenes, resolutions, and sequels, and it occurs in his nonprehistoric novels, such as *Princess of Mars* and *Tarzan of the Apes*, as well.[4] But the pattern is especially interesting in his ersatz Darwinian chronicles where the abduction of the potential "wife and mother" occurs in a context where procreation is an explicit element in the battle for species survival. Burroughs, of course, was not the only American writer working in a social Darwinist vein; Theodore Dreiser, Jack London, and Hamlin Garland each mobilize a Social Darwinist perspective derived from Herbert Spencer. But Burroughs not only crudely applies "Darwinian" principles in his fictional characterization of society; he also creates a world—a paleontological nightmare where humans and dinosaurs coexist—populated by what the popular mind would associate with the basic characters of the theory of evolution.

King Kong owes much of its narrative structure and several of its plot elements to the prehistoric story as it was popularized by Burroughs. The military/war theme is introduced in the beginning of the film with a discussion of the excessive amount of munitions that Denham has loaded onto the ship; the mention of "gas grenades," in particular, seems to allude fleetingly to World War I. Denham's group, in the tradition of the prehistoric story, is a technologically savvy team, and Driscoll, pursuing Kong with only a knife, stripped, so to speak, of his technology, is also in the Burroughs' lineage—it is as if modern man must prove his superiority in primitive terms before he can reap the benefits of his technology. Also, at least initially, Kong, the King, is presented as a tyrant who exacts merciless tribute; he holds the natives in a reign of terror and, in this, is like the Weiroo, and the Mahars of Pellucidar. On the other hand, he is also akin biologically to the various, partly sentient ape-men that populate many prehistoric tales. Although nothing is made of it, the technologically superior whites do liberate the human natives. This is not the crux of *King Kong,* nor is it a theme that receives any emphasis. Yet one can still see submerged in *Kong* the structural elements of the species liberation plot.

Kong generates action much in the manner of Burroughs. The second part of the film is organized around two abductions of Ann Darrow by a nonhuman, eventually followed by two rescues. Kong performs the function of the tyrannical, nonhuman races à la Burroughs. Also, Kong seems to be a race of one, which effectively makes that race, like the Weiroos, entirely male. *Son of Kong* (1933), aside from being an occasion of lewd jokes and speculation, may, in part, seem so misconceived because it tampers with the implied myth of the earlier film—that King Kong is absolutely singular and unique, the only one of his kind, profoundly alone, and ultimately a fit object of pathos for that reason—like the Frankenstein monster. Of course, the fundamental structural device of abduction/rescue in Kong diverges from its use in Burroughs because first, rather than follow the exploits of the rescuer, *Kong* stresses the *heroic* exploits of the abductor; and second, the virtues of the abductor—not only courage but gentleness, and certain ingratiating anthropomorphic traits, including childlikeness, confusion, and even timorousness as regards Darrow—overshadow the abductor's earlier identification as a cruel tyrant, as a force of pure evil. Nevertheless, large chunks of the film derive their narrative coherence, their pretext and resolution, from the abduction/rescue structure whose internal logic resembles the relation of a question to an answer.

Moreover, *Kong*'s primary method of filling in the actions that transpire between pretexts and resolutions—its plot complications, in other words—is also straight Burroughs: viz., a series of rough-and-tumble confrontations, hair-raising battles between Kong and various other contestants, often undertaken to protect the heroine. These are very repetitive and to hold our interest they depend to a large extent on how inventive the narrative is in finding more and more outrageous sparring partners for *Kong*. And, of course, *King Kong* is quite amazing in this regard.

But perhaps *King Kong*'s most important debt to Burroughs is its tendency to mold the prehistoric tale in such a way that it suggests itself as an exemplification of a Social Darwinist view of our society. In Burroughs, Caspak and Pellucidar are literalizations of Social Darwinist metaphors as applied to politics. Burroughs' American readers could have assimilated his imagery unblinkingly; they had already been accustomed for decades to hearing politicians, clergymen, and popular lecturers, like Edward Livingston Youmans, invoke Darwinian rhetoric to describe civil society.[5] *King Kong* does not refer its Darwinian imagery to politics; yet its portrait of ill-tempered monsters struggling tooth-and-claw for survival does relate to another aspect of society—the economy. The third scene of the film—Denham's search for a starlet (even if he has to marry one)—makes this reference unavoidable. Denham sadly peruses a queue of women at a soup kitchen; he saves Darrow, caught pilfering fruit, from the law, and the Depression looms large in their subsequent discussion, which not only dwells on her unemployment but which intentionally (although, finally, fallaciously) suggests that Denham's proposition is just that, an offer of prostitution or white slavery to a woman at the mercy of a depressed economy. For all the ensuing sound and fury, it is hard to shake the memory of these early scenes; the detail makes the Depression an unforgettable character in *King Kong*. Also, the plot of *King Kong* is subtended by the same fantasy that one finds in early 1930s musicals; like *Forty-Second Street*, *Gold Diggers of 1933*, and *Footlight Parade* (all 1933), *Kong* holds out the prospect that a show, in this case a movie, is just the panacea the characters need to chase the Depression away. The presence of the Depression in the film thus leads one to connect the jungle imagery to the economy. That is, the breakdown of the marketplace brings up the issue of the marketplace, which, in *Kong*, is juxtaposed with (later collapsed into) the prehistoric world. And the marketplace, as represented by that great emporium, New York City, is identified with the jungle.

The use of the Social Darwinist idiom to describe the economy and the operation of the marketplace was established by the late nineteenth century. Darwinian metaphors provided an attractive argot for robber barons.[6] Nor is Social Darwinism simply the language of financial giants. Small businessmen and free agents still attempt to glowingly excuse, at least to themselves, mercantile improprieties on the grounds that in the jungle anything goes; surviving is what counts.

At the same time, Darwinian metaphors could and can still be used pejoratively; business and the marketplace may be excoriated as a jungle or as ruled by the law of the jungle, as it was by Upton Sinclair in 1906. Of course, Protestant America had a pre-Darwinian prototype for condemning business via bestial imagery in Martin Luther's maledictions on usurers, who, he said, "oppress and ruin the small merchants, as the pike the little fish in the water, just as though they were lords over God's creatures and free from all the laws of faith and love." And another negative, although not morally strident, use of the jungle metaphor is that of an anxious, dispirited mood which accepts the competitiveness, heartlessness, and treacherousness of the marketplace as a necessary but bitter fact of life. In this sense the jungle metaphor is a sign of resignation that acquiesces to the pronouncements of the robber barons not with jubilance but with a twinge of lost innocence. The jungle is perilous, exhausting, with potential tragedy on every side (not only for others but for oneself), a battlefield on which the bottom line, survival, is the most one holds out for. This possibility of the jungle/business metaphor is, of course, most serviceable in times of economic crisis when "survival" comes to feel like a characterization of everyday life. That this jungle/business metaphor can be either honorific or horrific is less important for an initial understanding of *King Kong* than the fact that the Darwinian jungle was a readily accepted figure for the market in the culture in which *Kong* was made. For this is what makes the otherwise oxymoronic combination of the prehistoric jungle and the entrepot of world capitalism so singularly appropriate. Kong carries the battle for survival, with all its prehistoric trappings, to the heart of New York.

The leisurely pace of the first part of *King Kong*—in other words, the ocean voyage—is actually quite deceptive. A great deal of thematic work is being done throughout this section, even if the narrative seems to be merely lolling about. From the very first scene, with the guard and the theatrical agent, the audience's expectations are thrown in gear. At first, this is done through unexplained incongruity. The watchman says the voyage is crazy, that Denham is crazy, and that the crew is three times larger than the ship requires. Why? Our questions are intensified in the very next scene. More unexplained incongruities are introduced in the captain's cabin when, in the course of discussions about insurance, possible government inspection and Denham's inability to acquire a starlet, we learn that these difficulties stem from the fact that the ship is carrying enough ammunition and gas bombs to

King Kong, *1933. The giant ape battles for survival in the jungle of New York City.*
From the editors' collection.

blow up the harbor, and that even the skipper doesn't know where
they're headed. Denham's secrecy is used to explain why Denham
must find his own actress but the secret itself remains unexplained,
pulling the audience ahead along an arc of anticipation. Throughout
the introduction, the theme of the secret continues, the careful escala-
tion of the mystery distributed in such a way as to periodically revital-
ize our flagging interest by reminding us of the secret that the film
promises to reveal. At first, Denham is coyly vague about the secret;
Darrow asks their destination and he liltingly says, "a long way off."
Then he becomes evasive: when Driscoll asks what they're going to do
when they reach the island, Denham retorts, "How do I know, I'm not
a fortune teller." At the same time, Denham suggests that he knows
more than he cares to say. He keeps harping on the "Beauty and the
Beast" slogan; indeed, he even remarks to himself, at one point, "I'm
going right into a theme song here." The allusion to "Beauty and the
Beast" supplies only a hazy forecast of things to come but it gives us
just enough information to prime expectancies.

Denham ups the ante somewhat in the scene where he discloses the location of the island. It is as if his previous vagueness were getting a little threadbare, and, to remedy the problem, a few more details are added to tweak the spectator. The information is, however, still vague and only suggestive. Map in hand, he ominously points to the wall of the island: "The natives keep that wall in repair. They need it." Somewhat elliptically, he moves to the subject of why the natives need the wall by asking if the captain has ever heard of Kong. The captain thinks it's a native god and Denham defines Kong teasingly and obscurely, mostly through negation: "Well, anyway, neither beast nor man. Something monstrous, all-powerful, still living, still holding that island in a grip of deadly fear," and "I tell you there's something on that island that no white man has ever seen." When Driscoll sarcastically observes that Kong might not like his picture taken, Denham has a smart-aleck answer prepared, one he delivers with know-it-all nonchalance: "Well, now you know why I brought along those cases of gas bombs." This partially answers one of our earlier questions but at the price of an even greater mystery: what in the world could Kong be?

This mystery is first raised in the dialogue but is then accentuated visually in the next scene, the screen/scream test. This sequence is virtually a template from which much of the rest of the film will be struck. Darrow, in medium shot, stands in a satiny medieval outfit, her eyes downcast, fiddling with her fingers like Lillian Gish. Following Denham's offscreen directions, she, prophetically, looks higher and higher, and finally starts screeching repeatedly, at the timbre that has earned Fay Wray a reputation for having the greatest lungs in the history of film. This one shot is the germ of numerous similar ones in the second half of the film, although at this point we don't realize that Denham, figuratively speaking, is shooting much of the film to be. Denham's directions heighten our curiosity but supply us only with affect rather than details. He says, "Now you look higher. Still higher. Now you see it. You're amazed. Your eyes open wider. It's horrible, Ann, but you can't look away. There's no chance for you, Ann—no escape. You're helpless, Ann, helpless. There's just one chance. If you can scream—but your throat's paralyzed. Scream, Ann, cry. Perhaps if you didn't see it you could scream. Throw your arms across your face and scream, scream for your life." As the peals of terror still echo in our ears, the camera cuts to Driscoll, who asks our question for us: "What's he think she's really going to see?" Diabolically, the camera dissolves to a low-angle shot of the ship swathed in fog—so we can

barely see anything. Imagery of fog or mist recurs throughout the rest
of the film with grey-miasmic connotations of obscurity, primordial-
ness, fantasy, dreamlikeness, and ghostly presence. At this point in the
film, it coincides with the approach to the island, capping off the theme
of mystery, the major narrative motor thus far, with the fog as a visual
correlative for the unknown, the faintly perceived, the vague outline
wrapped in uncertainty.

The ship approaches Kong's island in a thick fog that marks the
threshold or passageway into a new realm. The pace of the ship seems
slow and gliding. The tone of this imagery, if not downright supernat-
uralist, is that of quiet, pregnant danger, as the adventurers float, virtually blind, into the unseen/unknown. The visual opacity in and of itself
raises apprehensions; the dialogue about what they will see quickens
its banefulness. Asked how he will know the right island when he sees
it, Denham says that it has a mountain shaped like a skull. Death lurks
in this soup. Next, the sense of unknown menace—menace, in large
part, *because* it is unknown—jumps a notch when Denham resolves
the ambiguity of some offscreen sound effects: "It's not breakers, it's
drums." The traditional horror film makes a special moment of the
approach toward unseen danger—for example, the doorways in *Psycho*
(1960) and *The Exorcist* (1973). The threshold, and the unseen/
unthinkable thing beyond it are perhaps the prime, interrelated themes
of the classical horror film. In Kong, the island itself is made into the
object of this anxiety; instead of an unseen chain clanking in the night,
drums beat in the fog; it might be the wind, it might be the breakers.
Instead of preparatory ghost legends, we are told that the island itself
is the image of death.

Another major theme that is broached in the opening sequences is
that of self-advertisement. Through the conceit of the film-within-the-
film, *Kong* constantly informs us about how we are to take it. *Kong*,
more or less, writes its own reviews, telling us what to think about it
as it goes along. Denham's comments about the film he's going to
make, and Denham's remarks about the adventure he's engaged in
rebound, so to speak, from inside the film and stick to *King Kong* itself.
No other film has ever been as self-congratulatory as *Kong*. It is a
swaggering, arrogant film that spends much of its time telling us how
great it is, yet its blustering, gigantic view of itself is not off-putting;
somehow it accords with the circus-exaggerated energy that is its most
distinctive quality. Denham starts the proceedings with, "I'm going to
make the greatest picture in the world. Something that no one has seen

or even heard of. They'll have to think of a lot of new adjectives when I get back." Played by Robert Armstrong with the manner and gusto of a carny barker, Denham convinces Darrow to be his star by saying, "It's money, adventure and fame. It's the thrill of a lifetime." Denham is the epitome of the advertising huckster; his obsession with "Beauty and the Beast" is that of a salesman trying to find a tagline for a new product. What Denham manages to advertise most is King Kong. Arriving at the native ceremony, he reminds us, "Holy mackerel, what a show," while Darrow asks us, "Isn't this exciting?" *Kong* is the quintessential American film—its self-image is so enormous. Denham can only speak in superlatives; Darrow is "the bravest girl"; or, to Capt. Englehorn, "I tell you, this Kong is the biggest thing in the world." It is, of course, very difficult to separate our reactions to Kong and to *King Kong*, a fact that their titular identification only exacerbates. Thus, when Denham abandons the film project for something more ambitious, viz. Kong, it has the effect of praising the movie he (Denham) is in—"We came here to get a motion picture and we found something worth all the motion pictures in the world." Denham hatches the ultimate ad for *King Kong* immediately after he gasses the beast into submission—"in a few months, it will be up in lights on Broadway: *Kong, The Eighth Wonder of the World.*" And, naturally, it is, just as quick as you can say "dissolve."

King Kong is the sort of film that is apt, in current critical parlance, to be designated reflexive. It not only contains the film-within-a-film conceit, but it could be argued that it bares its own devices—the screen test as meta-filmic gesture—and it displays, indirectly, the hysterical cadences and hyperbole of Hollywood advertising. Undoubtedly, the element in *Kong* that most tempts us toward a reflexive interpretation is the fact that so much of it is devoted to the subject of putting on a show. The film begins as the story of a movie and turns into the story of a theatrical. Also, the film-within-a-film conceit turns the native dances into the kind of exotic, ethnic extravaganzas that were popular in the '30s and '40s and date back at least to the Chicago World's Fair, and to the San Francisco Fair of 1893, while the procession leading Darrow to the sacrificial alter strikes the viewer as pure, staged spectacle. The capture of Kong reminds one of the culture hero Frank Buck, whose *Bring 'em Back Alive* was published in 1931; Buck, of course, was famous for supplying zoos and circuses with wild animals for exhibition, and the Kong show at Madison Square Garden is of the nature of a circus feature—one recalls Ringling Brothers Barnum and Bailey's famous gorilla Gargantua, billed as the largest ape in captivity. Also, there is the surge of media hype throughout *King Kong*, and one feels that had Denham completed his own film its potentially prurient content could have turned it into an exploitation vehicle following in the footsteps of Congo Pictures' *Ingagi* (1930), a film that promised "documentary" footage of a woman being sacrificed to an ape.

Yet for all the references to cinema and show business that one can find in *Kong*, it seems mistaken to identify the film as a significant example of reflexivity. Its primary function is not to make us aware of the processes of filmmaking. Rather, the show business topics and allusions function expressively, supplying a mood and an energy, an increment of brashness and excitement and shameless vulgarity. If *Kong* were not so profane in its handling of myth, so boisterous in its self-advertisement, it would not be so perfect a reflector of its time and place. Its celebration of naive, unselfconscious opportunism and of an imagination at once grandiose and shallow, fantastical, and pragmatic, presents a mirror of pre–World War II America, and not an unflattering one. For in its vulgarity—just like an American to crucify a god and then sell tickets to it—there is strength and vitality. And it is that quality or feeling of an admixture of hokum and enthusiasm, superficiality and profound energy, that the movie and show business motifs serve to project. The show business razzmatazz and self-advertising serve to incarnate the *geist* of unsophisticated American dynamism.

The character of Denham is central to this effect. In a number of senses, it is his story. It is Denham who persistently embellishes and editorializes on the action. He is a hustler and a loudmouth, sanctimonious but pragmatic, a P. T. Barnum type. And although, at times, we are meant to resent him—why does he take these risks? why doesn't he leave well enough alone?—he emerges positively because he is driving, manic, an artist/businessman, a dreamer/doer whose conceptions—outlandish, insensitive, sensational in the most trivial way, awesome, enterprising, and empty-headed—consume every ounce of his estimable energy. He is a sincere confidence man, an American *par excellence*, a rapacious innocent. We can view Denham nostalgically, overlooking the horrible things he does, and admire his untroubled, ignorant vitality, his arrogant energy. The show-biz hoopla is as much an end in itself as it is a means for the Denham character. Promotion becomes a way of being-in-the-world, if not introspective, at least intense and active, something that *Kong*'s first audiences could recognize as a source of American pride and a behavioral model, although not one exactly strong on morals. Denham predates *The Ugly American*. He is just an American, aspiring, noisy, crude but alive.

Denham is a combination of two familiar 1930s movie figures: the newspaperman à la *It Happened One Night* (1934) and *The Front Page* (1931) and the show business artiste à la *Twentieth Century* (1934) and myriad backstage musicals. Denham is related to the newspaper image not only because he is a documentary filmmaker of sorts, and, consequently, some kind of purveyor of facts, but because he thinks and talks like a movie newspaperman—for example, the journalists at Madison Square Garden "stumble" on the "Beauty and the Beast" routine and Denham hurriedly okays it as if he'd never heard it before. Denham is also cut from the same cloth as someone like the Jimmy Cagney character in *Footlight Parade*. Both the newspaperman and the show person (whether actor, actress, impresario, or director) in 1930s movie iconography stand for a special race of people who think (and speak) faster than mere mortals. Their diction is slangy, rapid, rhythmic, and sarcastic, and they represent a wiseacre, cynical view of the world that sizes up and sees through things, that lays it on the line with jazzy candor to the everyday types in the films. Show business and journalism, in the movies of the period, at least, give one a special purchase on the truth; they are ways of being-in-the-world that can be described under the rubric of *knowingness*. That Denham combines the iconographic movie authority of the journalist and show person, of course, gives the self-advertisement of *King Kong* all the more weight.

A third major theme is also set in motion in the captain's cabin in New York—that of a defensive attitude toward women, enunciated in almost boyish extremes of contempt. Denham mewls questioningly whether anyone thinks he wants to "haul a woman" along on his adventure and whether there isn't adventure in the world "without a flapper in it." This theme of disdain for women is developed during the ocean voyage. One part of the theme unfolds apace with the budding Driscoll/Darrow romance which begins when Driscoll accidentally cuffs her—Darrow should have known enough to abandon ship right then and there—and then tells her to stay below for the duration of the journey. Initially Driscoll informs Darrow that merely by being around, she causes trouble. With a manifestly adolescent fear of sex, Driscoll says, "You're all right but women can't help being a bother—made that way, I guess." Driscoll's resistance gradually turns to ambivalence and then into infatuation. Finally there is a mutual profession of affection, sealed by a kiss, followed by Darrow's abduction, which sends the story hurtling into the primal jungle of Kong. The latent fear of sexuality, of its being *unleashed*, of its darkness and danger, is more or less confirmed by the plot. Once sexual attraction is acknowledged, the film goes on a Dionysian rampage; the forest functions as a metaphoric primal scene conjoining sex and violence, rape, rage, death, and clawing frenzy, just as our adventuresome boys subconsciously suspected it would from the start.

The second half of the fear-of-sex theme is developed through the "Beauty and the Beast" motif, which holds the rather unlikely proposition that sex is unmanly and unmanning. Denham's favorite metaphor in his "Beauty and the Beast" myth is "going soft." Denham explains to Driscoll that it's "the idea of my picture. A beast was a tough guy. He could lick the world. But when he saw Beauty she got him. He went soft. He forgot his wisdom and the little fellows licked him." When Denham catches wind of the Driscoll/Darrow romance, he equates Driscoll with the beast in his forthcoming film: "You're a pretty tough guy, but if Beauty gets you. . . ." Again, the "going soft" metaphor predominates: "What's the matter, Jack, you going *soft* on me?"—"You have gone soft on her, huh?"—and, "I've never seen it fail, some big hardboiled egg gets a look at a pretty face and bang, he cracks up and goes *sappy*." Considering the Driscoll/Kong equation, we can retrospectively hear Driscoll's outraged protest—"think I'm gonna fall for any dame?"—as a baleful prediction, since Kong does take the plunge in the biggest and most lethal way.

After the discussion with the theatrical agent in the captain's cabin, Denham decides to find a leading lady on his own. There is a longshot of Times Square, a fitting choice for a film redolent with show biz and movie imagery. There are dissolves to a cab, then Denham debouching from it, and a cut to what Denham sees—a flashing neon sign, "Women's Home Mission." Denham overhears the best the women can expect here—soup at night, and coffee and sinkers in the morning. The women speak with joking bravado, which amplifies the ruefulness of the scene. As they kid about their lack of basic necessities, the Depression intrudes in a particularly forceful way. Basic necessities also weigh heavily in the next two scenes. Denham pays for the fruit that Darrow attempted to steal, and we get our first view of her opalescently, angelically lit face, looking up, predictably enough. He brings her to a drugstore/coffee shop. The camera pans along the counter, noting the fulsomely packed shelves of goods—everything Darrow needs/wants—and Denham brings her a cup of coffee. She is unemployed and her complete destitution generates its opposite, voiced by Denham: a dream of fortune, riches versus rags. The Depression details of privation anchor and call forth, so to speak, the Depression fantasy of wealth and fame.

In the captain's cabin, Denham attempted to compare the dangers of New York to the dangers a woman might encounter working in his film. The subsequent "Depression" scenes make the dangers of New York apparent—life at the level of economic necessity and powerlessness at the hands of monied males. The invocation of the Depression and unemployment elicits metaphors of the cruel marketplace. Darrow is struggling for existence, for survival. The economic circumstances are of the desperate, competitive variety which the common, pejorative metaphor of "the jungle" describes. The film does not state this metaphor outright at this point, but with these "Depression" scenes, it hovers on the horizon, awaiting the lavish, figurative jungle/city condensation of the second, "island" half.

Darrow's sacrifice on the island bears a number of strong formal relations to Kong's exhibition in New York. Darrow is tribute paid to the local tyrant; Kong is a product to be marketed. Both are exchange commodities. Kong, especially, recalls the imagery of a slave being auctioned. Darrow is presented to Kong as a novelty (remember Denham's racist "Yeah, blondes are scarce around here") just as Kong is presented to New York. Both presentations are preceded by elaborate ceremonies. And the presentations have strong visual correspondences with each other—both have raised platforms, bonds, "crucifixion" imagery, and audiences. The massive gate on the island is matched by the massive curtain in the theatre. The torches on the island become the flashbulbs in New York. If Darrow is a white speck on a dark field, then Kong is a black figure on a white ground. Thematically, in both these rituals, the sacrificial hosts are displaced and thoroughly alienated characters.

The equation of Kong, who is introduced as the ultimate rapist, with Darrow, an archetypal victim, is not as perverse as it first appears. Both are proper objects of Depression pathos. Darrow has been brought to the brink of this fate worse than death by unemployment. Kong is the victim of the modern jungle. I say this not only because Manhattan is a place we are wont to refer to as a jungle but also because it bears certain resemblances to Kong's homeland. Both are islands, a fact about Manhattan that is underlined in one of the shots of the planes taking off from New Jersey. Manhattan, like Skull Island, also once had a barricade at its foot, commemorated as Wall Street. Kong, enslaved by the market and sold for the price of a ticket, is conquered by the modern jungle. His bewilderment at its machinations is palpable in his last moments. He falls as precipitously as the economy had in the world outside the film. By the end of *King Kong*, he garners our sympathy because he is exploited as a commodity, displaced for the sake of business, befuddled, and smashed to a pulp in the modern jungle as the result of the antics of hucksters. Kong is not only the biggest country bumpkin ever to be crushed by the city; he is also a metaphor for the Depression Everyman, lowered in the course of Denham's promotional bid for the show biz pot of gold.

The rescue party reaches the gate just as Kong carries Darrow off. Driscoll, recoiling, catches sight of the beast from behind. The whites split up and a heavily armed platoon trails Kong into the jungle. We get our first view of the primordial world along with this martial-looking rescue squad. In the initial shots, the jungle is in soft focus, grayish in a way that suggests a misty background. The flora dwarfs the men; it's everywhere, huge, enveloping. The forest is primeval and wild enough—in the sense that it is dense—but it is more mysterious than it is physically forbidding. It is soft and seems darkly comfortable, a feeling accentuated by the relaxed jungle march music. If not exactly Edenic, it nevertheless has some seductive power.

The animals in the forest are another matter. First, the rescue party comes upon a grazing stegosaurus, which they polish off handily with their gas grenades. The monster's charge is back-projected in front of the resolute humans. One can't avoid feeling aware of this back-projection—in other words, can't resist some awareness of a screen within a screen—in this scene and many succeeding scenes. Despite Willis O'Brien's skill, the space of many of the shots sporting battling, back-projected behemoths in the background and tiny humans in the foreground seems curiously disjunct. The monsters inhabit tangibly different spatial zones than the humans. They appear, at times, like visions, imbued with an aura of irreality, which, in the long run, works in Kong's favor as yet another dimension of dreamlikeness.

The rescue party loses its mastery of the jungle quickly. They stay on Kong's heels until they reach a steamy swamp. They hear Kong sloshing across but cannot see through the fog. The jungle has suddenly become less inviting. The thick mist reminds one of the impenetrable haze that surrounded the island. The swamp is desolate and murky, the shoreline forebodingly strewn with broken logs. Like the earlier fog, this mist is also a threshold, the entry into the real terrors of the island. As the tiny raft poles across the water in a grey long shot, the theme of invisible menace oozes quietly from the image. The sea serpent one might have anticipated earlier appears: a brontosaurus rises slowly from the milky slime, water dripping from its jaws almost obscenely. The brontosaurus provokes the same kind of terror as the denizens of the deep in such films as *The Creature from the Black Lagoon* (1954), *Jaws* (1975), and *Shock Waves* (1977). It stalks its earthbound prey under a watery cloak of invisibility. It is most fearsome when it disappears; it can strike from any direction. From this point on in *King Kong*, danger can come from anywhere.

After overturning the raft, the brontosaurus chases the crew ashore, periodically chewing their heads and casting the bodies aside like play soldiers. The dinosaur's gait is noticeably abrupt and jerky, a characteristic of O'Brien's animation technique inherited by his epigone Ray Harryhausen and still apparent in the fantastical beings of *Clash of the Titans* (1981).[7] However, the visible unnaturalness of the monsters does not make them any less persuasive. Rather, it accents their otherness, a more appropriate effect for this type of film than a smoother, flowing naturalism would offer. When the cinematic seams show in *King Kong*, they fortuitously fit the overall expressive scheme of the film. The deviations from a norm of convincing realism in the special effects do not distract. We are, of course, aware of them, but integrate them as elements of the overarching strangeness of the film's fictional world.

The rescue party emerges from the twilight, dreamlike swamp into a nightmare, discovering that the island is nothing so much as a treasury of phobias. Giant snakes curl underfoot and dinosaurs swoop from the sky. Men are decapitated, eaten, crushed, hurled, and dropped from deadly heights, not to mention what the creatures of the island do to each other. Kong is strangled, pecked, burnt, gassed, stabbed, slashed, speared, and machine-gunned. The dazzling range of brutality in *King Kong* as well as the scale of the carnage make it quite a ferocious film. But its ferocity is as much a function of its pacing as it is of its individually brutal sequences. From the swamp onward, the narrative is basically a relentless series of fierce battles with few lulls in between. And these battles are basically stations amid three different chases. The longest pause between violent actions is Kong's unveiling in New York. Most of the rest of the dialogue sets up functionally and efficiently for the next (action-packed) scene: no sooner does Driscoll vow that Kong will never get Darrow again than we hear Kong's resounding leitmotif on the soundtrack; a split second after the radio announces that Kong is on the Empire State Building, Driscoll recites his plane plan, and then we dissolve to the airfield. The story moves breathlessly in a series of flabbergasting adventures paced at a velocity that has few if any rivals. From the abduction on, the narrative, often preceded and ably fleshed out by the subliminally informative leitmotifs, skyrockets ahead (again like a dream) with little or no time for explanatory exposition—so what are these battling dinosaurs doing here in this day and age? The intensity of each fray on its own is raised exponentially by their tight conjunction along the pullulating trunk of the narrative. If the studied conflicts of prehistoric beasts define the world of *King Kong* in terms of the law of the primeval jungle, then the pacing of the film implies that the battle for survival is ceaseless, uninterrupted, and without quarter.

What little time is spent on character nuance in the second half of the film is given over to Kong. At first, he is simply grisly, arriving offscreen in order to allow time for the vague suggestions we've heard previously to come to a boil. In the intentionally darkened American prints,[8] we see his silvery outline, and his eyes and teeth pop out of the blackness like the front of a car at night. Kong looks something like the devil in Gustav Doré's illustrations for Dante's *Inferno* (and in unexpurgated prints of the film, he munches on humans just as Dante's demon snacks on Judas). Initially, Kong's glistening white maw is the most striking thing about him in his first close-up, but the camera quickly moves in on his eyes; it is hard to tell whether the rapidity of the camera movement is meant to register Darrow's shock at first seeing Kong or vice-versa. This is the first step in Kong's anthropomorphization.

Kong growls at the natives and pounds his chest to assert his majesty. But most of the scene is spent revealing other attributes of Kong. His reaction to Darrow is questioning and quizzical. Rather than tearing her off the altar, he undoes the bonds like an awkward child with a delicate toy. You want to say he's gentle, in his clumsy way. He picks her up with two hands—carefully?—and he looks like a delighted though slightly confused kid with a doll. This image, Kong as child, is the film's first lever on the audience's sympathies toward Kong, its first appeal for an endorsement. The image is used later for comic effect. Driscoll stabs Kong in the finger and the big bruiser sits like one gigantic lump of a crybaby trying to find the pin prick. The mood shift involved in this scene is quite radical since this spate of comedy comes right after one of the most violent and harrowing incidents in the film, the sequence where Kong rolls the rescue party off the log bridge. In a matter of seconds, the film moves from Kong at his most vicious and threatening, a mountain of thundering anger, to Kong playing cat-and-mouse like a curious infant with Driscoll in the cave. The child image of Kong also grounds his adoring attitude to Darrow—Kong seems just the right age for a case of puppy (ape?) love. And, out of necessity, Kong's passion is pregenital, restricted to adolescent petting, stroking, and sniffing.

Kong's heroic stature is developed in his battles with the island's dinosaurs. Through these contests, we come to regard Kong as Darrow's protector. While Kong is nursing his finger, Darrow is beset by a Tyrannosaurus Rex. She unfurls a volley of bloodcurdling screams. Kong rouses and there is a shot of him leaping over a fallen log—the animation is done in the style of countless movie heroes "coming to the rescue." Kong and the dinosaur circle each other before the clutch. Kong's manner of fighting is more than simply anthropomorphic; it is undeniably Anglo-Saxon. Kong lobs roundhouse punches at the reptile as well as slapping a headlock on the beast and flipping it. Willis O'Brien's experience as a sports cartoonist and his early animated films of clay boxers undoubtedly come into play here. Admittedly, Kong bites the Tyrannosaurus Rex and, in the end, cracks its jaws apart. Nevertheless, Kong's generally humanized, "Americanized" fighting style invites us to side with him, whereas the reptile, who only kicks, scratches, and bites, is clearly the very image of a "dirty fighter." Kong comes off as a gentleman and a sportsman compared with the dinosaur.

Kong goes on to defend Darrow from the snake and the pterodactyl. If Kong is childlike in some cases, he is a child's fantasy of a male mate, a muscular superhero for whom sexual relations are a series of strenuous exercises in which the big fella (Superman, Tarzan) snatches his beloved from the jaws of death. Perhaps the reason why Kong postulates a sexually impossible liaison is that its reference is not to adult sexual relations but to a son's overweening affection for his mother. Darrow is Kong's bride since every son wants to marry his mother, and their life together is as any twelve-year-old might imagine—he protects her and vanquishes all the enemies. Kong is as big as the island is egocentrically his; he is the king, the head of a monarchy, the easiest form of government for a young child to understand. Kong is the king a child might wish to be or fantasize that he is.

At the same time, *King Kong* is self-pitying. Darrow never stops screaming, no matter how many lizards Kong stomps. One function of this shrieking obbligato is to give the film a sense of unrelenting horror; Darrow never lets us forget how ghastly the situation is. But the screams also become significant as a rejection of Kong. Kong comes to symbolize, through magnification, the child's feelings of ugliness, and Kong embodies the fantasy that the ugliness is unjustly held against him despite the (contradictory) fact that he is transpicuously noble. And there is Driscoll, the miniature father figure who will win the woman back, although Kong is stronger and greater.

One might think that a better interpretation of the film would see Driscoll as the son-figure and Kong as the tyrannical father, outfoxed by his cunning, much smaller opponent. But this does not square with either the childlike image of Kong in the film nor with the pathos of the ending. Kong's size stands for a child's perception of himself as an emotional giant and an emotional powerhouse. Kong clutches the small white Darrow as the "motherly" Brobdingnagian monkey does Gulliver in the illustrations of Book II of Swift's masterpiece, by such as Granville and Pierre Bailly. Yet despite Kong's proportions and the possible iconographic reference, Kong is not a domineering parent but the adoring, rejected son. That he does not understand Darrow marks him not only as an object of pathos, but as an uncomprehending babe in the woods.

The portrayal of Kong as a child-lover provides the psychological foundation of Kong's most significant attribute, his rage. Above all else, it is the uncontained and uncontainable quality of Kong's fury—as he tears apart the native village and, later, midtown Manhattan—that rivets us to our seats. Nothing can hold Kong, not even chains of chrome steel. Nothing can halt him, not even the gigantic gate on Skull Island. When his beloved is filched, he goes on a rampage, tossing midget humans to and fro. His is the terrible rage of the child frustrated—frustrated when the mother-figure Darrow is taken away. If the diminutive humans stand for the child's contempt for adults, then the gargantuan scale of Kong is the objective correlative of the infantile belief in the omnipotence of the will. The film seduces us by rehearsing a fantasy. The absent mother, according to the fiction, *has been stolen*, and the fictional creature, Kong, is physically capable of wreaking the apocalyptic havoc that the ordinary child can only imagine. Anyone blocking Kong's path becomes a weightless beanbag, effortlessly crumpled, hurled, or torn limb from limb. Kong-as-god can be glossed as an infantile delusion of grandeur.

Although the mechanics of this imagery are primarily psychological, it is also possible to discern an associated social fantasy telescoped in the action. Darrow-as-mother represents a plenitude that has been taken from Kong which is analogous to the well-being and promise of prosperity that the Depression had snatched from the audience. Perhaps it was the pressure of the Depression that made the audience susceptible to the regressive myth in *Kong*. In any case, that myth itself can be turned on the Depression as an emotional organizing device. Denied Darrow, denied plenitude, Kong's rage appears boundless. He becomes a one-ape revolution, momentarily venting the pent-up fury and indignation of a frustrated audience, their feelings of powerlessness relieved in an orgy of power, as if indulging infantile flights of pandemonium were their only option.

But in the end, Kong's power is limited. As with the final Oedipal tragedy, Kong cannot possess the mother. Forces he cannot understand destroy him. If our commiseration with Kong is more maudlin than for Oedipus, it may be because the emotions *Kong* stirs up are more regressive. *Kong* is a cautionary tale. But like many cautionary tales, *Kong* offers two bonuses along with its admonition. First, before we are warned of the dangers of an infantile worldview, that view and our affection for it are given a run for its money—two islands shattered by the scorned child. And second, even death, the putative warning, has lost its unattractiveness since Kong's fall, because of its combination of inevitability, alienation, hopelessness, and bravery, becomes admirable if not glorious.

I have already noted that the events on Skull Island and those in New York bear strong similarities to each other: the sacrifice/the show; the snake/the subway; the mountain/the skyscraper; the pterodactyl/the bi-planes. Other correspondences include: Kong's breaking down the gate/Kong's breaking down the theater wall; rolling the crew off the log/tumbling the passengers in the subway; punching reptiles/punching the subway. Kong tosses native huts into the air, they sail upward offscreen, and then come crashing back into the frame. Exactly the same technique is employed when Kong demolishes the canopy, torn off a building facade in New York. Kong reaches into a cave carved into a vertiginous precipice to ferret out the obstreperous Driscoll; just as Darrow complains that with Kong loose in New York, it's like a horrible (recurring?) dream—"It's like being back on the island again"— Kong's paw smashes through the hotel window, clobbers Driscoll, and grabs Darrow. The crew's fall—stated with excruciating thuds—is echoed by Kong's plummet from the top of the Empire State Building which, in turn, strongly contrasts with the lovers' leap to freedom from the promontory (Driscoll does fall for a woman, although quite successfully). The repetition of musical leitmotifs also serves to identify disparate places on the two islands. For example, the same musical theme is played both when Kong examines Darrow in his lair and at the pinnacle of the Empire State Building, thereby equating the sites of the highpoints of Kong's bewilderment. Throughout the second half of Kong, a feeling of *déjà vu* pervades; it is the *déjà vu* of a persistent, haunting nightmare.

The basis of much of the doubling in *Kong* is the idea of transporting a prehistoric creature to civilization where it escapes, a motif derived from Doyle's *The Lost World*. In Doyle's book, this gambit is played for comedy. A baby pterodactyl flaps out of the window of a science convocation and nestles with cathedral-top gargoyles, probably mistaking them for relatives, before winging it back to South America. Willis O'Brien's version of *The Lost World* (1925) raises the dramatic stakes by replacing the pterodactyl with a brontosaurus who tramps disastrously about London before falling into the Thames. Kong is a descendant of *The Lost World*, and the relation between the prehistoric world and the modern world is developed with much greater complexity in *Kong* than in its forebear. Most of the comparisons between the two islands in *Kong* are done stylistically through the repetition of visual and narrative motifs. Furthermore, this equation has particular expressive power because it animates certain pejorative societal metaphors at a time of great economic crisis, and in a way that encourages the audience to see the allegory as a characterization of their adversity that depicts the situation of civil (market) society as immoral and implacable and shows defeat in the modern jungle as tragically heroic.

Kong is not only a cautionary tale as regards psychological matters; it is also a cautionary tale as regards economic behavior. In films like *Little Caesar* (1930) and *Scarface* (1932), pop tragedies with a rise-and-fall rhythm, 1930s audiences were treated to an ethnic warning about the danger of leaving one's place in society for the sake of ambition. As soon as the gangsters don ritzy airs, replete with laughable *nouveau riche* manners, they are headed for their downfall. They are out of their class in more ways than one and they will be brought low. Likewise, once Kong leaves his domain and penetrates the gate, the boundary between nature and culture, he is out of his element and, therefore, doomed. His final bafflement is thick enough to cut with a knife. On one level, *Kong* warns: stay on your own turf or the bastards will drag you down. Life in the modern jungle, exactly because it is a jungle, is precarious, even for a Kong—a piece of perennial American folk wisdom distilled to a higher proof by the experience of the Depression.

Kong is not just a conservative warning about individual behavior, it is also a reflection of an enduring American attitude toward civil society that is readily intensified by conditions of economic anxiety. The prehistoric imagery (especially the clashing dinosaurs) and the condensation of the jungle and the city draft the Darwinian metaphor of the struggle for existence as the sign of modern, competitive, urban (read "economic") life. But in *Kong*, the battle—marked as such by the use of warplanes—does not have the triumphant connotations it had for the robber barons. Rather, it suggests that the city as a jungle is a source of bitterness and sorrow that at the very least reveals regret over the loss of innocence modern civil life entails as well as fear concerning what feels like slim prospects for surviving in such an environment. As a child, I remember my father trying to explain business to me. He wanted to impress me with how difficult, dangerous, and horrible it was. Though at the time neither he nor I was aware of it, his tropes were all Darwinian. I barely understood his lecture beyond gleaning that business was a terrible place and that it was wearing him down. But the reference to jungles, competition, survival, teeth, and claws made me think, irresistibly, that business must be a lot like the world of *King Kong*.

NOTES

1. Specifically, *Journey to the Center of the Earth* is a fictional tour through Lyell's *Principles of Geology* with a touch of John Cleves Symmon's hollow-earth thesis, Charles-Claire Deville's theories of volcanoes, and a strong dose of Cuvier.

2. In the mid-1970s, AIP released two passable adaptations of Burroughs' prehistoric world tales under the titles of *The Land That Time Forgot* (1974) and *At the Earth's Core* (1976).

3. The centrality of the abduction of women is also manifest in Burroughs' Pellucidar series, a total of seven novels, beginning with *At the Earth's Core* (1914), which are also in the prehistoric vein. The fauna of the underground world of Pellucidar has many similarities with Caspak's. Besides various prehistoric species, there are Sagoths (ape-men), humans, and Mahars. The Mahars are superintelligent, winged reptiles who dominate Pellucidar and who kidnap

humans to serve as slaves and for vile rituals as well. The Mahars are as nasty as the Weiroos and perform a similar narrative function. Whereas the Weiroo are all male, the Mahars are all female. As a result of their science, they have learned to reproduce without males by using a secret formula. When a surface-side human hero, a savior-from-above figure, steals that formula, the Mahars literally become an endangered species.

The Mahars are virtually emotionless, cruel, highly intellectual and hypnotic, like many 1950s sci-fi aliens who, in turn, bear strong resemblances to certain earlier comic book, pulp fiction, and movie portraits of Nazis (and then Communists). The Mahars are also political tyrants, a protomaster race, who view humans suspiciously as potential threats. In *At the Earth's Core* and *Pellucidar* (1915), the surface-side human heroes (using their superior knowledge and technology) mount what we would call a war of national liberation which, given the prehistoric setting, is portrayed as a matter of species liberation in which the Mahars face extinction if the humans are the fittest. There is a long tradition of political allegory in lost world and Atlantean tales, both in the earlier satiric tradition and in the later adventure/melodrama strain. In the prehistoric tale à la Burroughs, the saga of a purportedly innate Anglo-Saxon loathing of tyranny is reinforced by biological metaphors which themselves reflect the Social Darwinist idiom that was used at the turn of the century to talk "scientifically" about politics.

4. *Tarzan of the Apes* (1914) shares certain structures with the prehistoric novels, employing abductions/rescues and repetitive confrontation complications, but it is also a more intricately designed and more interesting book than anything in the Caspak or Pellucidar series. This is not the place to explain why this is. However, *Tarzan* does seem worth considering vis-à-vis *King Kong*, since Kong is somewhat of a fusion of two characters in *Tarzan*. Kong is, at first, Terkoz the ape, the abductor of Jane, but gradually he comes to resemble Tarzan, not only because he is a forest god who torments the natives and because he is ostensibly some kind of jungle orphan, but because he defends Ann Darrow in the wilderness as Tarzan defends Jane; though, of course, Kong is not as "civilized" (he can't read) as Tarzan.

5. One index of the popularity of Social Darwinism in the United States was the Spencer fad: from the 1860s to 1903, 368,755 copies of Spencer's works were sold in America, quite a heady turnover for sociological tomes in the nineteenth century. Social Darwinism was enough a part of the American vernacular for discussing politics that Burroughs' virtual allegorization of it was accommodated unflinchingly.

6. For some examples, consider James J. Hill, "The fortunes of the railroad companies are determined by the law of the survival of the fittest"; John D. Rockefeller, "The growth of large business is merely the survival of the fittest. . . ."; Andrew Carnegie, "While the law may sometimes be hard for the individual, it is best for the race because it assures the survival of the fittest in

every department." For these speakers, as for many Social Darwinists, evolutionary metaphors were a means to justify the status quo.

7. Perhaps this is why Harryhausen has felt the need to invent a new fantastic species, the mythological robot of which Minoton in *Sinbad and the Eye of the Tiger* (1977) is a prime example.

8. American prints of *Kong* were darker than British prints in order to avoid the censor's disapproval of streams of visible blood that oozed down the gorilla's chest.

13

The Comic and the Grotesque in James Whale's Frankenstein Films

Syndy M. Conger and Janice R. Welsch

Both the *grotesque* and the *comic* are much discussed terms, and for much the same reason: their discovery in art or life is largely a subjective matter; both depend for their intensity, and even for their existence, on the perceiver. If we find something comical, it is largely because we temporarily become disinterested, spectators whose hearts are momentarily "anesthetized."[1] We distance it by concentrating our attention on the presence of incongruity, eccentricity, infirmity, or illogicality.[2] Similarly, if we find something grotesque, it is because we temporarily become alienated, spectators who feel threatened: we distance it by perceiving it, labeling it an unnatural, even satanic, fusion, distortion, or fragmentation. "The grotesque," as Wolfgang Kayser suggests, "is the estranged world," and one we find quite appalling: it is "an attempt to invoke and subdue the demonic aspects of the world."[3] Students of the grotesque as well as the comic point out the close alliance between the two: both surprise us and both underline life's absurdity. The comic inspires surprise by juxtaposing things seemingly incongruous; the grotesque evokes shock by fusing the seemingly incompatible, by creating a world "in which the realm of inanimate things is no longer separated from those of plants, animals, and human beings, and where the laws of statics, symmetry, and proportion are no longer valid."[4] A descriptive equivalent for the grotesque current in the sixteenth century emphasizes the unsettling dreamlike quality of the grotesque—"*sogni del pittori*" (dreams of painters).[5] The comic, according to Freud, also bears resemblance to the dreamlike.[6]

Although the response to both juxtaposition and fusion may be laughter, the laughter inspired by the grotesque is quite distinct from that produced by the purely comic; the latter may be liberating or therapeutic, but the former is "involuntary and abysmal." The grotesque evokes the realization of a world at once "playful" or "fantastic" and "ominous and sinister," "a world totally different from the familiar one" of the comic muse.[7] Yet because of their close proximity, and because of the subjective factor that frustrates definition, the grotesque and the comic constantly threaten to collapse into one another, the sinister into the silly. Gargoyles may produce shudders or giggles or both; so may Gothic novels or horror films. A major task of the serious artist of the Gothic, then, is to prevent an unplanned comic escape from the chamber of horrors.

Critics intent upon underscoring the serious implications of the novel *Frankenstein, or The Modern Prometheus* (1818) have not been particularly eager to explore the presence of the comic and the grotesque in the text. They have concentrated instead on reading the novel as religious allegory, or as political, philosophical, or feminist protest. Recently, however, Maximilian Novak has explored the relationship between the grotesque and the Gothic and used *Frankenstein* as one example, and Philip Stevick, in his analysis of the novel, has ventured to assert that it is profoundly comical. Novak finds the "'straight black lips' of Frankenstein's monster" reminiscent of the Renaissance woodcut skeleton with its combination of deathly terror and horrible grin. "This," concludes Novak, "is the essence of the grotesque and the essence of the Gothic."[8] In seeming contradistinction to Novak, Stevick believes that the novel *Frankenstein* stands in a great literary tradition, headed by *The Odyssey*, which combines "mythic seriousness . . . and laughter."[9] He focuses, in a sense, on the "horrible grin." As he reads the work, he is caught up in its linguistic claim to high seriousness,[10] but in retrospect its dreamlike qualities—its ineffectual hero, its fragmentary and illogical plot—seem absurd to him.

If Mary Shelley was at all aware of the potential dreamlike absurdity of the Gothic tale, however, she certainly made no visible attempt in her masterpiece to exploit it. The only laughter in the novel is the satanic laughter of the monster mocking Victor's midnight oath to

avenge the death of Elizabeth and others: "I was answered through the
stillness of night by a loud and fiendish laugh. It rung on my ears long
and heavily; the mountains reechoed it, and I felt as if all hell surrounded me with mockery."[11] Moreover, the clearest admission of the
presence of the grotesque in the novel is Victor's initial description of
the monster as "deformed," "ugly," "a mummy," as "a thing such as
even Dante could not have conceived" (52–53). After this scene, the
novel employs a number of traditional techniques to counterbalance, if
not to erase, this grotesque surface. The monster is seen in half light,
in darkness, or from a great distance. Walton first glimpses him
through the arctic mist "at the distance of half a mile; a being which
had the shape of a man, but apparently of gigantic stature, sat in the
sledge and guided the dogs" (17).

If here we are encouraged to grant the creature epic stature, we are
elsewhere invited to admire and even to sympathize with him; and
sympathy, according to Bergson, co-exists uneasily with the comic.[12]
The gigantic creature is given eloquence, intelligence, noble aspirations,
and a keen sensitivity to his outcast status; and when his story inspires
the pity even of Victor, who has hitherto hated him, the reader can
almost forget that the creature is an absurdly grotesque fusion of life
and death, a motley collection of disparate parts ("yellow skin," "lus-
trous black" hair, "pearly" teeth, "watery eyes," "dun white sockets,"
"shriveled complexion," and "straight black lips" [52]). The novel's
close is most effective in diverting attention from the monster's surface
absurdity: "'But soon,' he cried. . . . 'Soon these burning miseries will
be extinct. I shall ascend my funeral pile triumphantly, and exult in the
agony of the torturing flames. The light of that conflagration will fade
away; my ashes will be swept into the sea by winds. My spirit will sleep
in peace.'" (221). His closing remarks allow the monster rhetorically
to erase his monstrosity and bestow on himself a death of a hero.

Seen in this context, the 1931 and 1935 Frankenstein films of James
Whale are full of surprises, especially if we come to them from a recent
reading of the novel. We expect the grotesque to center on the creature;
but instead, we gradually come to realize that the grotesque surrounds
the creator and his associates, particularly his satanic partner Praetorius, and the laboratory scenes. We may not expect to laugh at all since
"there is no doubt that the book is as utterly serious in intent as it is
serious in execution,"[13] or we may expect to laugh only at minor characters "specifically designed as comic relief" because we have learned
that "terror and laughter are near neighbours in our reaction to the

iconography of the cinematic tale of terror."[14] We do laugh at Baron Frankenstein, the burgomaster, and a village gossip, but later, with considerable unease, we also find ourselves laughing at the monster himself, and with the amoral, manipulative Praetorius. Instead of insisting on the story's high seriousness, then, as the novel does, Whale's films openly acknowledge its comic and grotesque potentialities. Whale's striking response invites the viewer, on one level, to reflect on the absurdities and grotesqueries of modern technological society. This level of appeal, of course, Whale shares with such fellow Expressionists as Georg Kaiser, Franz Kafka, Edvard Munch, and F. W. Murnau. On another level, however, the films invite the viewer to reflect, in a way that Mary Shelley's novel does not, on the danger any artist encounters who dares to tell Gothic tales, the danger of having one's tales dismissed as ludicrous. With increasing audacity, and primarily through the character of Praetorius, Whale successfully faces that danger. This level of appeal ties Whale's films into another, older literary tradition of sophisticated and self-conscious Gothic tale-telling, one which begins with Ann Radcliffe and has among its greatest representatives Charles Robert Maturin, Herman Melville, Edgar Allan Poe, and Henry James.

Whale's *Frankenstein* plunges its viewer abruptly into a world of traditional grotesquerie. The graveyard is a visual catalog of objects which Kayser identifies as inherently grotesque: the *skeletal* figure of *death* with its *scythe*, the *vertiginous* angle shot of *hunchback* Fritz's *mad* stare through fence *stakes*, the barren, *twisted* branches behind him. The spectator is confronted immediately with a world at once distorted and sinister which fuses life and death, sanity and madness, and which accentuates fragmentation and dizzying distortions. Moreover, the viewer is frequently reminded of that world thereafter: by the jagged rocks and by the visual juxtaposition of hunchback and hanged man; by the distorted shadows in the crowded medical classroom, and by a skeleton's shadow and a death's head which guard the foot of the classroom stairs; and by the skulls that decorate Dr. Waldman's desk and bookshelf. The one skull on the desk seems to be a fourth partner to the conversation Waldman has with Victor and Elizabeth, and behind them is a row of macabre spectators, death's heads all slightly tilted to one side.

The workshop of the grotesque in *Frankenstein* is, of course, the laboratory of Henry. There mind, machine, and nature's lightning conjoin to animate inert matter in the form of a creature constructed by Henry "from the bodies I took from the graves, from the gallows, anywhere!" to be a walking emblem of the grotesque: unnatural in origin, body, and brain, and despite its initial gentle behavior, too deformed, enormous, and powerful not to seem threatening and sinister. The appearance of the laboratory, its giant instruments reminiscent of Bosch's implements of torture, encourages the conclusion that Henry's creation is actually a satanic parody of the divine creation. The *mise-en-scène* suggests that Henry, despite his protests to the contrary, is involved in "an attempt to invoke and subdue the demonic aspects of the world." Waldman guides viewers towards precisely this conclusion with his repeated warnings: "Mark my words, he will prove dangerous!" (103).

Caught between his absurdly idealistic dream ("Have you never wanted to know what causes the trees to bud? And what changes darkness into light?" [104]) and his grotesque realization of that dream (a fusion of dead limbs, abnormal brain, and electrified heart), Henry becomes the embodiment of the mad scientist, a type that has often been the nexus of comedy, and which was for Shelley a cause for sympathy, but which can, as Kayser suggests, be an experience of the grotesque in one of its most alarming forms: "In the insane person, human nature itself seems to have taken on ominous overtones. Once more it is as if an impersonal force, an alien and inhuman spirit, had entered the soul."[15] The novel does not deny Victor Frankenstein's madness; but it does romanticize it. Walton reports that Victor's "eyes have generally an expression of wildness, and even madness; but there are moments when . . . his whole countenance is lighted up . . . with . . . benevolence and sweetness"; and he concludes, "How can I see so noble a creature destroyed by misery without feeling the most poignant grief?" (20, 22). Even on the night of the creation, at the height of Victor's "enthusiastic madness," his terror, his remorse, his disgust, and his painful dreams all work to evoke our sympathy for, rather than alienation from, this misguided student. Whale, in contrast, seems interested in compelling his viewer to an alienating recognition of Henry's instability. Henry taunts Waldman, his fiancée, and Victor as they interrupt his experiment; he acknowledges his madness, but with a sarcasm that attempts to belie it: "A moment ago you said I was crazy. Tomorrow we'll see about that." We catch no glimpse of melancholy benevolence in his cold stare, and just after his monster begins to move, we must witness Henry's disconcerting ecstasy as he shouts, over and over, "It's alive—it's alive! . . . IT'S ALIVE!" If Whale does not leave us witnesses to this alarming frenzy for long, he has made it grotesque enough to imprint it on our memories.

He rescues us temporarily by immediately cutting to the sunny, flower-filled parlor of Henry's father; Henry's grotesquerie is thus displaced by the comic—but only for a time. Only after the creation scene does Whale introduce the comic. Its deliberate avoidance seems quite apparent in the initial gravedigger's scene—traditionally a comic interlude, like the Yorick scene in *Hamlet*, but in *Frankenstein* the humor is left unexploited. The viewer watches the pudgy, slightly fatuous-looking gravedigger intently but is given little open invitation to laugh. The comic reigns, however, in the house of the Baron Frankenstein. The baron, and his mundane conclusions—"I understand perfectly well . . . huh . . . there is another woman"—also seem reductive, hence comical, in this world thus far so consumed by the grotesque. The burgomaster, whose name Vogel ("bird") might bring a smile to the lips of any German speaker, is his comic foil: he is as formal as the baron is informal, as conservative as the baron is outlandish in dress, and equally preoccupied with the comic festival of marriage. Where the comic prevails in *Frankenstein*, the grotesque, although not altogether banished, is subdued. The baron's dress and his taste in interior decoration (tasseled fez, polka-dotted tie, oversized pipe, baroque chair, the mixture of living and artificial flowers) strike us as at least mildly grotesque, as do the blossoms under glass the baron presents on the wedding day. But his is the fanciful grotesque of seventeenth-century illustrations. The grotesque is temporarily domesticated by the world of the comic.

Once the father leaves his comfortable sitting room and pounds on the door of the castle laboratory with his walking stick, he seems to carry this comic spirit with him. He mocks the negligence of those in the castle for leaving a burning torch on the floor, he forces Victor to rally his spirits with a fatherly insult, and he declares to Waldman his conviction that the whole situation is "tommyrot." He does not know the gravity of his son's experience—Fritz has just been murdered, the monster subdued with an injection—and he administers brandy and vows to take him home and cure his woes as if he believed he were a modern *deus ex machina*.

The grotesque reasserts itself, however, once the monster murders Waldman and escapes the castle of his birth. He invades the world of the pastoral Maria, inferring by his own macabre, unspoken logic (a logic that fails tragically to distinguish between plant and human) that a girl can be tossed into a lake. (Remarkably, Whale conveys the logic—flower, soft and pretty, floats; girl, soft and pretty; therefore, girl will float—solely through the visuals.)[16] Thereafter, he enters the baron's castle, until now the stronghold of the comic, and leaves Elizabeth flung across her bed in Fuseli's memorable nightmare pose. Once the monster overpowers Henry, dragging him to the windmill and hurling him from the balcony, the comic spirit seems permanently banished from the tale. This final scene, with its unabashed apocalyptic resolution, is not simply a reassertion of the traditional grotesque of the graveyard where the story began. With its visual allusion to a Cervantic windmill, it is also a subtle infusion of the comical into the ominous, a new intertwining, and as such looks forward to the complex fusion Whale will achieve in *The Bride of Frankenstein*.

In his sequel to *Frankenstein*, Whale initially treats the comic and the grotesque much as he had in the earlier film. Gothic arches, flickering shadows, open fires, ornate furniture, coffinlike bureaus, stone lions, wooden cupids, and flowers in the Frankenstein castle remind us of Henry and his monster's grotesque world even while Henry seems to be integrating himself into a more socially acceptable relationship. Other settings—the cemetery, the crypt, Henry's laboratory, and the cottage of the hermit who befriends the monster—also suggest this strange, alienated world through the distorting diagonals and shadows of wooden beams, iron grilles, statues, skeletons, and scientific apparatus and the unsettling juxtaposition of nature and religion and the worlds of the living and the dead. Only one brief scene involving a shepherdess visually suggests another world, the pastoral world Henry and Elizabeth retreat to in *Frankenstein* for Henry's recovery after his monster kills Fritz. In *The Bride of Frankenstein* this bright idyllic setting is immediately shattered by the monster's intrusion, and we are returned to the dark, deformed world of the grotesque.

Emphasis on an ominous, fragmented world does not prevent Whale from a traditional use of comic relief and he quickly introduces two characters who, as S. S. Prawer would say, "drain off our laughter."[17] As in *Frankenstein*, one of those characters is a good-natured but self-important and patronizing burgomaster; the other is the opinionated, gossipy, and excitable Minnie, a servant within the Frankenstein household. The burgomaster ceremoniously dismisses the crowd after the burning of the windmill while reminding the villagers of their good fortune in having him to keep them safe—certainly an ironic reminder, given the mob action leading to the monster's entrapment as well as the

The dark, deformed world of the grotesque in The Bride of Frankenstein, *1935.
From the editors' collection.*

audience's anticipation of his reemergence. The burgomaster's age and size compared with the monster's underscore the comic overtones of his claims and reassurances as he wishes the townspeople pleasant dreams, or, in later scenes, unrealistically declares that he is in control.

Minnie is the burgomaster's most vocal challenger, demanding the satisfaction of seeing the monster's roasted remains. Her age seems at odds with her strident and childish petulance. She obstinately stays behind while the burgomaster ushers the other villagers home and is, therefore, one of the first to meet the resurrected monster. She reacts with an unbalancing double-take before running hysterically back to town shouting, "He's alive! The monster is alive!" thus echoing Henry's earlier frenzied exclamation. Though we know she should be believed we are not surprised when Albert the butler dismisses her as an "old fool," her extravagant theatricality provoking laughter as well as easy dismissal. Since she reacts with the exaggeration and abruptness of a mindless marionette, she is difficult to take seriously even when she is responding to a genuine threat. The frilly cap perched precariously atop her head only adds to her comic oddity.

Whale's invitation to laugh at several of his minor characters may not be surprising given the tradition of comic relief within horror works, but what is surprising is the opportunity he gives us to laugh at his monster. We might laugh involuntarily at him in *Frankenstein* because of our unease at seeing such a stiff, mechanical, and oversized creature identified with man, but he is so quickly and unjustly thrust into the role of criminal by Waldman and Frankenstein that we tend to view him primarily with sympathy and pity. His attempts to communicate with Henry and Maria evoke the same response. But in *The Bride of Frankenstein*, during the hermit sequence, Whale presents Henry's ungainly creation as laughable as well as sympathetic. Drawn to the hermit's cottage by his music, the monster is apparently so moved by his host's hospitality that he sheds his first tears. The hermit quickly perceives the monster's needs and gives him food, a place to rest, and most important, friendship. The monster responds enthusiastically, and given only minimal encouragement and coaching, he attempts his first words. Spoken with great effort by the awkward man-monster-child, the words are at once funny and poignant since he categorizes food, wine, and cigars "good" with as much ardor as he designates the hermit ("friend") "good." While he does so he wolfs his food, gulps his wine, and puffs so energetically on his cigar that, although we acknowledge his growing identification with what is human, we are reminded, too, of his grotesquerie. When he sits and listens to the hermit play violin, his huge frame dwarfs the stool that supports him and his arms move awkwardly in time to the music.

Although this image is comical, Whale's juxtaposition of the monster's ugly hulk and visceral reactions with his childlike innocence and his delight in the music elicits more than laughter. Because of the low intelligence of the monster we cannot laugh *with* him; our laughter is directed *at* him here, but his importance within the narrative and our sympathy for him make laughter at his expense uncomfortable. Whale's incorporation of religious symbolism further complicates our response. Earlier, when captured by the villagers, the monster was tied to a large pole and dropped onto a wagon, his position as he was raised above the crowd absurdly recalling Christ's crucifixion. In the scene with the hermit, a crucifix is frequently prominent and the hermit repeatedly expresses his gratitude to God for sending him a companion. Whale seems to ask us to take the budding friendship between monster and hermit seriously, while reminding us at the same time of the impossibility of doing so. He tries simultaneously to draw us closer to the monster with his growing capacity and desire for human identification and contact, and to distance us from him by inviting mockery. Since the "comic and the caricatural fringe of the grotesque"[18] to which Whale brings us conflicts with the sympathy and seriousness evoked, we feel disconcerted, unable to juggle our contrary responses.

Ultimately, the monster's identification with human desire and this association with Christian symbolism make him more grotesque. He is physically disproportioned and unnatural, and his growing consciousness and human activity only accentuate the "fusion of realms" he embodies. He becomes more threatening, more estranged, since he fits nowhere within the natural order. His physical abnormality may no longer seem sinister because of our growing familiarity with it and because of the sympathy the monster elicits, but in *The Bride of Frankenstein* the monster is actually more hideously deformed than in *Frankenstein*. The burns he has suffered intensify his monstrosity. When he resurrects himself from the well of the burnt windmill, he immediately kills the first people he sees, a solitary owl[19] the appropriate witness to the ominous events. Later he is captured and shackled to a thronelike chair on a raised platform within the village prison, further isolating him from society. He frees himself through rage and brute strength and resumes his search for a haven, finding it briefly with the hermit. When his bond with the hermit is shattered, the monster aligns himself with the dead and strikes his own fatal bargain with the demonic Praetorius.

Introduced in an early sequence, Praetorius controls the monster and the hero, the events and the unsettling comico-grotesque tone of *The Bride of Frankenstein*. His first appearance is heralded by an hallucinatory image of death that Elizabeth sees as she tries to dissuade Henry from looking further for the "secret God is so jealous of . . . the secret of eternal life." Praetorius's knock mingles with Elizabeth's hysterical laughter just when she collapses in fear after recounting a dream, a dream so powerful she relives it. She sees "a figure like death . . . reaching out for" Henry and points in the direction from which Praetorius will soon make his entry. She screams, "It's coming for you here! Henry! Henry! Henry." Whale cuts to Praetorius, his dark, sinister figure framed by bare, twisted branches and animated by his wildly blown black cape, before showing Minnie reluctantly scurrying to the door in answer to his knock. Praetorius's imposing presence and hyp-

notizing stare gain him entry despite Minnie's protests. As the door
opens the doctor's gaunt face with its piercing eyes gradually emerges
from the darkness and continues to compel Minnie. Shadows underscore both figures as Praetorius follows the maid to Henry's room.
Disregarding Minnie's injunction to remain at the end of the hall,
Praetorius instantly appears when Minnie announces him, a huge
shadow of his figure and a musical crescendo effectively punctuating
his sinister appearance. He promptly apologizes for his intrusion, bows
to Elizabeth, and helps Henry complete his introduction by volunteer-
ing the information that he "was booted out" of the university for
"knowing too much." When Elizabeth reminds him that Henry has
been ill and should not be disturbed, Praetorius assures her he is a doctor. Despite their gentility, the exchange presages the opposition
between them, an opposition based on Elizabeth's concern for Henry's
health and her desire that he return to his traditional role within society and Praetorius's disregard of the established social order.

After effecting Elizabeth's dismissal and ignoring Henry's anguish
and anger, Praetorius skillfully rekindles Henry's interest in the act of
creation. Praetorius's coolness and persistence in the face of Henry's
moral and physical distress, coupled with the rigidity and disdain
apparent beneath his barely civil response to Elizabeth, intimate Praetorius's estrangement from society as well as his unswerving determination. The intelligence and calculation with which he pursues his goals
make him particularly dangerous, especially since he is not hampered
by a conscience. He makes this clear again and again, sometimes with
great seriousness, at other times with levity, as when he toasts a "new
world of gods and monsters" before taking his homunculi from their
coffinlike box and displaying them for Henry.

The viewer is suspended between laughter and alarm as a grim-faced
Praetorius opens his miniature coffin and unveils and then wryly introduces his creatures one by one: a king gnawing on a drumstick, a chat-
tering queen, a disgruntled archbishop, a ballerina who dances to
Mendelsohn's "Spring Song," a preening mermaid, and a devil with
whom Praetorius particularly identifies. Charming as these miniatures
may seem, Kayser would quickly remind us that they are all technically
grotesques: they break the laws of proportion; they fuse the realms of
human and animal, land and sea, life and death; they link together the
natural (human body) and the unnatural (existence under glass); and
two specifically invoke the demonic, the replica of a Mephisthophelean
satan and the figure of the king, unmistakably reminiscent of Henry
VIII, who beheaded his discarded wives.

Frankenstein is properly repelled by Praetorius's show, accusing him of black magic, but the elder scientist is determined to force Henry to see his creations in a more playful light. His introductions are made with aplomb, relish, and wit; and he stresses—indeed, he has himself literally created—the comically infatuated king, the ridiculously disapproving archbishop, and the mundanely conventional mermaid and ballerina. Only in his commentary on the devil do the sinister implications of his experiment begin to surface: "The next one is the very devil. Very bizarre, this little chap. There's a certain resemblance to me, don't you think? Or do I flatter myself? I took very great pains with him. Sometimes I wonder if life would not be much more amusing if we were all devils and no nonsense about angels and being good." These darkly satanic reflections are muffled, however, by Whale's deliberate focus on the lovesick miniking climbing out of his glass enclosure and comically storming the queen's bell jar. When the king is rather unceremoniously picked up by the scruff of his collar and plopped back into his glass cage, the spectator is reminded that all this is Praetorius's show. He is a puppeteer; these are his puppets, as Henry and others will be soon. He is the master artisan and the machinator of these comico-grotesques. They, especially the lovely female creatures, all prefigure the final creation of Praetorius in the film, the bride of the monster: stunning yet repelling in her wooden gestures and expressions and in her electrifying coiffure.

Praetorius again suggests that he and Henry collaborate. They could "leave the charnal house and follow the lead of nature" to create a race. In doing so they would be following the scriptural admonition to "be fruitful and multiply." Praetorius's sophistical advice echoes to some degree Henry's remarks when thinking of his dream to create life: "What a wonderful vision it was. Think of the power—to create man!" The intensity and passion of Henry's articulation bring him to the brink of madness, his mania contrasting dramatically with Praetorius's wry intelligence and humor when speaking of the same desire. Henry's frenzied outburst and his absurd egocentrism, alarming as they are, are ultimately less threatening, less grotesque than Praetorius's because they reflect the seriousness of Henry's presumption and at the same time are readily identified with the ultimately ineffectual ravings of other fictional mad scientists. Praetorius's witty irreverence belies the gravity of his proposal. His casualness in identifying with Satan and death and in asserting his will while nimbly turning scripture to his own use is far more unsettling because of the unexpected mingling of serious matters and cavalier approach.

Praetorius's jocose irreverence is apparent in later scenes, especially when he meets Frankenstein's monster while enjoying a drink and a cigar beside an open coffin in a crypt. Again Whale brings together traditional images of the grotesque: the crypt, coffins, shadows, and dead bodies juxtaposed with religious symbols, the monster, and Praetorius's gallows humor. While the monster hides in the shadows, Praetorius dismisses two murderers hired to help open a coffin and then relaxes as though in the most natural setting. He graces the coffin with candelabra and a skull before unwrapping some food and pouring himself a glass of wine. As he salutes the skull and drinks a toast to "the monster," he laughs the "mocking, cynical . . . involuntary and abysmal laughter" Kayser associates with connoisseurs of the grotesque.[20] If we are appalled by Praetorius's continuing cynical disregard for what society holds sacred, here demonstrated by his studied necrophilia, we nevertheless admire his temerity in greeting the monster when he unexpectedly reveals himself. Soon the two are sharing a smoke while Praetorius amiably and adroitly questions the monster and wins his confidence.

The facility with which Praetorius masters Henry's creature recalls the ease with which he gained entry into Frankenstein's home, secured Elizabeth's dismissal, and aroused Henry's interest in the homunculi. Authoritative and self-assured, Praetorius proceeds with his plan to create a woman, even though Henry is hesitant. With the monster ready to back his genteel requests with force, Praetorius reappears at the Castle Frankenstein and again demands to see Henry alone. He enters on a level above Henry and Elizabeth, asserting himself both through his position and his words. He assumes agreement but is ready for Henry's refusal. Summoning the monster, Praetorius unscrupulously terrorizes Elizabeth and forces Henry to cooperate. When the monster kidnaps Elizabeth, Praetorius leaves no one in doubt about his authority, dramatically smashing a vase to gain attention and then charging Henry's servants "to do nothing and to say nothing of this episode."

Once at work on the second monster, Praetorius, with his cool, dispassionate demeanor, functions on the sidelines and in the background, allowing the more emotional, excitable Henry center stage. Praetorius facilitates Henry's work by sanctioning Ludwig to commit murder in order to provide the fresh heart that Henry needs, by helping to cover up the murder when Henry questions the source of the heart, and by controlling the first monster when he pressures Henry to work harder.

Praetorius controls events up to the moment the Frankenstein monster, rejected by his newly fashioned bride, places his hand on the lever through which he subsequently destroys himself, his bride, and Praetorius. Thus Praetorius, master manipulator and appropriator of supernatural powers, inadvertently brings about his own demise.

That Praetorius is destroyed along with the two manmade monsters is fitting, considering his own monstrousness. His demonic coldness isolates him from normal human relationships and from human values and emotions. Beneath his suave, authoritative manner, his precise logic, and his crisp, clever dialogue is "the very devil," a man apparently bent on revenge and self-vindication through the usurpation of godlike power. In blending the comic with the grotesque in the character and creations of Praetorius, Whale challenges viewers with a complex presentation of the serious amid satanic comedy. That blend is potentially far more unsettling than Henry's mad desire; and therefore, what dictates Henry and Elizabeth's escape and Praetorius's and the monsters' deaths may not simply be Hollywood's penchant for a happy ending. With those deaths audiences can relax in the knowledge that the grotesque, with its threatening nihilism and absurdity, is once more contained, while Henry is reclaimed by the community, its traditional values and sense of order intact.[21]

The faces of Henry and Elizabeth as they embrace and watch the castle crumble and burn, however, suggest that theirs is far from a fairytale happy ending. They, and the spectator with them, have gazed into the grotesqueries of the human imagination, and have come away from the experience subdued, reflective. Whale exerts himself, particularly in his sequel, to allow the viewer the chance to think repeatedly about the thematic implications of this Shelleyan myth. From the film's prologue, with Mary's assertion that her publishers did not understand the moral of her story, to the monster's words in the laboratory just before he pulls the lever, "You stay. You belong dead . . . ," Whale clearly allegorizes the literal and transforms surface absurdity into serious commentary on human ambition, madness, and modern science. Whale's bold exploitation of the comic and the grotesque deftly guides viewer responses, occasionally allowing for well-directed laughter, more often insisting on revulsion. That the film sports with the myth, then, or seems to, should not mislead us. In doing so, it reaffirms its belief not only in the power of this Promethean myth but also in the capacity of the Gothic mode to communicate that power.

NOTES

1. Henri Bergson, "Laughter," in *Comedy*, intro. by Wylie Sypher (Garden City, N.Y.: Doubleday, 1956), 63–64.

2. Wylie Sypher, "The Meanings of Comedy," in *Comedy*, 193–258.

3. Wolfgang Kayser, *The Grotesque in Art and Literature*, trans. Ulrich Weisstein (New York: McGraw-Hill, 1966), 188.

4. Kayser, 21.

5. Kayser, 22.

6. Philip Stevick, "*Frankenstein* and Comedy," in *The Endurance of Frankenstein: Essays on Mary Shelley's Novel*, ed. George Levine and U. C. Knoepflmacher (Berkeley: University of California Press, 1979), 221–30. Cf. Bergson, 87.

7. Kayser, 187. For discussions of the proximity of the comic and the grotesque, see Kayser, 38, 118, and Bergson, esp. 66–79.

8. Maximilian Novak, "The Fiction and the Grotesque," *Novel* 13 (1979): 51.

9. Stevick, 221, 224, 226, 229. *The Endurance of Frankenstein* provides up-to-date sophisticated examples of each of the approaches mentioned.

10. Peter Brooks, "'Godlike Science/Unhallowed Arts': Language, Nature, and Monstrosity," in *The Endurance of Frankenstein*, 205–20.

11. Mary Wollstonecraft Shelley, *Frankenstein, or The Modern Prometheus* (the 1818 text), ed. with variant readings by James Rieger (New York: Bobbs-Merrill, 1974), 200. Page numbers hereafter cited in text.

12. Bergson, 63.

13. Stevick, 221.

14. S. S. Prawer, *Caligari's Children: The Film as Tale of Terror* (New York: Oxford, 1980), 41.

15. Kayser, 184. Cf. Bergson's similar description of the automaton principle in comedy, 67–71, 79–81.

16. The comic potential of this scene is exploited in Mel Brooks' *Young Frankenstein* (1974).

17. Prawer, 41.

18. Kayser, 187.

19. See Kayser, 182, for the relationship of owls to the grotesque.

20. Kayser, 187.

21. For a discussion of this aspect of closure in genre films, see Thomas Sobchack, "Genre Film: A Classical Experience," and Judith Hess, "Genre Films and the Status Quo," in *Film Genre: Theory and Criticism*, ed. Barry K. Grant (Metuchen, N.J.: Scarecrow Press, 1977), 39–52 and 53–61, respectively. The essays are reprinted in *Film Genre Reader III*, ed. Grant (Austin: University of Texas Press, 2003), 103–14 and 42–50, respectively.

14

Film, Society, and Ideas: *Nosferatu* and *Horror of Dracula*

Lane Roth

Bram Stoker's novel *Dracula*, published in 1897, has found various expression in the cinema, notably in the German *Nosferatu, Eine Symphonie des Grauens* (*Nosferatu, a Symphony of Horror*, 1922), and the British *Horror of Dracula* (1958). *Nosferatu* appears to have been the first definitive, feature-length vampire film.[1] *Horror of Dracula* (the U.S. release title of what was billed, simply, as *Dracula* in Britain) was commercially successful enough to spawn a horror film cycle at Hammer studios from the late 1950s through the 1970s. Because the screenplay for the American *Dracula* (1931) was generated not from Stoker's book but from an intervening stage play,[2] *Dracula* will be excluded from the present comparison of *Nosferatu* and *Horror of Dracula*, which are more direct transliterations of the original novel. Discussion will focus on the climax of the storyline, Dracula's destruction, to contrast respective visual styles and depictions of the vampire and his adversary. These observations will in turn be related to each film's underlying philosophy and cultural matrix. In his discussion of novels and film, George Bluestone asserts that "in film, more than in any of the other arts, the signature of social forces is evident in the final work."[3] Identifying these social forces through the analysis of film is cognate to what Rene Wellek and Austin Warren term "the extrinsic

approach to the study of literature."⁴ This study will seek such relationships of correspondence between films and their societies and
ideas.

In Stoker's novel, Dracula is the Undead, a preternatural parasite
who exists by feeding off the blood of the living. Van Helsing is Dracula's nemesis. Both characters represent authority figures by being male,
having venerable titles (Count, Professor), and possessing the wisdom
of maturity. As antagonists, each vies to dominate the situation and
the lives of the other characters. Dracula is ultimately destroyed after
a thrilling outdoor chase and gunfight when a band of heroes, Van Helsing among them, ambushes a gypsy caravan transporting the vampire
in his coffin to Castle Dracula. Just as the approaching twilight signals
the return of the vampire's supernatural powers, the heroes' knives stab
and decapitate Dracula, who instantly crumbles into dust and vanishes.

Stoker's narrative evokes vivid images that have not been faithfully
translated to the cinema. For example, both *Nosferatu* and *Horror of
Dracula* modify Stoker's story by destroying the vampire at dawn
rather than at dusk. Further, the films reverse the place and means of
the vampire's death. Whereas the setting in the novel is natural (the
Borgo Pass) and the agent of destruction is cultural (a band of men),
the setting in *Nosferatu* and *Horror of Dracula* is cultural (interior bedroom, interior library) and the agent of destruction is natural (the sun).
Dawn is an apt substitute for twilight. Both represent transitions
between the dark of night when the monster is powerful and the light
of day when he is helpless. Given the oneiric nature of the film experience itself, however, ending a monster movie story at dawn is metaphoric of the completion of a nightmare, and so can be more reassuring
to the film audience as well as to the fictional characters.⁵ Also, given
the archetypal correlation of visual values (light versus dark) with
moral values (good versus evil), the rising sun symbolizes the ascend-
ance of universal Good which purges the evil vampire.

The dissolution of Dracula is treated very differently in *Nosferatu*
than in *Horror of Dracula*, however, and this difference and its implications will now be explored in some detail. It should be noted that
"Nosferatu" is Romanian for "undead," and that Count Dracula is
renamed Graf Orlok or Nosferatu in the German film. In an abortive
scheme to avoid paying royalties, the filmmakers appropriated Stoker's
property but changed the characters' names as well as the location and
time period of the story. Nosferatu's dissolution is briefly and blood-
lessly depicted in one shot. First, he laterally crosses the screen in

medium shot and becomes transfixed. Then he dissolves out of the image.

This visual treatment owes much to Expressionism, a contemporary movement that flourished in the cinema and the other arts. While the movement is not easily defined, Lotte Eisner explains that "Expressionism constructs its own universe, it does not adapt itself to a world already in existence. ('Every landscape,' Novalis said, 'is the idealized Body of some form of Mind.')"[6] Integral to Expressionism are stylized abstraction and distortion.

Nosferatu differs from most contemporary German Expressionistic films because of its use of natural locations outside the film studio, so that abstraction and distortion are often communicated by specifically cinematic techniques. For example, the forest through which Nosferatu's coach rides appears abstracted from the rest of nature because of its reversal of normal blacks and whites. This distortion was achieved not by artificially constructing or modifying the landscape, but by deforming its image through printing the negative film. That is, the distortion was obtained from the recording process itself. Similarly, to signify the vampire's supernatural speed, the shots of the moving coach as well as a later segment of Nosferatu loading coffins on a wagon were filmed with an undercranked camera.[7] Again, the use of the dissolve to signify Nosferatu's extinction relies entirely on cinematic distortion. These images are Expressionistic because they emphasize the role of the camera, representing a seeing subject, as shaper of perception. In philosophical terms, Nosferatu's reality is mind-dependent and subjective. In its visual surface and underlying philosophy, the film, as will shortly be made clear, is the opposite of the materialistic *Horror of Dracula*.

Unlike in Stoker's novel and later film tradition, the vampire in *Nosferatu* is particularly hideous, with rodentlike teeth and taloned hands, and lacks a Van Helsing to thwart him. While subsequent films were to associate the vampire with the bat, attacking a single victim, *Nosferatu*'s vampire is associated with the rat and the plague, which decimates the population of an entire city. *Nosferatu* is a portrait of moral malignancy on the social, not merely the individual, level. Van Helsing is conspicuously absent from Nosferatu, so that Graf Orlok is unopposed by any male authority figure. Whereas in the novel, the vampire's ultimate demise is effected by male attack, it is achieved by feminine surrender in the film.

The qualities of the vampire, the absence of Van Helsing, and the

Max Schreck as Nosferatu, 1922, a portrait of moral malignancy.
From the editors' collection.

new ending correspond to the cultural matrix of Germany at the time the film was made. Germany in 1921–1922 was politically and economically unstable. Following defeat in World War I and the overthrow of the traditional monarchy, the new Weimar Republic was Germany's first democracy, but many government officials, military leaders, and members of the electorate remained right-wing in reaction to real and imagined threats of Bolshevism and anarchy. Siegfried Kracauer recapitulates the situation: "The Germans obviously held that they had no choice other than the cataclysm of anarchy or a tyrannical regime."[8] What remained robust about the democracy was its freedom of artistic expression. According to Roger Manvell and Heinrich Fraenkel, "the abortive social upheavals manifest during the postwar years in Germany found more permanent outlet in the arts than in politics."[9] The artistic movement that flourished was, fittingly, Expressionism, which was "designed to *get away from actuality* and to satisfy the desire to probe seemingly fundamental truths of human nature and society by presenting them through fantasy and dramatized mysticism."[10]

Expressionism found a new artistic medium in cinema, and horror films like *The Cabinet of Dr. Caligari* (1919), *Der Golem* (1920), and *Nosferatu* were especially popular during the early, unstable days of the Weimar Republic. The German cinema inevitably reflected the unresolved cultural dialectic of tyranny versus chaos. Some films, according to Kracauer, exploited the motif of tyranny, "detailing its crimes and the sufferings it inflicted."[11] Predictably, horror films tended to approach the subject obliquely, so that the tyrant assumed a fantastic disguise and menaced the Germany of a more remote time. Hence the mythical Nosferatu draining German lives is depicted in the safety of the past.

The apparent ineluctability of tyranny to the Germans can be seen in the absence of Professor Van Helsing in *Nosferatu*. With no benign authority figure to challenge the tyrant, the only option the film offers is to witness the vampire tyrant's crimes and to submit to him. Yet good ultimately prevails and evil is destroyed, not by aggressive human action, but by a combination of ritual sacrifice and mystic event. Hutter's wife Ellen (Mina Harker in Stoker's novel) personally resolves to redeem her stricken village according to the prescription she has found in a text about vampire lore: "Only if a chaste woman can fearlessly make him miss the first crowing of the cock will he disintegrate in the light of dawn." Contriving to be alone in her bedroom as a voluntary offering to the vampire, Ellen is inevitably violated, but her submission succeeds in detaining Nosferatu past his curfew. The mystical power of the rising sun then dissolves the evil creature.

In *Nosferatu*, love may be considered more *agape* than eros. The ads for *Horror of Dracula*, by contrast, featured drawings of pneumatic, nightgowned nymphs disarrayed and distressed by a fearsomely fanged, feral fiend, with the caption, "Who will be his bride tonight?" And the film is very much like its advertising. In lieu of the mystical gloom and mist of the silent, black-and-white *Nosferatu*, *Horror of Dracula* exploits sound and color on a wide screen to portray graphic violence and sex. What *Nosferatu* suggests, *Horror of Dracula* gruesomely shows. Outwitted in a violent fight with Van Helsing, Dracula screams in agony as the morning sunlight sears his body, and he is seen in medium and then in close-up shots, suffering through progressive stages of decomposition as the sun rots his body to dust. The vampire's disintegration is no longer created solely by the camera itself, as in *Nosferatu*'s dissolve. Instead, the camera records effects created for it by the makeup department. The distortion originates from outside, rather than from inside, the seeing eye of the camera. The British shift of focus from the seeing subject to the seen object correlates with a new underlying philosophy: where in Nosferatu reality is subjective and mind-dependent, in *Horror of Dracula* reality is matter.

The sensory surface stimuli are related to a new version of vampire lore. In *Horror of Dracula* the vampire emerges from the supernatural-ism associated with the earlier film and the original novel. The new emphasis on recording physical things leads to an emphasis on physical things themselves. Dracula is stripped of his supernatural powers when Van Helsing dismisses the vampire's power of metamorphosis as a "common fallacy." This revision holds true for many Hammer Films sequels, but it is a rupture from the cinematic vampire tradition estab-lished by Universal Studio in 1931, which had Dracula, faithful to Stoker's book, changing shape at will into a bat, a wolf, or a wisp of smoke. Hammer leaves Dracula with only physical power. "Without a doubt, all my characters are human," director Terence Fisher stated in an interview.[12] The vampire's power over his victims is reinterpreted in clinical terms according to Van Helsing's diagnosis "that victims con-sciously detest being dominated by vampirism, but are unable to relin-quish the practice, similar to addiction to drugs."

Unlike the odious vampire in *Nosferatu*, who personifies pestilence and the corruption of tyranny, Christopher Lee's Dracula is well-man-nered and cultured, and looks proverbially tall, dark, and handsome. Decrying vampirism, Van Helsing refers to Dracula as "the perpetrator of this unspeakable evil." Vampirism and evil, in the context of *Horror of Dracula*, are metaphors for subversive sex. Dracula represents "the embodiment of promiscuity," according to Harry Ringel, who con-cludes that "it is fitting that Van Helsing, Dracula's nemesis in the film, is a self-avowed bachelor."[13] Between this antimony of promiscuity and abstinence lie the other Victorian characters. Ringel observes that "aside from Van Helsing, however, nobody *does* anything in *Horror of Dracula*, besides getting rest, advising others to get some rest, or watching those who are resting. Such a world is too ripe for the sort of sexual dalliance which Dracula both embodies and ignites."[14]

The forces of good in opposition to Dracula are similarly divested of magical properties. Sunlight remains fatal to vampires, but is demys-tified when Van Helsing explains that "vampires are allergic to light." Likewise, the preventative power of garlic is attributed to the vampire's being "repelled by odor." Consonant with his clinical metaphors, Van Helsing is here addressed as "Doctor." Reducing what was heretofore magical to medical terms redefines the myth in the material world understandable to the British in the late 1950s. The film's tension arises from Dracula's visual collision with victims who oppose him in gender, value, and texture. Respectively, these can be polarized as male/female, dark/light, opacity/translucence: Dracula is cloaked in black, whereas the women are diaphanously décolleté. Given these conflicts, sex in *Horror of Dracula* is inevitable and expressed, as Carlos Clarens comments, through "a blatant, almost athletic display of sadism and necrophilia."[15]

Sexual dalliance constituted a threat to the status quo of the England of Victoria and of 1958, the release year of *Horror of Dracula*. Alexander Walker recalls that among the major challenges to the British social structure between 1956 and 1958 were increased (a) political disillusion following the Suez crisis, (b) consumerism from intensified TV advertising, (c) potential for social mobility via legislated educational opportunities for the working class, (d) public discussion, stimulated by the Wolfenden Report, of sexual abnormalities, and (e) liberalization, from 1958 on, of film censorship. Walker concludes that "sex came into prominence as part of this release of commercial energy concurrent with political disenchantment."[16] The label "Angry Young Men," generally applied to proletarian critics of British "class traditions and sexual mores,"[17] derived from the successful 1956 stage play, *Look Back in Anger*. According to Walker, it was not until the commercial success three years later of *Room at the Top* (1959) that this social and sexual awareness breached "the diehard conservatism" of the British film industry.[18]

In a sense, however, *Horror of Dracula* preceded this movement as its horrific underside. As a fantastic drama in a plush period setting filmed in color, dealing with the leisure class, *Horror of Dracula* seems contrapuntal—on the surface—to *Room at the Top* and to successive dramas in squalid modern settings filmed in black and white, dealing with working class heroes. Both types of films, however, are similar in their materialistic preoccupation with physical setting as an index of social status. By its implicit criticism of society's ruling class, *Horror of Dracula*'s attitude is congruent with that of *Room at the Top*, released the following year.

The protagonists of these British realistic films are "bitter, brutal, angry, tough . . . [whose] tragedy is usually that their only talent is loving, and society does not reward that kind of talent."[19] If the "Angry Young Men" are lovers who are debilitated by society, Dracula is a lover who debilitates society. He seems to be the only character who is sexually aware, and that is his strength. His female victims are enraptured, not repelled, by his salacious savagery. Certainly the mocking smile on Mina Holmwood's face after she returns from her first tryst with Dracula tells us that her virtuous husband Arthur's affectionate kisses on her forehead are anemic compared to the carnivorous concupiscence of the count. Christopher Lee's portrayal of a virile vampire represents the power of sexual promiscuity in the late 1950s to subvert the traditional British class structure. Although Dracula is an aristocrat, the probable audience composition for *Horror of Dracula* was more working-class than aristocracy, and audience members may have identified him as the hero. If Dracula was merely an unambiguous villain, why is his coffin so archetypally white instead of black?

Revenge is a common motive in *Horror of Dracula*. Jonathan Harker is the initial aggressor who comes to Castle Dracula to kill his employer. Count Dracula, the affable host, has hired Harker to index his books. When Harker stakes Dracula's mistress, then Dracula infects him and sets out to replace his destroyed mate with Harker's fiancée, Lucy Holmwood. Because Van Helsing has destroyed his former ally, the now-vampiric Harker, he is intent on destroying Dracula. Van Helsing is aided by Arthur Holmwood in staking his sister Lucy. Again thwarted, Dracula seeks revenge against Arthur by seducing his wife, Mina. Dracula's motives are thus no worse than his antagonists'. His desire to get out of life what he thinks is rightfully his, all the while frustrated by the established order, is not a marked departure from the desires of the "Angry Young Men."

Robin Wood's recent essay on sexuality in *Nosferatu* and the British remake of *Dracula* (John Badham, 1979) advocates "that it is time for our culture to abandon Dracula and pass beyond him, relinquishing him to social history."[20] The future of such a durable popular cultural artifact, however, is hard to forecast. Wood's prescription could have been written in 1948, when Dracula and his heirs were considered permanently buried by *Abbott and Costello Meet Frankenstein*, to be superseded by the science fiction films of the 1950s. Yet in 1958, *Horror of Dracula* unexpectedly began a new Dracula cycle. That cycle is now ended, and the public attention has again shifted toward the science fiction film. The most recent American variation of the count is *Love at First Bite* (1979), set in contemporary New York City with George Hamilton as the disco Dracula. This spoof would indicate that the Bela Lugosi version of *Dracula* is no longer taken seriously by modern movie audiences. As the lyrics of the song that begins *The Hunger* (1983), a female vampire film, reiterate, "Bela Lugosi's dead." The horrifying vampire that Lugosi portrayed, however, may be merely dormant until some future film incarnation, attuned to current society and ideas, once again revives Count Dracula. Because interrelationships among films, societies, and ideas are complex, and difficult to define or predict, the future of any film genre or subgenre remains speculative.

NOTES

1. For additional information on *Nosferatu*, see Lane Roth, "Dracula Meets the Zeitgeist: *Nosferatu* (1922) as Film Adaptation," *Literature/Film Quarterly* 7, no. 4 (1979): 309–13. For a survey of vampire films, of which hundreds have been produced worldwide, see Ron Borst, "The Vampire in the Cinema: Vampire Film Checklist," *Photon*, no. 19 (n.d.): 25–49; also Borst's "The Vampire Cinema: Additions and Corrections," *Photon*, no. 21 (1971): 24–44. For fuller discussion, see Donald F. Glut, *The Dracula Book* (Metuchen, N.J.: Scarecrow, 1975).

2. The successful stage play written by Hamilton Deane and John L. Balderstone premiered in 1927 in New York City. An earlier version, written by Deane for English audiences, opened in 1924 in Derby and in 1927 in London.

3. George Bluestone, *Novels into Film* (Berkeley: University of California Press, 1966), 35.

4. Rene Wellek and Austin Warren, *Theory of Literature*, 3rd ed. (New York: Harvest, 1977). See especially the introduction to part 3 (73–74), chap. 9 (94–109), and chap. 10 (110–24).

5. But not necessarily so, as *Night of the Living Dead* (1968) subversively demonstrates.

6. Lotte Eisner, *The Haunted Screen: Expressionism in the German Cinema and the Influence of Max Reinhardt*, trans. Roger Greaves (Berkeley: University of California Press, 1969), 153.

7. Movement recorded at an "undercranked" or slower speed will look accelerated when projected at standard speed.

8. Siegfried Kracauer, *From Caligari to Hitler: A Psychological History of the German Film* (Princeton, N.J.. Princeton University Press, 1971), 88.

9. Roger Manvell and Heinrich Fraenkel, *The German Cinema* (New York: Praeger, 1971), 13.

10. Manvell and Fraenkel, 13. Emphasis added.

11. Kracauer, *From Caligari to Hitler*, 77.

12. Quoted in Harry Ringel, "The Horrible Hammer Films of Terence Fisher," *Take One* 3, no. 9 (1973): 11.

13. Ringel, 11.

14. Ringel, 11.

15. Carlos Clarens, *An Illustrated History of the Horror Film* (New York: G. P. Putnam's Sons, 1967), 142.

16. Alexander Walker, *Hollywood UK: The British Film Industry in the Sixties* (New York: Stein and Day, 1974), 40, also 39–44.

17. Walker, 44.

18. Walker, 44–45.

19. Gerald Mast, *A Short History of the Movies* (Indianapolis, Ind.: Pegasus/Bobbs Merrill, 1971), 407.

20. Robin Wood, "Burying the Undead: The Use and Obsolescence of Count Dracula," *Mosaic* 16 (Winter/Spring 1983): 186. Reprinted in *The Dread of Difference: Gender in the Horror Film*, ed. Barry Keith Grant (Austin: University of Texas Press, 1996), 364–78.

15

Ritual, Tension, and Relief: The Terror of *The Tingler*

Mikita Brottman

It has long been a commonplace of horror film criticism, ever since the publication of Robin Wood's "An Introduction to the American Horror Film" in 1979, that the experience of watching a "trashy," low-budget B-movie can be far more profound than those available to the spectators of more "serious" cinema.[1] Those critics and scholars interested in nuanced acting, narrative elegance, and thematic complexity unhesitatingly write off the exploitation films of William Castle as unadulterated schlock—a brand of suspense that is thoroughly unsubtle, relying on a surface facetiousness and tongue-in-cheek aplomb, enlivened by moments of sudden, shrill shock. Yet, at the same time, Castle's movie *The Tingler* has been mentioned by critics, directors, and scholars—including John Waters, Barry Keith Grant, Howard Gensler, Christopher Sharrett, and David Sterritt—as one of the most memorable moviegoing experiences of their youth. An investigation of this paradox will reveal there is more to *The Tingler* than hokum-laden jolts and low-cost gimmicks.

One of the most important aims of film scholarship is to concretize and vivify the symbolic nature of the half-thoughts and semi-awarenesses that the plot of a film makes manifest, however superficial, sporadic, or facetious they may be. Interestingly enough, in an interview with *Cinefantastique* less than two years before his death, Castle remarked on his fascination with contemporary theoretical analyses of his 1950s and '60s horror films, which, as Castle points out with some pleasure, "are being treated with increasing respect, and taken very seriously today at the universities where they study them."[2] He goes on to make some other observations:

> It's a very strange thing. I definitely feel that possibly in my unconscious I was trying to say something. I never expected that they would put under a microscope pictures that I had made in the fifties and sixties and look for hidden meanings. Nevertheless, that is what is happening. . . . And I think about inner meaning, truly, it is possible that deeply buried within my unconscious was the feeling of trying to say something. . . . And I get this from *The Tingler*.[3]

The tendency to take Castle's films seriously is clearly not widespread enough for movie director John Waters, whose retrospective of Castle's work in *American Film* is in part an attack on critics for being slow to elevate "this ultimate eccentric director-producer" to cult status.[4] But, in fact, Waters was behind the times. *Cahiers du Cinéma* had published a brief but serious article about Castle's work by way of obituary in 1977, remarking on some of the ways in which films like *The Tingler* stand as realizations of the spectacular "happening-cinema" conceived by the Futurist movement system of traumatization, "where the spectacle unfolds not only on the screen, but also in the room, with special effects that allowed the audience to be played with like puppets." Comparing Castle's work to that of Italian horror auteur Dario Argento, *Cahiers du Cinéma* praised *The Tingler* for its radical use of color in an otherwise black-and-white film, describing the film as "unfolding at the limits of psychodrama," and "in the popular psychoanalytic style of Tennessee Williams." "For Castle," *Cahiers* rightly concludes, "only the spectacle counted."[5] Although it was obviously intended as no more than a bravura commercial ploy, *The Tingler* is, in fact, a deeply complex and interesting film, and in wiring up his cinema seats with electrical cables, Castle was actually—albeit unknowingly—extending the principles of experimentation with theater, audience, and spectacle initiated by Fillippo Marinetti and his Futurist followers in the late 1920s.

THE ABOMINABLE SHOWMAN

Born in New York City in 1914, William Castle broke into show business at the age of 15, getting a small part in a Broadway show by falsely
representing himself as a nephew of Samuel Goldwyn. He went
through a wide spectrum of acting, producing, and writing jobs before
going to Hollywood at the age of 23. After a transitional period as a
dialogue director, he began directing on his own. The first picture he
directed was *The Chance of a Lifetime*, which, when it first appeared
in 1942, was hailed by *Variety* as "probably the worst directed picture
in the history of motion pictures." But Harry Cohn at Columbia gave
the twenty-nine-year-old Castle another chance. *The Whistler* (1944),
a thriller, was a commercial success, and the respect Castle earned as
the film's director enabled him to pursue a successful career. He
directed dozens of low-budget films, showing some flair for crime and
action situations.

It was not until the late 1950s, however, that Castle really came into
his own by setting himself up as an independent producer, director,
and—most importantly—showman. He specialized in chillers and
schlock-horror films, most of which were panned by critics for "poor
taste," but still fared handsomely at the box office. His most ambitious
and best-known film was his 1968 adaptation of Ira Levin's *Rosemary's
Baby*, which he produced, but wisely left Roman Polanski to direct.
Later in his career, Castle also produced a number of television shows,
portrayed a producer in Hal Ashby's *Shampoo* and a director in John
Schlesinger's *Day of the Locust* (both 1975); he finally died of a heart
attack in 1977, on the set of the film he was producing for MGM.

But the Abominable Showman, or the King of the Bs—as Castle
came to be known at Columbia—is probably best remembered for the
series of low-budget horror films he made between 1958 and 1962, for
it was in these successful but exploitative chillers that the director
formed a personal bond with his audience through a wide series of
feisty, carnival-style gimmicks. Early experiments with widescreen 3-
D features an on-camera appearance (to introduce himself and to prepare the audience for the forthcoming cinematic experience) and
encouraged Castle to play around with various promotional ploys and
exploitation devices that guaranteed his films their box-office success.
"I've modelled my career on P. T. Barnum," he once boasted, and his
influence on the subsequent history of exploitation cinema is undeni-

able. John Waters, himself the proud inventor of Odorama, has referred to Castle as King of the Gimmicks, confessing that "William Castle was my idol."[6]

Castle's most bizarre and ambitious experiment in audience participation was without a doubt the device of Percepto. During all first release screening of *The Tingler*, Castle instructed movie theater managers to wire up small electric motors, similar to handshake buzzers, to a certain number of seats. At a specific point in the movie, a specially planted female stooge would burst into hysterics and have to be carried out by a (fake) nurse in uniform. Moments later, the projectionist would push a button activating the electrical charges on the wired-up seats, allowing certain unfortunate movie spectators to be hit at the base of the spine by a brief electrical jolt.

Like many of Castle's other gimmicks, Percepto did not always function as the director might have anticipated. The most common anecdote, recounted by Castle in his autobiography *Step Right Up!*, involved a cinema whose management, having dutifully installed the Percepto equipment the night before *The Tingler* was supposed to be shown, decided to test the device on a group of older ladies who were watching *The Nun's Story* on the last night of its run, with predictably hysterical results.[7] Waters tells an anecdote about a showing in Philadelphia where one beefy truck driver was so incensed by the Percepto buzzer underneath his chair that he ripped his entire seat from the floor and had to be subdued by five ushers.[8] Other Castle fans remember their suspense being broken by the broadcast announcement that "the Tingler is wanted in the lobby." John Waters describes his experience of *The Tingler* as "the fondest movie-going memory of my youth":

> I went to see it every day. Since, by the time it came to my neighborhood, only about ten random seats were wired, I would run through the theater searching for the magic buzzers. As I sat there experiencing the miracle of Percepto, I realized there could be such a thing as Art in the cinema.[9]

SCREAM! SCREAM FOR YOUR LIVES!

First released in 1959, *The Tingler* features a suave Vincent Price as Dr. Warren Chapin, a research scientist deeply involved in experimentation on the cause and often lethal effects of human fear. Chapin suspects that many people who have died from extreme fear were killed by a parasite that takes shape within the vertebrae—"the tingler"—which can be prevented from materializing only by the victim's screams. However, if the victim is not able to release the tension caused by this fear by screaming, the tingler takes shape and cracks the human spine.

Chapin's lab assistant (and sister-in-law's fiance) Dave Morris (played by Darryl Hickman) catches live dogs and cats for the doctor to use in his experiments on the pathology of human fear, but Chapin is more interested in human subjects. His first victim is his spiteful cheating wife, Isabelle (Patricia Cutts), whom he frightens into unconsciousness at gunpoint. Studying X-rays of her spine, he and Dave discover the bony shape of the tingler emerging from Isabelle's vertebrae. Next, Chapin attempts to experiment on himself by locking himself in his laboratory and injecting himself with 100 micrograms of liquid LSD, recording his hallucinations, and trying desperately not to scream. Skulls and skeletons come to life; he has trouble breathing; the walls close in on him; his tingler emerges, but the doctor finally gives in to his tension and destroys it with a scream.

Eventually, Chapin finds the perfect experimental subject—a paranoid deaf-mute woman (Judith Evelyn) with a morbid terror of blood. With a little unexpected help from her avaricious husband, Olly (Philip Coolidge), the deaf-mute is trapped in her apartment over a silent movie theater and slowly frightened to death by a series of shocks—windows slam suddenly closed; a rocking chair starts rocking of its own accord; a hideously masked stranger appears to pursue her with a hatchet; a beckoning hand emerges from the depths of a blood-filled bathtub (bright red Technicolor in an otherwise black-and-white film); and the woman's death certificate appears on the door of the bathroom cabinet: "Cause of Death: FRIGHT."

Upon determining the reason for the woman's death—that she had indeed died of fear—Chapin is granted permission from the seemingly innocent Olly to perform an important experiment. In the laboratory in his home, the doctor manages to remove the tingler from the body's spine with a pair of forceps, and we are given our first glimpse of its spiny, powerful form—in silhouette only—however, Chapin is operating behind a strategically placed screen. Almost immediately, the tingler attacks Chapin's arm, falling off only when he screams. The tingler (recaptured and picked up gingerly with a pair of forceps) is then placed in a special locked box while Chapin and his wife toast his suc-

cess. But Isabelle (who wants him dead so she can marry her lover) has
drugged his wine, and he falls unconscious on to the couch while his
vengeful wife goes to release the tingler, which crawls onto the doctor's
prone body, choking him around the neck with its spiny pincers until
disempowered at the last moment by the screams of Isabelle's sister,
Lucy (Pamela Lincoln).

Finally convinced that he has "violated the laws of nature," Chapin
takes the tingler to Olly's house to place it back in the body of Olly's
dead wife. However, during the process the tingler escapes, slips under
the floorboards, and makes its way into the silent-movie theater below.
On the loose, it attacks a girl in the audience, causing widespread hysterics. Dr. Chapin's voice is heard from the darkened screen informing
the audience that the girl is being taken care of, and that everything is
under control. Moments later, a second tingler attack takes place, this
time on the projectionist. The lights dim again, and the projected silhouette of the tingler crawls across the screen. Chapin addresses the
audience once more, this time to encourage everyone to "scream for
your lives!" until the tingler is thwarted, the danger has passed, and,
claims Chapin, "We can now return to our picture."

The scientist replaces the lethal organism in the body of its host and
leaves for the police station. Olly, left alone, finds himself sealed in the
apartment with the corpse. But the dead woman, in a perfectly timed
postmortem muscular spasm, sits up and directs an icy stare at her husband. In the film's final ironic twist, Olly falls dead to the floor. *Cause
of Death, FRIGHT.*

While Castle's experiments with audience, theater, and spectacle in
The Tingler were surprisingly radical, the film itself is rather typical of
the direction of American horror movies in 1959. Universal Studios
was exhausting its series of horror "classics," and the genre was gradually succumbing to the influence of the British Hammer style, which
relied heavily on gore effects and placed less importance on plot. Horror was becoming more and more distinctly a B-movie genre, and the
influence of Hammer would soon lead to Roger Corman's Poe cycle
of the 1960s, many of which also starred Vincent Price. In addition,
The Tingler is closely influenced by the horror-comedy tradition of
the 1940s, typified by such Universal fare as *Abbott and Costello Meet
Frankenstein* (1948).

The unapologetically ludicrous plot of *The Tingler* is held together
only by the presence of Vincent Price, who also starred in another of
Castle's gimmicky shockers, *The House on Haunted Hill.* In both

The Tingler, *1959, on the loose in the movie theater. Still courtesy of the editors.*

movies, the courtly Price plays a smarmy, effete sadist who nevertheless always manages to evoke audience sympathy as the wronged or injured party. Somehow, he remains urbane and avuncular while plotting an ingeniously violent revenge on his tormentors. The character played by Price in these two films has much in common with the prissy, effeminate gigolo he played in *Laura* (1944), a playboy kept by an older woman; it also looks forward to his elegantly sneering turns in Roger Corman's Poe cycle, the best of which is perhaps *The Masque of the Red Death* (1964). Indeed, one might argue that the barely suppressed male hysteria and homosexual panic of Price's Corman roles finally came to fruition in the 1973 movie *Theater of Blood*, in which he plays a number of roles, including that of a gleefully gay male hairdresser named Butch.

ANIMAL BODY DOUBLES

The Tingler lays bare a shared fascination with the physiology and the workings of the human body—both the bodies on screen and the participating bodies of the cinema audience—and it is this fascination that allows the critic to access the film's conscious and unconscious implications. The terror of the tingler relates to our own understanding of the ancient commonality of the human body, its failings, ruptures, and weaknesses.

The pattern that starts to emerge from a close analysis of *The Tingler* is that bodies form the close relationship between the symbolic order and the bodily order, disclosing how each gives form to the other in a dynamic intermingling of meanings that constitutes the basis for the history of human cultures and the symbolic importance of their narratives. To chart analogues between the symbol structure of contemporary narratives and the belief systems of earlier societies is not, as it first may seem, an attempt to cast a net further and wider for random connections, but rather an effort to look more deeply at the history of the human body, with its secret and disguised level of conscious understanding.

A number of primitive cultures also tell stories like that of *The Tingler*, involving versions of the animal-double motif. Some societies accept it as a matter of certainty that many people have secret animals like the tingler living inside their bodies. These are either people with the power to temporarily assume the form of an animal, or animals that can assume a human form. For example, animal-doubles like the tingler feature prominently in the Navajo skinwalker legends, and also in stories told by the Mandari, as well as by neighboring communities of the Nile frontage.

The salient point here is not that either Castle or his scriptwriter, Robb White—who, incidentally, found the whole tingler story quite ludicrous[10]—deliberately based the tingler on an ancient tradition. White was simply fitting a screenplay to Castle's compulsive quest for a new gimmick. But the narrative that they evolved together, like many of the narratives of popular culture, happens to tread upon a very ancient and well-worn path through the cognitive map of the human psyche. Budget limitations, the need for an exploitative trick, and minimal concerns with the niceties of plot and characterization meant that the story of the tingler could bypass the psychic censors habitually constructed by a cinema audience that had come to expect a certain level of realism and coherence of plot, and instead appeal directly to the audience's unconscious. Indeed, the first spectators of Castle's tricksy film, assailed directly by an ancient myth, were as reportedly ill-prepared and as violently disturbed as the victims of the vengeful parasite itself.

In Mandari culture, to take but one example from anthropology, man-into-beast transformations are held to be an example of witchcraft with a highly specific purpose. Beast-men are deliberately summoned by someone who, like Dr. Chapin in *The Tingler*, feels himself injured and denied a just hearing through the customary channels. In most of the societies that acknowledge them, beast-men are a recognized (if rarely used) ritual sanction that backs up traditional control; often they are considered to be a legitimate (but dangerous) way of drawing attention to wrongs. The danger lies in the fact that the user, employing the beast-man in the hope of gaining redress, runs a calculated risk if widespread harm is thought to have resulted.

A series of stylized domestic incidents in *The Tingler* makes it quite clear that Dr. Chapin's wife is continually unfaithful to him. She is absent when he returns home from the pathology lab, for example, and does not get back until the early hours of the morning, when Chapin spies her kissing her lover goodbye. In another scene, he enters the house only to hear the back door slam, and finds two stained wine glasses and a gold tie clip on the hall table. Isabelle, in turn, complains that her husband spends so much time at his laboratory that she has no choice but to be unfaithful. "You know, Warren, you've lost contact with living people," she tells him. "There's a word for you." "There's plenty for you," interrupts Chapin. Later, the Higgins's marriage is shown to be equally dysfunctional. "You know what it's like, Doc," complains Olly. "*She'd* have killed *me* if she could."

In this respect, it is interesting that the only two tinglers that are actually exposed to us in this film—the first in the silhouette of the X-ray machine, the second "in the flesh"—belong to the film's two main female characters, Isabelle Chapin and Martha Higgins. In cultures like the Mandari, the distance between people and animals is seen to be narrowed, directly and menacingly, whenever peril results from female sexual misbehavior. One result of this is the "animal accident"—mauling, trampling, and snake and scorpion bites—which befalls the promiscuous woman's close male relatives. In *The Tingler*, Chapin is almost choked to death by the tingler that his wife has let out of its cage and unleashed upon him. Our own culture charts associations between promiscuity and animality through metaphor and analogy. Unregulated sex (promiscuity, adultery, incest) is regarded by most cultures to be animal-like, and leads to animal-related dangers. Illicit sex is often regarded as something that takes place outside the home and bedroom. Similarly, sexual behavior metaphors in most cultures, including our own, are animal-based. It is also important to note that such animal-double motifs are not exclusive to the myths and legends of primitive and tribal culture. Western culture has plenty of animal-doubles of its own. Vampires and werewolves have long been a staple of horror movies, and elsewhere, superheroes like Batman and Spider-man are extensions of the same theme.

According to anthropology, the traditional animal-double inhabits ambiguous areas of the social structure domain, habitually presiding at funerals and ghost sacrifices. It has been suggested that the animal-double presides over areas of social and cultural life that are by nature ambiguous, unpredictable, and dangerous. In the same way, Castle's tingler is associated with murders, autopsies, and funerals, as well as the nether worlds of neurosis, paranoia, and mistrust, and the ambiguous domains of death and sex. As the narrative unfolds, we come to learn that the tingler presides over a night-world of psychosis, adultery, theft, bribery, corruption, broken promises, broken marriages, and wife-murder.

Significantly, the animal-double does not always take the form of an animal (in the zoological sense); it may equally take the form of an insect, fish, or bird. The tingler is a kind of hybrid parasite—a cross between a worm, a lobster, and a centipede. Castle describes it in his autobiography as "sort of like a lobster, but flat, and instead of claws it has long, slimy feelers."[11] While there are plenty of examples of ani-mal-doubles that take the form of shellfish or insects, it is worth exam-ining the fact that these categories of creatures are in themselves ambiguous or liminal. Shellfish, reptiles, and insects are the equivocal residue of the animal world, not quite animals and not quite fish, con-sidered by some cultures to be the animal enemies of human beings.[12] Some anthropologists have suggested that insects are considered abject and interstitial because they are generally not rated as food (in most countries at least), whereas reptiles and shellfish are determined to be freakish and ambiguous because their cold-bloodedness distances them from our far greater affective closeness to warm-blooded animals and birds. In this light, it is somewhat ironic that insects, reptiles, and shell-fish are referenced metaphorically in many societies to describe the kind of witchcraft accusations that occur within a domestic situation, where people all live closely together, as in the Kwahu proverb "only the insect in your own cloth will bite you."[13]

The Tibetan version of the animal-double is an apparition, either unconsciously or voluntarily created, of a *tulpa*, the only difference being that African versions of the animal-double generally depict the body from which it withdraws as remaining inanimate. Alexandra David-Neel's description of the tulpa in her book *Magic and Mystery in Tibet* suggests that it can be "either alike or different from its creator;" it does not need to be specifically invited to appear; and the author of the phenomenon generates it unconsciously and is not necessarily in the least aware of the apparition being seen by others.[14] Like Castle's tingler, the tulpa is perhaps best described as a spontaneously materialized "thought-form creation," a "magic formation generated by a powerful concentration of thoughts."[15] Unlike the animal-double, the tulpa can actually take any shape at all, however nebulous, and has tangible properties discernible to others. David-Neel describes one tulpa she came into contact with as a "foggy form," "a soft object whose substance gave way under [a] slight push."[16]

In fact, Castle's tingler has perhaps more in common with the Tibetan tulpa than with the more traditional African forms of animal-double. Like the tingler, the tulpa is induced to appear by various powerful emotions and causes or by a powerful concentration of thoughts, and, also like the tingler, the phenomenon is almost always produced without the conscious cooperation of its author. Even more significantly, once the tulpa is endowed with enough vitality to be capable of playing the part of a living creature, it tends to free itself from the body of its maker and from its maker's control. Tibetan occultists claim that this happens nearly mechanically, just as a child, when its body is fully formed and able to live apart, leaves its mother's womb. "Sometimes," remarks David-Neel, "the phantom becomes a rebellious son and one hears of uncanny struggles that have taken place between magicians and their creatures, the former being severely hurt or even killed by the latter."[17]

In the narrative unconscious, the tale of the tingler matches legends recounted by Tibetan magicians about the particular kind of tulpa that is expressly intended to survive its creator, and is induced specifically for that very purpose. Magicians and occultists relate many cases similar to Chapin's, in which the tulpa is brought forth in order to fulfill a mission, but escapes and does not come back, "pursuing its peregrinations," as David-Neel explains, "as a half-conscious, dangerously mischievous puppet."[18] And because it is the materialized form of such violent and overpowering emotions, once the tulpa has been visualized and animated, it is extremely difficult to dissolve. As part of an experiment in meditation, David-Neel summoned up a tangible illusion of her own, whose form grew gradually fixed and lifelike and became a kind of guest, living in her apartment.[19] Her tulpa eventually escaped her control and took on a life of its own, even to the extent of materializing to others, who took it for a real being. According to David-Neel, the tulpa was not easily destroyed. "I ought to have let the phenomenon follow its course," she writes, "but the presence of that unwanted companion began to prove trying to my nerves; it turned into a 'day-nightmare,' so I decided to dissolve the phantom. I succeeded, but only after six months of hard struggle. My mind-creature was tenacious of life."[20]

An interesting twist in the links between the tingler myth and the tulpa narrative is that, although the tingler is evidently an embodiment—rendered sensible to others—of Martha's mortal fear, the *author* and *master* of the tingler is not Martha, but Dr. Chapin. It is Chapin who discovers, summons, induces, and extracts the tingler, simply using Martha's body and emotions as the vehicle for his experiment. Some magicians argue that the discord and uproar wreaked by the unruly tulpa is a result of its performance of the unconscious aggression of its creator in the conscious, physical world. If this is true, then whose unconscious aggression does the escaped tingler embody? Is it Martha, the neurotic deaf-mute, projecting her bitterness and envy on to the able-bodied teenagers in the audience by forcing them to scream and scream again, rending and tormenting their vocal chords? Or is it Dr. Warren Chapin, the cuckolded husband, obsessed with his wife's infidelity, wreaking vengeance in the dating teenage couples in the movie theater by crawling up the girls' skirts, making them cry out in abhorrence and disgust?

DEFECATION AND THE POWER OF THE SCREAM

Interestingly, a number of primitive and tribal cultures conceive of the animal-double as fecal in form and consistency. If the province of this creation is to negotiate those ambiguous areas of culture, society, and the body, it is wholly befitting that the animal-double should emerge from the indistinct boundaries of the human body. In direct opposition to everything we consider human, the animal is a category inhabiting all those dark, shadowy cracks and crevices of human culture and the human body—not inside but outside, not the womb but the anus, not birth but defecation—and sometimes neither here nor there but *in between*, which inevitably connects it to the interstitial nature of the horror genre itself. Noël Carroll, in his book *The Philosophy of Horror*, describes the horror genre as interstitial in nature. Its monsters are frequently neither man nor beast, neither living nor dead, or else a result of such other-worldly processes as magnification (*King Kong, Night of the Lepus*) or reduction (*The Fly, The Incredible Shrinking Man*). Others belong to the category of the psychologically or morally interstitial (such as the psychopath, serial killer, or child murderer), sharing the category of those frightening bodily products (blood, excrement, tissue fluid) which, when appearing outside the bodily confines, are by necessity interstitial, and thereby out of place, corrupt, and taboo.[21]

It is surely not stretching the imagination too much to acknowledge that there is obviously something rather fecal about the tingler. After all, it is a wormlike protuberance that gradually emerges from the anal inner space, and its arrival is heralded by a range of physical perceptions and sensations both pleasant and disturbing. The emergence of the tingler involves agonized writhings, expressions of pain and relief, groans and wrenching sounds, followed by the sudden expulsion of a solid object from the space at the bottom of the spine. In fact, *The Tingler* is perhaps the most extreme of a whole subgenre of horror movies whose threats are fecal in nature, from the oleaginous slime of Chuck Russell's *The Blob* (1988), the body-burrowing parasite of Ridley Scott's *Alien* (1979), and the drain-dwelling leeches of David Cronenberg's *Shivers* (*The Parasite Murders/They Came from Within*, 1974) to the amorphous entity of Frank Henenlotter's *Basket Case* (1982).

Vincent Price's Dr. Warren Chapin is both shaman and conjurer, producing from behind a screen—as though by sleight of hand—a living fecal animal from the body of a dead person. Speaking symbolically, the tingler is not just feces, but feces from a corpse—a product that occupies the highly marginal and ambiguous character of the rotten, provoking the same feelings of revulsion as other dirty matter, such as sweat and urine, but impelling, at the same time, a strong element of fascination. Interest in feces is usual in animals and is a familiar part of the development of the child's psychological life. Feces is the first substance that the child can give or refuse to the outside world—an attribute that is soon shared by substances of far more interest to the child, including gifts, money, and genital compulsions. Feces, like other liminal substances such as sweat, saliva, urine, menstrual blood, and sexual excretia, have long been associated symbolically with magic, bewitchment, and the defilement and castration of both body and soul; hence, in most cultures at least, the careful rituals of cleansing after defecation, urination, coitus, menstruation, and childbirth.

Given this powerful preoccupation with bodily cleanliness and the careful avoidance of contact with impure matter, it seems ironic that the only living tingler in the film emerges from the body of a deaf-mute woman with an acute obsessive-compulsive cleanliness complex. Mrs. Higgins is terrified by fears of contaminations; she refuses to shake Chapin's proffered hand on the grounds that she's just finished washing her own. Olly complains that his wife is afraid of the germs on people's hands, and, consequently, their bill for towels comes to five dollars a week. As the fecal attributions of the tingler imply, despite our revulsion from feces and from dirty matter in general, much of our cultural symbolism and narrative mythology revolves around this theme. A dirty fecal animal with "the strength of a hydraulic press" and the power to kill any human being it encounters, the tingler embodies our ambivalent attitude toward fecal power and contamination, toward the terrifying involuntary processes our bodies undergo, and toward the nightmarish emissions they produce.

In *The Tingler*, the ability to produce human scream prevents the emergence of this fecal creature from the anal space. The fecal animal, "the force that makes your spine tingle when you're scared," has somehow transformed itself into a human voice. The metapsychology of the inner space of the human body image is so complex and multi-faceted that it allows for plenty of cathexis, both concrete and symbolic, between different bodily openings, inner spaces, and the contents hidden behind these openings. In fact, the entire structural foundation for the inner body image is created by the cathexis of various sensations and actual functions of the body simultaneously with phase-specific images and figures of speech that are connected with the body.[22] So, for instance, the sound of the human voice can easily be imaginatively experienced as feces, flatus, or urination—especially in cases of psychosis where the image of the body, especially its inner space, is disturbed. In relation to the top half of the inner body image, the lungs, larynx, and ears compose an inner-space entity, the "excrement" or product of which is the human voice, words and sounds—we react to important experiences by taking a deep breath, as though to internalize the auditory experience better, and our reaction to experiences we dislike or despise often involves expiration. Thus, in relation to the metapsychology of the human body image, it seems quite natural that a fecal image from the anus should be cathected into the inner space of the human voice.

According to Dr. Chapin, the tingler is a parasite that feeds off the stress and tension experienced in the spinal column at moments of intense fear. This tension can be released only by screaming, which, in turn, cuts off the tingler from its source of strength and renders it powerless. Scream, and you are safe. Fail to scream, and your body is lost to the tingler. When Dr. Chapin exhorts the onscreen audience to "scream for your lives!" to disempower the escaped tingler, he is also encouraging the screams of the by now hysterical *actual* cinema audience, whose panic-stricken reaction to random jolts of electrical energy should ideally, at least according to Castle's plan, serve as a promotional device to excite and encourage the crowds waiting in the lobby for the next showing.

The escaped tingler embodies not only the link between oral and anal expulsiveness, but also the basic notion that there are anal feelings at the movies, and that these feelings are specifically activated by this film. Put in its most simple terms, the human fear of losing control of one's defecatory functions—embodied by the sight of an enormous, swollen fecal animal, alive and on the loose—is cathected into the socially legitimate chaos of ritual screaming (itself inspired by the screams of the onscreen cinema audience). As I suggested earlier, uncontrolled defecation and an ungovernable vocal spasm are essentially different manifestations of the same bodily impulse, the significant difference being that chaotic defecation is considered horrific and polluting, whereas ungovernable screaming—especially when participating in the public viewing of a horror movie—fits into a legitimate social category, and has a communally accepted social function. To view *The Tingler* as it was originally screened is therefore to take part in a socially endorsed ritual of mass cathexis, where the threat of contamination is faced head-on, displaced, and, at least temporarily, "overcome." And for those audience members fortunate enough to select seats rigged up with Percepto-buzzers directing an electrical jolt at the base of the spine, just at the top of the buttocks, the experience can only have been doubly exciting and doubly hysterical. Perhaps the dynamics of this socialization procedure make it easy to understand why watching *The Tingler* is recalled by so many film lovers as one of the most intense and exhilarating moviegoing experiences of their youth.

FILM AND FECES

The Tingler is a tale of warning. It is the story of assault by a fecal animal-double that comes to life inside the body at the peak of terror, extending "from the coccyx to the sternum," and which, when released outside the body, takes on a life of its own and crawls around frantically, causing a violent anal jolt when it attacks. This fecal creation is the product of massive unreleased tension and can be calmed only by the cathexis of this defecatory neurosis into the vocal release of the scream. On one level then, this is a film about what Philip Rieff has described as "the triumph of the therapeutic," a trait of which is the widely held belief—almost a commonplace, by 1959—that emotions we fail to get "out" somehow remain repressed "within" us until they find their own way "out," possibly of their own accord, and possibly in a rather frightening and dangerous way.[23] The popular secularization of Freudian psychoanalysis allows for the expression of certain kinds of so-called repressed desires and urges to become increasingly acceptable in the name of a process of psychic cleansing. As it has become increasingly common during the last thirty years to attribute such repressed complexes to triggering childhood events (usually sexually or emotionally abusive parenting), the disclosure and display of such drives has met with increasing approval.

But *The Tingler* is a more involved film than a reading based on this very simplified therapeutic model might suggest. This is not a film about the expression of repressed fears in a tension-breaking psychic catharsis. Because it cannot be "attributed" to a single triggering event, because it will never become socially acceptable and because its effect is universal, the defecatory obsession is not really a neurosis we can "get in touch" with or "come to terms" with, like other unconscious urges have come to be characterized. Horror at the perverseness of our bodily emissions is not just a repressed impulse waiting to return, but part of the neurological disease of being human. *The Tingler* is a bodily nightmare in which a fecal animal, swollen to frightening proportions, is given a life of its own and let loose upon the unsuspecting world of consciousness. The plight of an unfortunate neurotic deaf-mute whose unreleased tensions grow so great they overcome her is simply the signal impelling the process of cathexis in the cinema audience from anal neurosis to oral expulsion and back again. Contrary to therapeutic fashion, however, this cathexis neither alleviates nor endures. The relief expressed in the scream of the spectator is nothing more than a socially admissible ritual of momentary release. In Castle's fantasy, the scream destroys the neurosis. But in the waking reality of our bodily lives, this crapulous preoccupation, like all the best monsters, like the fecal process itself, is totally indestructable.

NOTES

1. Robin Wood, "An Introduction to the American Horror Film," first published in *American Nightmare: Essays on the Horror Film,* ed. Robin Wood and Richard Lippe (Toronto, Festival of Festivals, 1979): 7–28. Reprinted in this volume.

2. Cited in Bill Burgess, "William Castle," *Classic Images* 111 (September 1984): 42–44.

3. Burgess, 42–44.

4. "Isn't it time for a retrospective? A documentary on his life? Some high-falutin' critique in *Cahiers du Cinéma*? Forget Ed Wood. Forget George Romero. William Castle was best. William Castle was God." John Waters, "Whatever Happened to Showmanship?" *American Film* 9, no. 3 (December 1983): 57.

5. "Even the spectator who remains glued to his seat is nevertheless involved. The effects stopped at nothing." Alain Garel, "William Castle Obituary," *Cahiers du Cinéma* 21 (1977): 70–71.

6. Waters, 55–58.

7. William Castle, *Step Right Up! I'm Gonna Scare the Pants Off America* (New York: Putnam's Sons, 1976), 57.

8. Waters, 57.

9. Waters, 57.

10. In fact, the idea of the tingler was fashioned not by Castle but by his screenwriter, Robb White, who very quickly came to be embarrassed by it. "I hated them," said Robb White of the series of films he made with Castle. "I mean, they're so dumb! God, there's not a worm in your backbone when you get scared!" Cited in Bryan Senn and John Johnson, *Fantastic Cinema Guide* (London: McFarland, 1992), 345.

11. Castle, *Step Right Up!,* 57.

12. See, for example, John Halverson, "Animal Categories and Terms of Abuse," *Man* 11, no. 4 (December 1976): 4–14.

13. Wolf Bleek, "Witchcraft, Gossip and Death: A Social Drama," *Man* 11, no. 4 (December 1976): 526–42 .

14. Alexandra David-Neel, *Magic and Mystery in Tibet* (London: Souvenir, 1967, reprinted London: Unwin, 1984), 217–18.

15. David-Neel, 217–18.

16. Ibid., 218. David-Neel is referring here to the tulpa produced by a

Tibetan painter's depiction of a wrathful deity, witnessed by David-Neel but not by the painter himself.

17. David-Neel, 218.

18. David-Neel, 200.

19. "In order to avoid being influenced by the form of lamaist deities, which I saw daily around me in paintings and images, I chose for my experiment a most insignificant character, a monk, short and fat, of an innocent and jolly type," writes David-Neel. Later, she observed that "the features which I had imagined, when building my phantom, gradually underwent a change. The fat, chubby-cheeked fellow grew leaner, his face assumed a vaguely mocking, sly, malignant look. He became more troublesome and bold. In brief, he escaped my control." (221).

20. David-Neel, 220.

21. Noël Carroll, *The Philosophy of Horror, or, Paradoxes of the Heart* (New York: Routledge, 1990).

22. Tor-Bjorn Hagglund and Heikki Piha, "The Inner Space of the Body Image," *Psychoanalytic Quarterly* 49 (1980): 256–83.

23. Philip Rieff, *The Triumph of the Therapeutic: Uses of Faith After Freud* (New York: Harper & Row, 1968).

16

AIP's *Pit and the Pendulum*: Poe as Drive-In Gothic

Rick Worland

At least as far back as D. W. Griffith's *The Avenging Conscience* (1914), the biographical legend and literary output of Edgar Allan Poe have had special resonance for the horror film, this despite adaptations that often have little to do with the writer's actual work. The macabre themes, gothic atmosphere, and the "unity of effect" achieved in Poe's short stories made them especially good candidates for adaptations on stage and screen. In 1959, when American International Pictures (AIP) decided to answer rising competition in the exploitation horror market from Hammer and other producers, they turned to Poe's proven marquee appeal. Roger Corman, virtually AIP's house director, was by this time an experienced craftsman with more than two dozen inventive but quickly produced pictures to his credit, and was eager to move into features with higher budgets and better production values. AIP provided the means, resolving to make one quality color feature for about $270,000 instead of two black-and-white quickies for $100,000 apiece. They also engaged Vincent Price, fresh from a string of successful horror roles, to personify some of Poe's tormented protagonists. *House of Usher* (1960) was the initial result.[1] Between the startling innovations of *Psycho* (1960) and the end of censorship in 1968, *Pit and the Pendulum* (1961), Corman's second Poe adaptation, epitomized the increasing tension between graphic violence and submerged sexuality in Hollywood horror. The dark irony, madness, and undercurrents of morbid eroticism in Poe's most famous tales allowed Corman and his collaborators to fuse the author's carefully crafted literary works with the dynamism of popular art in ways both original and characteristic of gothic tradition.

The canons of gothic literature, including Poe's particular contributions to the form, were often more disturbing, their willingness to revel in gore and corruption of the flesh more frequent than was possible in the classic Hollywood horror films of the 1930s and '40s when the medium was heavily censored. What we might term the Euro-American "gothic revival" of exploitation horror in the period from approximately 1957 through 1967 (the films of Hammer, AIP, and certain Italian productions) constituted a mannerist phase that upheld genre traditions while pointing to new formal and thematic possibilities. AIP's cycle combined Poe's settings with gothic ambiance and color cinematography to counter Hammer's bloodier, more callous reworking of *Frankenstein* and *Dracula*. Changing social standards alongside institutional shifts in the film industry after World War II, particularly new audience patterns and the erosion of censorship, made these colder, more graphic movies both possible and popular.[2] A broader historical view rescues this work, particularly AIP's Poe series, from the critical rejection or incomprehension with which it has often been greeted.

The reception of Poe's work follows two major currents: a critical tradition that dates from the mid-nineteenth century; and popular conceptions derived from mass culture adaptations. In 1950, the poet W. H. Auden suggested that Poe greatly influenced three literary genres (and by extension, genres of popular cinema): the horror tale, science fiction, and the detective story.[3] The claim for Poe's centrality to science fiction seems debatable but his importance in the other two forms is unquestioned.[4] Poe penned nearly seventy short stories, but as Julian Symons notes, his international reputation rests on no more than twenty of these, of which all save four detective stories are tales of terror.[5] Unfortunately, the gulf between elite and popular conceptions of Poe remains wide. A 1971 scholarly overview of Poe's career, which begins by noting with approval the author's appeal to a wide range of readers, snidely observes, "Even the cultural hucksters live off [Poe's] fame; we all remember the occasion—a school assembly, a record, or a low-camp film—when some aging actor first terrified us with 'The

Cask of Amontillado' or 'The Pit and the Pendulum.'"[6] The critic's last barb seems squarely directed at the series of Poe films Vincent Price starred in from 1960 through 1965, though popular adaptation of Poe extends back much further. We all remember, indeed. Poe's abiding fame is bolstered by popular culture as much as the labor of teachers and scholars. Through the media of commercial theater (notably the *Grand Guignol*) and motion pictures, Poe became a virtual "brand name" connoting brooding horror.

In 1909 (Poe's centennial year), Biograph released a film to nickelodeons titled *Edgar Allan Poe* directed by D. W. Griffith. In this biographical vignette, Poe (Herbert Yost) nurses his dying wife Virginia (Linda Arvidson) while struggling to compose "The Raven." The film's basic premise is more important here than its director's famous name. Biograph's *Edgar Allan Poe* illustrates as well as reinforces how the individual and literary biographies of Poe intertwine in the popular imagination, a folk narrative in which the writer's personal demons yield up his somber poetry and chilling tales before finally killing him. A few years later, Griffith directed the more elaborate *The Avenging Conscience*, which does more than adapt Poe: it attests to the affective power of his fiction to inspire dark acts of madness in the reader, represented by the protagonist (Henry B. Walthall) who, after reading "The Tell-Tale Heart," is driven to murder the uncle who blocks his marriage to a woman he nicknames "Annabel" after Poe's "Annabel Lee." Griffith deepened a familiar melodramatic plot by drawing on the repertoire of visual effects explored in trick films to portray the deranged man's subjective delusions. This thread continued in Universal's *The Raven* (1935) where Bela Lugosi plays a sadist obsessed by Poe's work, especially "The Pit and the Pendulum," who has constructed a dungeon in which to torture innocent and not-so-innocent victims such as co-star Boris Karloff.[7] The tut-tutting scholar above could find a rather high camp film when the deranged Lugosi throws back his head and inexplicably exclaims, "Poe, you are avenged!," before being crushed in another of his own homemade torture devices. AIP's trailer for *Pit and the Pendulum* began with a drawing of Poe and the legend, "From the torture and pain experienced in the dark, depraved depths of his personal hell, comes one of the world's classics in terror. . . ." Besides obvious ballyhoo, the traditional emphasis on Poe's inner turmoil and his work's supposed capacity to afflict the reader/viewer with irrational impulses may have motivated the psychological subjectivity and distorted visuals in increasingly fluid interpretations of his tales.

Poe's 1842 tale is set entirely in the torture chamber as the narrator, a nameless victim of the Inquisition, is consigned to slow death under the implicit gaze of his coldly sadistic judges. In the blackness of the cell, he avoids a drop into a deep adjoining pit piled with earlier victims, and suffers other torments before being strapped to the pendulum. In the most vividly repulsive segment, the prisoner lures a swarm of rats to chew the bindings off his body before the swinging blade slices him in half. Set in a manmade Hell, the tale actually describes how a resilient man staves off panic and hopelessness to counter virtually every trap laid for him before a melodramatic rescue at the last second. The spectacle of a frantic prisoner watching the scimitar blade descend became the animating scene—and promotional image—of Corman's film. Following the common logic of exploitation movie production, the scenario was seemingly written backwards from this point: How did a man end up in this nightmarish predicament? Who is he? Who put him there? To this, the script adds the spare-no-one principle of the *Grand Guignol* where the virtuous are as likely to be arbitrarily and viciously punished as the guilty. *Pit and the Pendulum* opens in sixteenth-century Spain with Francis Barnard (John Kerr) approaching the grim seaside castle of his brother-in-law, Don Nicholas Medina (Price), upon learning of the death of his sister, Elizabeth Barnard Medina (Barbara Steele). Initially refused entry, his suspicion grows when he meets the troubled Nicholas in the castle's lower depths engaged in some mysterious task in a locked room. Nicholas' sister Catherine (Luana Anders) and Dr. Charles Leon (Antony Carbone) reveal that Nicholas suffers a double agony. As a child he witnessed his father (Price in a double role), a merciless Inquisitor, murder his mother and uncle after accusing them of adultery. His mother was walled up in the dungeon to die slowly. Since Elizabeth's death, Nicholas is tormented by fear that she was accidentally entombed alive. Incidents suggesting that Elizabeth's restless ghost has returned lead the group to break into her crypt to learn the truth, where to their horror, they find her stiffened corpse tearing at the coffin lid. Eventually we learn this was all an elaborate ruse by the still-living Elizabeth and her lover, Dr. Leon. Unhinged by these events, Nicholas seemingly becomes his father and repeats the revenge on the treacherous lovers. Unfortunately, Francis Barnard is mistaken for the uncle and tortured on the bladed pendulum machine. Catherine rescues him and Nicholas falls into the pit and dies. Never seen alive by the survivors, Elizabeth is left to perish in an Iron Maiden when Catherine seals the torture chamber and departs.

The action of Richard Matheson's *Pit and the Pendulum* script begins almost exactly like his previous effort, *House of Usher*, with an incredulous outsider arriving at a creepy gothic manse and becoming unwittingly involved in a perverse relationship between a doomed woman and the master of the house played by Vincent Price. This basic structure was Poe's, the framing situation of "The Fall of the House of Usher." In the first outing, Phillip Winthrop (Mark Damon) becomes the character of Poe's nameless narrator, now described as the intended of Madeline Usher (Myrna Fahey); in the second film, Francis Barnard arrives to visit his sister's grave after learning of her (apparent) death. Apart from the title, though, *Pit and the Pendulum*, unlike the first movie's fairly close adaptation, took little from Poe besides the background of the Spanish Inquisition and a victim's torture on the eponymous machine. Instead, *Pit and the Pendulum* became a second take on *House of Usher*, improved at least in terms of the horror film with superior production values, a compelling monster (Price as both his father and the adult Nicholas overcome by the father's sinister influence), and a *Grand Guignol* flavor upon the opening of Elizabeth's crypt and the harsh fate the treacherous wife ultimately suffers.

A famous anecdote has AIP head Sam Arkoff expressing doubt about the commercial appeal of *House of Usher* because the story, unlike *I Was A Teenage Werewolf* (1957) et al., had no monster. Roger Corman says he quickly responded, "The house is the monster," and the film confirmed his grasp of this fundamental gothic convention.[8] From shots of the long fissure running down the building's outside face as Poe described, to a moment when the top edge of a banister crumbles to dust under Phillip Winthrop's fingers soon after Roderick catches him kissing Madeline (the script's invention), the decay of the actual house of Usher and of the Usher family line is associated. Upon Madeline's (apparent) death near the beginning of Poe's tale, the narrator says he learns "that the deceased and [Roderick] had been twins, and that sympathies of a scarcely intelligible nature had always existed between them." "The Fall of the House of Usher" has been interpreted as concerning an incestuous love between Roderick and Madeline, although Poe is vague about this throughout. In fact, making the film's male outsider Madeline's suitor actually brings Roderick's sexual jealousy into sharper relief. (Poe's narrator was Roderick's childhood friend and has never met Madeline.) Still, Price's understated portrayal of Roderick's dissolute attachment to his sister makes Corman's *House of Usher* nearly as elusive as Poe about the ultimate rationale for the place's final collapse. *Pit and the Pendulum*, however, allows the actor to wallow in grief and Oedipal guilt in act one, then explode in gleefully histrionic revenge in the climax.

AIP's Poe series has often been undervalued in part because of critical dismissal of Vincent Price. Writing in the mid-1960s (when the series had in fact concluded), genre historian Carlos Clarens winced that "the mind boggles at the thought of having the Complete Edgar Allan Poe translated into Vincent Price star vehicles," a judgment shared by many critics at the time and since.[9] But Price's acting range was greater than he was often given credit for. He was not (at least not always) just a rampant, hammy performer. In the gothic mode alone, given the right script and direction he could play quietly tragic (*House of Usher*); do broad comedy well (the "Black Cat" segment of *Tales of Terror* [1962]); or project genuine malevolence (*Witchfinder General/Conqueror Worm* [1968]). With his rich mid-Atlantic inflections and rubbery, expressive face, Price struck a chord with AIP's target audience, teenagers who detected the smile below the surface of his large villains. AIP's James H. Nicholson had "wondered if the youth market was there for a film based on required reading in school."[10] The Poe movies might indeed have been the "tasteful," that is, ponderous, adaptations *House of Usher* sometimes suggested. Instead, they were lively and engaging thanks in no small part to their star. Price's work may be enjoyed for its charismatic audacity or as camp but rarely deserves to be dismissed out of hand.

Though the combination of lurid promotion and an increasingly popular star drew patrons to theaters, Corman's cinematic skill was the decisive factor in the success of the Poe series, especially his practiced ability to stretch meager budgets and get most of the money up on the screen. This is all the more remarkable in that he pursued a conscious decision to restrict the films mainly to claustrophobic interiors in the controlled environment of the studio. ("I told my cast and crew I never wanted to see 'reality' in any of these scenes. If I did go exterior there should be something out of the ordinary."[11]) The only exteriors in *Pit and the Pendulum* are ominous shots of waves crashing against rocks used as transitions between scenes; even the bleak castle perched on an outcropping beside the sea was a matte painting. Corman says this strategy conformed to Poe's emphasis on the psychological interiority of his characters, realized on screen, for example, by using the ocean to invoke a Freudian symbol of the unconscious. Yet eschewing the too-familiar hills and ravines of Los Angeles locales for the soundstage also followed the tradition of expressionist films set in artificial, self-contained worlds. The more immediate reference point though, was Hammer's gothic chillers from *Curse of Frankenstein* (1957) forward, which typically used gray skies and bare, autumnal trees for exteriors and subdued color schemes in interior décor, the better to bring out the bloody red and veiny blue gore of the horror scenes. With the help of talented collaborators, especially production designer Daniel Haller and cinematographer Floyd Crosby, Corman could match Hammer's production values. Poe's fatalism and Price's élan countered the moody English gothic style with the dynamism of Hollywood exploitation movies.

Valdine Clemens' account of gothic literature underlines the importance of "the originating image of the ancient castle as bastion of personal or cultural identity under assault."[12] The atmosphere of physical decline in gothic horror, both in the decaying structures in which they are set and the often-unspecified wasting aliments of major characters, imply psychological regression and breakdown. Adapting insights of psychoanalyst C. J. Jung, Clemens argues that this image of the past in decrepitude, combined with the gothic's defining sense of foreboding allows (or can be a symbol for) access to the unconscious.[13] *Pit and the Pendulum*'s evocation of psychological regression starts with the opening credits, an abstract display of red, purple, blue, and yellow blobs of color slowly spreading and overlapping, punctuated by laconic interjections of electronic tones and timpani, which gradually blend with the sound of rolling surf. Visually, these running splotches of color recall the long-established cinematic convention of starting or ending dreams or flashbacks with blurry dissolves. The torpid mood continues as Francis Barnard's carriage halts under darkening skies so that he and the viewer can take in the sight of Castle Medina. He is actually put out a distance from the castle by a silent driver who refuses to approach any nearer. As in many versions of *Dracula*, the wary coachman who recognizes the territory of an unseen monster signals a clear boundary between the outer world and the essentially interior realm of gothic terror. Corman has literally stranded us in an alternate, mental landscape.

After this credit sequence, a servant initially refuses Barnard entry, another warning that ought to have been heeded; and a device that not only deepens the mystery of the gothic edifice but begs an irresistible, often fatal human curiosity. The servant's nervousness and hushed tones seem at once reverent and fearful. The attempt to bar visitors

from the ancient house implies that something awful lies within, a
secret the residents try to hide with a mixture of apprehension and
guilt. The gothic milieu is characterized foremost as one in which an
oppressive past dominates the present and the dead won't stay buried,
sometimes literally. At first, the past's baleful influence can neither be
acknowledged, assimilated, or rejected. Gothic tales often suggest a
neurotic drive to sustain the horror or secret sin in perpetuity. An outsider's introduction may expose the secrets of the terrible place and
cause its destruction; or it may claim additional victims. *Pit and the
Pendulum* manages both with a *Grand Guignol* twist.

Following this somber buildup, though, Vincent Price's entrance is
indeed rather campy. As Catherine Medina leads Francis below to his
sister's crypt, they jump at the loud rasping and groaning of machin-
ery. When Francis approaches the door from which it emanates, Nicholas suddenly emerges in a fit of anger and guilt, as if nearly caught in
some venal sin. The source of the racket we can probably guess from
the movie's title, yet Price, with his typical air of exaggerated gravity,
simply intones, "It's an apparatus that must be kept in constant
repair." Still, Nicholas' entrance from what we intuit as the torture
chamber foreshadows the collapse of his personality under his father's
malignant influence. In the wake of *Psycho*, Price's performance here
and in other scenes hints that his father has already partly overtaken
his mind when the film begins. Nicholas' quick move to lock the door
repeats the servant's attempt to turn away the visitor from the castle
itself that, true to gothic convention, only promises the story will turn
on the secret in the forbidden room.

The balance of the first act, suggesting that Elizabeth's ghost is
returning to haunt Nicholas, presents a series of eerie incidents enlivened by Corman's penchant for moving camera and busy compositions: a maid hears Elizabeth's ethereal voice calling in the bedroom
Nicholas has kept preserved as a memorial (or another neurotic compulsion), music from the harpsichord, which only the departed could
play fills the halls at night, and her locked room is later ransacked as if
in great fury. The harpsichord sequence begins with the camera moving in on Elizabeth's crypt, then passing a family altar with its crucifix,
subtly implying she has risen from the dead, before continuing
through the castle's empty rooms. These gliding camera moves suggest
the passage of the ghost itself, a technique traceable to Paul Leni's *The
Cat and the Canary* (1927). Still, we are reluctant to accept this as the
work of spirits because hoaxes and red herrings are the stuff of innu-

Vincent Price chews up the scenery in Pit and the Pendulum, *1961.*
From the editors' collection.

merable gothic potboilers, and casting inclines us to consider Price's
character the monster instead of a victim. (The harpsichord sequence
ends ambiguously with Francis and the others finding the terrified
Nicholas near the instrument.) The subsequent discovery by Francis of
a secret passageway between Nicholas' room and Elizabeth's that
would have allowed him to stage these incidents seems to confirm the
doubt. (The secret passage is another gothic cliché that can as yet symbolize an active if hidden part of the house's psychological anatomy.)
Increasingly angry, Francis charges that Nicholas may have had a hand
in his sister's death.

In response, Nicholas reluctantly permits access to the torture
chamber to convince Francis it was really "the miasma of barbarity
which permeates these walls" that gradually destroyed an idyllic marriage, culminating in Elizabeth's mysterious death inside a rusty Iron
Maiden repeating "Sebastian," the name of the dread father. In gothic
tales, physical descent equals psychological descent. Sebastian's dun-

geon is of course concealed in the castle's depths, entered by further descending a long stone staircase. Inside, we regard a dusty, cobwebbed space replete with the rack, cages, stocks, braziers, and other nasty instruments. Price recounts the room's horrific history in a performance that conveys Nicholas' near paralysis with guilt at his father's crimes. The setting inspires the first of two flashbacks that convey a queasy sense of half-recalled nightmare through comparatively simple means—a blue filter and a wavy anamorphic lens, Vaselined at the rim to create areas of blurry focus. Taking advantage of the Panavision frame, Corman begins each flashback with a rectangular iris that shrinks down to black before a wipe opens onto the stylized images of the past. The use of this odd iris to introduce what will eventually be revealed as Elizabeth's faked death recurs in the movie's final shot framing her terrified face inside the Iron Maiden. The evocative set design, camerawork, and clever visual style display Corman's command of both genre convention and film technique.

The more disturbing childhood flashback sequence as narrated by Catherine Medina paints Nicholas as another victim of their father's evil, depicting the Oedipal murder of the mother while the boy Nicholas cowers in helpless fright. Still, our initial sense that Vincent Price is really the monster is partly satisfied in this second flashback where even through the distorted visuals and a black hood, we recognize the star in his dual role as the Inquisitor. Sebastian's cruel smiles and explosion of violence as he beats his brother Bartolome to death with a poker before turning angrily to his wife expose the beast we suspected was there. Yet the ambiguity of Price's character deepens when Dr. Leon tells Catherine and Francis that Nicholas was twice victimized: their mother was not only tortured as the boy watched but walled up and abandoned to a slow death; and that this trauma has led him to fear Elizabeth may have been buried alive. An ostensibly sympathetic male character that can never be fully trusted or embraced, another significant gothic motif, creates a sense of unease that lingers despite any nominal happy ending.

The ominous mood of *Pit and the Pendulum*'s early scenes, including the flashbacks, rely on the indirect, suggestive style Val Lewton's unit perfected. Yet a hardy independent company founded to channel exploitation movies to drive-ins could not go far into costume-drama refinement or indulge in foreboding atmosphere alone without losing its major audience. After Hammer's example, AIP needed to deliver harsher and more graphic effects, too. This occurs when the group exhumes Elizabeth's body to dispel Nicholas' fear, another stalwart gothic trope. Expert editing punctuated by dissonant harp glissandi convey the group's approach to the crypt, the blows of their picks as they break in, a scurrying rat, and Nicholas' eyes widening and rolling as he flashes back to his mother's terrible death. The sense of mounting delirium climaxes when the sarcophagus is forced open and we catch a quick look at a greenish, ossified woman, decaying skull and hands thrown back as if in a frozen shriek. Our minds quickly conjure the stifling blackness of her death, the stench at the moment of its exposure. While the shattered Nicholas, alternately shouting and whispering, "True! True!," is led away by the doctor, Francis steels himself to initiate what we want—one more glance at the desiccated corpse. The *Grand Guignol* had come to the American drive-in.

The poster art for *House of Usher* presents a cross-sectional view of Madeline's suffocating panic inside the oblong shape of a buried coffin—an effective come-on whose promise the movie failed to deliver. Indeed, the suspense and shock of the exhumation scene alone in Corman's second Poe movie surpassed the climax of the first where the prematurely interred Madeline Usher awoke and pursued Price's Roderick with bloody, outstretched fingers. Corman repeated this scenario in *Pit and Pendulum* to set up an even more baroque finale. His mind now deteriorating, Nicholas follows Elizabeth's beckoning voice into the castle's depths. He returns to the opened crypt from which Elizabeth rises in diaphanous shroud to stalk her terrified husband through the moldy corridors, finally cornering him in the torture chamber as he collapses. With her raven-haired beauty and wide-set, magnetic eyes, Barbara Steele became a cult favorite in a dozen Euro-American horror films in the 1960s. She might alternately play a seductive monster or tormented victim, sometimes both in the same movie, as in her startling debut in Mario Bava's *Black Sunday* (1960), making her screen persona in the genre a feminine parallel to the ambiguous gothic male Price enacts here.[14] Fittingly, when Nicholas finally drops and falls silent with loopy smiles of longing and delight, he seems weirdly aroused by the presence of her supposed "corpse." Along with their enhanced production values, AIP's Poe movies were testing the limits of both graphic horror and kinky sex.

The debunking of supernatural explanation in the early scenes works to catch us off guard for exposure of the real plot, immediately followed by its inversion as the scheme to drive Nicholas mad succeeds only too well when he transforms from simpering victim to deranged

avenger. Elizabeth and the doctor are embracing in front of their cata-
tonic dupe when he revives fully possessed by the delusion that he is
the heartless Sebastian. Addressing the pair as Isabella and Bartolome,
he begins to reenact the father's vengeance. The "mistake" in *House of
Usher*, casting Price as a quietly passive if decadent villain, is spectacularly corrected here as he starts an operatic performance near the top
and then builds. Nicholas seizes Elizabeth for an as yet unknown
agony; trying to escape, the frightened Dr. Leon retreats to the semi-
darkness of the lower chamber, the one containing the apparatus of the
title, and stumbles into the pit to his death. Price's relish of the Inquisitor's evil becomes black comedy when he hears Francis Barnard calling
for him and turns to respond, *"There* you are, Bartolome!"* Corman
and Price hereby abandon the tenuous literary fealty of their first col-
laboration for a spectacle firmly planted in the traditions of popular
horror.

   The unsuspecting Francis is knocked cold and awakens on an expressionistic set rivaling some of the best designs of the 1920s and '30s. Art
Director Daniel Haller husbanded his resources and ingenuity for the
construction of this multilevel chamber where another stone stairway
leads down to the wooden table on which Francis lies bound. In longshot we see that the pendulum sits on a lower outcropping surrounded
by a rocky pit, an optical composite shot that conveys the literal rock
bottom of the castle's psychological depths. State of the art at the time,
the artificial matte shot has aged gracefully to embellish an almost surreal clash of art and hallucination. In a nod to Poe, Haller realized the
author's description of the surrounding walls bearing "figures of fiends
in aspects of menace" by painting hooded Inquisitors staring with slit-
ted yellow eyes. These stark monochromatic figures recall the painted
backdrops and distorted settings of *The Cabinet of Dr. Caligari* (1919)
and other expressionist works, an effect Corman compounds by shooting oblique angles and canted frames in the manner of 1920s German
cinematography. This calculated return to traditional styles though,
adorns a movie linking the genre's past to the violent extremes that
would predominate by decade's end. Through the first half of the
1960s, the subdued and coded sexuality prevailing in Hollywood movies since the mid 1930s largely continued, even in exploitation fare. We
can observe the transition beginning, though. With the influence of the
Production Code rapidly waning, Corman upheld the conventions of
gothic horror by pushing the boundaries of violence and lurid content
while minimizing direct acknowledgment of the perverse sexuality ani-

mating the story itself. Although the Production Code had once strictly prohibited scenes of torture, for instance, *Pit and the Pendulum* was blatantly marketed on the spectacle of just such an episode. Moreover, given the sexual ambiguity of Vincent Price's star persona, the sight of a handsome young man at the mercy of this domineering older man lent a homoerotic charge to an already sado-masochistic scene. That in the mind of Nicholas the identities of both parties are confused by Oedipal trauma, sexual betrayal, and frustrated desires ripened the possibilities for a rash of psychosexual interpretations. This was appropriately sensational stuff for the drive-in after all, despite the ruffled collars and literary gloss.

The scene's hallucinatory air, the sense of a plunge into dreadful fantasy is again relayed through visual style. As Francis slowly awakens, his point-of-view shots show Nicholas, now clad in his father's black executioner's garb, through the wavy lens, contorted angles, and blue tints Corman employed in the flashbacks. The protagonist's disorientation motivates the style but also suggests that Sebastian—the tale's true ghost—has burst into the present to devour both his son and another innocent. The man Francis suspected from the start of involvement in his sister's death was actually blameless until the machinations of that still living sister drove him to become a monster that turns on them both. The irony at least would have suited Poe. Less suitable to the author's literary champions, but perfect for the time and place the movie would be seen, is Price's elaborate taunting of his captive, with broad gestures and lip-curling recitation of every syllable comprising a veritable gothic aria: "Do you know where you are, Bartolome? You are about to enter Hell. Hell! The labyrinth, the infernal region; the abode of the damned; the place of torment. Pandemonium. Abandon. Thoth! Gehenna! Naraka! The pit!—and the pendulum!," he coos, indicating the suspended blade with its gears and chains. While Price cannot be faulted for the script's excesses, the scenery-chewing vigor is all his. Still, the performance blends smoothly with Corman's eccentric compositions and quick editing (including inserts of the glaring Inquisitors cut to the cadence of Price's recital), making it perhaps more unnerving that Francis' tormenter is not some horned demon (as in *The Avenging Conscience*) but a slightly ridiculous madman.

A well-mounted episode of suspense follows as Francis struggles while the blade inexorably descends. Corman's montage combines with vivid sound effects that make the blade's long swishing arcs seem at once quick and massive. As the scene progresses, cross-cutting between the captive, his tormenter, and Catherine knocking at the door, then rushing to get help, we are inclined to expect a last-minute rescue of the innocent and the death of the monster, possibly caused by the pendulum itself. Corman, however, is a step or two ahead of us again. Francis is indeed delivered seconds after the blade swipes the first shallow gash across his white shirt (the fatal wound visually antici- pated with a bright red gag covering his mouth), and Nicholas falls into the pit as he grapples with the servant. But throughout this skillful sequence, Corman has been preparing a genuine shock, one that sepa- rates this movie from earlier genre traditions. As Catherine and her ser- vant are helping Francis up the stairs and the music rises, Corman cranes down into the pit where we see Nicholas' body, bloodied eyes open, arms outstretched, beside the corpse of Dr. Leon, a camera movement and position that, allied with the dramatic catharsis, con- ventionally indicates the final shot of the movie. But then, we cut back to Catherine closing the upper door with the resolute words, "No one will ever enter this room again," at which the camera whip-pans right to reveal the traumatized Elizabeth tied and gagged inside the Iron Maiden.

Roughly ten minutes elapses on screen between the time we see Nicholas throttling Elizabeth and spying the metal box and our final glimpse of Barbara Steele's panicked expression inside the cage as the survivors depart—a period encompassing the pursuit and death of Dr. Leon, Francis' torture on the pendulum, Catherine fetching the ser- vant, and his struggle with Nicholas just in time to save Francis. This busy action manipulates the audience to forget about the figure who initiated all this so that when we last see her helpless, unable to call out and left to the living entombment she had earlier convinced Nicholas she had suffered, we gasp. Corman enhances the jolt by swiftly fading down with the rectangular iris (and as rapidly fading-in the blue tint of the flashbacks), which momentarily conforms to the small aperture of Elizabeth's prison so we can regard her terror, before closing to black. Our simultaneous grasp of her fatal entrapment with the rough justice that has transpired creates a rush of unsettling responses that deny complete catharsis even as it deftly ties up the plot's last loose end. In conjunction with the final chords of Les Baxter's shrill, pulsing score, this device becomes a cinematic equivalent of ringing down the curtain that matches the operatic intensity of the movie's last act.

This ending was far more cruel and sardonic than horror films of the past, such as Universal's *Dracula* (1931), *Frankenstein* (1931), or *The*

Black Cat (1934). There the destruction of the monster and the formation of a heterosexual couple conveyed a normatively satisfying sense
that goodness has prevailed both for the individuals and society.
Instead, *Pit and the Pendulum* conformed to the tenor of Hammer's
influential *Curse of Frankenstein* where Peter Cushing's amoral baron
is rebuffed by his friend, the only one who could confirm the murderous, artificial creature actually existed, and sent to the guillotine. We
are at once chastened by his fate and grimly satisfied that the true monster has been punished. Neither film's ending is affirmative in conventional terms. Francis Barnard and Catherine Medina are hardly a
couple; the movie gives no attention at all to a possible romance
between them and so avoids that familiar emblem of redemption and
hope. Rather, *Pit and the Pendulum* furthers the bloody warfare centered in the nuclear family that *Psycho* unleashed, psychosexual violence that would be enacted again and again in the horror genre for the
next twenty-five years, signaled here by the awful end of Steele's devi-
ous Elizabeth.

Corman ultimately directed eight Poe adaptations, seven with Vincent Price, which cannily mustered notable variations on proven elements of the first two movies. These ranged from the well-produced
Tales of Terror (1962) that capitalized on the European vogue for
anthology films made up three or four short episodes, to the purely
comic *The Raven* (1963) that teamed Price with horror veterans Peter
Lorre and Boris Karloff. Stretching the notion of adaptation even further, *The Haunted Palace* (1963) simply attached a Poe title to a tale by
modern horror author H. P. Lovecraft. *The Masque of the Red Death*
(1964) inspired critical opprobrium as an allegedly pretentious attempt
to copy the brooding art cinema tone of Ingmar Bergman, notably *The
Seventh Seal* (1956). (Corman's New World would later distribute
Bergman's *Cries and Whispers* [1972], as well as other European art
films by such directors as François Truffaut and Federico Fellini.) Yet
with its striking production design (Haller again), sumptuous cinematography by Nicolas Roeg, and downbeat ending, Corman was carrying the stylistic and thematic givens of early '60s gothic horror to their
logical ends. Corman finished the series with *The Tomb of Ligeia*
(1965), another outlandishly baroque piece including a thinly-veiled
drug hallucination/nightmare sequence that anticipated the topical—
and usually more highly praised—counter-culture movies (*The Wild
Angels* [1966], *The Trip* [1967]) that he would turn to afterwards. Poe's
startling scenes and dark irony were perfect for the AIP treatment that

extracted and expanded on their latent melodramatic qualities, inspiring the overwrought characters that were meant for the right star's
uninhibited performances. All this was harnessed by a director whose
cinematic flair at once satisfied and transcended the demands of the
exploitation movie. Discounting *Pit and the Pendulum* for infidelity to
its literary source is pointless. Corman, Price, and Poe represent one of
the most memorable collaborations in the history of the horror genre.

NOTES

1. Roger Corman with Jim Jerome, *How I Made a Hundred Movies in Hollywood and Never Lost a Dime* (New York: Random House, 1990), 78. See also
Sam Arkoff with Richard Turbo, *Flying through Hollywood by the Seat of My
Pants* (New York: Birch Lane Press, 1992), 91–92. Posters and ads for Corman's first adaptation used the abbreviated title, *House of Usher*, although
Poe's full original title appears in the movie's opening credits. For clarity, I will
use the shorter title to refer to the movie version.

2. For a detailed history of the social and economic shifts in film production and exhibition that shaped the genre in this period, see Kevin Heffernan,
*Ghouls, Gimmicks, and Gold: Horror Films and the American Movie Business,
1952–1968* (Durham, N.C.: Duke University Press, 2004).

3. W. H. Auden, "Edgar Allan Poe," *Forewords and Afterwords by W. H.
Auden*, ed. Edward Mendelson (New York: Random House, 1973), 210–12.

4. To say Poe wrote stories that can now be counted as science fiction is
not the same as asserting his importance in the evolution of the form. For a
wary discussion of Poe's place in the development of science fiction, see John
Trensch, "Extra! Extra! Poe Invents Science Fiction!," in *The Cambridge
Companion to Edgar Allan Poe*, ed. Kevin J. Hayes (Cambridge: Cambridge
University Press, 2002), 113–32.

5. Julian Symons, *The Tell-Tale Heart: The Life and Works of Edgar Allan
Poe* (New York: Harper and Row, 1978), 210.

6. William I. Howarth, "Introduction," in *Twentieth Century Interpretations of Poe's Tales*, ed. Howarth (Englewood Cliffs, N.J.: Prentice Hall, 1971),
1–2. For a recent and more sympathetic survey of the exchanges between Poe,
his work, and its many popular transformations to the present day, see Mark
Neimeyer, "Poe and Popular Culture," in *The Cambridge Companion to
Edgar Allan Poe*, 205–24.

7. Although Universal's *The Black Cat* (1934) and *The Raven* also did little
with Poe except appropriate a couple of his famous titles, it is notable that the
studio as yet affirmed the author's centrality to the horror form even as it was
establishing the classic parameters of the film genre.

8. Corman, *How I Made a Hundred Movies*, 78.

9. Carlos Clarens, *An Illustrated History of the Horror Film* (New York: Paragon Books, 1979 [originally published in 1967]), 151.

10. Corman, *How I Made a Hundred Movies*, 78.

11. Corman, 81. The most inspired effect here was the opening for *House of Usher*, where Corman rapidly shot Phillip Winthrop's horseback approach on the site of a just-extinguished brush fire in the Hollywood hills that had left a landscape of gray ash and blackened trees, a vivid rendering of the blighted terrain Poe describes surrounding "the melancholy House of Usher."

12. Valdine Clemens, *The Return of the Repressed: Gothic Horror from* The Castle of Otronto *to* Alien (Albany: State University of New York Press, 1999), 7.

13. Clemens, 2.

14. AIP distributed the Italian horror film *La Maschera del Demonio* (1960) in the United States as *Black Sunday*. The trailer for *Pit and the Pendulum* touted Steele's starring role in that earlier movie.

17

The Idea of Apocalypse in *The Texas Chainsaw Massacre*

Christopher Sharrett

It would be questionable to argue that the apocalypse of the contemporary horror film is the product simply of a particular set of crises occurring in America during the past several decades. While it is true that many of the themes of the horror film are responses to recent American experience, especially the delegitimation of authority in the wake of Vietnam and Watergate, this apocalypticism must be viewed against the backdrop of a long history of millennialism in American art. It is important to understand how this line of thinking has been implicated in the cinema's meditation on the ongoing collapse of bourgeois culture, a collapse in line with systems of apocalyptic belief, and a strain of pessimistic (or "counter-revelatory") apocalyptic thinking finding a culmination in the horror genre. Certain strains of thought reveal themselves in such an investigation, including a familiar critique of capitalist civilization from a rightist or nihilist perspective (the two have close affiliation), which Tobe Hooper's *The Texas Chainsaw Massacre* (1974) just nearly bypasses.

The development of apocalypticism in horror may be associated with an intellectual tradition distinct from the visions of catastrophe and utopia in, say, science fiction. The horror film, particularly since *Psycho* (1960) and *The Birds* (1963), has become heavily involved in

asking questions about the fundamental validity of the American civilizing process. This critical process was already under way in James
Fenimore Cooper's *The Pioneers*, carried forward to a more pronounced degree in the novels of Sinclair Lewis, Theodore Dreiser,
Nathanael West, Fitzgerald, and others, and in forms such as the revisionist Western, such as Peckinpah's *The Wild Bunch* (1969). There has
been an adjacent effort by scholars like Leo Marx who, at least tangen-
tially, touch on the idea of apocalypse by examining how technology
has destroyed the Edenic vision of America.[1] More specific, highly
reactionary critical insights have relied on strained notions of entropy
to explain how the energies expended on the development of the frontier would eventually implode as America established its boundaries
and built its cities.[2] Such theories have a relationship to Spengler's
deterministic notion, much appreciated by earlier geopolitical thinking, of a society degenerating from the purer epic moment of Culture
to Civilization. The point to be made here is that the failure of America's sense of divinely ordained "mission,"[3] the development of pessimism and the fixation by many American artists on a nonregenerative
apocalypse, suggests a kind of wish-fulfillment calling for an end to
history, a divine intervention meant to destroy what cannot be revitalized or what has worked against the earlier collective (that is to say
white, male, capitalist) beliefs of society.

The American horror film became tied in the 1960s and '70s to an
ongoing process of debunking the myths of utopia underneath the
American civilizing process, but with a far grander, cataclysmic, and
mythically based approach (even if myth is viewed rather tongue-in-
cheek) than other genre films of the last thirty years of the twentieth
century, including the revisionist Western.

Tobe Hooper's *The Texas Chainsaw Massacre* represents a crucial
moment in the history of the horror genre, when the form develops a
specific relationship to the historical and cultural tendencies of
America already touched upon and to a distinct period of discontent
in American society. Although Hooper's film has been analyzed
(incorrectly) as being a forerunner of the "slasher" films of the 1970s,[4]
its scope is far broader, more significant, and distant from the formulas
of the slasher cycle.

Robin Wood has discussed *Psycho* as "a key work of our time,"[5] one
that could be deciphered and accepted by a mass audience in a world
that has witnessed the death camps, the rise of the nuclear age, and the
impact of psychoanalysis on everyday human interchange. If *Psycho*

began an exploration of a new sense of absurdity in contemporary life, of the collapse of causality and the diseased underbelly of American Gothic, *The Texas Chainsaw Massacre* carries this exploration to a logical conclusion, addressing many of the issues of Hitchcock's film while refusing comforting closure (Hitchcock's ham-handed psychoanalytic ending) and placing them within the apocalyptic perspective inherited by genre art.

Begun by a group of young Austin filmmakers working through a private backer and on a minimal budget,[6] *The Texas Chainsaw Massacre* was meant, according to Hooper and scriptwriter Kim Henkel, to comment on the "moral schizophrenia of the Watergate era."[7] There are indeed ways in which Hooper's film works as a metapolitical document, although perhaps not necessarily of the most progressive order. Andrew Britton went so far as to remark that *The Texas Chainsaw Massacre* is "close in feeling" to Coppola's *Apocalypse Now* (1979) in that both works involve the viewer in a "collusion with triumphant barbarism."[8] D. H. Lawrence's approach to apocalypticism seems applicable here,[9] since both Hooper's and Coppola's films reflect the traditional Christian apocalyptic belief that an end to secular history is the proper resolution to crisis, a collective expression of resentment and an attempt to "remind" civilization of its sacred destiny. *The Texas Chainsaw Massacre* may tend to conflate a cynical nihilism with criticism of the order of things, thus making it close to an embrace of the mystical/reactionary apocalyptic, but its refusal of consolations, and its clever attention to overturning comforting notions of America embodied in genre conventions, removes it from this sensibility.

The apocalyptic sentiment of *The Texas Chainsaw Massacre* is evident first in its consciously misleading "documentary" aspect. On one level the film is meant to be approached as a "true story" with the chronicle function of "docudrama," but its hyperbole defies the assumptions of such forms, its reality centered on images suggesting a pandemic sickness in the population of America distinguished only by degree. *The Texas Chainsaw Massacre* is, in fact, based on a real historical event (which also inspired *Psycho* over a decade earlier) and is able to condense a number of historical incidents into its text to give the film poetic resonance. The notion of the film being a re-creation of actual crimes interlocks with a broader sense of the story's historical incidents having "cosmic'" significance (the sunspot opening credits and references to astrology and mysticism). Here the film's apocalypticism surfaces, but with witty skepticism.

The plot is deceptively simple and clearly traditional. It is the Hansel-and-Gretel story of apparently innocent youth stumbling upon unexplained and unimaginable evil. Sally and her boyfriend Jerry, along with Kirk and Pam and Sally's crippled brother, Franklin, take a trip through East Texas in Kirk's van. Their ultimate destination is unclear—we assume they are on a vacation outing. When they hear radio reports of atrocities at a local cemetery, the young people detour to see whether the grave of Sally's grandfather has been defiled. When everything is discovered to be in order, the five continue with a trip that takes them past sprawling cattle pens; Franklin delights in detailing the new mechanization used in livestock slaughter. Franklin's monologue rambles on, interrupted by Sally's quotes from the recent issue of her astrology magazine. Kirk stops the van to pick up a very ragged hitchhiker.

In short order we are aware that the hitchhiker is insane. He jumps into Franklin's discourse on meat processing, then takes a Polaroid snapshot of the travelers. He suddenly mutilates himself with a penknife and destroys the snapshot by fire in a hysterical, yet noticeably ritual manner. He jumps from the van, smearing his bloody hand on a rear fender, forming what later appears to a terrified and perplexed Franklin to be a hex sign.

The five continue on their way, ending up at a ruined mansion that once belonged to Sally's grandfather. We learn that the grandfather was once in the cattle business. The two couples tour the crumbling house while the wheelchair-bound Franklin remains outside. As Sally muses over the torn wallpaper she remembers from childhood, Franklin discovers bizarre artifacts of feathers and animal bones. Kirk and Pam wander away from the mansion to an old swimming hole (now dried up) and then to a ramshackle farmhouse on another property. Kirk assumes the house is occupied and attempts to buy gasoline.

We are shown images of the surrounding grounds: barren trees and shrubs are adorned with tin cups and plates (apparently to be cleaned, pioneer-fashion, by the sun and sand); toys and lawn furniture are strewn about in disuse. Kirk discovers a number of abandoned vehicles in a camouflaged yard behind the house. When Kirk enters the house in search of assistance, he is savagely murdered by a huge man in a leather mask. The man is never referred to by name but is listed in the credits as "Leatherface." Leatherface eventually captures, kills, and mutilates Jerry, Pam, and Franklin. We learn that Leatherface is a member of a family of wildly psychotic cannibals, including the crazed hitchhiker and an older man who operates a service station/luncheon-ette at which the youngsters stopped earlier. Sally is the only survivor of a night of murder and madness; she is captured and tortured by the cannibals in a grisly parody of the Mad Tea Party, but manages to escape and, after a harrowing pursuit down a back road, is rescued by a passing truck driver. The final image is of a berserk Leatherface alone on the highway against a setting sun, wildly swinging a chainsaw over-head in frustration.

The simplicity of the film is particularly noteworthy in its absence of any extraneous element and its de-emphasis of dialogue. In fact, the second half of the film is almost totally lacking in speech, the sound-track filled with Sally's screams, the insane mutterings of the cannibals, and the constant whir of Leatherface's chainsaw. Despite these charac-teristics the film has an obvious structural and thematic relationship to *Psycho*; making a distinction between the two films is where a discus-sion of *The Texas Chainsaw Massacre* really begins. While Hitchcock seems concerned with showing how various forms of repression lead

The Texas Chainsaw Massacre, 1974. Leatherface in his final rampage.
From the editors' collection.

to compulsive/schizophrenic behavior (which Hitchcock views with the humor associated with the average layman's disdain for psycho-analysis),[10] Hooper concentrates on the idea that insanity is such a widespread phenomenon of modern society that no discipline can contain it. Hooper goes to greater lengths than Hitchcock in referring to images associated with the American landscape: the family home, the vacation trip (which might also be associated with the westward movement of pioneers, or simply the American fascination with the road), the town church and cemetery, the fascination with strange hobbies and cultish beliefs, the culling of childhood memories, the squabbling among siblings, the allusion to professions and industries long entrenched in the American economy, all serve in building Hooper's sense of an overwhelmingly catastrophic situation that is rapidly moving toward an explosion. As with *Psycho*, Hooper's film spends its first half in a prologue to what is to follow, and one that goes to greater lengths than Hitchcock's in connecting its banal horrors to its outrageous ones. As with Marion's story, Franklin, his sister and their friends, and the world surrounding them, suggest the cruelty of the "normal" world. With Hooper, however, this world comes across as barbaric, the circumstances of the surrounding Southwest society (and that beyond) more accentuated to drive home its savagery. The civility of *Psycho*'s modern Southwest culture of bank offices and used car lots is replaced by the aridity and degeneration of postindustrial civilization, and the manifest cruelty of family and community.

Hooper, like Hitchcock, draws on a specific event in recent history for *The Texas Chainsaw Massacre*'s "documentary" aspect. The gruesome crimes of Ed Gein, a Wisconsin handyman who, in 1957, was discovered to be a mass murderer and cannibal is the now well-known source material for the novel by Robert Bloch that became Hitchcock's *Psycho*. The details of the Gein crimes are more faithfully rendered in Hooper's film, particularly in Leatherface's fetishism, his use of human skin as a mask, and the artworks made of human and animal remains.

The Ed Gein murders and related crimes of the quiescent '50s set off some intellectual activity outside of cinema and popular novels. Social psychologists struggled for ways to explain these atrocities to a complacent public of the Eisenhower years.[11] New studies of repression in relation to Middle America appeared, one of the most telling of which did not reach the public until over fifteen years after the Gein crimes. Michael Lesy's *Wisconsin Death Trip*, a kind of photo-monograph originally accepted as a graduate thesis at Rutgers University, was published during a period of renewed interest in the pathological element of American culture, particularly the atmosphere of the 1950s.[12] The text of this book is thin, the work relying very much on a collection of nineteenth-century portraits of small-town Wisconsin residents. In his research Lesy discovered that numerous bizarre crimes (arson, murder, myriad forms of sexual "deviance") occurred in the same rural communities that produced the serene images Lesy unearthed from newspaper offices and private collections. What connection, if any, could there be between these images and the "real" history of Wisconsin (and, by extension perhaps, a large segment of rural America)? By excluding any mention of Ed Gein, certainly Wisconsin's most notorious criminal, Lesy seems to suggest that the individual crime is only symptomatic of the general breakdown of a society, and it is because such crimes are seen as remarkable that the reason for aberration remains enigmatic.

Hooper's conclusions on this subject are far more forceful than Lesy's. In examining his photographs and Wisconsin history, Lesy relies on theories of repression derived from Freud, Erikson, even Max Nordau. Lesy's explanation of midwestern crime (which is not so different from Robin Wood's analysis of *The Texas Chainsaw Massacre*)[13] is that frustration set in among a group of already deracinated people disenfranchised by entrepreneurial capitalism and long since psychologically torn by the in-built contradictions of Protestant theology and the capitalist work ethic. The rise of the major East and West Coast cities and the principal commercial power bases further alienated these people, giving rise to the fragmented nature of the American character and creating the fabled "silent majority" of Nixon, a group presented to us as a frightening and vengeful social class. The crimes and generally bizarre fixations of the Wisconsin people can be seen, according to Lesy's research, as apocalypticism in nascent form, as a need to provoke crisis in the hope of effecting change and possible renewal. This apocalypticism begins on an individual, microcosmic scale, but its psychological origins become transpsychical and symbolic of a crisis in the general community. An extension of the crisis Lesy outlines is a tendency toward self-destruction that is collective in its appearance and consequences, and represents the perceived need for a total assault on society when change is thought to be impossible or too threatening to consider.

It is on this terrain that Hooper films *The Texas Chainsaw Massacre*. Hooper parts company with Lesy in the filmmaker's belief that the forces bringing about the dissolution of society are overwhelming; psychoanalysis and anthropology must be seen merely as the only tools we have to deal with certain phenomena. The "cosmic" nature of Hooper's film is suggested early through the images of solar fires against the opening credits. Images of a huge sun, a moon, and their micro/macrocosmic relationship to other images (such as the eyeball of a terrified Sally filmed with a macrozoom lens) recur throughout the film; we are reminded of the moon in Poe's "The Fall of the House of Usher," and how the "orb of the satellite" glares through the crumbling Usher facade. Like Poe, Hooper is concerned with showing how an edifice viewed from a distance seems intact, but a close inspection reveals not only numerous flaws but the general infirmity of the structure.

Hooper's modernism is key to describing his apocalyptic vision. The cosmic upheaval he portrays is apparent in his sound/image conjunction, the overlayering of the soundtrack, the nonlinear nature of his editing, and the de-emphasis of the spoken word. As we read the credits during the solar fire sequence, we hear the voice of a radio announcer (emanating, we discover, from Kirk's van) detailing a terrible discovery in a cemetery: two corpses have been unearthed and assembled in a surrealist, sodomic position to form a grotesque tableau (surrealism again offering the subversive element that the horror film absorbs so spontaneously). The way we are informed of this horror suggests it is unlikely that the broadcast set the plot of the film into motion, since Sally, Franklin, and their friends were apparently already traveling in the van at the time the broadcast occurs. Although Hooper makes the broadcast recede on the soundtrack as we are introduced to the young people, we are able to hear news of other calamities: the discovery in another part of the country of a body with genitals missing (making determination of sex difficult); incidents of international terrorism; oil spills; wholesale arson in a major city. The rather nondiegetic aspect of the broadcast creates the catastrophic atmosphere that quickly encompasses the film. At each instant Hooper establishes the idea of an Evil Age and the collapse of causality. The documentary-style prologue (with the monstrous graveyard tableau) is both amplified and subverted by the lack of explanation for all that follows; there seems no obvious reason for the trip by the young, bickering "family" in its latter-day covered wagon, for the existence or behavior of the cannibal family, for their attack on the young people, or for Sally's eventual rescue.

In his analysis of this film, Robin Wood, advancing his "return of
the repressed" thesis, argues that Leatherface and his family are products of oppression by industrial capitalism. They are, after all, out-of-
work slaughterhouse workers whose skills are rendered obsolete by
technology. Their cannibalism is, according to Wood, a logical extension and a proper metaphor for consumerism in capitalist society.[14]
Wood's thesis is very reasonable, but one continually wonders if the
film's vision offers an authentically progressive critique, or if, as Britton argues, it colludes with the hopeless, entrenched barbarism of
American society. Progressive critiques of bourgeois society need not
offer an explicit Marxist alternative (it may be said that Buñuel and
Pasolini often made horror films refusing progressive solutions, instead
pointing out a catastrophic vision that is the logical outcome of capitalist society); perhaps more compelling for a progressive reading of the
film is the denial of causality and emphasis on barbarism and ritual
structures, suggesting an apocalypse both primitive and modernist in
spirit. The primitive aspect is associated with the ritual atmosphere surrounding the film's horrors and the foregrounding of a situation of
chaos; the modernist aspect denies the primitive belief in a cyclical view
of history and asserts instead an absolute dead end without the possibility of renewal or transformation, which seems to be a reassertion of
the bourgeois embrace of apocalypse. But the absolute sense of dissolution tends to dismiss such readings. The film's conveyance of modernism's dismissal of myth and ritual, in particular some of the
foundational myths of the American West and the American civilizing
experience, is at the heart of its profound radicalism.

We can also, for several reasons, call *The Texas Chainsaw Massacre* a
film of "primitive apocalypse" with both "sacred" and "profane"
impulses. The film is about a world dissolving into primordial chaos,
set in an archetypal wasteland where the sustaining forces of civilization are not operative. The cannibal motif, which occurs in a number
of films following Hooper's success, suggests a number of ideas about
the resuscitation of primitive culture that need to be dealt with in
detail. The profane element of the film is the localization of the cataclysm precisely in the historical situation of the American Southwest
in the late twentieth century. In this area Hooper achieved a minor
coup when he cast John Henry Faulk—the blacklisted radio personality of the 1950s—as a kind of aging prophet presiding, with a few
drunken redneck elders, at the cemetery Sally and Franklin visit.
Nearby, an aging drunken man lounging in a tire says: "Nobody listens

to an old man . . . they laugh . . . there's them that laugh and know better!" Faulk's presence gives the brief scene some resonance. The drunk can be seen as a chorus, as chronicler of the grotesquerie that encompasses the world of the film. But if Hooper is inserting a chorus here, it is ironic, for it seems to give the lie to the idea of insightful rural folk with their homespun wisdom and common-sense philosophy; the terror that we see overwhelming the country is a culmination to the notion of the violent disruption of the security and stability of rural and suburban life (compare the sense of shock at organized crime's takeover of rural America, precipitating the "hero's" savagery in *Walking Tall*, 1973), and we are reminded of the often barbaric historical backdrop that preceded this civilization. Beyond this, the acceptance of the drunk as a conventional chorus is to accept the workings of insight, reason, and causality in the film, which are clearly elements Hooper wants to show have been demolished.

It must be emphasized that Hooper's apocalypse is not one associated with conventional notions of revelation or the reconstitution of society. The secularism and pessimism of *The Texas Chainsaw Massacre* might be seen as close in feeling to the "vengeful" religious impulse of the Christian apocalypse as interpreted by Lawrence. What remains is the notion that what cannot be changed must be destroyed totally to escape the "terror of history"[15] and the disappearance of any shared cultural beliefs, a concept also running through the films of David Cronenberg, Scorsese's *Taxi Driver* (1976), and Coppola's *Apocalypse Now*.

Hooper's disposal of cyclical thinking in *The Texas Chainsaw Massacre*'s apocalypticism is the refusal of belief in a theory that allows for the possibility of change, of one that offers a faith in human ability to perceive a role in history and eventually effect control over it. If there is anything "cyclical" to Hooper's worldview, there is a complement to Frank Kermode's notion that human need to apprehend crisis occurs throughout history, that the beginning and end of the individual life must be seen as having a "fictive concord with origins and ends, such as give meanings to lives and to poems. . . . The end they imagine will reflect their irreducibly intermediary preoccupations."[16] In the context of such thinking, cyclical theories of history can only express skepticism at the concept of a divinely motivated end to history and a spontaneous resolution to humanity's travails.

The unnerving and, to many, dissatisfying dénouement to Hooper's film—the image of Leatherface swinging his chainsaw against a sunset—is abrupt and genuinely cataclysmic. One imagines the character as the camera apparatus in Michael Snow's *La Région Centrale* (1971), with the filmmaker's point of view registering a world careening off-kilter. Unlike the "explanatory" ending of *Psycho*, there is no comfort to *The Texas Chainsaw Massacre*, so in this way at least Hooper subverts the "sense of an ending" that Kermode feels is basic to the impulse to bring history under control through the mediation of art. Hooper prefers to create a crisis, to present a world returning to chaos (usually a precondition for regeneration), an Evil Age in primitive and Eastern eschatologies. Yet, as if to offset the Evil Age motif he creates early in the film, Hooper introduces an eschatological sense a little kindred to the thinking of antiquity: the gods, if they exist, are capricious, and intervention itself is to be distrusted. Although we can assume that the world of this film is the consequence of a long historical process, there is nothing to suggest (as there is in *Psycho*) that anything can be recuperated and a new epoch begun. The *deus ex machina* rescue of Sally at the end of the film expresses this very clearly. There is a truly horrific concept here, more profound than in conventional Western apocalypticism, since Hooper reiterates the link established by critics such as Jan Kott between the ancient and contemporary absurdist worldviews.[17] Hooper's vision is compatible with the Greek view that human tragedy is tied to powerlessness in confronting fate, that the dissolution of one's age into chaos is not of one's own making.[18] In this sense the "moral schizophrenia" the filmmakers are describing cannot be easily understood through Marxist/Freudian methodologies alone, since these methods propose a system of belief and a kind of faith that is indeed millennic.

The atmosphere of an Evil Age that gives the film its force depends finally on its main horrific element—cannibalism. Noteworthy here is René Girard's comment that "cannibalism has not yet found its Freud and been promoted to the status of a major contemporary myth. Some filmmakers have tried, to be sure, to bring cannibalism into fashion, but their efforts to date have been less than successful."[19] Girard is in error here, although it is unclear whether he is opting for humor. A number of Freudian studies have analyzed the introduction of cannibalism into art, and if we are to judge by the sheer number of films with cannibalism as a theme *(Night of the Living Dead*, 1968; *Frightmare*, 1974; *Raw Meat* [aka *Deathline*], 1972; *Cannibal Holocaust*, 1979; *Zombie*, 1979; and so on), this form of horror has indeed been "successful," at least in terms of eliciting a response from the mass audience. Cannibalism has always been implied as a theme in horror, especially in the werewolf and vampire films; analysts have referred to oral attacks on the victim as emblematic of regression to the infantile stage, where attempts to satisfy libidinal impulses overlap with the instinct for nourishment and survival.[20] George Romero's *Night of the Living Dead* (1968) was the first work to literalize the theme of cannibalism, to show the relation of cannibalism to the death wish, and to illustrate the image of society feeding on itself. But it is *The Texas Chainsaw Massacre* that gives cannibalism a mythic as well as political dimension that allows it the broader resonance as a metaphor in the horror genre.

Mircea Eliade has noted that ritual cannibalism is the consequence of a tragic religious conception.[21] In many areas of mytho/anthropological study, cannibalism has been associated with regenerative functions. On a symbolic level the consumption of "sacred" flesh (the Eucharist)[22] involves replenishing the spiritual aspect of a culture and reminding society of its sense of communion. Most studies in cultural anthropology note that anthropophagy occurs in a period when a given society perceives its breakdown and finds a need to descend to an extreme level of experience through collective violence or sexual orgy, which leads to or is associated with cannibalism. This descent recapitulates the origins of the world in turmoil, when the sacred time of the gods crossed into the profane world. Eliade also notes that cannibalism has never been seen as "natural" behavior in primitive society, but rather is always "cultural behavior, based on a religious view of life."[23] The act of cannibalism in primitive society always suggests a hearkening back to the cosmic origins of the world to regain the primeval force that sparked the beginning of history. In Western mythology we are reminded of the war of the Titans in antiquity, of Cronus devouring his children, and the epic clashes of families, as in the house of Pelops. Cannibalism can signify not only the consuming of the spiritual power of the gods (making a connection to sacred time) but ultimate revenge on a foe or his progeny by devouring his strength and redressing a long-term historical debt.

In Western civilization there is no question, of course, that cannibalism has always had evil connotations. The actual consumption of the human being (rather than a symbolic ritual) has signaled societal inversion, as we learn as far back as Porphyry's *De abstinentia*.[24] The apocalyptic literary tradition has likewise associated cannibalism with barbarism and the dissolution rather than revitalization of society.[25] The torture of Sally in Hooper's film is particularly ritualistic in nature and in keeping with traditional associations of cannibalism with rite and the apocalyptic spirit. Sally is a victim, but her relative anonymity and the arbitrariness of her selection suggests she is a scapegoat. Girard has noted that "the mechanism of the surrogate victim is redemptive twice over; by promoting unanimity it quells violence on all fronts, and by preventing an outbreak of bloodshed within the community it keeps the truth about men from becoming known."[26]

Of course the cannibals, while they constitute a group, are insane; yet because the psychosis is shared, the actions each member takes can be said to reflect the perceived "best interests" of their society. The "sacrifice" of Sally mimics aspects of ritual or, rather, the converse of ritual, since we discover that this violence, which is familiar to us at least through the art form we observe, is empty of any signification in the sense formerly associated with collective violence. Hooper focuses not so much on what the cannibals do to Sally (which is relatively little) as on the extremes of her terror and the way the cannibals project their hate and collective violence upon her. Sally is by turns honored and vilified, as in primitive ritual, to a point where she is literally driven insane. Leatherface and his crazed brother delight in tormenting Sally during her initial phase of shock and pleading; she is mocked for thinking that pity and reason have anything to do with the needs of the society to which she now belongs. But even this mockery falls apart since the cannibals are in so little control of themselves that they cannot even conclude the murder of their victim. The real ritual dimension may be Hooper's refusal to accede to the most important conventions of the genre and of drama itself; the catharsis meant to be reached by the work is denied, destroying a common code shared by the audience. Just as the blood Sally might shed has no role in "replenishing" Hooper's horrific wasteland, the cynicism under the film's notion of sacrifice must be recognized. The use of Sally as ritual scapegoat becomes dark humor, meaningless since the cannibal clan has a cohesion lacking in the "normal" world of Sally's friends.

While our understanding of *The Texas Chainsaw Massacre* benefits from attention to various disciplines, it would be extreme to argue that the filmmakers have done a schematic reworking of violence and cannibalistic ritual as understood by cultural anthropology. It would be equally extreme, however, to ignore the scholarship that has informed us how cannibalism, on a metaphoric level, operates in Western consciousness. Certainly the increased recurrence of the subject in the horror film, even if reduced to the gratuitous qualifications of the "splatter" film, can be understood solely by recognizing the threads of this theme in cultural experience, the springs that make it work.

The "cosmic" opening of the film against the backdrop of solar fire, the sense of rampant evil, the uses of classical devices such as a chorus, the references to astrology, and the idea of totemism as iconographic emblem, all create Hooper's mythic dimension. Sally's preoccupation with astrology, underlined by visual references to the sun and moon, further enhances it. Her statement that "Saturn is in retrograde" reminds us that the Age of Aquarius actually signaled a time of chaos and regression.[27] More important, the references to Saturn develop the fundamental definitions of the Evil Age as a period when reason and all language/symbol systems break down. Sally is alienated from her friends by her astrology fetishism; this situation is sensible since astrology is associated with the "old religion" of sorcery, the nemesis of Christian humanism and the rise of the scientific method. Only Franklin, Sally's crippled, temperamental, and possibly psychotic brother, is enthralled with her remarks. He is equally enthralled and frightened by the bloody mark the hitchhiker leaves on the van, finding in it some magical code or curse. When he asks for an explanation of it, Pam replies, "I guess everything means something." In fact, Pam's thinking must be turned on its ear—nothing has meaning since reason has collapsed into a condition of hysteria.

Franklin, Sally, and their friends (with the mimetic doubles[28] of Leatherface, his brothers, and their clan) are offered as the film's challenge to demarcations of Self and Other basic to genre film. There is the Sally/Franklin blood relationship, which compares to the blood ties of the cannibals and repeats the traditional construct of warring clans. Within this is the notion that Franklin, presumably the eldest male of Sally's clan, is paralyzed—paralysis as a figure for impotence can be underscored by Franklin's cowardice. Franklin would most likely be the strongest member of the group (physically) were it not for his ailment, but he is now forced to ask for his sister's help to maneuver his wheelchair. Our first sense of evil in the film (outside of the prologue) comes through Franklin; he is the first to respond to the hitchhiker's "curse" and the one who discovers and is alarmed by the otherwise meaningless bone fetishes in the ruined home of his grandfather. He is also the first to buy (unknowingly) a piece of barbecue at the roadside stand owned by one of the cannibals, causing him to enter into a tacit contract with the opposing, barbaric clan. Although he discards the meat, we recognize that the descent into barbarism is shared.

After he witnesses the hitchhiker's self-mutilation, Franklin tells Kirk
in wonderment, "That must really take somethin', y'know, to just go
and do that . . . I mean, that takes somethin'." Franklin equates the act
with a test of will, like the blood-brother rite of the American Indian;
it is of course closer to Watergate burglar G. Gordon Liddy's famous
hand-singeing with a candle to prove his masculinity. Franklin embodies the apocalyptic gesture in microcosm—that is, the tendency to self-
destruction to provoke a crisis in oneself when there is no resolution
to the frustration of interchange in the exterior world. The blubbering
cowardice and psychopathology of Franklin and the insanity of the
cannibals form an important and complementary dichotomy. Franklin
is the only obvious Southwesterner of Sally's group; he knows tales of
his region and is the identifiable "pioneer stock" figure. As such, he
and the cannibals together represent the film's idea that the drives that
propelled this civilization forward can now be seen as reduced to
obsessive/compulsive and self-destructive behavior. This situation is
especially pathetic in Franklin's case, since he is reduced to little more
than a target for abuse by his peers, and although his peers are ostensibly more vital, they are nonetheless shallow and idiotic. Franklin's
whining is close to Leatherface's squealing and cowering at the hands
of his family, especially the bullying eldest brother, the mad cook.
Both Franklin and Leatherface (a real "leatherstocking" figure) are the
frontier process at the end of the road, the pioneering American family
as self-destructive (and comical in its cruel lunacy).

Sally is ultimately the focal point of unreason in the film, and the
fact that most of the truly horrific moments of the film involve her
defines her as a scapegoat whose punishment might provoke catharsis.
The hysteria of the film might be associated with the link between language's collapse and the reign of the female principle. This hysteria
doesn't reveal the film's sexism, but suggests hysteria as the only logical response of a totally disempowered civilization, where all social/
political structures have collapsed. Sally's screams overwhelm the film.
They do not abate as the film ends, the madness not expelled. Sally's
hysteria is signaled early on as she attempts to restore order but cannot
even locate her grandfather's grave. Her interest in astrology seems a
more legitimized, systematic superstition than the meandering anxi-
ties of her brother. She is enraptured by the filthy wallpaper in her
grandfather's mansion—on which she envisioned zebras in her childhood—while Kirk simultaneously spots a swarm of insects. She is
trapped in a delusory realm of the imaginary, while Kirk at least intuits

the reality of the current environment. The hysteria, of course, is not Sally's alone. Here and elsewhere the film's description of its world has little in common with the slasher cycle, with its incessant punishment of the female and reactionary notions of gender. The hysteria of *The Texas Chainsaw Massacre* prefigures the arrival of male hysteria, or the free-form hysteria that would dominate the genre cinema of the ensuing decades, especially the Angry White Male films delineating the terrible vengeance wrought by male displacement in the postindustrial age.

The ease with which Sally and her friends enter onto the landscape suggests the casual acceptance of a dead world. The crumbling mansion and defiled graveyard are curiosities to them, and some images privileged for the viewer (sick and dying cattle, a dead armadillo on the road, surrealist junk in the cannibals' backyard) pass the young people unnoticed. The cannibals' onslaught sets up a warfare between clans that is an attempt at final expiation in a decadent universe, but it is an onslaught that goes nowhere. It has been suggested several times that the action of *The Texas Chainsaw Massacre* simply dissolves, as in absurdist drama.[29] The chase sequence at the conclusion, for example, goes in a circle, as Leatherface pursues Sally from the cannibals' homestead to the old man's gas station, where she is captured and brought back to the homestead. Circularity is also seen in the implied sense of routine in the cannibals' daily lives, the feeling that they carry out a perverse mirror reflection of ordinary lower middle-class existence, something Hitchcock suggests about Norman Bates early in *Psycho* when we first catch a glimpse of him in his mother's clothes, walking routinely past the bedroom window as Marion looks up from the motel porch. A key emblem of *Chainsaw*'s circularity and of the collapse of time is a pocket watch with a nail driven through it, a Dadaist piece of sculpture swinging from a shrub, along with pots and pans being washed clean by the sun pioneer-style on the cannibals' lawn. A more literal collapse of time is seen at the dinner party where Sally is tormented: it is night when the party begins, dawn when Sally crashes through a window and escapes, and late afternoon as she is pursued down the road by Leatherface and his hitchhiker brother. All of this points to the concept of repetition as an element of the void which contains the world of the film. Repetition is evident in the traditional sense of a refusal to confront obsessional behavior, as a means of covering up or preventing a cathartic process from taking place. The ritual violence of the film has important implications when considered against the backdrop of repetition on a broad social level, as a form of collective experience denying the foundations of crisis.

I have spoken of the cannibalism of the film (which is never actually seen since all we witness is the consumption of rather generic sausage, pointing to the metaphoric value Hooper gives to cannibalism) as representative of a process of inverting all values, myths, and symbols of a culture. The cannibals' meal, rather than a communion, suggests the utter fragmentation and atomization of society, beginning with basic identity and communication. The most ferocious (and yet meek) of the group, Leatherface, is, like Franklin, the subject of constant torment and humiliation. The perpetual harangue that makes up the cannibals' conversation (the old man's famous "Look what your brother did to that door!") refers in its reflections of the average family to the heteronomy of patriarchy prevailing in American life. We do not fully understand the blood ties of the cannibals, except that Leatherface is brother to the hitchhiker and the old cook; Grandpa and Grandma can hardly be distinguished from the rest of the gruesome artifacts filling the house. The sadistic old cook would seem to be the father, but this is unclear although irrelevant (Hooper later said that he is actually the eldest brother); it is certain that he is head of the clan, and as such, is another Old Man Clanton who sees his role almost solely in terms of defending the rights of his faction against poachers, city-slickers, and any other form of intruder. Like the terrible renegade criminals of folklore,[30] the old man and his tribe become recluses, people dangerous or obsolete to society, as Wood argues. Here Hooper's narrative is self-aware, reminding us how the alienation of such people is fetishized and even valorized by popular culture. By extension, alienation itself becomes an accepted state of being—the valorization of Manson, Ed Gein, and others by pop culture makes the point sufficiently.

The clan construct reminds us that the story takes place in Texas, a state brimming with folklore and the key signifiers of the frontier experience: the Alamo, Davy Crockett, cattle drives, frontier justice, Indian wars. Again there is inversion; Leatherface's mask is of human skin, not buckskin. If Leatherface's mask (which is certainly a prominent piece of the film's iconography) is an extremely pathological fetish, it is so because of the perverse ritualism of the film. In referring to primeval time and the savage origins of history, the fetishism of the film re-creates the lampshades of Buchenwald rather than the knife scabbards and buckskin jackets of Daniel Boone and Davy Crockett. Instead of early America's epic conjunction of Culture with Nature, the cannibals' fetishism represents the total refusal of participation in the object-world. (It is worthwhile to note that the fetishism of the Nazis was part of a new tribalism and an attempt to summon up the gods of a primeval world.) In art, one connotation of the mask is the adoption of a persona signifying specific identity in terms of its relationship to the overall group. Georges Bataille has pointed out, however, that the mask can also be a symbol of chaos and the breakdown of social order, a denial of the "open face" of human exchange.[31] Leatherface's mask does not have the social function of some ritual acts; it merely serves to cover up and terrorize by reminding the spectator of corruption, the degradation of the flesh, disease, insanity, death. The mask signifies the cannibals' distance from their own acts, a fact first represented in their insanity. Their total immersion in the chaos of violence prevents them from seeing any end product of their action, a notion further uniting them to the normal world of American culture. Since there is evidence that the violence of the story has occurred many times earlier, there is an explanation (metaphorically) for the insanity of the cannibals in the basic notion of repetition as a process of flight from recognition.

The terminal states fetishism can reach is emphasized also in the "saving" of Grandpa as a human fetish, a living corpse who is kept around as a reminder of the old days before the new transformation of labor. Grandpa is remembered as the best killer in the slaughterhouse ("Nobody could beat Grandpa"); there is no irony that Grandpa, the wizened ruler of the wasteland, is given the job of killing Sally and drops the hammer. That the patriarch's past glory is associated solely with killing is a wonderful summary statement on American history. Actions constantly evaporate; the horror of the violence carried out is equaled by the comedic failure of the violence showing the absurdity of the hunter/prey construct basic to American history and folklore.

The film suggests that we "discover" something about America as Sally and her friends stumble upon the cannibal household. We are reminded that what takes place in this film occurs at an unusual time when the stars have taken on special characteristics. The civilizing spirit has run its course; its energies are depleted, its myths not only dead but inverted and forced to show the consequences of their motivating force. This is underneath Sally's shock as she falls into the artifacts and debris of the cannibals' living room. What is most unnerving and forceful in the film's initial power is the implication that the purer, epic moment of the American civilizing process is revealed to have had from the beginning the impulse of barbarism, and that this very impulse is what made it work. We witness also the implications underneath the "deliberate regression" to early, primeval culture lauded by Romantic art and so much an attribute of American myth.[32]

Hooper's apocalyptic landscape is Texas, not Wisconsin. It is a desert wasteland of dissolution where once vibrant myth is desiccated. The ideas and iconography of Cooper, Bret Harte, and Francis Parkman are now transmogrified into agribusiness yards of sick cattle, dilapidated gasoline stations and fast-food joints, defiled graveyards, crumbling mansions, and a ramshackle farmhouse full of psychotic killers. *The Texas Chainsaw Massacre* has perhaps become recognizable as a statement about the dead end of American experience simply because it jibes with the "diminished expectations" of the population in the 1970s and '80s (we cannot help but see how rightfully diminished those expectations were from the vantage point of the new millennium).

While Hooper's film suggests that there is no millennic transition as understood by religious and other established institutions, the acceptance of *The Texas Chainsaw Massacre* as an apocalyptic work may be based on audience need to fulfill through its art a growing pessimistic inclination. This same inclination has already called for a massive criticism and deconstruction of mythology in general, a process associated with the climate of postmodernity. It may be repeated that as we might understand the apocalypse of *The Texas Chainsaw Massacre* by drawing on structural anthropology and such constructs as scapegoat killing, it is important to realize how the film is a denial of such interpretation as it is a denial of ritual processes themselves. The comedic aspect of the film has always been perceived by critics and audiences; the comedy enhances rather than deflates the film's terror. The comedy, in so horrific a work, suggests that the rules of the form (and of drama itself—even as we are aware that tragedy and comedy have long since been merged), providing as they do a comfortable sense of organization and closure, are delusory if art is supposed to "mimic" reality. The reality that Hooper's art imitates is resistant to any rational ordering system, perhaps its most profound subversion; art can no longer be intellectual recreation through the contemplation of order. The idea of "redemption" that patriarchal occidental humanity has assigned to the spirit of art, underlined by the "great works" continuing the concepts of sacrifice and revivification of society, is parodied here. The patently absurd reenactment of scapegoat killing (which indeed has a rough correlate in *Apocalypse Now*) in Hooper's film is one of cinema's strongest statements of the general bankruptcy of myth and communal belief in the contemporary world.

NOTES

1. Leo Marx, *The Machine in the Garden: Technology and the Pastoral Idea in America* (New York: Oxford University Press, 1964).

2. Brooks Adams, *The Law of Civilization and Decay* (1924; rpt. New York: Vintage-Knopf, 1959).

3. Ernest Cassara, "The Development of America's Sense of Mission," in *The Apocalyptic Vision in America,* ed. Lois P. Zamora (Bowling Green, Ohio: Popular Press, 1982), 64.

4. See, for example, Ellen Farley and William K. Knoedelseder Jr., "The Real *Texas Chainsaw Massacre*," *Los Angeles Times* (September 5, 1982), 4.

5. Robin Wood, *Hitchcock's Films* (New York: A. S. Barnes, 1965), 144.

6. The full production history of the film is detailed in Farley and Knoedelseder, "The Real *Texas Chainsaw Massacre*," 30. See, also, Danny Peary, *Cult Films* (New York: Delta, 1981), 347.

7. Farley and Knoedelseder, "The Real *Texas Chainsaw Massacre*," 31.

8. Andrew Britton, "Sideshows: Hollywood in Vietnam," *Movie*, nos. 27/28 (Winter 1980/Spring 1981): 13.

9. D. H. Lawrence, *Apocalypse* (New York: Viking, 1932).

10. There are, of course, numerous worthwhile studies of *Psycho* in print. A good beginning is James Naremore, *Filmguide to* Psycho (Bloomington: Indiana University Press, 1973).

11. The facts of the Ed Gein crimes are recounted in Jay Robert Nash, *Bloodletters and Badmen: A Narrative Encyclopedia of American Criminals: From the Pilgrims to the Present* (New York: M. Evans and Co., 1973), 206. An intelligent essay on Gein is David Schreiner, "Ed Gein and the Left Hand of God," *Weird Trips*, no. 2, 20. The comic book aspect of this magazine should not deceive the reader; the article by Schreiner is valuable.

12. *Wisconsin Death Trip* (New York: Pantheon Books, 1973) may be seen as a form of popular scholarship serving as an exegesis of a political/religious belief system that came to the surface (and came apart) in the 1950s and thereafter. In the 1930s the crimes of Dillinger, Pretty Boy Floyd, and Bonnie and Clyde were seen as aberrations brought about by extraordinarily difficult economic times; the crimes of Charles Starkweather, Ed Gein, et al. in the 1950s spurred a revisionism in sectors of American Studies that looked to psychopathology as the evidence of something awry in the entire American civilizing experience.

13. Robin Wood, "An Introduction to the American Horror Film," *The*

American Nightmare (Toronto: Festival of Festivals, 1979), 19–22. Reprinted in this volume.

14. Wood, 20.

15. Mircea Eliade, *The Myth of the Eternal Return, or Cosmos and History*, trans. Willard R. Trask (Princeton, N.J.: Bollingen, 1971), 139–59. The term refers to primitive man's need for repetition to avoid the prospective confrontation with the meaninglessness of profane existence.

16. Frank Kermode, *The Sense of an Ending: Studies in the Theories of Fiction* (New York: Oxford University Press, 1966), 22. See a discussion of Kermode in Bernard McGinn, *Apocalyptic Spirituality* (New York: Paulist Press, 1979).

17. Jan Kott, *The Eating of the Gods* (New York: Vintage, 1971).

18. Debra Berghoffen, "The Apocalyptic Meaning of History," in *The Apocalyptic Vision in America*, ed. Samora, 17.

19. René Girard, *Violence and the Sacred*, trans. Patrick Gregory (Baltimore, Md.: Johns Hopkins University Press, 1977), 277.

20. This is discussed in relation to the horror film in, for example, David Pirie, *The Vampire Cinema* (London: Crescent Books, 1973), 16–18.

21. Mircea Eliade, *The Sacred and the Profane*, trans. Willard R. Trask (New York: Harcourt Brace Jovanovich, 1957), 106.

22. This idea is discussed in Richard Slotkin, *Regeneration through Violence: The Mythology of the American Frontier* (Middletown, Conn.: Wesleyan University Press, 1973), 48, passim.

23. Eliade, *The Sacred and the Profane*, 103.

24. Discussed in Marcel Detienne, "Between Beasts and Gods," in *Myth, Religion & Society,* ed. R. L. Gordon (Cambridge: Cambridge University Press, 1981), 218.

25. Zamora, "The Myth of Apocalypse and the American Literary Tradition," in *The Apocalyptic Vision in America*, 126.

26. Girard, *Violence and the Sacred*, 42.

27. Wood, "An Introduction to the American Horror Film," 20.

28. Girard, *Violence and the Sacred*, 143–68, who advances the notion of violence (such as in sadism and masochism) requiring a reciprocal contract; violence requires that the victim see the oppressor as having demonic/supernatural power, causing the victim to internalize the means of oppression and continue the cycle of violence.

29. See, for example, Peary, *Cult Films*, 348.

30. Jay Robert Nash's book allows us to view this material against a long history of valorizing crime in America.

31. Georges Bataille, "Le Masque," *Oeuvres Complètes* 2 (Paris: Gallimard, 1970), 403–06.

32. The genealogy of this thinking is traced in Robert Harbison, *Deliberate Regression* (New York: Alfred Knopf, 1980).

18

Archetypal Landscapes and *Jaws*

Jonathan Lemkin

Jaws appeared in American theaters in June 1975, preceded by a massive "media blitz," yet reviewers initially dismissed the film. "*Jaws* is, at least, the old standby, a science fiction film," said Vincent Canby of the *New York Times*, who saw nothing extraordinary about the film at all. "It opens according to the time-honored tradition with a happy-go-lucky innocent being suddenly ravaged by the mad monster, which in *Jaws* comes from the depths of inner space—the sea as well as man's nightmares. Thereafter *Jaws* follows the formula with fidelity. . . . It's a noisy, busy movie that has less on its mind than any child at the beach might have."[1] After the film grossed more than $90 million in its first two months, the *Times* published a second review calling the film "nothing more than a creaky old monster picture."[2] Stephen Farber continued to affirm that *Jaws* "was strikingly similar to another movie in release this summer, William Castle's *Bug*, about giant, incendiary cockroaches that overrun Los Angeles after an earthquake."[3]

But Canby, Farber, and the other reviewers missed the point. *Jaws* proved to be the second most popular film in history, grossing, as of January 1, 1980, more than $130 million. It is not a standard science-fiction film, or a monster movie about giant exploding cockroaches. For unlike the aforementioned *Bug*, and other formula monster movies, *Jaws* is not a film set in Los Angeles, New York, Washington, D.C., or even the plains of the midwest; it is about America—perhaps an

America that does not exist and never did, but one the audience recognizes nonetheless. The "real" America is at best a series of widely scattered and discrepant regions, each with its own unique characteristics, often dependent on the natural topography of the landscape. As early as 1792, J. Hector St. John de Crèvecoeur pointed to this as being an early and seminal characteristic of America in his *Letters from an American Farmer*:

> British America is divided into many provinces, forming a large association, scattered along a coast 1500 miles extent and about 200 miles wide. This society I would fain examine, at least as it appears in the middle provinces; if it does not afford that variety of tinges which may be observed in Europe, we have colours peculiar to ourselves. For instance, it is natural to conceive that those who live near the sea, must be very different than those who live in the woods; the intermediate space will afford a separate and distinct class.[4]

Spielberg distills elements from a variety of American landscapes into one ideal, mythic landscape. In the process lies the power of the film to evoke a place that everyone in the audience recognizes as "America."

In an essay on symbolic landscapes and idealizations of American communities, D. W. Mienig claims that "Every mature nation has its symbolic landscapes. They are part of the iconography of the nationhood, part of the shared set of ideas and memories and feelings that bind a people together."[5] *Jaws* is a perfect example: the landscape in the film is an environment that never really existed, except in the collective conscious of the vast majority of Americans. The setting is the archetypal American coastal town—absolutely the earliest American image, the settlements of the pilgrims on the coast of New England. It is the predecessor of the American rural ideal, and in that sense, the truest America. It is also a creation of nostalgia, a *pure* American community, which is nothing less than mythic.

But this is only half the story. Spielberg also makes powerful use of another aspect of the environment—the beachfront and ocean. Not only in American culture, but in almost all cosmologies, the ocean is the predecessor of all, even the pure small town. And while the ocean may too be pure, it is not necessarily gentle. As W. H. Auden points out in *The Enchafed Flood*:

> The sea or the great waters, that is, are the symbol for the primordial undifferentiated flux, the substance which became created nature only by having form imposed or wedded to it.

The sea, in fact, is that state of barbaric vagueness and disorder out of which civilization has emerged and into which, unless saved by the efforts of gods and men, it is always liable to relapse. It is so little of a friendly symbol that the first thing which the author of the Book of Revelations notices in his vision of the new heaven and earth at the end of time is that "There was no more sea."[6]

There are two crucial points to be recognized in the collective perception of the sea as an unfriendly environment. First, the sea is a place of the unknown: the life that lies beneath its surface, however dreadful, is greater than the visible. Herman Melville expressed this dread of submerged malignancy well in *Moby Dick*: "As this appalling ocean surrounds the verdant land, so in the soul of man there lies one insular Tahiti, full of peace and joy, but encompassed by all the horrors of the half-known life."[7] And on a much more personal and frightening level, as Spielberg notes, "When you're out swimming and you turn to tread water, half of your body is under the surface and you can't keep tabs on what's happening down there around your feet."[8]

Second, the sea is a place beyond the rule of man, whose influence stops at the shoreline. There are no demarcated borders to fight over, only arbitrary claims; it is beyond the subjugation of humanity. "The sea does not belong to despots. Upon its surface men can still exercise unjust laws, fight, tear one another to pieces, and be carried away with terrestrial horrors," argues Nemo in Jules Verne's *Twenty Thousand Leagues Under the Sea*; "But at thirty feet below its level, their reign ceases, their influence is quenched, and their power disappears. Ah, sir, five in the bosom of the waters. There is only independence. There I recognize no master's voice. There I am free."[9] Beyond human control, the sea takes on all the aspects of wilderness that the virgin forest or desert might possess. And it is as archetypal and immediately recognizable as any other wilderness. As long as corpses wash up on the beach, we will fear the sea as uncontrollable, formless wilderness. In 1865, upon viewing corpses washed ashore from a shipwreck, even Henry David Thoreau decried the ocean as "wilder than a Bengal jungle." "Serpents, bears, hyenas, tigers, rapidly vanish as civilization advances, but the most populous and civilized city cannot scare a shark from its wharves." The beach Thoreau found no more than "a morgue" where "the carcasses of men and beasts together lie stately upon its shelf, rotting and bleaching in the sun."[10]

In addition to the general disease generated by its symbolic value as evil and wilderness, the issue is further complicated by the dual nature of the sea. The maternal significance of water and the sea has always been one of the clearest symbols in mythology,[11] although, as Jung points out, the mother archetype is not an easy symbol to deal with. The qualities associated with it are not only "all that is benign, all that cherishes and sustains," but also "anything secret, hidden, dark; the abyss, the world of the dead, anything that devours, seduces, and poisons, that is terrifying and inescapable like fate."[12] In *Jaws*, this dichotomy is clear; the sea is at once both the warm, soft days of summer and the evil and danger lurking just beneath the surface. There is a beautifully visual cue of this between the first scene of the shark attack on the "summer girl," Chrissie, and the introduction of Chief Brody. At the end of the shark attack, the camera looks out on the evilly gleaming night sea, awash with death, and slowly, on the same horizon line, there is a lap dissolve to the same ocean and the same sky, but now cheerfully gleaming in the clean blue morning: Jung's loving and terrible mother has come to rest in the sea.

For all the neat categorizations of mythology, the sea is still a region entirely beyond the control of man; we may label it and classify it, but that is all. And it is between this archetypal uncontrollable wilderness and the archetypal American landscape that Spielberg spins his tale. His challenge is to structure two distinctly different landscapes into the film. In the first ten minutes he introduces them both, details them, and forces them upon the audience. *Jaws* opens on a beach at night—a group of summer teenagers gather by a fire, a primitive source of heat and fight, and unwittingly carouse in reach of Thoreau's morgue. Not only is the sea a place of wilderness, so too is the beach. The evershifting, infertile sands are an object of chaos beyond the control of man and thus also tend toward evil.[13] Like the ocean, it is a place both barren and beyond the pale of law. One edge of the beach plunges irrevocably into the sea, or perhaps just as malevolently, rises from it. At once, then, Spielberg thrusts his characters in a liminal zone and exposes them to danger.

One young woman leaves the relative safety of the fire-lit circle; she runs along the beach until she reaches the water's edge, disrobing as she goes, abandoning the vestiges of civilization and returning to a wild state herself. In the truest sense of the word, she has become *bewildered* by the landscape. She enters the water and becomes the shark's first victim. Yet with the environmental preamble afforded no viewer is shocked, for despite the cinematic violence, the film has not lied. No

Jaws, 1975. The monster shark in the underwater wilderness.
Still courtesy of Jerry Ohlinger's Movie Material Store.

gigantic flaming cockroaches suddenly appear; she entered a place of known evil and the virulence there overcame her. "She should have known better," is the implied moral. In the final shots of this first shark attack, Chrissie begins to cry out for help, first to any one who might hear, and then to God. With no response forthcoming, she reaches for her one possible succor, a buoy floating behind her. Under-lining man's impotence in this environment, it points out that the best that can be managed against the primitive power of the sea is a device to warn of the danger present. The beach and the ocean have been little more than a dark blur on the screen; but already they have been identi-fied as a place where evil is hidden but ever-present. There are no happy families in sailboats and no bronzed surfers in this environment, only fools and corpses. Thus the archetype of the sea is powerfully introduced in the film's opening.

The sea introduced, it is now left for elucidation as Spielberg unveils his consummate manmade environment, the fictional village of Amity, a summer town located somewhere off the coast of New York state. With few exceptions this environment no longer exists on the eastern coast of the United States, and in any case it is not the modern conception of the beachfront. But it *is* the idealistic prototypical conception. And the small town that Spielberg locates there is a place of safety in the midst of the wilderness. As John R. Stilgoe points out in his comprehensive work *Common Landscape of America, 1580 to 1850*:

> For colonial New Englanders the word *town* was rich in peculiar spatial significance. It denoted a self-governing, nearly self-sufficient agricultural community inhabiting a discrete, carefully bounded space shaped from wilderness chaos and through continuous corporate effort maintained in equilibrium against the wild beasts and plants—and supernatural evils like witches—that threatened to overwhelm it.[14]

The bright clean world of Amity Island—a world of white picket fences and gleaming white houses—is a purified version of the original Puritan settlements. The neatly maintained fences demarcate the community order, the sprucely painted houses the worth of each homeowner. The web of sanctity spreads out until it reaches the lighthouses that appear throughout the film marking the limits of order. Like the buoy in the opening scene, the lighthouses warn man away from the dangers of the sea. "The towers, however, marked more than dangerous shoals and narrow channels. They announced the end of the locally controlled complex of structures and man-made spaces that most people recognize by the word neighborhood."[15]

Spielberg not only creates this American environment, but takes it one step further. He extends his American archetype by combining it with the archetype of the sea by placing the community on an island. Auden considers the island to be "an enclosed place of safety . . . a private place where the writ of the law does not run" and "the earthly paradise where there is no conflict between natural desire and duty."[16] The village of Amity is suspended in the primordial innocence of an island, and like Defoe's island in *Robinson Crusoe* or Cooper's in *The Crater, or Vulcan's Peak*, it is threatened only by its antecedent—the chaos and wilderness of the sea.

After the introduction of the sea and the first shark attack, Spielberg reveals his American landscape through the film's protagonist, Chief Brody. Brody's relationship to his environment is crucial; he is a man who has just fled New York City, the land of muggers, rapists, and corruption. He has come to Amity for "a healthy place to raise the kids," for the ideal of simplicity and innocence. In short, he has left

New York for this mythic America, the earthly paradise where "one man can make a difference."

Brody, though, is a man who does not like the water; he sits in his car on the ferry to the mainland. Yet so strong is the draw of this archetype that he has braved the island. What Brody is unaware of is that he has simply exchanged one wilderness for another; he has bartered away the city for the sea. And the sea threatens to take away all he has gained. It is this shattering of the American archetypal landscape which forms the emotional framework of the film; the shark attacks are horrific and examples of cinematic expertise, but they mean more than what is there on the "surface." On a larger scale, Meinig's symbolic landscape is being threatened. Spielberg threatens to tear America apart with this shark and, as it will become clear, it is this attack on the American environment that helped bring forty million people into the theaters, not just the blood washing up on the beach.

Yet despite Brody's best efforts, the blood does wash up on the beach again, this time as the young Alex Kitner is attacked in the midst of a crowd of bathers. After this attack, the town finally recognizes that a problem does exist and the local populace gathers in the town council chambers to discuss the issue. It is here, in the midst of their inefficient discussion, that the audience is first introduced to the character of Quint. Like the woodcutter of the fifteenth-century European village of *Grimm's Tales*, Quint has been in the wilderness too long. He is no longer one who dwells on the land or belongs there. He is an outsider, and the public fears him as such, much the way the settled public of James Fenimore Cooper's *Leatherstocking Tales* felt the life of a hunter to be "of vast disadvantage for temporal purposes, and it totally removes one from within the influences of more sacred things."[17] Indeed, to the townspeople of Amity, Quint seems to have gone a bit wild himself: a hairy, scruffy denizen of the sea, he now lies outside the hegemony of the Amity landscape. He demands respect and even fear from the mayor, a man who can bluster and shout his way through controlling the indigenous population, but finds that Quint, much like the shark, must be treated on a different level. Quint's alignment with this gathering, and indeed the land itself, is at best tenuous, but he still stands as the townspeople's most direct link with the primal power of the sea. The outcome of the meeting, however, is nebulous, as Quint's offer to hunt down the shark is "taken under advisement." For now, at least, the townspeople decide to deal with the problem themselves. But Brody, despite his compliance with

the decision, decides to find his own help, aligned with the environment of the sea, and so he calls in an expert from the Oceanographic
Institute.

The next morning, the ineptitude of the landspeople on the sea is
revealed as they overload their boats and try to hunt the shark with
explosives. In the midst of this tumult Brody's expert from the institute
arrives. The expert, Hooper, comes equipped with a long history of
shark study and an extraordinary array of technical wizardry. It is
unclear whether his boat would be more at home at sea or on a pad at
Cape Canaveral. The information he provides will create an important
catalyst to prod Brody on to action—yet it seems evident from the
moment of his arrival that he has come from the wrong environment
to do battle with the sea and the evil presented there in the form of the
great white shark. His knowledge of the sea is from the second-hand
flash of a diode. Hooper does not spring from the days of the British
navy tar, nor of the tattooed merchant marine; he negotiates the sea
through electronic artifice, not by battling it on its own primitive
terms. While Hooper may play an important role in the eventual eradi-
cation of the shark, it is clear that he will not take a major role in its
actual demise. At this point, *Jaws* divides into two films; the first half
is the attack on the beaches of the archetypal coastal town, and the second half, the captain and crew in pursuit of their prize, the great white
shark. Just as neatly it divides into the final conflict of the two archetypal landscapes.

The film also makes it clear that there is only one man present who
can fight the shark on its own terms, in its own environment. Brody
and Hooper realize this and visit Quint's house/dock to procure
Quint's services in eradicating the shark. The room is bedecked with
trophies of Quint's triumphs against the sea; his one view of the harbor
is literally through the jaws of a giant shark—Quint negotiates the
environment of the sea from within it. He appears to be the only logical
choice to battle the shark, for he fights the primitive force of the sea
with a primitive force of his own. But the origin of his strength is the
sea itself. As far back as 1738, Lord Bolingbroke, in his essay on "The
Idea of a Patriot King," described the source of power of the archetypal sailor: "Like other amphibious animals, we must come onshore;
but the water is more properly our element, and in it we find the greatest security, so we exert our greatest power."[18] But Quint has allowed
this force to overpower the part of him that belongs to the land and the
community of men.

After their first battle at sea with the shark, Quint, Brody, and Hooper spend the night afloat awaiting the shark's return. After an evening's drinking, Quint tells the tale of his rescue from the U.S.S. *Indianapolis*, torpedoed and sunk with 1,100 men on board, only 316 of whom survived the subsequent shark attack. Quint survived, although death, it seemed, passed within a fin's width. Somewhere in the five days he floated, waiting and hoping for salvation, Quint resigned himself to his own death; his life no longer belonged to him but to the sea. He has sworn never to wear another life jacket, and indeed, as the *Orca* begins to flounder, he does not, but only hands them to Hooper and Brody. There are three black circles painted on the forecastle of the Orca: two of them have life rings hung and centered, while the third, representing Quint, contains a set of shark jaws. Quint has quit the land and aligned himself with the sea. After the shark attacks the boat and it begins to founder, Brody rushes to the radio to signal to land for help, but Quint suddenly appears and beats the radio into pieces with a baseball bat. If they are going to sink and die, so be it, but they will not depend upon society for help in the briny wilderness. Quint's alignment with his environment is complete; and in the eyes of Brody, Quint has gone mad—or more appropriate, in his case—*wild*.

Aligned now totally with the sea, and his bond with the land severed, Quint can never return to Amity, the island of friendship. Instead, he joins the sea as the shark takes him as its next victim. For Hooper and Brody, the ship is now the last vestige of union to the land. And yet the shark threatens to destroy this too. Just prior to Quint's death, Hooper descends into the sea, his plan to fight the shark in its own environment. But Hooper's "anti-shark cage" proves to be less than effective, and as his technology fails him he is forced to take refuge in the very environment in which he hoped to triumph. He, as Quint had once been, was the survivor of a near shark attack, swimming to shore as a youth, as a shark devoured his boat.

He has spent the rest of his life since that incident studying sharks. His alternative to staying at Amity and battling the shark was spending eighteen months at sea aboard the *Aurora*, a "floating asylum" for shark scientists. He, too, has only a tenuous alignment with the land. Only Brody is left to do battle with the shark. Unlike Quint and Hooper, his stake in returning to the land is high. He has declared Amity his home, and has ventured into the wilderness to defend it. While the sailor or denizen of the sea may accept death on the waters as his inevitable fate, the land dweller has never taken it quite as well.

As Gonzalo cries out in Shakespeare's *The Tempest* as the ship founders in the storm: "Now would I give a thousand furlongs of sea for an acre of barren ground; long heath, brown furze, anything. The wills above be done, but I would fain die a dry death."[19]

As the ship sinks and the shark cruises in search of its next meal and victory, all that is left Brody is the primitive instinct of survival—no complicated strategies, no premeditated plan of action, only the desire to endure. And reduced to this primitive level, Brody, in his final attempt to survive, his last gesture of defiance against the sea, triumphs. He triumphs not in denying his bond with the land, nor in attempting to retreat to safety, but in fighting to defend himself and his environment against this interloper. And thus Brody and his environment are saved.

The success of *Jaws* was phenomenal, but its success lay in more than just its cinematic virtue. The film is a consummate collision between wilderness and community as it pits the two immediately recognizable archetypes against each other. In this nation of immigrants, the archetype of the sea as a place of wilderness has been part of American subconscious beliefs since the first pilgrims crossed the water seeking sanctuary. Whether in metaphor or actuality, all (European) Americans have braved the wilderness to reach these shores. Amity, unlike the sea and wilderness, exists only on the screen; but it also exists deep within the subconscious beliefs of Americans. For all its cinematic scares, *Jaws* did not ask its viewers to do anything difficult or frightening; it demanded the acceptance of no new ideas. The film simply reinforced the audience's already preconceived notions about these two archetypes, and in this sense, it was both a comforting and comfortable film. What is said to the audience was, in effect, "You're right. You were right all the time." The film reinforces our already preconceived fears of wilderness and the unknown and bolsters our belief in the purity and sanctity of America. The supposedly helpless and hydrophobic Chief Brody overcomes the wilderness; he triumphs over chaos. Thus, the ending of this film is immensely satisfying. The audience is given exactly what it wants.

Jaws in many ways is a propaganda film for America. It draws on deep, submerged beliefs, manipulates them, and feeds them back to us. Spielberg threatens America with his shark; the wilderness and the unknown hidden there threaten the sanctuary and community that is America. But typical of most horror films, *Jaws* can only toy with beliefs and anxieties we already have. We may not recognize them, but

like the shark, they prowl unceasingly beneath the seemingly calm surface of consciousness. We want to believe that America will triumph
over all unknown obstacles, through ferocious battle perhaps, but triumph nonetheless. By aligning his protagonist with a symbolic, idealized landscape of America, Spielberg insures that on some level his
audience will understand and be reassured of Brody's eventual triumph—America, or course, cannot fail. *Jaws* provided its audience
with a satisfactory solution to the conflicts presented: the shark dies,
Brody prevails, and two submerged beliefs are brought to the surface
for 120 minutes, reaffirmed, and then allowed to sink quietly from
where they came. The audience leaves the theatre calm and inwardly
pleased—they were right, after all.

NOTES

1. Vincent Canby, "If You Are What You Eat," *New York Times*, 21 June
1975, 19, col. 2.

2. Stephen Farber, "Only Difference Is the Hype," *New York Times*, 24
August 1975, 11, col. 1.

3. Farber, 11.

4. J. Hector St. John de Crèvecoeur, *Letters from an American Farmer*
(New York: Dutton. 1975), 40.

5. D. W. Meinig, ed., *The Interpretation of Ordinary Landscapes* (New
York: Oxford University Press, 1979), 164.

6. W. H. Auden, *The Enchafed Flood* (New York: Random House, 1950), 7.

7. Herman Melville, *Moby Dick* (New York: The Modern Library, 1926),
181.

8. Andrew C. Bobrow, "An Interview with Steven Spielberg," *Filmmakers
Newsletter* (Summer 1974): 34.

9. Jules Verne, *Twenty Thousand Leagues Under the Sea* (London: Thomas
W. Cromwell, 1976), 234.

10. Henry David Thoreau, *Cape Cod* (New York: Thomas Crowell, 1966),
161 and 165–67.

11. Sigmund Freud, *The Interpretation of Dreams*, Vol. 5 of *The Standard
Edition of the Complete Psychological Works of Sigmund Freud* (London:
Hogarth Press and the Institute of Psychoanalysis, 1962), 399 ff.; and Karl
Abraham, *Dreams and Myths* (New York: The Journal of Nervous and Mental
Disease Publishing Co., 1913), 23, as cited by C. G. Jung in *Symbols of Trans-
formation* (Princeton, N.J.: Princeton University Press, 1973), 16.

12. C. G. Jung, *Four Archetypes* (Princeton, N.J.: Princeton University
Press, 1973), 16.

13. John R. Stilgoe, "A New England Coastal Wilderness," *Geographical Review* (April 1981): 33.

14. John R. Stilgoe, *Common Landscape of America, 1580 to 1850* (New Haven: Yale University Press, 1982), 57.

15. Stilgoe, 109.

16. Auden, *The Enchafed Flood,* 21.

17. From *The Pioneers* by James Fenimore Cooper, published 1823, as cited by Henry Nash Smith, *Virgin Land: The American West as Symbol and Myth* (Cambridge: Harvard University Press, 1970), 63.

18. Lord Bolingbroke, from "The Idea of a Patriot King" (1738) in *Flowers of the Sea*, ed. Captain Eric Bush (London: George Allen & Unwin), 1.

19. William Shakespeare, *The Tempest*, I:i, 71–74.

19

Biological Alchemy and the Films of David Cronenberg

Mary B. Campbell

The horror films of Canadian director David Cronenberg manifest a deeply artful understanding of the genre in which he is working. He has produced a series of generic creations that have the complex structure and distressing power of "serious" art, without the strategies of subversion and ironic rearrangement on which most European directors rely in their attempts to exploit generic expectations (as in Antonioni's *Blow-Up* [1966], Herzog's *Nosferatu* [1979], Godard's *A bout de souffle* [*Breathless*, 1959]). This is because he has understood the content of his genre, and felt out its conventional materials in such a way as to extend their resonances into the realm of viable metaphor. Such *topoi* of science-fiction horror as mutation, telepathy, epidemic, and sexual metaliberation become, in his trembling hands, the precise pathology of the human condition. Horror and science-fiction genre pieces are effective, of course, because their structures and images have evolved in adaptive response to an audience whose dreams and nightmares can be told in such terms. Cronenberg simply makes conscious, and thus capable of organized significance, what the makers of B movies have been producing in their sleep.

The classic horror plot irritates more than one source of fear: we fear vampirism because it transforms human beings, and being contagious, it spreads uncontrollably. Neither this disease nor the ones that create zombies are simple play-offs between body and invader. Some people are more potently transformed than others, reveal different symptoms, carry more responsibility for the spread of the condition. Sometimes the disease itself alters its nature as time goes on: in *Zombies* (1964) the problem begins as a fatal, plague-like disease of which the peculiar symptom is that the body becomes a zombie after death; by the end of the film, all deaths are followed by this empty resurrection, and the bite of a zombie can induce it even before death. In most B horror movies, our fears of transformation, uncontrollable contagion, and unnatural complexity are left as separate strands, each contributing its separate share of anxiety to our fragmented experience. In Cronenberg's films, these strands are woven together into a strong, single rope. My suggestion is that there is a traditional system where all these elements figure in an organic unity of purpose, and that consciously or not, Cronenberg has drawn on the structure and world view of the ancient science of alchemy to produce his opus of modern dread.

Cronenberg's films belong among the currently crowded ranks of paranoid fictions, along with the novels of Thomas Pynchon and William S. Burroughs, and films like *Zombies, Dawn of the Dead* (1978), and *Invasion of the Body Snatchers* (1956). The paranoid vision most characteristic of our culture at the present moment is that of an autonomous technology, spinning its own dreams beyond our control, thoroughly international, tended to by an invisible network of powerful human servants.[1] In *The President's Analyst* (1967) this technological system is identified, with comic reductiveness, as the phone company. Cronenberg's paranoia is a step beyond that of *The President's Analyst* in its images, and seems to deal with a deeper fear—a fear of the mindlessly autonomous Life Force itself. This may be a logical extension of the animism that has lately accompanied our view of the technological monster, which is perceived by many as self-generating and self-maintaining. It is a short step from Harlan Ellison's nightmare of the malign computer which exterminates a redundant human race[2] to the nightmare of human behavior reduced to the mechanical activity of propagation.

Though his focus is biological, and usually sexual, Cronenberg does involve technology in his plots. Unlike the creators of *Zombies* or *Dawn of the Dead*, he always gives us a culprit, and that culprit is always a scientist—in fact, a doctor. Technology out of control is not his primary fear, but it is implicated: his doctors never intend the catastrophic effects of their research and inventions, and are always destroyed by them. As doctors, they are ostensibly figures of control. Of all technologies, medicine is the one that seems most harnessed to the individual will and discretion of its practitioners—a perception which is clearly exploited for its horrific potential in Michael Crichton's *Coma* (1978). But Cronenberg's doctors are in the grip of a technological enthusiasm stronger than human will or discretion, and their zealous tinkering with Nature reaps from her a calamitous revenge. Nature, like technology, can run rampant, and more than any specific cause it is this effect of rampancy that we have come to fear.

We live in an age in which all things threaten to run rampant, in which "spiraling" is an adjective full of terror: we have spiraling inflation, a spiraling arms race, spiraling unemployment and population growth. Spiraling surpluses—of children, capital, technological know-how—encourage spiraling shortages of food, wages, employment, satisfaction. And yet the spiral is one of our most ancient and universal cosmological symbols. With all the figure implies of unlimited growth and expansion it must at one time have been a symbol as hopeful and life-affirming as those of the sun or the lotus. And it was God Himself who commanded us to "be fruitful and multiply." Our technologies have been developed in obedience to this injunction; they have been systems of techniques that enable multiplication, profusion, abundance, increase (along with techniques that encourage the *spread* of this or that).

Though the generativeness of Nature has been the positive model for this urge to expand, we have always been impatient with the slow pace of natural production and propagation, and with what seems to us Nature's parsimony. Technical methods of vitalizing nature have as their ancestor the age-long practice of alchemy. Indeed, alchemy and the more ancient metallurgies from which it developed are the primal manifestations of man's impulse to speed up and exaggerate the inevitable but slow generation of perfect natural things. The alchemists, though far happier than Cronenberg about it, shared with him an intensely sexualized vision of the physical world and its inner relations. Mineral gold was thought to be generated in the womb of the Earth where it matured, recapitulating a value-laden periodic table, from "base matter" into gold. In the speeded-up process of the alchemist, the Philosopher's Stone was considered a seed which, implanted in the "menstruum"—the base matter—effected the conception of alchemical gold. The Stone itself, sometimes called the "hermetic Androgyne," was the child of the "Royal Marriage" between gold (the male element) and silver (the female element). The alchemist was a priest, who officiated at and more or less consecrated these reproductive rituals.

In our world, the mushroom cloud and the population explosion have altered forever the joyful connotations of fertility. And the alchemical conception of "spirit," which informed and animated dead matter, has been replaced by atomic radiation, which poisons and causes mutations. The spirit in the Philosopher's Stone which multiplied gold here multiplies cells, and we call the result cancer. The medieval alchemist known as the Pseudo-Lully thought he could turn the sea to gold with his little Stone: we know we can turn the sea into a radioactive poison with ours.[3] Since the chemists learned to turn uranium into plutonium, and to retrieve more plutonium from reactor wastes than they put in in the first place, the notions of transmutation and infinite multiplication have resonances that are more fearful than benign.

The population explosion more than any other current dilemma has the power to dim our reverence for the reproductive cycle as a paradigm for universal relations. For many years human fertility has stood in the way of prosperity, and even of survival. Like the technological machine we have spawned to smooth over the difficulties of survival, it has turned on us and yet we remain enslaved to it, reproducing against our own self-interest. In Cronenberg's world, sexuality, like technology, is a destructive enthusiasm, an agent no longer of Eros but of Thanatos.

The element we fear in both the population explosion and the creeping hegemony of the technological network is the single-minded drive towards self-multiplication. This drive is at once an awesome and mindless force: seen in its light, the human beings through which it operates are merely its puppets, robbed of self-direction and individual identity. The reduction of human action and motivation, by whatever means, to this mechanically biological imperialism is a classic theme of the horror genre. Zombies, vampires, immaterial extraterrestrials looking for a physical species to colonize—all frighten us, particularly with their ferocious urge to multiply their kind by transforming ours. The sexual and technological spirals have begun to vie so strenuously with each other for first place among our anxieties that it is difficult to say which of the two dilemmas a recent film like Philip Kaufman's *Invasion of the Body Snatchers* (1978) dramatizes: is the film an animistic image of the victory of technology, or a mechanized image of human procreation?

This blending or crossing of the two essential categories of the animate and the inanimate might be perceived as establishing itself in the real world, where computers play chess and write short stories for *Omni*, and people walk the streets with plastic hearts and larynxes. (What else could be meant by the scenes of intercourse between humans and machines in such recent films as *Demon Seed* [1977] and *Star Trek—The Motion Picture* [1979]?) A confusion like this might be perceived as establishing itself in the real world between the two essential categories of the animate and the inanimate. The worldview of alchemy confused these two categories too, joyfully. Its operations were based on the idea of a fully animated and fertile universe, in which even crystals had gender, and which needed only the skills of human technicians to increase its fertility. Alchemy's transformations and multiplications confirmed and celebrated this view of nature. Cronenberg, at one time in his life a biochemistry major, gives us creepier transformations and more destructive multiplications, looking at alchemy's gender-suffused mutabilities through very dark glasses.

These dark glasses are not worn merely by morbid choice. The logic which used to buttress our individual joy in procreation has been undermined by the economic facts of modern life.[4] The family remains an emotional unit, but it is no longer a mutually necessary and supportive economic unit. As a higher level of social organization, procreation is still functional, serving capitalism by the production of cheap labor, and to the capitalist (as capitalist, not as husband or suffering modern man) "growth" is still a good word. But the capitalist/human being is finally realizing the threat embodied in the myth of Midas: his kiss turns children into gold.[5] Cronenberg is surely aware of the ease with which his organic allegories of fatal growth can be felt as metaphorical reflections of economic catastrophe: "growth economies" and "limits of growth" are catch phrases of our historical moment. And transformation is a key concept in the worlds of finance and business, where interest and capital are the gold produced by modern economic alchemy from the dung of cash and human labor.

But Cronenberg's images are so elemental that our experience of them goes beyond (or remains beneath) the plane of ideological critique. Though his vision is comprehensive, and his symbolic network coherent as a displaced image of modern social schizophrenia, he is at bottom a poet, that is to say, concerned with the bodily facts and primal fears of individual human experience. The literal level of his nightmare is the foundation on which his dark social vision is reared: it is his good fortune as an artist that his personal fears and obsessions are so metaphorically applicable to this moment in history.

Cronenberg's horror films are about sex, and although some of them can be seen as sociologically motivated explorations of modern sexual mores, they are tied together by a more biological focus. They are *horror* movies, after all. As such, they are generically bound to titillate us at a more basic level than that of sociological commentary. Sexual promiscuity is not terrifying, but bodily transmutation is.

His films present us with a series of sexual Worst Possible Cases. *Shivers* (1975, aka *They Came from Within, The Parasite Murders*) offers a disease which, transmitted sexually, is a parody of pregnancy and birth. Animate, liverlike parasites are generated in the victim's body and leap out through his or her mouth in order to multiply their kind in another body. Instead of the fever with which a body normally attacks its invader, the concomitant symptom here is lust, and thus the spread of the disease is assured. This is the Kissing Disease *par excellence*. What is especially horrifying is that the victims purposely infect each other, with all the single-minded eagerness of a horde of Club Med aficionados. The events of the film are seductions and orgies; the transformed participants become puppets in a sexual drama that blindly seeks to perpetuate and extend itself. (The film offers, among other things, a phobic prophecy of the recent panic over herpes, sensationalized by *Time* magazine as the perfect science-fiction disease. The estimated twenty million American sufferers of this disease could be enlisted as evidence for the uncanny timeliness of Cronenberg's phobias—as could the caption of the *Time* cover story photograph of a herpes virus, "This thing has a life of its own." The story makes much of those who purposely spread the disease: "Says a Los Angeles woman: 'When I first got it I wanted to pass it on to everyone for vengeance until everyone had it and it became normal.' . . . A Midwestern woman says she has infected 75 men in three years.")[6]

Rabid (1976) again ties together sex and the idea of dehumanizing transformation. The culprit in this case is a plastic surgeon who has developed something he calls "neutral field tissue." This skin tissue can be grafted onto any part of the body, where it will then contract the genetic material specific to that part. It is an inversion of the Philosopher's Stone, which turns all matter into something like itself, but based on the same idea of a prime material, something unspecific and formless in itself. The skin grafts performed on the thighs of the antiheroine, cleverly cast porn star Marilyn Chambers, cause her in some mysterious way to grow a new organ in her armpit—something that looks rather like a vagina but contains a sharp, cartilaginous plunger that sucks blood. Chambers' metabolism is so transformed that she can be nourished only by blood, and without it she goes into agonizing withdrawal pains. And the new organ is inconveniently placed so that she can use it only during sexual encounters. In these encounters she infects her partners/victims with an incredibly virulent and rapidly fatal form of rabies.

In both *Shivers* and *Rabid*, transformations involve transference and confusion of sexual characteristics, resulting in ominous parodies of the Androgyne: men parodically giving birth to monstrous lumps of flesh in the former, a woman with a phallic organ that sucks in fluids rather than expelling them in the latter. The Androgyne has been celebrated as a psychic ideal by Jungians, but images of its physical corollaries are here made monstrous, the symptoms of fatal diseases. In Cronenberg's tangled weave of sexual profligacy, epidemic disease, and gender-oriented transformation, a causal sequence can be inferred: it is as if the libidinal unleashings occasioned by the new diseases led inevitably to a blurring of sexual identity, as if the logic of intercourse concluded in the erasure of difference.

The director is tapping into another set of conventional images: the hermaphroditic and androgynous bodies of the grotesque tradition, with its graftings and fusions of species, its imaginary organs and proliferation of bodies and body parts. But, as he does with his exploitation of alchemical images and ideas, Cronenberg here sidesteps the joyful, or at least playful, impulse of the tradition he invokes.[7] The physiological freedoms of his bodies (liberated and liberating in the grotesque canon) signal a return to chaos, just as their sexual license does. The contagion of the Philosopher's Stone (the "hermetic Androgyne"), through which base matter was refined and brought closer to its highest potential, here reduces the already spiritualized matter of the human body to a lower, less differentiated state. The fear of blending will reappear in the closing moments of *Scanners* (1980), when the long, incestuous battle-embrace of two telepathic brothers results in what seems an actual exchange of bodies.

If in Cronenberg's first two movies contagious diseases evoke or mimic the behaviors of sexual life, in *The Brood* (1979) the two are identical; that is, the main character's disease is literally her ability to make babies. Cronenberg's apparent indictment of the sexual cycle is at its most outrageous here because he retains so much of the familiar:

women do make babies, those babies are jealous of Dad, and their daughters do inherit their capacity. In making the disease genetic in its transmission he makes it much more nearly identical with the reproductive cycle (an image maintained also in *Scanners*).

The difference between the afflicted mother's disease and natural female fertility are once again explicable in alchemical terms. The alchemist/psychiatrist has uncovered and encouraged in his patient a seemingly inborn technique of parthenogenesis. This hermetic Androgyne manifests her deep angers by giving birth to broods of violent automatons. Conception is immaculate, gestation a matter of hours, and the children reach the physical stature of five- or six-year-olds almost immediately. What is creepiest about this woman's weird fertility is that she conceives her broods alone. She has found one of those magical tricks that get us around the contingencies of real life. We have always felt guilty about such tricks and gifts (witness the myths of Prometheus and Midas, and papal injunctions against The Pill). In the decline of alchemy, disbelief in its efficacy was preceded by the belief that it produced only "fools' gold," a material that shared one or two

The monstrous parthenogenesis of Nola Carveth (Samantha Eggar) in The Brood, *1979. From the editors' collection.*

aspects with gold but wasn't the real thing. Similarly, the partheno-genic offspring here have the bodies of children, and the loyalty of children to their mother, but nothing else. They are zombies, like the rabid crowds of transformed adults in the earlier films, but zombies by their own nature. Mass production of children reduces their value, their individuality, even the level of their reality—as it does with everything else. The last laws passed against the practice of alchemy in England were designed to protect the market value of gold by restricting its untamed production *ex nihilo*.[8] When the uncontrollable mother floods the market with her brood, the only solution is her destruction. It is not, however, a final solution: her "natural" daughter has inherited her licentious fertility.

Scanners encompasses and fuses the whole range of terrors imagined in Cronenberg's other films, focusing most closely on the terrors of intimacy. It might seem peculiar that the telepathy of the Scanners is the side effect of a fertility drug administered to their mothers, but it is metaphorically logical. Sexual intercourse and pregnancy tend to render ambiguous the otherwise clean biological outlines of our identities. The sense of blurring in intercourse is reflected in such terms as *death,* the old slang word for orgasm, and *sexual union.* Abortion legislation is complicated precisely by our inability to agree on the point at which mother and fetus become separate individuals. These states of "union" are usually voluntarily chosen, but the mergers with which the Scanners have to deal continually are inadvertent, a kind of metasta-sizing intimacy that drives one of the first of them to drill a hole in his forehead and "let the voices out." In the last scene, one Scanner actually invades and takes over the body of his brother. The scene is an image simultaneously of telepathy, incest, and the disintegration of identity.

Telepathic power is seen in the science fiction tradition as a major step towards the ultimate pinnacle of mental evolution: bodily tran-scendence. It is with telepathy that we "become as gods," eat the forbidden apple of knowledge, complete the interrupted construction of Babel. If "the proper study of mankind is man," it promises us unmediated and unlimited knowledge of each other, removing the last intellectual "limit of growth." But Cronenberg's dark picture of this power expresses more than an intellectual vertigo. The doctor who has invented the fertility drug ("Ephemerol"), of which this power is a side effect, defines telepathy as "the direct linking of two nervous systems separated by space"—an ominous and paranoid description of the sexual act. And this technologically induced evolutionary advance finds its point of entry in the reproductive cycle: in an inversion of *The Brood*'s scenario, a woman is inseminated by two partners, her man and modern science, in order to produce offspring with more rather than less of "the human potential." The fertility drug does not seem to produce more numerous offspring, but offspring with more numerous powers. And these powers are a curse, recapitulating and extending the hazards already inherent in sexual intimacy, attacking from another angle the endangered value—primary for Cronenberg—of identity.

Taken as a whole, Cronenberg's *oeuvre* so far presents the images of sexual life as a kind of cancer unleashed by precisely those scientific practitioners whose function should be to control and regulate it. There is a doctor at fault in each of these films, a doctor searching for a magic trick that will render nature more vital and generative than it already is. The doctor in *Shivers* invents an aphrodisiac; in *Rabid*, an infinitely mutable tissue; in *The Brood* a technique of expressiveness that stimulates parthenogenic births; in *Scanners*, a fertility drug. The errors of these zealous medical experimenters seem to be compounded of an unbridled enthusiasm for the generative and regenerative powers of modern technology and the belief that more is better. What they get from their mistakes is unbridled generation and regeneration, and more than they had counted on.

Each of the mistaken scientists is destroyed by his own creations. But the deaths of the doctors are not the climaxes of these films, for the doctors are not sufficiently responsible agents. In the best of them, the climax is our sudden awareness that this new biological network is in fact uncontrollable, as uncontrollable as the natural propagation of any species. The final moment in *Shivers* shows the infected condominium dwellers surging out of their parking lot at dawn to infect the rest of the world; at the end of *The Brood*, the natural daughter of the unnatural mother sees, in a moment of distress, growths on her arm which signify that she has inherited her dead mother's terrible faculty for embodying emotion. What had seemed a learned behavior, and therefore controllable, turns out to be a genetic trait, and therefore potentially rampant.

Near the end of *Scanners* we discover that pregnant women all over the country had been taking Ephemerol. Their fetuses are already Scanners, reaching out to touch the minds of other Scanners while still hidden in the womb. Meanwhile, the adult Scanners have smelled power and felt the addictive succor of their forced grouping. One is not permitted to imagine their disbanding, and there are countless recruits on the way. *Rabid* milks irony out of the uncontrollability topos: in the last scene we are shown the body of Marilyn Chambers being dumped anonymously into a trash compacter. As the Typhoid Mary of the new disease, she has seemed the source of its catastrophe. But we know that it is too late now to stop the spread of the rabies. With or without her, the infected will go on biting the clean, with such suddenness and speed and violence that quarantine and curfew will be no more effective than they are in any other horror movie.

The myth at the bottom of all this is not ultimately Mary Wollstonecraft Shelley's *Frankenstein* (1818), although that was the first tale of modern times to connect the fears of science and transformation that define Cronenberg's use of the genre. The myth lurking here is the story of Midas, who cannot control the extranatural power to transform, and the contagion of whose touch will turn the whole world to gold. Midas frightened the alchemists, who wrapped their practice in secrecy and spoke in codes to keep it under control. But the desire of Midas was in them, as the Pseudo-Lully indicates when he boasts of his ability to turn the sea to gold. Cronenberg's scientists are secretive too; the difference is that DNA is more amenable to the techniques of modern technology than dung and lead were to those of the ancient and medieval worlds. It is harder to keep a secret that works, especially when an important factor in the process is contagion.

The metaphor of these films, in which their thematic concern with meaningless and uncontrollable reproduction is rooted, is their literal subject—the new diseases we fear that genetic research will create. The key to their fearfulness is that the diseases are either animate in themselves, or so alter the metabolism and consciousness of their victim that he/she seems to have abandoned our species, embodied the disease. The diseases could be seen from their own perspective as new life forms— and we are asked to see them that way. In William S. Burroughs' great paranoid novel, *Cities of the Red Night*, the contagious disease that is taking over the world (and which is credited with having originated the Caucasian race as a mutation) is described by a doctor as follows:

> We know that a consuming passion can produce physical symptoms . . . fever . . . loss of appetite . . . even allergic reactions . . . and few conditions are more obsessional and potentially self-destructive than love. Are not the symptoms of Virus B-23 simply the symptoms of what we are pleased to call 'love'? Eve, we are told, was made from Adam's rib . . . so a hepatitis virus was once a healthy liver cell.[9]

Fear of the Other is endemic to Cronenberg's genre. What he has done in these films that is so radically horrifying is to locate the Other in those strands of our experience and ourselves which are in fact the least personal and individual, but which remain nevertheless "part of nature, *part of us.*"

Cronenberg's films, in linking reproduction, transformation, and disease so tightly, present a supremely alienated view of our biological life: it is a conspiracy to exist, assured of success because it is symbiotic with our individual emotional hungers for love and for children. Even the high priests of abstraction—scientists in their antiseptic labs—are ultimately henchmen of the ravening Life Force and its pure urge to multiply.

NOTES

1. Cf. Langdon Winner, *Autonomous Technology: Technics-out-of-Control as a Theme in Political Thought* (Cambridge, Mass.: MIT Press, 1977), chap. 1.

2. Harlan Ellison, "I Have No Mouth, and I Must Scream" in *Alone against Tomorrow* (New York: Macmillan, 1971), 3–19.

3. *"Mare tingerem, si mercurius esset."* Quoted in John Read, *Prelude to Chemistry: An Outline of Alchemy, Its Literature and Relationships* (New York: Macmillan Company, 1937), 148.

4. In older economies based on agriculture and small, family-run businesses, families necessarily worked together to ensure the means of survival. The industrial welfare state allows and promotes economic self-sufficiency: children are economic parasites within the family, who leave when they are of age to become productive, and social security has shouldered most of the responsibility for maintenance of the elderly. Perhaps it is this uncoupling of the emotional and the practical that has led to the family's centrality as an image of the monstrous in the horror films of the last twenty years. Robin Wood's 1978 article, "The Return of the Repressed," in *Film Comment* 14, no. 4 (July–August 1978), 25–32, argues persuasively for the image of the family as "one of the great composite monsters of the American cinema." I would add that the family can only have come to be seen and felt as monstrous in a society where our experience of it is almost completely limited to the emotional sphere.

5. I would like to thank Professor Frank Knobloch, of Brockville, Indiana, for pointing out to me the economic aspect of my thesis in a letter of May 3, 1982.

6. "The New Scarlet Letter" and "Battling an Elusive Invader," *Time* (August 2, 1982), 62–69.

7. Cf. Mikhail Bakhtin, *Rabelais and His World* (Cambridge: MIT Press, 1968). Chap. 5, "The Grotesque Image of the Body and Its Sources," is an erudite and fascinating critique of the pleasure principle operating in the bodily images of grotesque art, from Pliny to Rabelais.

8. "It is ordained and established, That none from henceforth shall use to multiply Gold or Silver nor use the Craft of Multiplication. . . ." in *The Statues of the Realm*, Vol. 2, ed. A. Luders et al. (London, 1816), 144.

9. William S. Burroughs, *Cities of the Red Night* (New York: Holt, Rinehart, and Winston, 1981), 25.

20

The Enemy Within: The Economy of Violence in *The Hills Have Eyes*

D. N. Rodowick

Work on the imaging of the family in the horror films of the '70s has been one of the more productive and interesting areas of recent film criticism. However, it has not been the high-class, big-budget fantasies that have attracted the most attention, but rather those films that situated themselves in the margins of the industry: the exploitation films. This tendency of current film criticism is complicated by the fact that the exploitation film, and especially the low-budget horror film, is often considered as presenting an ideological alternative to mainstream film practice. This idea is not quite so paradoxical if we consider a few general points. First of all, exploitation films are commonly independent productions. Financed, produced, and often distributed outside of the mainstream corporate/studio system, they are less subject to the possibility of creative controls and restrictions than their more glossy cousins. Second, the necessity of working quickly and economically, although often responsible for shoddy production values, in many cases breeds stylistic innovations as well. The third, and most significant point, I think, is the fact that these films bank not on stars or other manufactured and quantifiable guarantees of box office returns, but on

I would like to thank Robin Wood for his encouragement and comments in the preparation of this essay.

the subject of exploitation itself. The idea of exploitation is not so insidious when we consider that all commercial films manufactured within the capitalist mode of production are exploitive of someone or some class, a fact that is often elided. The low-budget film certainly has no monopoly on the exploitation of sexuality, violence, or class, but considering that the mainstream film often refuses to address these problems as problems, or else only considers them in an oblique fashion, we can see that the exploitation film by the very nature of its economy opens up the possibility of attacking problems and subjects of representation forbidden to mainstream films.

In this manner, I would like to suggest that what I consider to be the most interesting of these films are those able to exploit the idea of exploitation in a way that exposes this contradiction rather than effacing it. Stephanie Rothman's films, for example, are exemplary in this respect. However, I would be guilty of a gross misrepresentation if I did not point out that for every *Terminal Island* (1973) there are probably fifty films like *House of Psychotic Women* (1973). Even so, I would be willing to risk exaggeration by claiming that, with respect to their exploitation of women and women's sexuality, *House of Psychotic Women* is not substantially or qualitatively different from *An Unmarried Woman* (1978).

With these introductory remarks in mind, I would like to concretize these observations in an analysis of *The Hills Have Eyes* (1977), which like Wes Craven's earlier film, *Last House on the Left* (1972), banks on the exploitation of violence in order to attract its audience. However, I do not consider the representation of violence in either of these films to be unproblematically exploitative. What interests me is the degree to which films such as *The Hills Have Eyes*, *The Texas Chainsaw Massacre* (1974), and *Martin* (1976) clearly accept that an "ideology" of violence is an essential, if repressed, component in the figuration of the bourgeois family. Briefly, the contention of these films is that, in its struggle for survival and/or revenge, the Family manifests a degree of violence which equals or exceeds that of its "monstrous" aggressors, effectively implicating the Family in the monstrosity it is trying to combat. Moreover, what is ultimately most distressing about Craven's films is not the excessiveness of their violence (one could name many mainstream films that exceed *The Hills Have Eyes* in graphic violence), but rather, the consistent and self-conscious undermining of representational codes that contain the manifestation of violence, guaranteeing its service to authority and the eventual reinforcement of established ideologies and institutions. One could, in fact, briefly list a series of general conventions that structure the exploitation of violence in the commercial film in order to confer upon that violence the rationality of bourgeois ideologies. For example:

1. The violence of authority (that is, the armed forces, the law, a man whose rights of possession are jeopardized) is always justified to the extent that it preserves social, political, and moral order. The violence of justice is never "excessive," but balanced against the force of transgression of the law.
2. Since bourgeois society cannot, or does not, conceive of itself as being inherently or unjustifiably violent (or even exploitive for that matter), the source of violence is most commonly seen as coming from the outside. Thus the figuration of violence is always projected onto an irrational and anarchic other who, inconceivably, cannot accept or is blind to the "rationality" of a vision of the bourgeois cultural order as a kind of social utopia.
3. This third notion is in actuality the division of numbers 1 from 2, in that this projection of violence onto the other splits the film-text, structuring the narrative as a series of oppositions where the representation of violence may be circulated as part of the text's economy of pleasure: criminal violence is consumed by legal violence in a closed circuit established by the undermining and restoration of stable ideological positions. This structure permits the vicarious pleasure of violence without implicating the audience or challenging any normative ideologies or institutions.

The disturbing power of *The Hills Have Eyes* lies precisely in its global transgression of these conventions. What the film gradually reveals is that there is no comfortable distance between the Carter family and the "monster" family that threatens them. The Carters are depicted as the product of a culture where violence is an everyday fact, even a way of life. This is most clearly stated in Big Bob's speech after their family car and trailer are wrecked in the desert, where he summarizes his twenty-five years on the police force as a history of ridicule where he was even shot at by his own men on two occasions; and even taking all this into account, he states that he never came so close to being killed as by his own family. As representatives of the "dominant ideology" they embody no positive values. They are WASPish, prototypically reactionary, and undoubtedly Republicans: in an interview Craven constantly refers to them as the "Whitebreads."[1] In this manner, the status of bourgeois ideology is immediately questioned as a normative value; in fact, by the end of the film it is not clear who is more monstrous: the Carters or the monster family that doubles them in the film. The conflict depicted in *The Hills Have Eyes* is neither precisely the struggle for survival between two apparently mutually exclusive cultures nor a structured opposition between a positive and a negative set of values whose outcome is predetermined. Instead, a structural correspondence is drawn between the two families. We are encouraged, I think, to understand them as being two sides of the same coin; or better yet, the violent "monster" family could be characterized as the latent image underlying the depiction of the Whitebreads. The monster family remains mysterious and unknowable only as long as the Carters are unable to recognize the potential violence of the desert landscape in which they have been stranded. Furthermore, the gradual pictorialization of the monsters takes place in direct proportion to the violence they provoke, and concomitantly, this violence initiates a system of exchange wherein their defeat can only be read ironically: instead of celebrating the triumph of the bourgeois family, the final moments of the film only serve to inscribe them in the place of their victimizers.

In *The Hills Have Eyes*, the representation of violence is not comfortably consigned to a purely external threat; it is omnipresent in the textual landscape, even if it is unrecognized as such at first by the Carters or the viewer. The figuration of the desert is exemplary in this respect, for it perfectly reveals the irony wherein the consumer fantasies of the Carters only serve to blind them to the reality of their situation. They project onto the desert the mirage of the silver mine, Bob and Ethel's twenty-fifth anniversary present, beneath which is concealed the reality of a nuclear testing site that shelters the incomprehensible danger they must soon face. In this manner, the Carters' fictional journey takes place as two simultaneous movements, both of which are aimed at shattering their fragile vision of the bourgeois universe in order to reveal the stark and violent reality it conceals. The first of these movements can be thought of as a vision of the future in which the promised land of modern capitalism is stripped of its tranquil veneer to reveal a wasteland exploited as the site of an absolute technological aggression. But this journey is also a regressive one in which the Carters, as middle-class "everymen," are returned to an archaic and violent past. Harsh and primeval, the desert is literally a "testing-range" that incorporates and entraps the self-enclosed, self-

Pluto (Michael Berryman) meets one of the Whitebreads (Dee Wallace) in The Hills
Have Eyes, *1977. Still courtesy of Jerry Ohlinger's Movie Material Store.*

sustaining space of bourgeois domesticity represented by the Carters' trailer.

This double movement is more forcefully reproduced in the structural correspondences and exchanges that unite the two families. For example, on the one hand, the choice of mythological names for the monster family situates them as part of an archaic past, an older system of social economy whose presence lies dormant in the Whitebreads. On the other hand, descending from Old Fred, the monsters are also a product of white society and thus represent a future which blossomed from the rubble of the collapsed boom town economy of the silver mine. Significantly, Ruby is the only one of Jupiter's children without a mythological name, as well as the only one who desires to leave the "pack." Her identification with the outside world is the reverse side of a trajectory in which the surviving Whitebreads will finally be identified in the place of their aggressors; in the opening sequence of the film she is as forcefully drawn out of the desert as the Carters are drawn into it. Moreover, according to the logic of the film, the capital of this exchange is violence. Finding a broken window with blood on it at the "Oasis" gas station, a concerned Doug tells Old Fred he'd better check his "grandchildren." Although the presence of danger is deflected from Doug's comprehension by the projection of his own familial values onto an understanding of the situation, his assumption nonetheless contains an element of truth.

However, the structural correspondences between the two families are more forcefully organized through the manipulation of point of view and offscreen space. In fact, the differential coding of point of view immediately splits the two families in terms of aggressors and victims. In this manner, vision is exercised as power in the text. Even though early on most of the Carters are given strongly marked point of view shots, their vision either just misses the relevant action or else is simply blind to it—their aggressors are so at home in the hostile environment of the desert that they blend with it completely. Moreover, the Carters' blindness to the reality of their predicament is compounded by the constant feeling of being watched, of being "more than uncomfortable," and of sensing an ominous presence that always seems to be just beyond the limits of vision.

On the other hand, the monster family is initially represented as having a kind of omniscience which is all the more striking because of their invisibility. Their absolute dominance of the power of vision in the text is maintained by merging their point of view with that of the camera.

Their surveillance of the Carters takes place as a variety of longshots or extreme longshots whose subjectivity is marked either by the use of offscreen sound, their communications by walkie-talkie, or by the activation of foreground space, most commonly the desert shrubbery that evidently conceals them from view. In fact, as the Carters begin their journey into the desert, their progress is marked as a literal incorporation into the vision of the monsters. From this point through the first attack on their wrecked trailer, it is often impossible to tell whether a shot is objective or from the point of view of one of the monsters. An image which was potentially neutral could be charged with danger by the tell-tale walkie-talkie communications of the monster lookouts. They dominate offscreen space so completely that one feels that an attack could come from any side of the frame at any time.

This particular distribution of aggressors and victims across the organization of vision is not a stable system, however. It will be subject to disturbance and reorientation according to an economy of violence which is governed in a world of scarcity by the struggle for survival and assertion of patriarchal right. The logic of this conflict orchestrates the gradual pictorialization of the monsters according to the violence they provoke.

Here I would like to briefly outline the terms of this logic of violence, orchestrated as the assertion of patriarchal right in the desert. The first movement of this logic culminates with the murder of Old Fred. The initiatory violence of the film is represented as a primal event, consigned to a textual prehistory as narrated by Old Fred to Big Bob. It is here that Fred tells of Jupiter's birth and the destruction of Fred's home, wife, and daughter, the signs of which are still present in the rubble that surrounds the "Oasis." Jupiter's first appearance is motivated by this narration, and just as he still bears the mark of the tire iron that Fred laid across his face then, Jupiter now repeats this violence by beating Fred to death with a tire iron and pinning him to a shack with it.

After Fred is killed, and this initial, murderous Oedipal conflict is exhausted, a second movement of violence devolves upon the defeat of Big Bob who, being a retired police official, is the literal representative of bourgeois authority in the text. In a sense, this conflict superimposes itself on the murder of Old Fred. As a grandfather, Big Bob is capable of occupying Fred's place in conflict with Jupiter. However, there are even more direct correspondences between Big Bob and Jupiter himself: they are both fathers, the heads of their respective "clans." What are the consequences of the struggle between the two? After leaving the trailer to look for help, Big Bob is captured and eventually crucified and immolated. We might note that the sequence of actions between Big Bob's crucifixion and immolation are alternated with images of the disintegration of familial order on both sides: on the one hand, there are Ruby's attempts to run away and join the Carters, her eventual recapture and bondage; and on the other, the disunity, nervousness, and lack of communication among the Carters. Furthermore, by the time Big Bob is finally killed, we have had our first looks at both Pluto and Mars. It is significant that we first see Mars directly after the explosion which immolates Big Bob, for being Jupiter's eldest, he fulfills his father's murderous heritage by killing Big Bob's wife and eldest daughter. The scenario described in Fred's "primal event" is thus completed a second time.

With Big Bob dead, the obligation of revenge, survival, and assertion of patriarchal right over the desert falls to Doug Wood, his son-in-law. Moreover, the murder of Doug's wife and the theft of his child threatens to complete the cycle of violence a third time. It is at this point that the trajectory of aggression takes a different turn. Entering a regressive phase, it is channeled back along the path it originally traveled in a cycle of revenge initiated by the Whitebreads. The film moves toward a resolution, but this will not mean the restoration of order and ideological stability. It is, rather, a movement of equivalence in which the Whitebreads will be identified with the ideology of "violence" previously reserved for the monsters. This is signified in the excessiveness and the imagination of their vengeance, and it also takes place in a structural movement in which they are inscribed in the point-of-view positions of their aggressors. For example, Beauty, one of the Carter's German Shepherds, is the first to die and be consumed by the monsters (a fate that appears to be only temporarily deferred for the infant Katy) and, therefore, Beast is the first to go into action. The first strongly marked point-of-view construction in the cycle of violence is given to him as he watches the radio communication between Mercury on the cliff and Pluto and Mars with the baby. Moreover, Beast's killing of Mercury and the theft of the walkie-talkie is the first instance of violence returned against the monsters. In this manner, he ruins the pleasure of their victory, and by co-opting their means of offscreen communication, he enables Doug to even up the odds somewhat.

Thus, in the final movement of the film, a structure of action is set up that alternates Pluto and Jupiter's approach to the trailer with Doug and Beast's approach to the monsters' camp. However, the power of vision and offscreen space is at a stalemate here. Doug's point of view organizes the beginning of the sequence. He sees the danger to the trailer, but he is unable to communicate that danger over the interruption of Pluto's radio imitation of Air Force Rescue. From here on, the cycle of revenge must play itself out along the lines which the economy of violence has already carved out for it in the text. Briefly, here is the logic that orchestrates that revenge:

1. Beast kills Pluto. First through an exchange of leg wounds, then by ripping Pluto's throat out, Beast avenges the death of his mate, Beauty, at Pluto's hands. It might also be said that Beast's capacity to kill, his cunning, and his immediate, instinctual response to danger, serve to represent the dormant capacity for violence now being drawn out of the Whitebreads.
2. Bobby and Brenda kill Jupiter. The aesthetic of violence is an important factor in the contemporary horror film. In this respect, brother and sister exhibit a considerable degree of imagination—the grotesque use of their dead mother as bait in a motorized lasso trap, and rigging the trailer to explode, hopefully consigning Jupiter to the same fate as their father. But Jupiter is not so easily defeated. For the most part, Brenda's point of view has orchestrated this scenario, but as she and Bobby approach the burning trailer, Jupiter comes screaming from offscreen space and the two teenagers are forced to bring him down through a sheer excess of physical violence: Brenda with an ax, Bobby with his gun.
3. With Jupiter dead, along with the rest of his masculine line, the fight between Doug and Mars can be read as the ultimate struggle for parental authority. Mars's death, and the struggle that leads up to it, are even more gruesome and brutal than with Jupiter. It is also interesting that killing Mars takes the efforts of both Doug and Ruby, just as it took both Brenda and Bobby to kill Jupiter. But what kind of conclusion does this violence serve? The film does not end with Doug reunited with his child or his brother and sister-in-law. While Ruby screams hysterically, Doug repeatedly and brutally stabs Mars's dead body, carried away by the force of violence that consumes him. The film is ended here, its resolution suspended on this moment.

In conclusion, we should take into account two factors concerning the conditions of violence in the film. First of all, violence in the film is predominantly violence against women. It is true that the struggle for patriarchal right is given the most representational weight by the film, but we must not forget that this conflict takes place against a backdrop which includes the deaths of Fred's wife and child, Ethel Carter, and Lynn Carter Wood; the attempted rape and murder of Brenda; Ruby's bondage; as well as the kidnapping of the infant Katy, the "tenderloin" baby. Second, if violence against women seems gratuitous, excessive, and meaningless in any commercial cinema, this is due in part to the passive roles delegated to them in most narrative structures. Violence is meaningful *for* men because it is the struggle *over* women.

In the final analysis, I'm not sure whether I would consider *The Hills Have Eyes* to be a progressive text. It seems to take only small steps in exposing a particular vision of bourgeois culture in terms of the violence that founds it. But like the best work of George Romero, Larry Cohen, and a few others, it does seem to expose a gap, an internal dislocation in which a particularly repressive ideology may be read within the textual system of the film. What are we left with at the end of this film that has been characterized by a violent nihilism, anarchic struggles for power, and the consideration of women as either objects of exchange (to be killed, raped, or literally consumed) or the transmitters of a culture that is better left forgotten? Here is a brief inventory: Brenda and Bobby Carter, an orphaned society; Mama and Ruby, a widowed matriarchy; Doug and Katy, a widowed patriarchy. In a very real sense, the freeze frame that suspends the film is also the signifier of an ideological stalemate which marks not the triumph and reaffirmation of a culture, but its internal disintegration.

NOTE

1. Tony Williams, "Wes Craven: An Interview," *Journal of Popular Film and Television* 8, no. 3 (Fall 1980): 13.

21

Halloween: Suspense, Aggression, and the Look

Steve Neale

Through an analysis of some aspects of John Carpenter's *Halloween* (1978), this article proposes to consider some of the textual, cinematic, and psychoanalytic mechanisms involved in the horror film and particularly in its moments of suspense.

The narrative of *Halloween* is simple and straightforward, basing itself on a series of barely differentiated repetitions both at the level of enunciation and at the level of the enounced. In the opening scene, Michael Myers kills his sister Judith at their house in Haddonfield on Halloween night. Fifteen years later, Michael escapes from the asylum in which he has been kept since the killing, eluding his psychiatrist, Sam Loomis, who is convinced that Michael will return to Haddonfield to repeat his crime. The film then introduces a further set of characters during the course of the following day, principally Laurie Strode, an adolescent girl of about the same age as Judith; Tommy, a young boy for whom she is due to baby-sit that Halloween night; and Laurie's school friends, Annie and Lynda. Laurie seems to be being followed by Michael, who appears a number of times during the course of the day, though he remains unseen by any of the other characters. Later that night Annie, Lynda, and Bob (Lynda's boyfriend) are killed by Michael, who, when disturbed by Laurie, pursues her into her house. She seems twice to have stabbed him to death, once with a knit-ting needle, once with coat hanger, but he attacks again for the third time, at which point Loomis rushes into the house and shoots Michael. However, when he looks out the window for the body, it is gone.

The film begins with Michael entering a house, climbing the stairs and stabbing a teenage girl to death. It ends with Michael entering Lau-rie's house and failing after a repeated series of attacks—and a repeated series of apparent deaths. Altogether we see four killings, all set in Haddonfield on Halloween night. Each killing involves either strangu-lation and/or stabbing with a huge, phallic knife, and in the assembly of the elements it repeats, each killing implies punishment of a woman who asserted a sexual appetite. The film is careful to avoid in its multi-ple series of repetitions an overstatement of the principles behind them—hence the variation provided by the killing of a male. However, Bob, unlike Judith, Annie, and Lynda, is neither stalked at length nor signified as the object of Michael's voyeuristic gaze; structurally, his death functions largely as a preliminary to the killing of Lynda. It is noteworthy, in this respect, that neither Michael nor the spectator sees Laurie in a state of undress. She is differentiated from the others in that she is depicted as both sexually timid and inexperienced. In babysitting on Halloween night while her friends anticipate a night of sex, she is cast in the roles both of virgin and mother, two roles that are signified elsewhere as exempt from Michael's aggression. Of the four adolescent women who are attacked, it is therefore, logically, Laurie who survives.

At the level of enunciation, *Halloween* works through a codification of violence and suspense across four distinct and separate textual sec-tions: the first scene (the murder of Judith); the second scene (the escape from Smith's Grove asylum); the sequences set in Haddonfield during the course of the following day; and the sequences at night with the murders of Annie, Bob, and Lynda and the final attack on Laurie. In each of these sections aggression and suspense are articulated differ-ently. A cumulative and repetitive elaboration eventually weaves them all together until they establish a system across which the repeated vio-lence of the last section is played out. Judith's killing is shown in a sin-gle shot, marked, in retrospect, as having been taken from Michael's point of view. The camera hovers outside the house, peering through the window as Judith and her boyfriend go upstairs to her bedroom for sex, then moves to the side entrance and into the kitchen to pick up a Halloween mask and a knife from the kitchen drawer as the boyfriend comes down the stairs and leaves through the front door, up the stairs, and into her room for the killing, then down the stairs again and finally out the front door to confront the parents. Then there is a reverse cut to a crane as the camera swoops back to show Michael, six years old, dressed in Harlequin garb and clutching the knife in his hand.

The second scene, set at night like the first one, opens with a dialogue sequence between Loomis and a nurse as they drive toward the asylum in the rain. Through the windshield they see a number of the inmates wandering around and Loomis realizes something is wrong. He gets out of the car to investigate. Through the rear window of the car a figure briefly appears as it leaps onto the roof. An extended sequence follows in which the figure (Michael) attempts to get into the car. Throughout this sequence the camera is positioned at various points inside the car. The tension is elaborated spatially around the question as to *where* Michael will appear and attack, and temporally around the question as to *when* he will do so. Eventually, while the nurse is looking in one direction, Michael's hand appears behind her through the car window to smash it and to grab her by the throat. She struggles free and escapes from the car. Loomis runs to her aid as the car drives off in the distance.

Suspense, aggression, and violence are articulated in two different ways in these scenes. The opening scene turns upon an elaborate, unidentified point-of-view shot. Tension and suspense arise as a conjunction of a number of different mechanisms and processes. The shot functions so as to interweave three separate looks: that of the camera, that of the spectator and that of what is at this point still a character unknown to the viewer, although it is known to Judith and her parents. They call it by name: Michael. But the audience does not know who Michael is. There is disjunction in knowledge among the audience, the characters and the narrative subject. The tension lies exactly in the way this disjunction is articulated across the specific, unstable combination of looks involved in the construction of the shot. This tension gradually accumulates throughout the span of the shot until it culminates first in an act of apparently motiveless violence and second in the shock involved in the cut that gives the spectator the identity both of the killer and (hence) of the camera's point of view. For if the cut serves at last to separate the first two of the three looks from the third (a condition of mainstream narrative film), and to provide simultaneously the knowledge desired but frustrated during the span of the opening shot, it undermines any position of relative certainty that may have been reached after the killing itself by identifying the killer not as some psychopathic adult male, as the convention would have dictated, but instead as a tiny, wide-eyed child. Overall the scene functions, firstly, to set the narrative in motion by disrupting diegetic equilibrium and by introducing elements which will be elaborated in the form of repetitions throughout the rest of the film (night, killing, Halloween, lengthy point-of-view shots, aggression, and suspense); second, as a consequence, to "suspend" the spectator's knowledge, position, and sense of certainty (with the exception, of course, of the certainty that knowledge, position, and certainty will come with the film's resolution); and third, to associate marked but unmotivated point-of-view shots with Michael and thus with the agent of violence and aggression in the film. Such shots will function henceforth to signify Michael's potential (if not actual) presence and therefore danger to those characters who are caught as objects in the frame demonstrating the incidence of this look.

The second scene at the asylum involves similar elements of aggression and suspense, but they are articulated differently. The conversation in the car between Loomis and the nurse serves both to introduce the characters and to indicate an ellipsis in diegetic time, while remarking Michael as agent of violence and threat. Point of view is again identified with narrative disruption but this time with a number of crucial differences. Firstly, the conjunction is operated from a specified point of view (that of Loomis) and its object is displaced in relation to the agent of disruption itself (we—and he—see not Michael but other inmates of Smith's Grove asylum wandering in the road). Second, the point of view is that of the subject of diegetic violence (i.e., Loomis', not Michael's, point of view). Third, point of view here does not coincide with an act of aggression. It simply inaugurates the suspense of its possibility. When Michael first appears (fleetingly, as he jumps onto the roof of the car), he is the object only of the looks of the camera and the spectator. These looks, however, are both mapped onto each other and differentiated through recourse to a compositional device that recurs frequently throughout the film: the use of a frame internal to the image-frame. In this instance, the rear window of the car acts as a frame within the frame of the image. At this point, the nurse is looking out of the car's windshield: her look as (potential) victim and our look as spectators are thus disconnected, but she shares our knowledge of Michael's presence, having heard him as he lands on the roof. With the camera from this point on being in the car, the knowledge and the view of the nurse and of the spectator are suspended, and a tension is constructed precisely around their lack. When Michael's hand appears, it appears to the spectator but not to the nurse. It then immediately begins its attack. The tension increases as it is focused on the question as to whether the nurse will be killed, before it's relaxed when she escapes from the car. Again, then, suspense and aggression are functions of a lack of knowledge and adequate viewpoint on the part of the spectator. They are articulated here, however, not around a point-of-view shot as such, but rather around fields of vision as marked by the frame. Importantly, whereas point of view (specifically the point of view of the agent of aggression) coincided in the first scene with the death of its female object, here the system of frame, field of vision, camera and spectator look results in aggression and violence directed at the female victim, but not resulting in her death.

Although sharing a suspense and aggression articulated in terms of (a lack of) position, knowledge, and an omniscient look on the part of the spectating subject, the first two sections are marked by distinct modes of cinematic construction, the one centering on point of view, the other on space, field of vision, and frame. These two modes are then woven together into the systems that compose and articulate the third section: the daytime sequences in Haddonfield that follow Michael's escape. The sequences consist essentially of the introduction of Laurie, Tommy, Annie, and Lynda. Laurie and Tommy walk to school discussing Halloween and pausing on the way at the old Myers house. Next we see Laurie in her classroom during an English lesson, then Tommy in the playground with some other boys after school. Laurie walks home with Annie and Lynda, then goes up alone to her room. It is these sequences upon which I wish to concentrate, since it is they that are marked strongly by suspense and threat. They are interspersed with and followed by Loomis' discovery of the body of a truck driver whose clothes have been taken by Michael, Laurie, and Annie going for a drive to come upon a store robbed by Michael of a Halloween mask and a knife, and Loomis's visit to Judith's grave to find that her headstone is missing.

In all the sequences I want to discuss, Michael appears in a distinct and particular manner. He appears in two different ways: first, united by a disjunction in knowledge between ourselves as spectators and the other characters in the story (who are all at this point ignorant of Michael's existence and hence of the threat he poses), and second, by the fact that the menace he represents is at no point translated into physical violence. We see him on the one hand as the object of Laurie's point of view, in which case he appears in full figure in all but one instance. In each case, point of view and looking are re-marked through a set of compositional devices: framed by the schoolroom and car door windows while seated at the car; framed on the left of the image by a hedge behind which he subsequently disappears while Laurie walks home with Annie; and, finally, framed by Laurie's bedroom window as he stands in the garden next door. In each instance, too, these point-of-view shots are repeated in a classical structure of shot-counter shot, and each time there is such a repetition Michael's figure has vanished from the frame. A potential victim's point of view once again inaugurates threat (with the aggressor in full view), but this time there is not only no death, but also no attack. The shot-counter shot system serves to weaken Laurie's certainty, while, through its systematicity, increasing and stabilizing ours. However, if our knowledge of Michael's general presence and of the danger he embodies is remarked over Laurie's, our ignorance as to his precise whereabouts is articulated as his refusal, so to speak, to stabilize as the object of her gaze; we share with her an inability to frame him stably in our look, an ignorance as to where, when, and whether he will appear. On the other hand, we glimpse him briefly from behind, appearing in momentary fragments: the back of his head, a shoulder, a trunk, and a leg. In these instances, the codification of an unmotivated point of view with Michael's threatening look becomes an important aspect of the system. A series of lengthy traveling shots that track the characters from a distance, or, as we cut to a camera inside the Myers house while Tommy and Laurie pause outside to discuss its evil nature, a shot marked as point of view through the internal frame provided by the window in the door, indicate Michael's presence and generate a tension across the gap between, on the one hand, the knowledge and look of the spectator and the characters, and on the other hand, a knowledge on the part of the spectator that Michael might be the subject of the camera's point of view and an absence of a look that would confirm or deny that possibility or that would specify definitively his spatial location. In each case but one (the shot that tracks Laurie and Tommy from across the street as they walk in the direction of the Myers house on the way to school), these shots are held until a fragment of Michael's body appears in the frame.

What is interesting about the cinematic construction of these appearances is that although point of view is strongly marked, none of the shots in question turns out to be a point-of-view shot in the strict sense, in other words, a shot designated as being from the exact position of one of the characters (in this case, Michael's). The function of this is threefold. First, the structure of these shots serves effectively to combine the point-of-view system inaugurated in the first scene with the framing system predominant in the second one: threat and aggression are a function both of Michael's point of view and of the limits on our vision as spectators provided by the articulation of the frame. The look of the camera, of Michael, and of the spectator are codified first as identical and then they separate. Second, this identification and separation generate an aggressive tension in relation to the frustration of our knowledge and, hence, of a position from which we can stably dominate the process of the text. We are offered a position from which we can ubiquitously dominate all the characters except one, Michael, whose elusiveness increases over us, so to speak, as our position increases in elusiveness with respect to the characters he is watching. They are identified as under threat as we are positioned as lacking a place from which we can be sure where Michael actually is or what he might do. Finally, the combination of point of view and framing in this particular section, while functioning to articulate suspense and threat, actually never coincides with an act of aggression as such. The system threatens, so to speak, but never attacks. It is in the final section that the aggression breaks loose.

This last section of the film combines elements of the system of the cinematic articulation of suspense elaborated during the course of section three (itself a combination in a number of respects of the systems that marked scenes one and two) with a number of other elements from the opening scene (nighttime, a voyeuristic gaze at the female victims in a state of seminudity, sexual activity, sequences set in enclosed, interior spaces). What it adds, increasingly, is Michael's presence within the frame as a stable and consistent object of the look of the viewer as distributed across a series of shots in this sequence. Rather than give an exhaustive description of this section, I would simply like to emphasize one or two movements and aspects of its composition. First, there is the darkness, which functions largely to amplify at a number of points our difficulty in seeing where Michael is, increasing the frustration of our knowledge as to his position and of our wish for an omniscient gaze. Second, there is the continual frustration of the possibility of seeing Michael on the part either of his victims or, more important, of Laurie. Where in the previous section she had seen him, albeit fleetingly (she indeed was the only character to do so), here he is never the object of the point of view until he attacks her in the bedroom where Lynda is killed as she discovers Annie's body on the bed with Judith's headstone. The only character who *does* see him is Tommy (as, again, he is framed in point of view through a window), and when Tommy persuades Laurie to take a look, he has gone (the shot-counter shot system of the previous section being split here across two points of view). Finally, there is the elaboration of the inscription of Michael's body in the frame as the object of the point of view of the spectator, of Lynda, of Laurie and, last, of Loomis. Michael stabilizes, first, as the object of the look of the spectator, appearing at length in full figure as he stares up at the body of Bob. Next, he appears to us and to Lynda from Lynda's point of view, but draped in a sheet and wearing Bob's glasses, so that Lynda in fact thinks he is Bob while we know it is Michael. The tension in the shot is not, then, a function of a disjunction of looks but solely a function of a disjunction in knowledge between the spectator and Lynda. Finally, he is caught in Laurie's gaze and in ours as he appears in full figure to attack her, pursuing her into her house and there attacking her again.

Throughout this sequence, as there has been before in this section as

Halloween, 1978. Michael Myer's presence becomes more emphatic.
From the editors' collection.

well as in other parts of the film, there is a play of coincidence and disjunction between the knowledge of the audience and the character, together with a play of mapping/separation between the audience's and the character's points of view. This tension is further amplified at a number of points by a lack of knowledge as to Michael's precise spatial location. Having twice survived apparent death (in both instances reviving and attacking Laurie from behind while we watch him approach), Michael finally is caught in Loomis' sight, something which has been missing since Loomis' initial appearance in the film. Loomis shoots straight at the camera. This is followed by a cut to a reverse angle as Michael pulls off his mask and staggers toward the window. Cut to the ground outside as he falls—once again apparently dead.

Loomis's gun shot into the camera in a sense recalls and reverses the opening shot. While there the camera, spectator, and Michael were united in a point of view that traced the initial aggression; here we have the reverse angle, so to speak, in which the aggression is erased by an act of aggression in return in which the violence is directed *toward*, rather than away from the camera, in which the camera is the object rather than the subject of attack. But not quite, because this time the camera is not signified as Michael's point of view. It is at the right angle, but too close. There is a disjunction between the spectator's look and Michael's. An aggression is returned, as it were, against both Michael *and* spectator, but because the two are *separated* across the look of the camera at the point of Loomis's shot, it becomes possible, according to the logic of the film, for Michael to survive (and for the spectator to carry on looking as the shots are fired). When Loomis looks out the window for Michael's body, we see, with him, that it is gone. The music signals the return of the possibility of aggression and threat. The diegetic source of violence has not definitely been destroyed; but then neither has its source in the desire and position of the spectator. Nor has it been erased from the enunciative mechanisms of the text. That last sequence, the empty frames, the possibility that Michael has survived and will attack again, is a final aggression by the film against its spectators. This aspect of the functioning of the film, its generation of suspense in terms of an aggression distributed within and between the spectator on the one hand and the text itself, so to speak, on the other, requires some further comment.

Some of the textual, cinematic, and psychoanalytic mechanisms involved in the generation and codification of aggression in film have been discussed by Jacqueline Rose, in an article on *The Birds* (1963) in

Screen and by Kaja Silverman in an article in *Framework*.¹ The former discusses aggression and diegetic violence in terms of paranoia and narcissism, the latter in terms of a masochism involved in the relationship between the subject and the text. Each of these is important, and it is clear, for example, that paranoia is a perennial commonplace in the horror film and in the thriller (two genres which depend especially upon a violent suspense) and that the former in particular, in working, in Rose's terms, "to excite displeasure," must involve, of necessity, a degree of masochism, in the relationship between film and spectator— perhaps more, indeed, than any other mainstream genre. What I want to do here is to specify in a little more detail these and other structures involved and inscribed in the systematization of aggression and suspense in *Halloween*.

As we have seen, each moment of suspense in *Halloween* is marked both by a lack of knowledge on the part of the spectating subject (articulated in terms of point of view and the field of vision offered by the frame) and also by a knowledge on the spectator's part that exceeds that of the characters under threat of attack. In other words, the sequences in the film in which these structures of knowledge and looking are present coincide with an intense inscription of threat, aggression, and potential or actual diegetic violence. What is at issue, in a sense, is control of the frame. The distribution of that control across the instances of the spectator, the film's subject of enunciation and its characters is articulated very precisely around the figure of Michael: will he appear? when, where, and in relation to whose look? Control and dominance are worked out between the spectating subject and the subject of enunciation of the film in terms of a diegetic aggression involving, first, characters who are marked as victims and whose status as such is heavily stressed, because up to the end of the film there is no question of these characters being in a position to defend themselves and to return the aggression directed against them; and, second, involving a character whose only function and motivation (for the film as well as in the film) is that of inflicting violence and death. A fact that again is heavily stressed: Loomis's function, in a sense, is precisely to speak and define this fact. As such, this structure can be said to be both paranoid and sado-masochistic. Paranoia is articulated in the relationship between film and spectator and between the spectator and the fictional figure of Michael. None of the other characters, with the exception perhaps of Loomis, can be described as paranoid: they are neither aware of Michael's presence nor are they prone to fantasies of persecution. It is the spectator who is prone to such fantasies, investing the film itself and the figure of Michael with an omnipotence and aggressiveness that cannot be fully controlled.

What is perhaps particularly interesting, given Rose's comments on the paranoid structure of shot-reverse devices turning on point-of-view inscriptions, is that here paranoia is a function of a similar cinematic system, with point of view once again playing an especially significant role. Unlike the sequence she describes in *North by Northwest* (1959), however, here, where aggression is a function of a repetitive meeting of the points of view of two different characters, and paranoia is latent in the reversibility of the positions of subject and of a tension in the distribution of several instances of looking across the points of view of Michael, on the one hand, and of the characters subjected to his and our gaze on the other, what is significant about the spectator's position within the sado-masochistic aspects of the structure is that it is constantly split between the twin poles of sadism and masochism. And this split is inscribed in the text in terms of a shifting series of polarized identifications. The spectator identifies with the film and what it fantasizes as its subject of enunciation insofar as that subject is invested with omnipotence and control. The viewing subject also, of necessity, identifies itself as subjected to that omnipotence and control as well as to the aggression it implies. The identifications of the spectator are thus split between the polarities of a sadistic, aggressive, and controlling position and a masochistic, suffering, and controlled position. These identifications are in turn and simultaneously structured and put into operation across the positions occupied by characters in the film. The spectator identifies with Michael and with the characters aggressed by him. In moments of suspense, where the spectator's subjection to the aggression implicit in that instance is most marked, the spectator's loss of a position of control is translated either into an acute anxiety or eventually into an act of extreme diegetic violence.

Two points emerge from these remarks. The first is that *Halloween* (and the horror film in general) is dependent not so much upon the generation of *unpleasure* as upon the generation of a very particular kind of pleasure—the masochistic enjoyment of the infliction of an aggression, pleasure in subjection to another, or rather a masochistic pleasure in combination with its sadistic opposite. The second point, a concomitant of this, is that although suffering persecution and attack, the spectating subject does not turn *its* aggression against the film as such. On the contrary, the film is enjoyed, and this seems to involve the representation of violence and aggression in the film itself. The spectator's aggression is thus articulated across a series of specific representations and across the complex of positions of suffering, of violence and the infliction of violence, of death and the infliction of death, that those representations entail.

Two final points: Why the predominance of women as victims of the aggression and violence, not only in *Halloween*, but also in the genre to which it belongs and in the recent cycle it seems to have inaugurated so successfully? And why its own particular and insistent structure of repetition? There is a clear and immediate answer to the first of these questions. Patriarchy positions women as subject to men (and their violence) and *Halloween* simply rehearses and restates that ideology as an assertion both of male aggression and male power and of male fear of women and female sexuality. Nuanced somewhat (one male character, Bob, is killed in the film, and the spectator, female or male, is subject also to the aggression in the film), the question then is one to do with the textual mechanisms involved in that rehearsal and restatement. The first of these revolves around an ideological identification of femininity with a position of passivity. In *Halloween*, as we have seen, the spectator's identifications are split. One side of that split involves occupying a passive position as object of aggression and control, a position articulated across the diegesis as identification with those characters marked also as objects of an omnipotent violence and threat. That particular identification is amplified insofar as ideologically such a position is generally identified as feminine, an identification mobilized and put to work in the film. The other side of the split involves an identification with the opposite position of omnipotence and control, articulated in the film in terms of an omnipotence vis-à-vis its victims and a concomitant identification with Michael as its agent. Conversely, then, the spectator here identifies with an agent of active control who, conventionally fantasized, is male, is specified and stressed in the film as male. The thing to note about this is the extent to which active/masculine and passive/feminine have to be constructed while the spectating subject is perfectly capable of oscillating between the two. Indeed, the film is absolutely dependent upon that possibility of oscillation. In order to be undermined and challenged, however, it is important to note that these specifications cannot simply be reversed, for that would only activate the fantasy of the castrating woman, the phallic mother, common enough in other horror films and, perhaps, as a final point of speculation, a fantasy that ultimately underpins this text as well.

There are two reasons for such a statement. The first concerns the mechanism of "identification with an aggressor" involved in the relations between the spectator and the film in general, and the spectator and the character of Michael in particular. In their entry on the mechanism in *The Language of Psychoanalysis*, Laplanche and Pontalis first note the specific sense given to the term by Ferenczi: "The aggression he has in mind is the sexual attack by an adult who lives in a world of passion and guilt upon a supposedly innocent child."[2] It is worth remembering Michael's initial appearance as a supposedly innocent child inflicting an attack upon an adolescent girl who is not, being "guilty" of sexual desire, and who occupies the position of the mother in a sequence resonant of the primal scene. Also it is worth noting in respect of Ferenczi's formulation that Laurie, the victim who survives, is specified precisely as sexually innocent. Laplanche and Pontalis go on to describe Lagache's view that identification with the aggressor is involved in the formation of the ideal ego: the subject identifying with an adult whom it endows with the trait of omnipotence. The relationship is a dual one, sado-masochistic in character, with the aggression reversible and ambivalent (in endowing the adult with omnipotence the subject is itself placed in an aggressive, omnipotent position, since the former is thus "misperceived, subjugated, even abolished altogether").[3] The model for this omnipotence is basically, initially, the mother, which would suggest that both Michael and the fantasized subject of the film, insofar as they are invested with traits of aggressive omnipotence, are invested also with the traits of the phallic mother.[4] If identification with an aggressor is involved in the formation of the ego ideal, and if the ego ideal is an "ideal of narcissistic omnipotence constructed on the model of infantile narcissism,"[5] then it is also involved to some extent in paranoia, which itself involves narcissism, aggression and fantasies of an omnipotent other. It is also characterized "by a passive homosexual current, and hence a 'feminine' position on both man and woman,"[6] and, as we have seen, such a position is crucial to *Halloween*. Once again, the model for the persecuting and omnipotent other is ultimately the image of the mother.

If *Halloween* is thus marked by this image, it is marked also by its insistent repetitions. What do these repetitions repeat? First, an ideology of women that it marks at a number of levels of its text; second, a fantasy that it shares with most other horror films and that it here renews through the very mechanisms of its suspense, aggression, and violence; and third, insofar as it consists almost solely of repeated variations of suspense across the instance of the look, and insofar as it consequently articulates a struggle for control in terms of a constant gaining and losing of a position of such control on the part of the spectating subject, it simply, obsessively, repeats, in a register of almost unmitigated aggression, a mechanism basic to the narrative process and to the suspense which is so fundamental to it.

NOTES

1. Jacqueline Rose, "Paranoia and the Film System," *Screen* 17, no. 4 (Winter 1967/77): 85–105; Kaja Silverman, "Masochism and Subjectivity," *Framework*, no. 12 (n.d.): 2–8.

2. J. Laplanche and J. B. Pontalis, *The Language of Psychoanalysis* (New York: Hogarth Press, 1973), 209.

3. Laplanche and Pontalis, 209.

4. The text functions as the mother, in other words, it reactivates in fantasy certain traces of the mother–child dyad, insofar as it offers the spectator security, comfort, and a narcissistic position of omnipotence itself. Where that offer is refused and withdrawn, so to speak, the mother becomes a source not of security and comfort but rather of terror and threat. It should be borne in mind, however, that both these functions occur in film as part of its symbolic process, and that the subject of that process has itself thus entered the Symbolic insofar as a separation from the mother has occurred involving the destruction of primal narcissism, the intervention of the Law, the father, and the terrors that he represents. These primal functions and fantasies—and the positions occupied by the subject within them—are thus not repeated exactly. They are rather evoked through specific representations. In *Halloween* it should be noted that their evocation coincides precisely with the representation of a father figure, Loomis, who is singularly weak and ineffectual despite the fact that as representative of the Law he alone knows the truth about Michael.

5. Laplanche and Pontalis, *The Language of Psychoanalysis*, 201.

6. Rose, "Paranoia and the Film System," 103.

22

Demons in the Family: Tracking the Japanese "Uncanny Mother Film" from *A Page of Madness* to *Ringu*

Ruth Goldberg

> The same old demons will always come up until finally you have learned your lesson, the lesson they came to teach you.
>
> —Pema Chödrön[1]

Spurred on by the unprecedented box office success of Nakata Hideo's terrifying *Ringu* (1998) and the popular and critical interest in landmark films like *Audition* (2000), the Japanese horror film has enjoyed a renaissance, producing some of the most provocative and satisfying of recent horror films and inspiring remakes and imitations all over the globe. "J-horror," as it has become popularly known, has developed a wide range of tropes and tendencies, offering something for every possible taste.[2] Jay McRoy has described the range of Japanese contributions to modern horror in detail: traditional ghost stories inspired by Kabuki dramas; the infamous *Guinea Pig* "snuff" films; modern rape/ revenge narratives like *Freeze Me* (2002); the frenetic postpunk *Tetsuo* (1988) and *Tetsuo II* (1992); goofy supernatural teen dramas including the enormously popular *Eko Eko Azaraku* (*Wizard of Darkness*, 1995) and *Uzumaki* (*Spiral*, 2000); and sophisticated noir fantasies such as *Gemini* (1999), *Chaos* (1999), and *Audition*, among many others.[3]

These are, on the whole, uncanny, disorienting, haunting films, and their popularity proves that the Japanese have been successful in translating their nightmares to the screen. These films can be read either in terms of cultural specificity or as "acts of translation" to foreign audiences, and, as Steffen Hantke has pointed out, both approaches are extremely problematic and limiting.[4] What Japanese filmmakers seem to have arrived at is a national rendering of the universally visceral experience that was defined by Freud as "the uncanny." The mechanisms Freud described in his essay "The Uncanny"—intellectual uncertainty, the return of the repressed, the appearance of the double, the eerie, atmospheric transformation of what is most familiar into something unfamiliar—are the preoccupations and constructs around which the horror film initially evolved. It is in this "return" to the themes and methods of the uncanny film that Japanese horror is often satisfyingly "old-school," evoking the early atmospheric works of Jacques Tourneur and James Whale. At their best, the films combine elements from Japanese mythology and Buddhist teachings on death, karma, and the supernatural with high technology and an ultramodern veneer, all of which blend together to create unique, nuanced, and terrifying films.

Japan actually has been turning out these edgy, innovative horror films for decades, but this body of work was largely unknown in the West until *Ringu* sparked new critical interest in "J-Horror," and introduced fans to Sadako, the faceless female ghost who has become the horror film's new icon. *Ringu*, as a representative example of the new Japanese horror film, lends itself to a close reading of the ambivalence about motherhood that haunts Japan in the form of a recurring cinematic nightmare, reflecting in microcosm the anxious tension between tradition and modernity that looms large in the nation's sensibility. It is the sharp and surprising contrast between the cinematic trope of the Uncanny Mother and the actual reverence of motherhood in Japanese culture that this article will primarily address. *Ringu* is a new landmark in what may be called the "Uncanny Mother film," a significant trope in the horror film generally, although a rereading of Japanese film history reveals that the Uncanny Mother has developed special significance and nuance in Japanese cinema.

A LOOK BACK

The popular understanding of the Japanese horror film generally begins with the campy monster films of the 1950s like *Gojira* (*God-*

zilla, *King of the Monsters*, 1954), and landmark films of the '50s and '60s that contain references to the supernatural or psychopathology, such as *Ugetsu Monogatari (Tales of Ugetsu*, 1953), *Jigoku (Hell*, 1960), *Onibaba (The Hole*, 1964), *Yotsuya Kwaidon (Ghost Story*, 1964), and *Mojuu (Blind Beast*, 1969). Beyond the literature on Japanese horror films of the '50s and '60s, a number of later films including *Tetsuo (Iron Man*, 1988) and *Evil Dead Trap* (1988) have been the focus of scholarship, leading up to *Ringu* and the '90s boom. Most reviewers trace *Ringu*'s roots back to the tradition of Kaidon ("weird tales") films, which are traditionally shown during the Buddhist "O-Bon" festival of the dead. In the literature on Japanese horror film there is minimal treatment of prewar horror outside of the Kaidon, which have largely been dismissed by scholars like Joseph L. Anderson and Donald Richie as being "cheap," "unimaginative," and "all the same."[5]

Yet configuring the history in this way is a mistake. Just as a history of the Western horror film would, of necessity, recognize the contribution of the German Expressionists and of the significance of *The Cabinet of Dr. Caligari* in particular, so a history of the Japanese horror film must begin with *A Page of Madness* (1926). Kinugasa Teinosuke's hauntingly beautiful avant-garde masterwork is the true predecessor of *Ringu* and an early example of what may be called the *bukimi-na haha-mono*: the "Uncanny Mother" film.

Noël Burch has mapped the parallels between *A Page of Madness* and *Caligari*, and has written convincingly about *Page*'s exalted position in the history of Japanese cinema.[6] What remains to be illuminated here is the way in which *Page* shows the beginnings of an idea of monstrous motherhood which has never left the popular imagination in Japan. The film unfolds as a surrealist meditation on insanity and the family. A man (Inoue Masuo) has taken a job as a janitor at an insane asylum to be near his wife (Nakagawa Yoshie), who has been committed there. Narrating in purely subjective terms, the film presents the desires, memories, and fantasies of the characters as interchangeably "real" and present. *A Page of Madness* shows the fracturing of the family, the janitor's gradual descent from grief into madness, and the eventual anarchy that ensues, all revolving around the Uncanny Mother, once familiar, now unfamiliar, who abandoned her family after trying to drown her infant son years earlier, and who has retreated into a world that no one else can access.

Perhaps most striking is the cultural background against which this enduringly resonant figure of the Uncanny Mother is posited. As

Masami Ohinata has written, "When Japanese hear the word *mother* they do not call to mind the real flesh-and-blood mothers of their personal experience but, rather, see a personification of 'devotion to children, parental affection, and self-sacrifice.' . . . People's devotion to the concept comes close to that of a religious faith."[7] The veritable cult of motherhood in Japan has been the subject of considerable scholarship, and even a cursory review of the literature makes clear that despite increasing Westernization, the breakdown of the multigenerational family unit, rising divorce rates, and the growing numbers of mothers working outside the home, Japanese cultural ideals of motherhood have not adapted to fit the changing social landscape. According to Susan Orpett Long, "The . . . Japanese cultural ideal of nurturance is the expectation that caregiving is a totalizing experience. Nurturing children, husbands and elderly parents has been considered a woman's major role."[8]

Ideals about Japanese motherhood have traditionally been reinforced by cinema: this is a culture in which the *haha-mono* ("mother film"), wherein saintly mothers are martyred in their undying devotion to their errant children, is a classic box-office staple. The flip side of the idealized representation of Japanese motherhood, found in the *haha-mono*, is the *bukimi-na haha*: the nightmare mother who has a special link to madness or the supernatural, and it is this figure that appears in *A Page of Madness* and is represented in many Japanese horror films leading up to *Ringu*.[9]

Among numerous examples, *Ugetsu*, *Onibaba*, and *Mojuu* stand out as three films of critical importance from different periods that illustrate the trajectory of the Uncanny Mother trope between *A Page of Madness* and *Ringu*. In Mizoguchi's lyrical *Ugetsu*, a mother returns from beyond the grave to reunite her son and husband and care for them one last time, the physical embodiment of her husband's guilt at having abandoned the family. In *Ugetsu*, Buddhist teachings about attachment and retribution are overtly pressed into the service of Mizoguchi's allegorical representation of the crisis in Japanese society. The husband is dishonest about his motivation for leaving the family, and it is at this moment that a demon appears, luring him away from his path and keeping him imprisoned until after his wife has died. When he is finally able to break free, it is too late, and the ghost's appearance at his homecoming is a last reminder that there was a moral lesson to be learned from the ordeal. Hearth and home, in *Ugetsu*, become "un-homelike" ("unheimlich") transformed by the presence of the ghostly mother who appears, at first, to be a familiar, comforting presence, but is actually an agent of the Uncanny who is meant to illustrate that there will be no rest until the husband learns what the demons have come to teach him.

In other groundbreaking films like Shindo Kaneto's dramatically innovative *Onibaba*, the mother is depicted as a murderous amazon predator who impersonates a demon in order to manipulate her daughter-in-law according to her will. This vision of motherhood could not be more diametrically opposed to the popular vision of the haha-mono. The mother is ultimately punished for her greed and attachment, at first entirely unable to pull off her demon mask and then horribly disfigured in the attempt.

Masumura's treatment of the Uncanny Japanese Mother in *Mojuu* begins to resemble the American "momist" visions of *Psycho* (1960) or *The Manchurian Candidate* (1962), insofar as the son is a monster because the mother made him into one. New Wave films like *Mojuu* begin to mark a shift in the Japanese vision of the Uncanny Mother. It is during this period that the element of blame comes overtly into play, and unnatural mothers who do not fulfill the ideals of Japanese motherhood are depicted as begetting monstrous children. Masumura's treatment of the subject is consistent with the visions of monstrous motherhood found in horror films around the world during this period of time,[10] and led directly to films like *Ringu* and *Dark Water* (2001), which kicked off the horror boom in Japan, proving the trope's enduring power. Perhaps what is most interesting to note is how much subtler *Ringu* is about blaming the mother, concurrent with more nuanced ambivalences about motherhood in contemporary Japanese society.

The small body of literature growing around Nakata's seminal film reflects the preoccupation of film scholarship with what these nightmares might tell us about the culture that dreamed them up. Reimi Tateishi reads the film on the level of national allegory, as a text about social anxiety located in the discourse on modernity and the ongoing tensions between Japan's cultural/mythological past and rapidly advancing hi-tech present a clash between Japan's gleaming metallic facade and the old "hungry ghosts."[11] Jay McRoy extends this argument, looking at *Ringu* as a reflection of anxiety over shifting gender roles and Japanese cultural norms about male violence against women.[12]

The most often repeated remark about *Ringu*, however, that it is like the *"Exorcist"* of Japanese horror films, veers away from a culturally specific reading, and raises questions about what lies underneath the film's surface, making it so terrifyingly resonant for the international audiences that have come to embrace it with an almost fetishistic devotion. Alvin Lu's statement ("Hideo Nakata's *Ring* is to these films what *The Exorcist* was to Seventies American Cinema's horror boom") was certainly nothing more than an off-hand comment—a kind of shorthand meant to articulate that *Ringu* had enjoyed astonishing box-office success, had sparked a resurgence of interest in the genre, and was followed by a slew of sequels and spin-offs precisely as *The Exorcist* had been in the United States in 1973.[13] However, the comment comes to have an uncanny ring of truth, for despite having been made twenty-five years apart in radically different cultural contexts and having overtly different plots, *Ringu* and *The Exorcist* are family dramas that explore identical conflicts and resolutions.

DEMONS IN THE FAMILY AND THE MOTHERS WHO LOVE THEM

Since the "same old demons" have resurfaced, it is worth addressing what they have come to teach us. Addressing two cult films with the same underlying trope almost becomes an issue of comparative mythology, and provokes questions about what is at the heart of the recurrent narrative. *Ringu*, like *The Exorcist* before it, is a film about two families that are peopled less by fully developed characters than by what seem like fixed energies which draw each other out and express themselves with the relentless fluency of archetypes. At the core, the films are about the standard family dynamics of guilt and ambivalence, secrets and lies, anger and repression. More specifically, they are tales about frantic investigations in which mothers search desperately for clues and answers about demon daughters and must ultimately learn a specific and unchanging lesson in order to restore the family to a state of balance.

In each film the dynamics of anger and ambivalence are encoded in the supernatural: the family members who live in the present must appease those who have passed on or have transformed into demons or ghosts. Otherworldly anger becomes symptomatic of the familial rift in communication and crisis over roles, and, as in many families, the symptoms become the means by which people communicate metaphorically. Both films are propelled by the mechanism of nightmare, in which the frantic search for insight into what appears to be an external threat draws the mothers to confront those conflicts at the very heart of the family. Toward this effort, each film provokes a kind of dialogue or interaction between a living family and a family of demons and ghosts, and this dialogue serves an internally therapeutic function within the film, exposing the primary conflict so that it may be understood and resolved. In this way, the tensions and connections between the doubled families begin to resemble the doubling/splitting/projection mechanisms of the dream work, by which different aspects of the dreamer that would normally be kept apart are allowed to encounter one another. The "explanation" of the films' supernatural menace supplies the means to rectify their external conflicts, but also points to an encrypted, interior level of meaning. It is this dualistic quality which gives these two films their nightmarish quality and validates the idea of examining both *Ringu* and *The Exorcist* on the level of dream.

These are morality tales, and their resolution comes at a high price to the guilty parties. Historically, the attention given to both films has placed the figure of the demon-child-as-monster at the center of the narrative. However, in both of these films, the "obvious" or "surface" monstrosity of the young girls serves only to misdirect the viewer's attention away from the films' true source of horror—a reactionary vision of the inept, "unnatural" mother as the root cause of the drama—represented as monstrous by virtue of her inability to fulfill her role as nurturer and protector. Unlike the absent fathers in both films, the mothers in *Ringu* and *The Exorcist* are forced to step back into their traditional roles in order to restore the family to a state of balance by the time the credits roll.

Robin Wood has long since identified the narrative tendency in which an emancipated female character is subjected to torture and pressed into the service of restoring the patriarchy. While the "monstrous emancipated mother" configuration of the formula may serve some of the same ends, the intricacies of its development and resolution within these two films presents a drastic shift from the kind of depictions of women that Wood was addressing (specifically the character of Ripley in *Alien* [1979]).[14] These are not feminist avengers, and they are not the archetypal castrating mothers which Barbara Creed has examined in her work.[15] *Ringu* and *The Exorcist* contain a radically different vision of the mother who is monstrous not by virtue of being controlling, but by virtue of being ineffectual. She is depicted as freakish in her hysterical inability to protect her children and fulfill her nat-

ural role as martyred homemaker, all of which stems from her desire
to have an independent identity. Her neglect, avoidance, and sublimated anger manifest in her children, turning them into monsters
through the mechanism of projection. In this way the films clearly
blame and punish the mothers for and through the horror which
ensues. This understated vision of monstrosity insidiously slips by on
the radar screen, enabling the critical and pervasive misreading of these
films as being "about" the daughters and not the mothers.

Seen in this light, the two films come to have three significant parallels: a specific variation on the monstrous mother theme which, in each
case, emerges out of and is contrasted against a cult of motherhood
(the Japanese *boseishugi* or "doctrine of motherhood" and the Roman
Catholic Church), an unconscious dialogue resembling the dream
work that occurs between the doubled families in each film (one a living family and the other a ghostly/demonic double), and the possibility
this dialogue creates for a therapeutic as opposed to apocalyptic resolution of the drama. All of these factors bear further scrutiny. In this
case, the devil is in the details.

'RINGU'

Ringu tells the story of television reporter Reiko (Nanako Matsus-
hima), a single mother who is determined to get to the bottom of an
urban legend about a cursed videotape that has the power to kill anyone who watches it exactly one week after the initial viewing. Reiko's
determination to unravel the unsettling story is reinforced by the
untimely death of her own niece, Tomoko (Yuko Takeuchi), after a
group viewing of the video the week before. Leaving her young son
Yoichi (Rikiya Otaka) to fend for himself at home, Reiko goes to a
hotel on the Izu peninsula where Tomoko is rumored to have initially
received the "curse" and watches the mysterious tape herself.

The video contains a surreal montage of disjointed images and
words, scenes of volcanic eruptions, a woman brushing her hair in a
mirror, the word *sada* (*chaste*), an abandoned well. After the viewing,
the phone rings and out of the receiver comes an unearthly buzzing
sound, "the keening wail of the supposed other world,"[16] as Reiko
becomes "cursed" to die a week later.

Frantic to find the connection between these events, she enlists the
aid of her reluctant ex-husband Ryuji (Hiroyuki Sanada), a mathemat-

Mother faces the horror in Ringu, *1998. From the editors' collection.*

ics professor with psychic abilities and a link to the spirit world. During the search for clues both Ryuji and Yoichi become "infected" with the curse. The search leads the divorced couple to the island of Oshima to gather information about Shizuko (Masako), a psychic who committed suicide by throwing herself into a volcano forty years earlier after being publicly accused of being a fraud. On the island they discover that Shizuko had a daughter, Sadako (Orie Izuno) ("chaste child"), the result of an adulterous union with the university professor who brought Shizuko's psychic talents to the attention of the public. Sadako was a monster, possessed of the ability to kill by the force of her sheer will. Left abandoned after her mother's suicide, the fiendish Sadako was murdered by her father—pushed down a well on the Izu peninsula, on the same the property where the video would first appear forty years later. Her rage has allowed her to manifest from beyond the grave through the conduits of technology, spreading her viral curse to anyone who watches the videotape, a montage of her memories and emotions. A hunt to find Sadako before the week is up results in Reiko descending into the well with only minutes to spare, calling for the ghost who emerges in the form of a weeping skeleton. Reiko cradles Sadako in her arms, crooning to the angry ghost-child as it dissolves and fades away. Reiko and Ryuji go their separate ways, believing the curse to have been lifted.

The landscape of Reiko and Yoichi's family life clearly establishes the case made by McRoy and Tateishi for reading *Ringu* in terms of anxiety over the Westernization of Japan. Unlike the traditional multi-generational Japanese household, Reiko and Yoichi live alone together in a sterile modern environment in which they do not communicate or show any affection. Reiko is consumed by her work life, and this is enabled by a kind of convenient lie in which both mother and son participate that Yoichi is old enough to be independent (to employ the clinical term, he is an entirely "parentified" six-year-old child—laying out Reiko's clothes for her, helping her dress, walking himself to school, heating up his own dinner, putting himself to bed), and that Reiko's neglect of Yoichi has no emotional consequences for either of them.

The dynamic of denial is reinforced by an atmosphere of repression and secrecy and is extended to every human interaction in the film through innumerable and seemingly insignificant details which accumulate to form an unnerving portrait of absolute alienation. Nobody communicates or expresses any strong emotions. Instead of comforting her grieving family in the wake of Tomoko's death, Reiko immediately reverts to her professional role as an investigative reporter (the natural role of the dreamer) and leaves home, consumed by the search for clues that might break the curse.

The irony of Reiko's fascination with the curse of Sadako is that it is only a dream conceit—the journey that all dreamers take in which the action appears to be external but ultimately can only be about a confrontation between the dreamer and his or her own demons. Reiko's fascination with a child-killing monster is what places her own child in harm's way. It is the logic of nightmare—that the demons will pursue you in exact proportion to the energy you exert in trying to avoid them. Reiko thinks that the curse has suddenly descended on her family from nowhere and goes on a journey to find out why, but she need not have left home—it was waiting there for her all along. The family is already cursed with the burden of secrets and lies, repression, and avoidance before the narrative even begins.

Into this fractured family comes a family of restless ghosts, symptomatic of or embodying the conflicts among the living characters and pointing the way toward resolution. Reiko and Ryuji have to leave the alienated, modern landscape and return to the traditional seaside village on Oshima in order to uncover the origins of the curse and the original family drama that loosed Sadako on the world. Returning to an earlier mode of living forces them to confront archaic/classical Japanese images of the supernatural—references to "goblins" and vengeful ghosts—and also exemplifies the film's implicit critique of the alienated Japanese social landscape and the loss of traditional family values. The ghost family, emissary of the family's unconscious on the one hand and the culture's surmounted beliefs on the other, indicates the level on which this drama must be played out: a living family that is so repressed they can barely look at each other encounters a spirit family raging out of control in which the emotions of anger, disgust, shame, and despair are acted out at their most savage and primal levels. True to dream-logic, the ghost family shares some important parallels with the living family, but every dynamic is extended or amplified to such monstrous proportions that each pair ends up resembling different aspects of the same conflict: two absent angry fathers, two abandoning mothers, two otherworldly children.

As if a dream solution for having abandoned her own child and devaluing her identity as a mother, Reiko makes it up to the demon daughter Sadako, plunging into the depths of the well to find and console her. Reiko's redemption comes in embracing her traditional role in the family, and in meeting the demon instead of letting it pursue her. In her descent into the well, Reiko expiates her maternal guilt and assuages Sadako's anger at her own abandoning mother. Sadako is the expression of everything that Yoichi holds inside, as she turns her rage at her parents' betrayal against the world—almost as if Reiko had conjured up a nightmare vision of her sweet, silent, parentified little boy.

The parallels of the two absent fathers are ultimately the most instructive. In what is perhaps the most spectacularly terrifying moment of the film, after they believe the curse has already been lifted, Sadako returns to claim Ryuji. Ryuji believes the danger is past after Reiko does not die when Sadako emerges from the well. He immediately takes leave of the family again, even though the ordeal has made it abundantly clear that Reiko and Yoichi need him around. A few days later he dies, a victim of Sadako's wrath. The film explains it away as a technicality—the curse is broken only if you make a copy of the tape and show it to someone else, and Ryuji didn't figure that out in time—but on another level Ryuji dies because he didn't learn the lesson the demon had come to teach him. Sadako's father imprisoned her in the well after her mother's suicide, and in the dream logic of the film with its doubled characters, the living father must atone for the dead one through a realization about his role in the family. Ryuji doesn't see the connection, doesn't learn the lesson about not leaving the people who need him, and so must die.

It is here that the film becomes unabashedly prescriptive. To break the curse you have to ask someone else for help; you have to communicate. The film resolves with Reiko turning to her previously estranged father to help her save Yoichi, affirming her dedication to the welfare of her son and a return to traditional family values. Where the father, Ryuji, is sacrificed to the child's anger, the mother, realizing she is fundamentally to blame, changes her life and restores order to the world.

CONCLUSION

It is against the backdrop of uneasily shifting social attitudes towards the cult of motherhood and traditional family values in the late 1990s that *Ringu* appeared and quickly became the highest grossing horror film in Japanese film history. It shares with its American counterpart *The Exorcist* the sense of being a modern morality tale directed at the mother who both takes the blame for the horror and assumes the onus for restoring the family to wholeness. The trope is complex and painful: it posits that into families riddled with secrets and lies, demons are born. Both stories pivot around an absent father, a repressed or deceptive, ineffectual mother who cannot openly express her anger within the context of the family, an atmosphere of secrecy, and a demon-daughter who embodies the family's collective rage. A variation on the old "Uncanny" theme of monstrous birth, *Ringu*, like *The Exorcist*, operates with the logic of the unconscious and the urgency of dream work: the primary family is doubled and between the two families a kind of therapeutic resolution is finally achieved, albeit at a terrible cost.

In both films the familial roles and patterns are rigidly constructed. In this moralistic trope, the fathers can only be sacrificed, the mothers only punished. Neither *Ringu* nor *The Exorcist* can envision a solution beyond punishment and blame, and the mother gets the lion's share of both. Both films are reactionary and create a kind of nostalgia for tradition, but the different endings of *Ringu* and *The Exorcist* may potentially reveal something about the differences between the cultures from which they emerged. By the end of *The Exorcist*, the bleak American facade of normalcy is restored, and this is where the two films differ most significantly. *Ringu* leaves us with a much more optimistic, expansive ending—the idea that some greater sense of connectedness is possible in a renewed appreciation of the traditional extended Japanese family. From Kinugasa's depiction of the delusional mother in *A Page of Madness* to Nakata's alienated working mother in *Ringu*, representations of Uncanny Mothers in Japanese cinema, although varied, remain essentially consistent—they embody the conflict and ambivalence over the changing ideas about women in Japan, and the Japanese family in transition.

The idea of "distant observers" looking to examine and understand these films within their cultural contexts rekindles the old argument over the merits of cultural specificity versus universality as analytic modes, and contains a series of implications for future currents within scholarship on the horror film. New work has begun to emerge on the relationship between horror and national cinemas,[17] work which appears to be divided between three approaches: scholars either feel compelled to look at the issue of cultural specificity and the nightmares of different cultures; to recognize that they are (at best) translating foreign texts and so choose to focus on those elements of horror which resonate across cultural divides and which might well form part of a universal human experience; to use elements of both approaches to arrive at a fuller understanding of the relationship between horror and national cinemas.

In the case of Japan, a culturally specific reading of J-horror through the lens of Zen Buddhist philosophy yields rich results, revealing a core preoccupation with the horror of attachment and of the enduring idea of the destructive and consuming "red thread of passion" that gives much of J-horror its pessimistic erotic bent. Taking the opposite approach, and looking at horror as a phenomenon that may transcend culture, one could read these films, although clearly emerging from a specific cultural context, as being rooted in the universal human experience of the body and in the horror of embodiment; of having been born and the certainty of death; and in the uneasy connection to the mothers who bore us and whom we will outlive. Situating the analysis of *Ringu* within the framework of Freud's essay on the Uncanny reveals a clear preference for the third and most expansive approach, which incorporates elements of the other two. Freud's meditation on the uncanny rests on a foundation of dualistic thought and is largely preoccupied with the fear of the occlusion of boundaries between pairs of ideas or states of being: between life and death, self and other, reality and dream, consciousness and the unconscious. These accumulate to form a laundry list of horrors all predicated on duality; and, in applying the uncanny to an analysis of Japanese horror film, it is easy to see how these dynamics of ambivalence would be particularly resonant within a society whose traditional philosophies maintain that anything short of embracing nonduality leads to perpetual suffering. Freud's essay on the Uncanny emerged from the same cultural context as German Expressionism, in the same time and place where the early horror films and modern understandings of horror in the West cohered. It is tempting to analyze the content of the uncanny and early German horror films through the lens of cultural specificity, and to argue that in them one can see the anxieties, tensions, and ambivalences of Weimar society; this is, beyond doubt, an effective framework in which to examine these cultural artifacts. However, in 1926, without ever having seen a German Expressionist film, Kinugasa used the techniques of Expressionism to create the uncanny masterpiece *A Page of Madness* in the radically different cultural context of Taisho Japan. How are we to understand this overlap and its recent recurrence in the J-horror boom? Perhaps this overlap of techniques and content, as well as the international popularity of these films, reveals universalities in the experience of horror and the uncanny, or perhaps looking at films in such a broad way renders them meaningless by virtue of factoring out the influence of culture. But the fact that Japanese horror films such as *Ringu* ultimately resonate with viewers both within and across cultures allows the expansive approach of mining the horror film for both its universal and culturally specific content to remain valid and productive.

NOTES

1. Pema Chödrön, *The Wisdom of No Escape and the Path of Loving-Kindness* (Boston: Shambala Press, 1991), 32.
2. Although horror has long been a staple of the Japanese film industry, it has been largely excluded from the canon of film scholarship until very recently, when critics and scholars have begun to champion the work, and its box-office success has made it impossible to ignore.

3. Jay McRoy, "Japan's Screaming: Recent Trends in Contemporary Japanese Horror Cinema," in *Nightmare Japan: New Essays on Japanese Horror Cinema*, ed. McRoy (Edinburgh: Edinburgh University Press, 2004), 1.

4. Steffan Hantke, "Japanese Horror under Western Eyes: Social Class and Global Culture in Takeshi Miike's *Audition*," in *Nightmare Japan*, ed. McRoy, 14.

5. As Anderson and Richie elaborate: "All contain the traditional Japanese ghost, usually female, with a heavily scarred face, blood running from the mouth, no legs, and long disheveled hair. These spirits usually return to haunt men who have done them wrong, or to redress old wrongs. They never return simply to haunt at large, and all have a single purpose—revenge." *The Japanese Film: Art and Industry* (Princeton, N.J.: Princeton University Press, 1982), 262.

6. Noël Burch, *To the Distant Observer: Form and Meaning in the Japanese Cinema* (Berkeley: University of California Press, 1979), 138–39.

7. Masami Ohinata, "The Mystique of Motherhood: A Key to Understanding Social Change and Family Problems in Japan," in *Japanese Women: New Feminist Perspectives on the Past, Present and Future*, ed. Kumiko Fujimura-Fanselow and Atsuko Kameda (New York: Feminist Press at the City University of New York, 1995), 205.

8. Susan Orpett Long, "Nurturing and Femininity: The Ideal of Caregiving in Postwar Japan," in *Re-Imaging Japanese Women*, ed. Anne Imamura (Berkeley: University of California Press, 1996), 162.

9. On a universal level, the horror film is largely preoccupied with the fractured family and metaphorical understandings of the forces of alienation and ambivalence. The Japanese horror film is no exception. What is worth noting is that, in this way, J-horror is entirely consistent with classical mainstream Japanese film. The family in crisis not a new theme, and directors as diverse as Yasujiro Ozu, Kenji Mizoguchi, and Akira Kurosawa have all employed representations of the Japanese family to illustrate the particular tensions in the society as a whole.

10. What makes *Mojuu* so unusual (aside from Masumura's wildly innovative aesthetic sensibility) is precisely its similarity to Western Momist films, despite having been made in Japan, and ostensibly being a meditation on the traditionally Japanese theme of the boundaries between torture and eroticism found in such classic films as Nagisa Oshima's *In the Realm of the Senses* (1976).

11. Ramie Tateishi, "The Japanese Horror Film Series: *Ring* and *Eko Eko Azarak*," in *Fear Without Frontiers: Horror Cinema Across the Globe*, ed. Steven Jay Schneider (London: FAB Press, 2003): 295.

12. McRoy, "Japan Screaming," 1.

13. Alvin Lu, "Focus on New Japanese Cinema," *Film Comment* 38, no. 1 (January–February 2001): 11.

14. Robin Wood, "An Introduction to the American Horror Film," in this volume.

15. Barbara Creed, *The Monstrous-Feminine: Film, Feminism, Psychoanalysis* (New York: Routledge, 1993).

16. Author's interview with Kevin Davies, New York City, June 30, 2003.

17. See, for example, Steven J. Schneider and Tony Williams, eds., *Horror International* (Detroit: Wayne State University Press, 2004), and Schneider, ed., *Fear without Frontiers*.

Select Bibliography

Included here are the most important works on the horror film genre. There are also many studies of individual horror films, directors, stars, and studios too numerous to mention.

Aylesworth, Thomas G. *Monsters from the Movies*. Philadelphia: J. B. Lippincott, 1972.

Badley, Linda. *Film, Horror and the Body Fantastic*. Westport, Conn.: Greenwood Press, 1995.

Barron, Neil. *Fantasy and Horror: A Cultural and Historical Guide to Literature, Illustration, Film, TV, Radio, and the Internet*. Lanham, Md.: Scarecrow Press, 1999.

Benshoff, Harry. "Blaxploitation Horror Films: Generic Reappropriation or Reinscription?" *Cinema Journal* 39, no. 2 (Winter 2000): 31–50.

——. *Monsters in the Closet: Homosexuality and the Horror Film*. Manchester: Manchester University Press, 1997.

Bernstein, Rhona. *Attack of the Leading Ladies: Gender, Sexuality, and Spectatorship in Classic Horror Cinema*. New York: Columbia University Press, 1996.

Boss, Pete. "Vile Bodies and Bad Medicine." *Screen* 27, no. 1 (January–February 1986): 14–24.

Brophy, Philip. "Horrality—The Textuality of Contemporary Horror Films." *Screen* 27, no. 1 (January–February 1986): 2–13.

Brosnan, John. *The Horror People*. New York: New American Library, 1977.

Brunas, Michael, John Brunas, and Tom Weaver. *Universal Horrors: The Studio's Classic Films, 1931–1946*. Jefferson, N.C.: McFarland, 1990.

Butler, Ivan. *Horror in the Cinema*. New York: A. S. Barnes, 1970.

Carroll, Noël. *The Philosophy of Horror, or, Paradoxes of the Heart.* New York: Routledge, 1990.

Clarens, Carlos. *An Illustrated History of the Horror Film.* New York: Capricorn Books, 1968.

Clover, Carol J. *Men, Women, and Chain Saws: Gender in the Modern Horror Film.* Princeton: Princeton University Press, 1992.

Coates, Paul. *The Gorgon's Gaze: German Cinema, Expressionism and the Image of Horror.* Cambridge: Cambridge University Press, 1991.

Cowie, Susan D., and Tom Johnson. *The Mummy in Fact, Fiction and Film.* Jefferson, N.C.: McFarland, 2002.

Crane, Jonathan Lake. *Terror and Everyday Life: Singular Moments in the History of the Horror Film.* Thousand Oaks, Calif.: Sage, 1994.

Creed, Barbara. *The Monstrous-Feminine: Film, Feminism, Psychoanalysis.* London: Routledge, 1993.

Crutchfield, Susan. "Touching Scenes and Finishing Touches: Blindness in the Slasher Film." In *Mythologies of Violence in Postmodern Media,* edited by Christopher Sharrett, 275–99. Detroit: Wayne State University Press, 1999.

Daniels, Les. *Living in Fear: A History of Horror in the Mass Media.* New York: Charles Scribner's Sons, 1975.

Dendle, Peter. *The Zombie Movie Encyclopedia.* Jefferson, N.C.: McFarland, 2001.

Dika, Vera. *Games of Terror: Halloween, Friday the 13th, and the Films of the Stalker Cycle.* Rutherford, N.J.: Farleigh Dickinson University Press, 1990.

Dillard, R. H. W. "Even a Man Who Is Pure at Heart: Poetry and Danger in the Horror Film." In *Man and the Movies,* edited by W. R. Robinson, 60–69. Baltimore: Penguin, 1967.

———, ed. *Horror Films.* New York: Monarch Press, 1976.

Doherty, Thomas. *Teenagers and Teenpics: The Juvenilization of American Movies in the 1950s.* Boston: Unwin Hyman, 1988.

Donald, James, ed. *Fantasy and the Cinema.* London: British Film Institute, 1989.

Douglas, Drake. *Horror.* New York: Macmillan, 1966.

Draper, Ellen. "Zombie Women When the Gaze Is Male." *Wide Angle* 10, no. 3 (1988): 52–62.

Dyer, Peter John. "The Roots of Horror." In *International Film Annual,* no. 3, edited by William Whitebair, 60–69. New York: Taplinger, 1959.

Ebert, Roger. "Why Audiences Aren't Safe Anymore." *American Film* 6, no. 5 (March 1981): 54–56.

Eisner, Lotte. *The Haunted Screen.* Berkeley: University of California Press, 1973.

Ellison, Harlan. "Three Faces of Fear." *Cinema* (U.S.) 3, no. 2 (March 1966): 4–8, 13–14.

Evans, Walter. "Monster Movies and Rites of Initiation." *Journal of Popular Film* 4, no. 2 (1975): 124–42.

————. "Monster Movies: A Sexual Theory." *Journal of Popular Film* 2, no. 4 (Fall 1973): 353–65. Reprinted in *Planks of Reason: Essays on the Horror Film*, edited by Barry K. Grant, 53–64. Metuchen, N.J.: Scarecrow Press, 1984.

Everson, William K. *Classics of the Horror Film*. Secaucus, N.J.: Citadel Press, 1974.

————. "A Family Tree of Monsters." *Film Culture* 1, no. 1 (January 1955): 24–30.

————. "Horror Films." *Films in Review* 5, no. 1 (January 1954): 12–23.

————. *More Classics of the Horror Film*. Secaucus, N.J.: Citadel, 1986.

Fischer, Dennis. *Horror Film Directors, 1931– 1990*. Jefferson, N.C.: McFarland, 1991.

Flynn, John L. *Cinematic Vampires: The Living Dead on Film and Television, from The Devil's Castle to Bram Stoker's Dracula*. Jefferson, N.C.: McFarland, 1992.

Fox, Julian. "The Golden Age of Terror." 5 pts. *Films and Filming* 22, no. 9 (June 1976): 16–23; no. 10 (July 1976): 18–24; no. 11 (August 1976): 20–24; no. 12 (September 1976): 20–25; 23, no. 1 (October 1976): 18–25.

Frank, Alan. *The Horror Film Handbook*. Totowa, N.J.: Barnes and Noble, 1982.

————. *Horror Movies: Tales of Terror in the Cinema*. London: Octopus, 1974.

Fraser, John. "Watching Horror Movies." *Michigan Quarterly Review* 29, no. 1 (Winter 1990): 39–54.

Freeland, Cynthia. *The Naked and the Undead: Evil and the Appeal of Horror*. Boulder: Westview Press, 1999.

Galbraith, Stuart IV. *Japanese Science Fiction, Fantasy and Horror Films: A Critical Analysis and Filmography of 103 Features Released in the United States, 1950–1992*. Jefferson, N.C.: McFarland, 1994.

Gelder, Ken. *Reading the Vampire*. New York and London: Routledge, 1994.

————, ed. *The Horror Reader*. New York: Routledge, 2000.

Gifford, Denis. *Movie Monsters*. New York: Dutton, 1967.

————. *A Pictorial History of Horror Movies*. New York: Hamlyn, 1973.

Glut, Donald F. *Classic Movie Monsters*. Metuchen, N.J.: Scarecrow Press, 1978.

————. *The Frankenstein Catalogue*. Jefferson City, N.C.: McFarland, 1984.

Grant, Barry Keith, ed. *The Dread of Difference: Gender and the Horror Film*. Austin: University of Texas Press, 1996.

————. *Planks of Reason: Essays on the Horror Film*. Metuchen, N.J.: Scarecrow Press, 1984.

Greenberg, Harvey R. "The Fractures of Desire: Psychoanalytic Notes on *Alien* and the Contemporary 'Cruel' Horror Film." *The Psychoanalytic Review* 70, no. 2 (1983): 241–67.

————. *The Movies on Your Mind*. New York: Saturday Review Press/Dutton, 1975.

Guerrero, Edward. "AIDS as Monster in Science Fiction and Horror Cinema." *Journal of Popular Film and Television* 18, no. 3 (Fall 1990): 86–93.

Halberstam, Judith. *Skin Shows: Gothic Horror and the Technology of Monsters.* Durham, N.C.: Duke University Press, 1995.

Halliwell, Leslie. "The Baron, the Count, and Their Ghoul Friends." 2 pts. *Films and Filming* 15, no. 9 (June 1969): 13–16; no. 10 (July 1969): 12–16.

———. *The Dead that Walk: Dracula, Frankenstein, The Mummy and Other Favorite Movie Monsters.* New York: Continuum, 1988.

Hanke, Ken. *A Critical Guide to Horror Film Series.* Hamden, Conn.: Garland, 1991.

Hardy, Phil, ed. *The Encyclopedia of Horror Films.* New York: Harper & Row, 1986.

Hawkins, Joan. *Cutting-Edge: Art-Horror and the Horrific Avant-Garde.* Minneapolis: University of Minnesota Press, 2000.

Hendershot, Cyndy. "Vampire and Replicant: The One-Sex Body in a Two-Sex World." *Science Fiction Studies,* no. 67 (November 1995): 373–98.

Higham, Charles, and Joel Greenberg. *Hollywood in the Forties.* New York: A. S. Barnes, 1968.

Hill, Derek. "Horror." *Sight and Sound* 28, no. 1 (Winter 1958–59): 6–11.

Hogan, David J. *Dark Romance: Sex and Death in the Horror Film.* Jefferson, N.C.: McFarland, 1986.

Hunt, Leon. "A (Sadistic) Night at the Opera: Notes on the Italian Horror Film." *Velvet Light Trap,* no. 30 (Fall 1992): 65–75.

———. "Pleasure and Excess: Vincent Price and the Horror Film." *Movie,* no. 36 (2000): 80–96.

Huss, Roy, and T. J. Ross, eds. *Focus on the Horror Film.* Englewood Cliffs, N.J.: Prentice Hall, 1972.

Hutchings, Peter. *Hammer and Beyond: The British Horror Film.* Manchester: Manchester University Press, 1993.

———. "Masculinity and the Horror Film." *You Tarzan: Masculinity, Movies and Men,* edited by Pat Kirkham and Janet Thumim, 84–94. London: Lawrence & Wishart, 1993.

Hutchinson, Tom. *Horror and Fantasy in the Cinema.* London: Studio Vista, 1974.

Jancovich, Mark. *Horror.* London: Batsford, 1992.

———. *Rational Fears: The American Horror Genre in the 1950s.* Manchester: Manchester University Press, 1996.

Jensen, Paul M. *The Men Who Made the Movies.* New York: Twayne, 1996.

Jones, E. Michael. *Monsters from the Id: The Rise of Horror in Film and Fiction.* Dallas: Spence, 2000.

Kaminsky, Stuart. *American Film Genres: Approaches to a Critical Theory of Popular Film,* chap. 7. Dayton, Ohio: Pflaum, 1974.

Kendrick, Walter. *The Thrill of Fear: 250 Years of Scary Entertainment.* New York: Grove Press, 1991.

Kennedy, Harlan. "Things that Go Howl in the Id." *Film Comment* 18, no. 2 (March–April 1982): 37–39.

King, Stephen. *Danse Macabre.* New York: Everett House, 1981.

Kinnard, Roy. *Horror in Silent Films: A Filmography, 1896–1929.* Jefferson, N.C.: McFarland, 1995.

Kovacs, Lee. *The Haunted Screen: Ghosts in Literature and Film.* Jefferson, N.C.: McFarland, 1999.

Landy, Marcia. *British Genres: Cinema and Society, 1930–1960.* Princeton, N.J.: Princeton University Press, 1991.

Lavery, David. "The Horror Film and the Horror of Film." *Film Criticism* 7, no. 1 (Fall 1982): 47–55.

Lazar, Moshe, ed. *The Anxious Subject: Nightmares and Daydreams in Literature and Film.* Malibu, Calif.: Undena, 1983.

Lee, Walt, ed. *Reference Guide to Fantastic Films: Science Fiction, Fantasy, and Horror.* 3 vols. Los Angeles: Chelsea-Lee Books, 1972.

Lenne, Gerard. "Monster and Victim: Women in the Horror Film." In *Sexual Strategems,* edited by Patricia Erens, 31–40. New York: Horizon Press, 1979.

Lentz, Harris, III. *Science Fiction, Horror, and Fantasy Film and Television Credits.* 2 vols. Jefferson, N.C.: McFarland, 1983.

———. *Science Fiction, Horror & Fantasy Film and Television Credits Supplement: Through 1987.* Jefferson, N.C.: McFarland, 1989.

London, Rose. *Zombie: The Living Dead.* New York: Bounty Books, 1976.

Lowry, Edward. "Genre and Enunciation: The Case of Horror." *Journal of Film and Video* 36, no. 2 (1984): 13–20, 72.

Lucanio, Patrick. *Them or Us: Archetypal Interpretations of Fifties Alien Invasion Films.* Bloomington and Indianapolis: Indiana University Press, 1987.

McCallum, Lawrence. *Italian Horror Films of the 1960s: A Critical Catalogue of 62 Chillers.* Jefferson, N.C.: McFarland, 1998.

McCarty, John. *John McCarty's Splatter Movie Guide,* Vol. 2. New York: St. Martin's Press, 1992.

———. *The Modern Horror Film.* New York: Citadel Press, 1990.

———. *Psychos: Ninety Years of Mad Movies, Maniacs and Murderous Deeds.* New York: Carol Publishing Group, 1986.

———. *Splatter Movies.* New York: St. Martin's Press, 1984.

McConnell, Frank. "Rough Beasts Slouching: A Note on Horror Movies." *Kenyon Review* 128 (1970): 109–20.

Manchel, Frank. *Terrors of the Screen.* Englewood Cliffs, N.J.: Prentice Hall, 1970.

Mank, Gregory W. *It's Alive! The Classic Cinema Saga of Frankenstein.* San Diego, Calif.: A. S. Barnes, 1981.

Modleski, Tania. "The Terror of Pleasure: The Contemporary Horror Film and Postmodern Theory." *Studies in Entertainment,* edited by Tania Modleski, 155–66. Bloomington: Indiana University Press, 1986.

Murphy, Robert. *Sixties British Cinema,* chap. 8. London: British Film Institute, 1992.

Naha, Ed. *Horrors from Screen to Scream.* New York: Avon, 1975.

Newman, Kim. *Nightmare Movies: A Guide to Contemporary Horror Films.* New York: Harmony Books, 1988.

Nicholls, Peter. *The World of Fantastic Films: An Illustrated Survey.* New York: Dodd, Mead, 1984.

Oliver, Mary Beth. "Adolescents' Enjoyment of Graphic Horror." *Communication Research* 20, no. 1 (1993): 30–50.

Pattison, Barrie. *The Seal of Dracula.* New York: Bounty Books, 1975.

Pendo, Stephen. "Universal's Golden Age of Horror." *Films in Review* 26, no. 3 (March 1975): 155–61.

Pinedo, Isabel. "Recreational Terror: Postmodern Elements of the Contemporary Horror Film." *Journal of Film and Video* 48, nos. 1–2 (Spring–Summer 1996): 17–31.

Pirie, David. *A Heritage of Horror: The English Gothic Cinema, 1946–1972.* London: Gordon Fraser, 1973.

———. *The Vampire Cinema.* New York: Crescent, 1977.

Pitts, Michael R. *Horror Film Stars.* Jefferson, N.C.: McFarland, 1981. 2nd. ed., 1991.

Prawer, S. S. *Caligari's Children: The Film as Tale of Terror.* New York: Oxford University Press, 1980.

Prince, Stephen. "Dread, Taboo and *The Thing:* Toward a Social Theory of the Horror Film." *Wide Angle* 10, no. 3 (1988): 19–29.

Rasmussen, Randy. *Children of the Night: The Six Archetypal Characters of Classic Horror Films.* Jefferson, N.C.: McFarland, 1998.

Riccardo, Martin V. *Vampires Unearthed: The Vampire and Dracula Bibliography of Books Articles, Movies, Records, and Other Material.* New York: Garland, 1983.

Rockett, Will H. *Devouring Whirlwind: Terror and Transcendence in the Cinema of Cruelty.* New York: Greenwood Press, 1988.

Russell, David J. "Monster Roundup: Reintegrating the Horror Genre." In *Refiguring American Film Genres: History and Theory,* edited by Nick Browne, 233–54. Berkeley: University of California Press, 1998.

Ryan, Michael, and Douglas Kellner. *Camera Politica: The Politics and Ideology of Contemporary Hollywood Film.* Bloomington: Indiana University Press, 1988.

Sanjek, David. "Fans' Notes: The Horror Film Fanzine." *Literature/Film Quarterly* 18, no. 3 (1990): 150–59.

———. "Twilight of the Monsters: The English Horror Film, 1968–1975." *Film Criticism* 16, nos. 1–2 (Fall-Winter 1991–92): 111–26. Reprinted in *Reviewing British Cinema, 1900–1992: Essays and Interviews,* edited by Wheeler Winston Dixon, 195–209. Albany: State University of New York Press, 1994.

Saunders, Michael William. *Imps of the Perverse: Gay Monsters in Film.* Westport, Conn.: Praeger, 1998.

Schneider, Steven Jay. "Kevin Williamson and the Rise of the Neo-Stalker." *Post Script* 19, no. 2 (Winter–Spring 2000): 73–87.

———. "Uncanny Realism and the Decline of the Modern Horror Film." *Paradoxa* 3, nos. 3–4 (1997): 417–28.

Schoell, William. *Stay Out of the Shower: Twenty-Five Years of Shocker Films Beginning with* Psycho. New York: Dembner, 1985.

Sconce, Jeffrey. "Spectacles of Death: Identification, Reflexivity, and Contemporary Horror." *Film Theory Goes to the Movies,* edited by Jim Collins, Hilary Radner, and Ava Preacher Collins, 103–19. New York: Routledge, 1993.

Senn, Bryan. *Golden Horrors: An Illustrated Critical Filmography of Terror Cinema, 1931–1939.* Jefferson, N.C.: McFarland, 1996.

Senn, Bryan, and John Johnson. *Fantastic Subject Guide: A Topical Index to 2,500 Horror Science Fiction and Fantasy Films.* Jefferson, N.C.: McFarland, 1992.

Sevastakis, Michael. *Songs of Love and Death: The Classical American Horror Film of the 1930s.* Westport, Conn: Greenwood, 1993.

Skal, David J. *The Monster Show: A Cultural History of Horror.* New York: Norton, 1994.

Smith, Gary A. *Uneasy Dreams: The Golden Age of British Horror Films, 1956–1976.* Jefferson, N.C.: McFarland, 2000.

Steiger, Brad. *Monsters, Maidens and Mayhem: A Pictorial History of Horror Film Monsters.* New York: Merit, 1965.

Sullivan, Jack, ed. *The Penguin Encyclopedia of Horror and the Supernatural.* New York: Viking, 1986.

Telotte, J. P. "The Doubles of Fantasy and the Space of Desire." *Film Criticism* 6, no. 1 (Fall 1982): 56–68. Reprinted in *Film Criticism* 11, nos. 1–2 (Fall–Winter 1987): 43–55.

———. *Dreams of Darkness: Fantasy and the Films of Val Lewton.* Urbana: University of Illinois Press, 1985.

Tietchen, Todd F. "Samplers and Copycats: The Cultural Implications of the Postmodern Slasher in Contemporary American Film." *Journal of Popular Film and Television* 26, no. 3 (Fall 1998): 98–107.

Trencansky, Sarah. "Final Girls and Terrible Youth: Transgression in 1980s Slasher Horror." *Journal of Popular Film and Television* 29, no. 2 (Summer 2001): 63–73.

Tropp, Martin. *Mary Shelley's Monster.* Boston: Houghton Mifflin, 1976.

Tudor, Andrew. *Image and Influence: Studies in the Sociology of Film.* London: George Allen and Unwin, 1974.

———. *Monsters and Mad Scientists: A Cultural History of the Horror Movie.* London: Basil Blackwell, 1989.

Turner, George E., and Michael H. Price. *Forgotten Horrors: Early Talkie Chillers from Poverty Row*. S. Brunswick: A. S. Barnes, 1979.

Twitchell, James B. *Dreadful Pleasures: An Anatomy of Modern Horror*. New York: Oxford University Press, 1985.

———. "*Frankenstein* and the Anatomy of Horror." *Georgia Review* 37, no. 1 (1983): 44–78.

———. *Preposterous Violence: Fables of Aggression in Modern Culture*. New York: Oxford University Press, 1989.

———. "A Psychoanalysis of the Vampire Myth." *American Imago* 37 (1980): 83–92.

Ursini, James, and Alain Silver. *The Vampire Film*. New York: A. S. Barnes/ London: Tantivy, 1975. Revised ed., New York: Limelight, 1993.

Vale, V., and Andrea June. *Incredibly Strange Films.* San Francisco: Research #10, 1986.

Waller, Gregory A. *The Living and the Undead: From Stoker's* Dracula *to Romero's* Dawn of the Dead. Urbana: University of Illinois Press, 1986.

———, ed. *American Horrors: Essays on the Modern American Horror Film*. Urbana: University of Illinois Press, 1987.

Warren, Bill. *Set Visits: Interviews with 32 Horror and Science Fiction Filmmakers*. Jefferson, N.C.: McFarland, 1997.

Weaver, James B. III, and Ron Tamborini, eds. *Horror Films: Current Research in Audience Preferences and Reactions*. Mahwah, N.J.: Laurence Erlbaum, 1995.

Weaver, Tom. *Interviews with B Science Fiction and Horror Movie Makers: Writers, Producers, Directors, Actors, Moguls and Makeup*. Jefferson, N.C.: McFarland, 1988.

———. *It Came from Weaver Five: Interviews with 20 Zany, Glib and Earnest Moviemakers in the SF and Horror Traditions of the Thirties, Forties, Fifties and Sixties*. Jefferson, N.C.: McFarland, 1996.

———. *I Was a Monster Movie Maker: Conversations with 22 SF and Horror Filmmakers*. Jefferson, N.C.: McFarland, 2001.

———. *Poverty Row Horrors!: Monogram, PRC and Republic Horror Films of the Forties*. Jefferson, N.C.: McFarland, 1993.

———. *Science Fiction Stars and Horror Heroes: Interviews with Actors, Directors, Producers and Writers of the 1940s through 1960s*. Jefferson, N.C.: McFarland, 1991.

———. *They Fought in the Creature Features: Interviews with 23 Classic Horror, Science Fiction and Serial Stars*. Jefferson, N.C.: McFarland, 1995.

Wells, Paul. *The Horror Genre: From* Beelzebub *to* Blair Witch. London: Wallflower Press, 2001.

White, Dennis L. "The Poetics of Horror: More Than Meets the Eye." *Cinema Journal* 10, no. 2 (Spring 1971): 1–18. Reprinted in *Film Genre: Theory and Criticism*, edited by Barry K. Grant, 124–44. Metuchen, N.J.: Scarecrow

Press, 1977. *Cinema Examined: Selections from Cinema Journal,* edited by Richard Dyer MacCann and Jack C. Ellis, 251–68. New York: Dutton, 1982.

Wiater, Stanley. *Dark Visions: Conversations with the Masters of the Horror Film.* New York: Avon, 1992.

Williams, Linda. "When the Woman Looks." In *Re-Vision: Essays in Feminist Film Criticism,* edited by Mary Ann Doane and Linda Williams, 83–99. Frederick, Md.: University Publications, 1983. Reprinted in *The Dread of Difference: Gender and the Horror Film,* edited by Barry Keith Grant, 15–34. Austin: University of Texas Press, 1996.

Williams, Tony. "American Cinema in the 70s: Family Horror." *Movie,* nos. 27–28 (1981): 117–26.

———. "Horror in the Family." *Focus on Film,* no. 36 (October 1980): 14–20.

Willis, Don. *Horror and Science Fiction Films: A Checklist.* Metuchen, N.J.: Scarecrow Press, 1972.

———. *Horror and Science Fiction Films II.* Metuchen, N.J.: Scarecrow Press, 1982.

———. *Horror and Science Fiction Films III.* Metuchen, N.J.: Scarecrow Press, 1984.

———. *Horror and Science Fiction Films IV (1984–1993).* Lanham, Md.: Scarecrow Press, 1997.

Wolf, Leonard. *Horror: A Connoisseur's Guide to Literature and Film.* New York: Facts on File, 1989.

Wood, Gerald C. "Horror Film." In *Handbook of American Film Genres,* edited by Wes D. Gehrig, 211–28. New York: Greenwood Press, 1988.

Wood, Robin. "The American Family Comedy: From *Meet Me in St. Louis* to *The Texas Chainsaw Massacre.*" *Wide Angle* 3, no. 2 (1979): 5–11.

———, and Richard Lippe, eds. *The American Nightmare: Essays on the Horror Film.* Toronto: Festival of Festivals, 1979.

Worland, Rick. "OWI Meets the Monsters: Hollywood Horror Films and War Propaganda, 1942–1945." *Cinema Journal* 37, no. 1 (Fall 1997): 47–65.

Wright, Gene. *Horrorshows.* New York: Facts on File, 1986.

Index

Note: Boldface page numbers indicate photographs.

About the Editors and Contributors

Mikita Brottman is professor of language and literature at the Maryland Institute College of Art in Baltimore. Her essays and articles have appeared in *New Literary History*, *The Chronicle of Higher Education*, *Film Quarterly*, *The Journal of Aesthetics and Art Criticism*, and elsewhere. She is the author of *Meat Is Murder*, *Hollywood Hex*, *Funny Peculiar*, and the editor of *Car Crash Culture*. A revised version of her book *Offensive Films*, in which her essay on *The Tingler* first appeared, is forthcoming from Vanderbilt University Press.

Mary Baine Campbell is professor of English and American Literature at Brandeis University, where she teaches medieval and early modern literature and culture. She is the author most recently of *Wonder and Science: Imagining Worlds in Early Modern Europe* and *Trouble*, a collection of poems.

Noël Carroll is Andrew Mellon Professor of Philosophy at Temple University, Philadelphia. He is the author of *Philosophical Problems of Classical Film Theory*, *Mystifying Movies: Fads and Fallacies in Contemporary Film Theory*, and *The Philosophy of Horror, or, Paradoxes of the Heart*. His essays have appeared in such journals as *Artforum* and *Millennium Film Journal*.

Syndy M. Conger taught Gothic literature in the Department of English at Western Illinois University, Macomb. The author of *Mary Wollstonecraft and the Language of Sensibility* and co-editor of *Icono-*

clastic Departures: Mary Shelley after Frankenstein, she has also published on Matthew Lewis, Horace Walpole, Ann Radcliffe, Jane Austen, Charlotte Bronte, and other writers. Recently retired from academia, she now lives and works in Iowa City with her husband and cats.

Richard deCordova was an associate professor of communications at DePaul University, after having received his Ph.D. in film and television studies from UCLA and spending one year at the Centre Americain du Cinéma in Paris. Richard was the author of *Picture Personalities: The Emergence of the Star System in America*. He passed away in November 1996.

Morris Dickstein is distinguished professor of English at the Graduate Center of the City University of New York, where he teaches courses in literature, film, and American cultural history. He is a senior fellow of the Center for the Humanities, which he founded in 1993. His books include a study of the 1960s, *Gates of Eden*, which was nominated for the National Book Critics Circle Award in criticism; *Double Agent: The Critic and Society*; and *Leopards in the Temple*, a social history of postwar American fiction. His recent essays and reviews have appeared in the *New York Times Book Review*, *Times Literary Supplement* (London), *Washington Post*, *The American Scholar*, *The Nation*, *Chronicle of Higher Education*, and *Partisan Review*, where he was a contributing editor from 1972 to 2003.

Lester D. Friedman teaches film and medical humanities at Northwestern University. His publications revolve around issues of multiculturalism, contemporary British cinema, and post–World War II American films. His latest books are *Cultural Sutures: Media and Medicine* and the forthcoming *Citizen Spielberg*. He is also co-editor of The Screen Decades series, a history of the American cinema from 1895–1999, to which he will contribute the volume on the 1970s.

Dennis Giles received his M.S. in radio, TV, and film from the University of Texas–Austin in 1972 and his Ph.D. in film from Northwestern University in 1976. His scholarship on the reception of film, film theory, and film history has appeared in such publications as *Film Heritage*, *Journal of Humanities and the Classics*, *Velvet Light Trap*, *Film Reader*, *Spirales*, and *Cinema Journal*. At the time of his death in 1989,

Dr. Giles was associate professor of communication at Cleveland State University.

Ruth Goldberg teaches at SUNY/Empire State College, New York University School of Continuing and Professional Studies, and the Escuela Internacional de Cine y TV in San Antonio de los Banos, Cuba. She has published on the horror film and Latin American cinema in the journals *Miradas* and *Kinoeye* and the anthologies *Fear Without Frontiers: Horror Cinema Across the Globe* and *Nightmare Japan*, among others. She is currently at work on a documentary film about the cult of Palo Mayombe in Cuba and the United States.

Barry Keith Grant is professor of film studies and popular culture at Brock University in Ontario, Canada. He is the author of *Voyages of Discovery: The Cinema of Frederick Wiseman*, co-author of *The Film Studies Dictionary*, and editor of numerous volumes including *Film Genre Reader, The Dread of Difference: Gender and the Horror Film, Documenting the Documentary: Close Readings of Documentary Film and Video*, and *John Ford's Stagecoach*. He is the editor-in-chief of the forthcoming *Schirmer Encyclopedia of Film* and editor of the Contemporary Approaches to Film and Television series for Wayne State University Press.

Bruce Kawin is professor of English and film at the University of Colorado at Boulder. His books include *How Movies Work, Telling It Again and Again: Repetition in Literature and Film, Mindscreen: Bergman, Godard, and First-Person Film, The Mind of the Novel: Reflexive Fiction and the Ineffable*, as well as three books on Faulkner and the fifth through ninth editions of the late Gerald Mast's *A Short History of the Movies*. He is also a poet and screenwriter, and he has been preparing a book on the horror film for many years.

Jonathan Lemkin is a screenwriter whose credits include *The Devil's Advocate* and *Red Planet*, as well as episodes of such television series as *Beverly Hills 90210, 21 Jump Street*, and *Hill Street Blues*.

Edward Lowry taught film studies at Southern Illinois University at Carbondale. He passed away in 1985.

Steve Neale is research professor in film, media, and communication studies at Sheffield Hallam University in England. He is the author of

Genre, Genre and Hollywood, co-author (with Frank Krutnik) of *Popular Film and Television Comedy*, and editor of *Genre and Contemporary Hollywood* and, with Murray Smith, of *Contemporary Hollywood Cinema*.

Dana B. Polan is professor of critical studies in the School of Cinema-TV at the University of Southern California. He is the author of several books on film, including *Power and Paranoia: History, Narrative, and the America Cinema, 1940–1950*, *The Political Language of Film and the Avant-Garde*, *The Confusions of Warren Beatty*, *Pulp Fiction* in the BFI's Modern Classics series and *In a Lonely Place* in their Film Classics series. He has just completed a historical study of the discipline of film entitled *The Beginnings of the American Study of Film*.

D. N. Rodowick is professor of English and visual/cultural studies at the University of Rochester. He is the author of *Gilles Deleuze's Time Machine*, *The Difficulty of Difference: Psychoanalysis, Sexual Difference and Film Theory*, and *The Crisis of Political Modernism: Critical Ideology in Contemporary Film Theory*. His work has appeared in numerous anthologies and journals, including *iris* and *camera obscura*.

Lane Roth is an associate professor in the Department of Communications at Lamar State University in Beaumont, Texas.

Sharon Russell taught communications studies at Indiana State University, Terre Haute. She is the author of several works on literature and film, including *Stephen King*, *Stephen King Revisited*, and *Guide to African Cinema*. She is currently working on a book about the author Chelsea Quinn Yarbro.

Christopher Sharrett is professor of communication at Seton Hall University. He is editor of *Crisis Cinema: The Apocalyptic Idea in Postmodern Narrative Film*, and *Mythologies of Violence in Postmodern Media*. His work has appeared in *Cineaste*, *Kino Eye*, *Journal of Popular Film and Television*, *Film Quarterly*, *Persistence of Vision*, and numerous anthologies, including *The End of Cinema as We Know It*, *Bad: Infamy, Darkness, Evil and Slime on Screen*, *Fifty Contemporary Filmmakers*, *The New American Cinema*, and *The Dread of Difference: Gender and the Horror Film*.

J. P. Telotte, a professor in the School of Literature, Communication, and Culture at Georgia Tech, teaches courses in media studies, film history, and film and technology. He co-edits the journal *Post Script* and is the author of a number of books on film and media, among them *Voices in the Dark: The Narrative Patterns of Film Noir*, *The Science Fiction Film*, and *Disney TV*.

Janice Welsch is professor in the Department of English and Journalism at Western Illinois University, where she teaches courses in film criticism and multicultural education. She has co-edited a number of anthologies including *Multiple Voices in Feminist Film Criticism* and *Cultural Diversity: Curriculum, Classroom and Climate*. She is currently working on a reference guide to films that focus on issues of race/ethnicity. She is a member of the Society for Cinema and Media Studies and recently received that organization's service award for distinguished contributions to the society and the profession.

Robin Wood is the author of numerous books, including *Sexual Politics and Narrative Film*, *Hitchcock's Films Revisited*, and *Hollywood from Vietnam to Reagan*, all published by Columbia University Press. He teaches a graduate course in film criticism each year at York University, Toronto.

Rick Worland is associate professor of Cinema-Television in the Meadows School of the Arts at Southern Methodist University. His teaching includes film history, documentary, popular genres including horror, westerns, film noir, and the cinema of Alfred Hitchcock. His work has appeared in *Cinema Journal*, *Journal of Film and Video*, *Post-Script*, and *Journal of Popular Film and Television* among others. He is the author of *The Horror Film*, forthcoming from Cambridge UP.

Bonnie Zimmerman has been professor of women's studies at San Diego State University since 1978. She served as chair of the department and graduate advisor, as well as chair of the University Senate. She was active in the National Women's Studies Association until 2003, and considers her 1998–99 term as president one of the highlights of her career. She is the author of *The Safe Sea of Women: Lesbian Fiction 1969–1989*, and editor of *Professions of Desire: Lesbian and Gay Stud-*

ies in Literature, *The New Lesbian Studies*, and *Lesbian Histories and Cultures: An Encyclopedia.* In addition, she has published numerous articles and book reviews, including the oft-reprinted "What Has Never Been: An Overview of Lesbian Feminist Literary Criticism." She is currently associate vice president for faculty affairs at SDSU.